I0821781

# Bridge Builder

# Bridge Builder

## An Insider's Account of Over Sixty Years in Post-War Reconstruction, International Diplomacy, and German-American Relations

BY

Walther Leisler Kiep

Purdue University Press
West Lafayette, Indiana

Printed in the United States of America.

**Library of Congress Cataloging-in-Publication Data**

Kiep, Walther Leisler, 1926-
Bridge builder : an insider's account of over sixty years in post-war reconstruction, international diplomacy, and German-American relations / Walther Leisler Kiep.
p. cm.
Includes index.
ISBN 978-1-55753-620-4 (pbk. : alk. paper) -- ISBN 978-1-61249-207-0 (epdf) -- ISBN 978-1-61249-206-3 (epub) 1. Kiep, Walther Leisler, 1926- 2. Statesmen--Germany--Biography. 3. Politicians--Germany--Biography. 4. Germany (West)--Politics and government. 5. Germany--Politics and government--1990- 6. Germany (West)--Foreign relations--United States. 7. United States--Foreign relations--Germany (West) 8. Germany--Foreign relations--United States. 9. United States--Foreign relations--Germany. I. Title.
DD259.7.K48A3 2012
327.43073092--dc23
[B]

2011047688

Cover: Walther Leisler Kiep with Richard von Weizsäcker, who later became President of Germany.

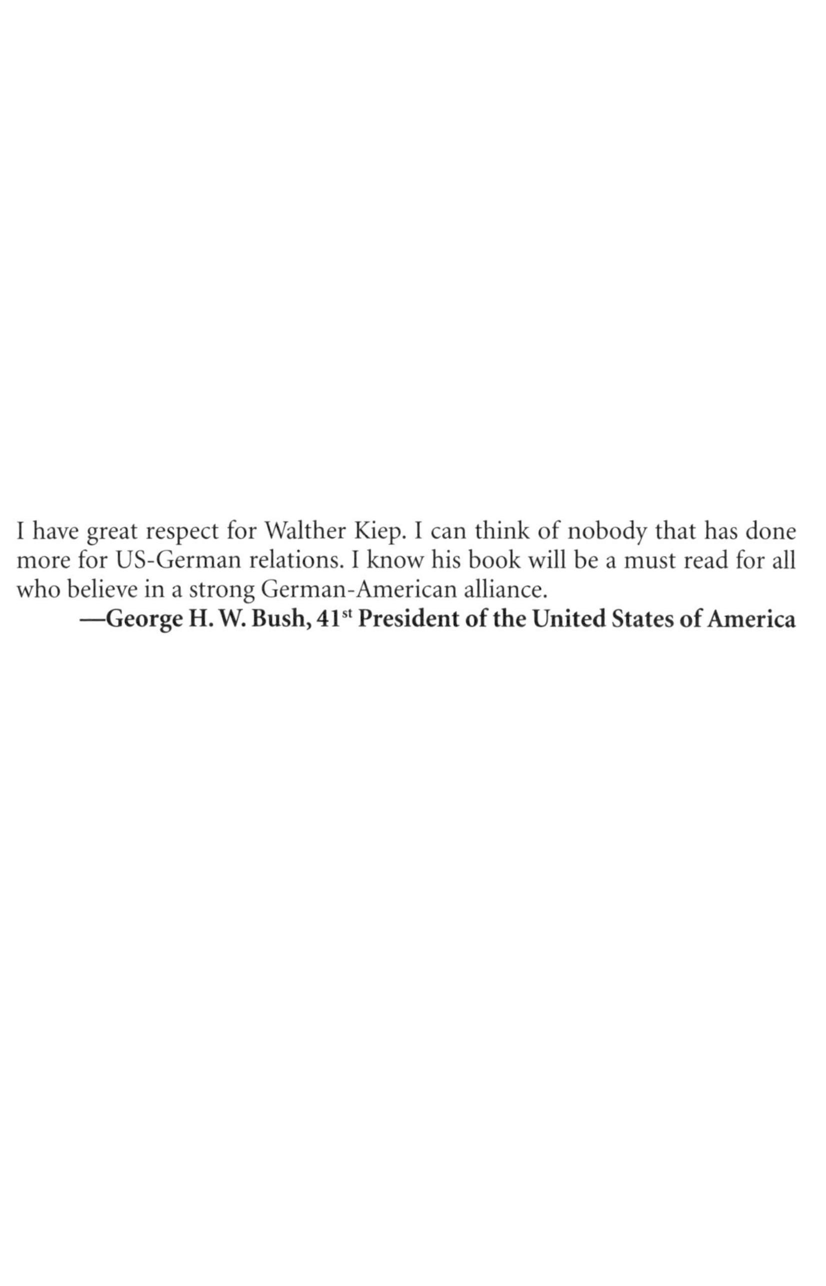

I have great respect for Walther Kiep. I can think of nobody that has done more for US-German relations. I know his book will be a must read for all who believe in a strong German-American alliance.

**—George H. W. Bush, 41st President of the United States of America**

# Contents

# List of Abbreviations

| | |
|---|---|
| AJC | American Jewish Committee |
| APO | Extraparliamentary Opposition |
| BND | West German Federal Intelligence Service |
| CDU | Christian Democratic Union |
| CSCE | Conference on Security and Cooperation in Europe |
| CSU | Christian Social Union |
| DC | Christian Democrats (Italy) |
| DM | deutsche mark |
| EC | European Community |
| EU | European Union |
| FAW | First Automobile Works |
| FDP | Free Democratic Party |
| FRG | Federal Republic of Germany |
| GDR | German Democratic Republic |
| GMF | German Marshall Fund |
| IAC | International Advisory Council |
| IMF | International Monetary Fund |
| INA | Insurance Company of North America |
| INF | Intermediate-Range Nuclear Forces |
| JFK | John Fitzgerald Kennedy |
| KfW | Kreditanstalt für Wiederaufbau |
| MBFR | Mutual and Balanced Force Reductions |
| NATO | North Atlantic Treaty Organization |
| NordLB | Norddeutsche Landesbank AG |
| NPD | National Democratic Party of Germany |
| NPT | Treaty on the Non-Proliferation of Nuclear Weapons |
| NSDAP | National Socialist German Workers' Party |
| OECD | Organization for Economic Co-operation and Development |
| PLO | Palestine Liberation Organization |
| RAF | Red Army Faction |
| RICO | Racketeer Influenced and Corrupt Organizations Act |
| SACEUR | Supreme Allied Commander Europe |
| SALT | Strategic Arms Limitation Talks |
| Stasi | East German Secret Service |
| SPD | Social Democratic Party |
| UN | United Nations |
| ZDF | Second Television Network (German public broadcaster) |

# Foreword

This lively personal/political saga by Walther Leisler Kiep is an ultimate European insider's account, rare in the English language. It constitutes an unusually valuable record of a half century of German and transnational politics. The author's breadth of personal contacts, his ease of access in European and world capitals, and his repeated availability for important special assignments combine to give the reader many fascinating behind-the-scenes glimpses of important financial, political, and diplomatic developments over recent decades.

The narrative covers the author's wide and deep personal involvement over many decades as an astute trouble-shooter at home and abroad. His ventures start in Europe, but extend to East Asia, the Middle East, and North America. Confidential missions take him to Communist East Germany, Turkey, Italy, Morocco, China, Japan, and often to the United States. Having spent his youth in Turkey where he maintained a close affinity, Kiep is even called upon to explain Turkey's importance to a skeptical Greek caucus in the US Congress.

The author enjoyed British as well as German citizenship, which helped pave the way for his early business success in post-war occupied Germany, his continued success with British-related activities in the Federal Republic, and his eventual receipt of honors from the Queen.

In addition, here is some vivid and entertaining writing by an accomplished storyteller. Kiep displays a disarming openness about his own unachieved ambitions for the German Chancellorship. The book is replete with insider portraits of Western leaders of the past half century. These well-written vignettes of politicians on both sides of the Atlantic benefit from, and are lent authenticity by, the author's lifelong habit of keeping daily diary entries of his private and public activities.

The significance of Kiep's "bridge building" role is demonstrated in a host of situations at home and abroad. Clearly many of his winning techniques were honed by repeated use. Serving as mediator/pacifier in big business conflicts like the Volkswagen-General Motors feud served him well in local, regional, and international disputes of a more public nature. His account of the origins and renewal of the highly successful German Marshall Fund of the United States, for instance, will be of special interest in the American NGO and foundation community. Kiep credits another NGO, the Bilderberg Group, with introducing him to other Western leaders who would be important to him eventually.

Kiep often found himself a dissenter in his own Christian Democratic party, although he remained—not without some grief—the CDU party treasurer for many years. His criticism is at times unabashed of some of his conservative colleagues. Flavorful verdicts like "obnoxious blockheads" and "such orchestrated mediocrity" add spice to his recollections.

An early believer in Ostpolitik, Kiep often found his sympathies more in tune with SPD chancellors like Brandt, Schmidt, and Schröder than with his own conservative faction in the Bundestag. Even while holding office as a cabinet minister in Lower Saxony, he found time to undertake sensitive missions in the German Democratic Republic, quietly laboring to lay the groundwork for future German reunification. His accounts of conversations with GDR officials from Erich Honecker on down are illuminating.

Famous names emerge effortlessly from these pages. All the post-war German Chancellors appear—Adenauer, Erhard, Kiesinger, Brandt, Schmidt, Kohl, and Merkel—as well as other distinguished German political figures like Scheel, Gerstenmeier, Barzel, Wehner, Biedenkopf, Richard von Weizsäcker, and Ernst Albrecht.

Important non-German world figures also emerge—from Souvvanna Phouma to Peres and Arafat; from Agnelli and Ecevit to Falin and Zagladin; and from Margaret Thatcher to Princess Diana.

There are sketches of American Presidents Nixon, Carter, and Reagan, as well as Bush 41, Clinton, and Bush 43. Kiep's American contacts also included Averell Harriman, Hubert Humphrey, John J. McCloy, Nelson Rockefeller, Henry Kissinger, Ted Kennedy, Cyrus Vance, Robert McNamara, Al Haig, and Warren Christopher, not to mention Volkswagen lawyers Vernon Jordon and Robert Strauss.

The book's final chapter is likely to be of particular interest to American readers. Starting in 1984 Kiep chaired Atlantik-Brücke for many successful years, and he has been honorary chairman since 2004. In his book the bridge builder pays a highly deserved tribute to Beate Lindemann who is also well known in America and who has inspired and managed most recent Atlantic Bridge programs. Despite, and during, occasional official ups and downs—like the Berlin-Washington split over the US invasion of Iraq in 2003—this organization helped keep German-American relations on an even keel. Its continuing investments in the future through its ventures like Youth for Understanding, the Young Leaders Program, and Atlantik Forum are especially noteworthy.

For anyone looking for an informed behind-the-scenes account of a critical era in world politics, and of German-American relations in particular, this book is a major addition to the existing literature.

—Thomas L. Hughes
Former US Assistant Secretary of State
President of the Carnegie Endowment for International Peace
Senior Fellow of the German Historical Institute

# Preface

Christmas 1945: Those were the days when we Germans first sensed and received signals from America indicating a certain feeling of compassion, concern, and even friendship. After the unconditional German surrender in May 1945, the American soldiers took over as victors who requisitioned homes, took prisoners, and excluded from public life Germans whom they considered to have been active in Hitler's rule.

At the end of the war over twelve million Germans from the East sought and found refuge in West Germany.

But around Christmas a feeling of compassion—an increasing desire and readiness to help—arose. Relatives and friends in America were the first ones to reestablish contacts with former friends in Germany, and larger organizations followed.

Forever should we be grateful to the senders of the famous CARE packages that helped many thousands of Germans to survive.

The Quakers and other charitable organizations from America came into defeated Germany and became active in helping to solve the basic needs of our people.

This was the foundation for a growing understanding between Americans and Germans, which in subsequent years developed into a far-reaching consensus in basic convictions and ideas, an understanding that proved its depth in the 1948 Blockade of Berlin as well as in America's defiance of the ultimative demands of the Soviet Union in the autumn of 1958.

The climax was, of course, the peaceful end of the Cold War in 1991, concluded by President George H. W. Bush, Soviet leader Mikhail Gorbachev, and German Chancellor Helmut Kohl, reluctantly accompanied by British Prime Minister Margaret Thatcher, French President François Mitterand, and Italian Prime Minister Giulio Andreotti. A new age—the arrival of the "Globalized World"—replaced the past. In the wake of this change the Soviet Union became Russia, with its population reduced from 290 to 142 million people. But the crowning event was the German unification and freedom for all Eastern European countries.

In all these years I kept writing my diaries, now over sixty-six volumes. It was during my summer holidays in Maine when I found time to read my notes about the darkest days in the history of my country—the total military, economic, and moral collapse. In the summer of 2007 I decided to write a book for my American friends describing my efforts to integrate the new Germany into the Western World.

—Walther Leisler Kiep
Vinalhaven, Maine
August 2011

# Acknowledgments

My sincerest thanks go to Gebhard Schweigler. Without his unwavering support, everlasting encouragement, and critical mind, the book would not be what it is.

Beate Lindemann, in spite of her full-time engagement in Atlantik-Brücke and Atlantik Forum, deserves my deep gratitude for having accompanied me on this long road.

John Bauman, former political counselor at the US Embassy in Berlin, lent me his lifelong experience on important aspects of American foreign policy and the long history of German-American relations.

Former German Ambassador Anna-Margareta Peters devoted much of her time to intensely reading the whole manuscript of this book.

My friend Jürgen Grossmann deserves my sincere appreciation for his successful bridge-building effort to Purdue University, his alma mater, which serves as the publisher of my book.

Last but not least I want to thank Sharon and Bob Philbrook for their friendship and hospitality during my many visits to their beautiful Island of Vinalhaven in Maine.

# Chapter 1

## A Long Road to Politics

The first American I ever met was Averell Harriman, one of the richest men of his time. Thus began a lifelong fascination with America. Many years later, I would meet Harriman again. He became a friend and mentor, even a role model as someone strongly committed to serving his country. Like him, I appreciated the good life, unabashedly. But I also worked hard so that others could enjoy a better life. Mine turned into a life of brokering deals and bridging gaps: between an ugly past and a better future, between the world of business and the realm of politics, between Europe and America, between East and West. This is the story of how I got there, and what happened along the way.

It must have been around 1933, just after Adolf Hitler came to power in Germany. My father was on the board of directors of the Hamburg-Amerika Linie (HAL), rebuilt to be one of the world's largest shipping lines after its near demise following Germany's defeat in World War I. Averell Harriman—the railroad, shipping, and banking tycoon—had acquired a financial interest in HAL some years earlier, thus greatly helping in its recovery. He came to Hamburg to talk business and to see his new friend, my father, who invited him to our home for dinner. I was seven years old. Decked out in our Sunday best—sailor suits for us boys—my older brothers, my older sister, and I were presented to the famous guest from America. We were used to such visits. Some years before, the Prince of Wales—the future Duke of Windsor—had honored my parents with a visit. After all, my father, who had grown up in Scotland, was a subject of His Majesty the King. He was also a proud German, who, having joined the German Navy in 1901 with Queen Victoria's personal permission, fought during World War I in every major naval battle against the Royal Navy. His German pride was sorely tested when he participated as a member of the German delegation in the Versailles peace treaty negotiations.

Still, Harriman's appearance in our house in Hamburg was a special occasion, even to us children. Alfons, our butler, was disappointed, though, as he confided to us nosy children afterward. The American visitor had disdained the fancy French wines offered at my parents' table and asked for a locally produced beer instead. People who preferred beer to a Bordeaux couldn't really be that rich. I remember sharing his puzzlement. Was this man in fact a superrich American? Or was he merely American: disdaining European luxuries and just enjoying a good beer? I was impressed and never forgot.

The next memorable Americans I met fell from the sky. Literally. It was a quite different event, but equally unforgettable.

The year was 1943. I was a typical teenager in a totally untypical situation: the middle of World War II. I had spent four years of the Third Reich period in Istanbul, where my father had accepted a position as adviser to the Turkish government regarding matters of building up a commercial shipping fleet. For me, it was a wonderful time. I was educated privately by a German teacher, whom I adored and who enriched my life immensely. I made many friends among similarly situated children of the international community. I grew to like Turkey, which was marked by a spirit of openness and liberalism. And I was far removed from the turmoil engulfing Germany and Europe. Alas, by 1940 my father's job had come to an end. My mother was eager to return to Germany because my two older brothers had meanwhile joined the German Navy. They went off to war in submarines, the most demanding—and deadliest—of sea services. Though my parents were anything but devoted nationalists, they could not stand the idea of hiding out in Turkey while their sons fought for Germany. So with a sense of foreboding and deep regret, they returned to Hamburg, where my father accepted a directorship in a local bank. Soon, Allied bombers began to attack Germany's major cities. Life in Hamburg became too dangerous, and our beautiful house was eventually destroyed. By 1943 we were forced to move to my grandparents' residence in the Taunus hills in Kronberg, just outside Frankfurt.

The war had caught up with us in many ways. The year before, in the fall of 1942, we had learned that my oldest brother, Claus, was missing in action. His submarine had disappeared off the coast of Newfoundland. My mother was devastated, my father stoic. I was, well, a typical teenager. While I mourned the death of my brother, I was more determined than ever to follow in his footsteps.

I had little sympathy for Hitler and his repressive regime. While on vacation in Kronberg in November 1938, I had personally witnessed the destruction of Jewish-owned properties and the humiliation of our Jewish neighbors during the pogrom of the *Reichskristallnacht*. While living in Istanbul, where the family read the London *Times* daily, we had been reasonably aware of what was going on in Germany. Later, like every other youngster, I was compelled to join the Hitler Youth, but I courted danger when I entertained my fellow *Hitlerjugend* with some pretty mean imitations.

That the war was not going well for Germany was no secret to us. My godfather Otto Carl Kiep, who also was my paternal uncle, quit Germany's Foreign Service after he realized that he could no longer represent Nazi Germany abroad. When Nobel Prize laureate Albert Einstein arrived in New York two months after Hitler's takeover in the spring of 1933, Otto Kiep, as German Consul General in New York, remarked at a huge welcoming reception in Manhattan to the American audience, regarding Einstein: "Your gain is our loss!" Otto Kiep left the United States, and after the outbreak of World War II in 1939, he joined the counterintelligence department under Admiral Wilhelm Canaris, which became one of the centers of resistance to Hitler. Eventually, he was arrested by the *Gestapo*, Hitler's notorious secret police, for allegedly undermining the German people's morale. When the plot to assassinate Hitler failed on July 20, 1944, Otto Kiep became linked to the conspiracy—in which he had not actively participated—because his name was found on a list of potential members for a post-Hitler government. After a show trial in Roland Freisler's *Volksgerichtshof*, he was sentenced to death and brutally executed. We were no friends of Hitler, nor had we any illusions about how the war would end.

However, I couldn't wait to join the *Kriegsmarine*—Germany's navy. That is where my father had served, where one of my brothers had given his life, and where my other brother was fighting. One by one, my friends went off to war. I wanted to be with them and contribute to the effort. Besides, some years earlier, when I was thirteen, I had developed a crush on Charlotte, the daughter of a neighbor down the street in Kronberg. I was still in love with her. She, however, was married to a highly decorated *Luftwaffe* pilot. I dreamed I could impress her with my own exploits in this war.

I had applied to join the navy even before I finished high school in the summer of 1943. But before I could begin my military service, I had to do what every other German was required to do: perform nine months of menial work in the *Reichsarbeitsdienst*. "National Socialism" was meant seriously by the National Socialist German Workers' Party (NSDAP). In order to instill a sense of national unity, social equality, and classless modesty, every German—male and female—had to report for a period of manual labor for some kind of community project at least once, even during the middle of a war that urgently required fresh recruits. Before we could carry a rifle, we had to handle a shovel. So off I went to help build a road.

While out working, we observed huge formations of Allied bomber aircraft streaming across Germany's skies—American during the day, British at night. One day, we saw one of the returning bombers burn, break up, and crash not far from where we were working. A couple of parachutes in the sky indicated that the bomber's crew had bailed out. Our *Arbeitsdienst* leaders quickly called us together, issued us some old Serbian rifles that were almost as long as ancient muskets, and sent us out in teams of three to find and capture any survivors of the crashed bomber.

My search group happened to run across two American airmen who had fallen from the sky. They were calmly sitting in the grass of a clearing in the woods smoking cigarettes, obviously glad that they were alive. We approached them cautiously, courageously pointed our rifles at them, and yelled one of the few English words we knew: "prisoner." They nodded, indicated that they were willing to surrender, and then offered us some cigarettes. We accepted the cigarettes somewhat sheepishly, put them away in our pockets for later use, and waited until military police arrived to take our "prisoners" away. I never forgot that typical American display of coolness under duress, and of friendliness in a critical situation.

I never did get to serve in the *Kriegsmarine*. Shortly after I had so "heroically" helped to capture American airmen, the boring nature of menial work caught up with me. I was detailed to load debris onto trucks. One day when I was not carefully watching what I was doing, the contraption that held the debris became overloaded and collapsed. I was buried underneath a pile of rubble, with only my feet sticking out. My fellow workers quickly dug me free; however, I had suffered a serious concussion, perhaps even a skull fracture, which kept me hospitalized for a while and which would cause excruciating headaches for months.

When I eventually reported for basic training, the navy doctors performed an extremely painful medical procedure that required pumping air into my head. They determined that I was unfit for duty and sent me home again.

In January 1945, I went once again to Stralsund on the Baltic Sea to report for naval duty. By now the Russian front was very close to Stralsund, and naval recruits were simply issued rifles and ordered into battle. As they were untrained and inexperienced, few of them survived. The navy doctors, however, examined me, declared me unfit once more, and told me to come back in June. On the train ride home, I was confused and despondent, but also scared when the train was strafed by Soviet fighter aircraft. The war was clearly lost, yet I so desperately wanted to prove myself in combat and to live up to my brothers' examples and reputations. Spared from having to fight in a near suicidal effort, I should have been deliriously happy, but instead I felt almost like a second-class German, kept from fulfilling my duty by what seemed to me a cruel fate. Only gradually would I learn to accept and to appreciate that fate.

To make matters worse—or better?—I learned in 1944 that my secret love's husband, the dashing *Luftwaffe* pilot and physician by by training Wilhelm Knapp, had died when his plane crashed while on a reconnaissance mission. Charlotte was now alone with her baby boy, Edmund. I was also aware that she had lost her mother, her sister, and her brother during the course of the war. I began keeping a diary, to which I entrusted my feelings and observations. I still make entries in my diary—by now more than sixty volumes—almost every day. A steady companion, it is now a treasured source of memories of a life fully lived.

Kept out of military service by my nagging *Arbeitsdienst* injury, and troubled by my youthful yearnings, I was persuaded by my more practical-minded father to start doing something useful. So I began an apprenticeship as an accountant and sales manager in a large Frankfurt firm. I hated it. Entering column after column of numbers and then reconciling them did not interest me, especially not with the world in flames and some kind of *Götterdämmerung* approaching on the horizon. But I stuck with it, and eventually I was glad that I did, as it provided me with a solid grounding in the basic principles of business. Soon that training would prove invaluable.

The end came in May 1945. Charles Dickens' cliché opening line rang true: "It was the best of times, it was the worst of times"—especially for a nineteen-year-old like me. My old world had come crashing down, leaving much of Germany in ruins and exposing its unfathomable moral corruption. Yet Germany's *Stunde Null*—its "zero hour," as it soon came to be known—was also a time of new beginnings. How to start anew? Our daily lives were filled with seemingly endless, but also endlessly fascinating, discussions of how to go about rebuilding not only our personal lives, but also our country. In the Frankfurt area—the heart of the American zone of occupation—so-called reeducation efforts began almost immediately. They were a constant source of amusement (What can those "uncultured Yankees" teach us?), but also an eye-opening experience: maybe we could, after all, learn something from American liberalism and democratic political processes.

I thought that the world was open to me. I seriously considered leaving Germany behind and immigrating to a place with fewer problems and more promises (and far away from everything that was troubling me). America was my dream destination. But I quickly discovered that the New World would not let me in; immigration was strictly limited, and underage Germans with no history of persecution by, or active resistance to, the Hitler regime simply were not welcome. So I considered Canada or perhaps South Africa. In the end, that proved to be too difficult as well. Besides, there were enough challenges and temptations in Germany. My parents needed support. Perhaps I could, even should, make it in Germany after all. Surely the massive rebuilding efforts offered plenty of opportunities for an eager young man. Maybe I could even enter politics and play an active role. Family members on both my father's side and my mother's side had been prominently active in local and national politics during the Kaiser years and during the Weimar Republic (my maternal grandfather had been a member of the Prussian parliament and a personal friend of Chancellor Otto von Bismarck). There were large shoes to fill.

My parents had also burdened me with the expectations conveyed by my middle name: Leisler. Jacob Leisler, an ancestor in my father's Calvinist family line, had left Hesse in 1660 for the New World as a nineteen-year-old, seeking freedom and prosperity—now there was an inspiration for another nineteen-year-old! He found both in New Netherland, at least for a while. He married a wealthy widow, went into business, and accumulated a fortune. New Netherland soon became New York, and Jacob Leisler became a subject of the British Crown. During the turmoil of the Glorious Revolution of 1688, Leisler formed a militia and led a rebellion that saw him emerge as governor of New York. He convened the first Intercolonial Congress in America in 1690 (to organize against Indian and French attacks) and drafted a constitution that foreshadowed America's democratic future. The British were not amused. A military detachment arrived in New York in March 1691 to reclaim it for the Crown. Jacob Leisler and his son-in-law were charged with treason and publicly hanged in May 1691. (Ironically enough, the Nazi regime had tried to reinvent and then portray Jacob Leisler as a German hero who gave his life in the fight against the British.)

Eventually, I convinced myself that it was indeed my turn, and that I was going to do it better. The defeat of Hitler's Germany presented us with the opportunity of national reconstruction on a grand scale. We had our doubts whether the occupation regime would actually lead to such an outcome—growing disagreements among the Allies and schemes such as the Morgenthau Plan, which called for an end to all industrial activities in Germany, tended to fuel such doubts. But surely without active participation by the Germans themselves, Germany would never reemerge from the desolation and destruction of the Third Reich. My decision to stay in Germany and make the best of "the worst of times" strengthened quickly into a resolve.

Fate intervened and I was to have my next memorable encounter with an American. He was Lieutenant Bentley of the 82nd Airborne Division, United States Army. He stepped into my life soon after Germany's unconditional surrender on May 8, 1945. I was at home in Kronberg when there was a knock on the door. In marched this lieutenant, who took a quick look around and calmly informed us that we had three hours to get out. Our house was being requisitioned for use by the US Army as temporary quarters for its officers. We packed up whatever we could in the short time allowed and moved down the street to stay with neighbors—Charlotte's family. Conditions were crowded, but I was under the same roof as my secret love. A few weeks later that house was requisitioned as well, so all of us had to move again, into even more cramped quarters. (Our living conditions were made worse, somewhat embarrassingly so to us, because my parents had taken in as a houseguest an old acquaintance, the sister of Kaiser Wilhelm II, whose castle in Kronberg had been requisitioned for use as an officers' club.)

A few weeks later, around nine o'clock in the evening, Lieutenant Bentley appeared again at our new domicile, accompanied by another man. In his gruff way, he brought us incredibly good news. "You are that Kiep kid, aren't you?" he asked after I had opened the door. I admitted that I was. Did I know the man who was with him? Did I ever: it was my older brother Jürgen! He had been trained to run two-men mini-subs as suicidal weapons for last-ditch attacks against enemy ships. We had not heard from or about him, and we were obviously greatly worried. To this day, my joy at seeing him again remains unmatched.

Jürgen, it turned out, was a lucky guy. First, almost miraculously, he had survived the suicidal madness of the "sea dog" mini-subs. Then, like many other soldiers at the end of the war, he had simply left his unit, destroyed all evidence of his military background, and sought to make his way home. Technically, he was a deserter who should have surrendered with his unit and become a prisoner of war. The occupation powers had to consider German military personnel on the loose as being potential resistance fighters, and thus, they were not kindly disposed to such people roaming around the countryside. My brother escaped detection and detention by riding a bicycle all the way from Hamburg to Kronberg, more than four hundred kilometers on worn-out and crowded back roads. When challenged, he claimed to be a Jewish actor. How he got away with such an incongruous disguise remains a miracle and a mystery.

Jürgen, of course, did not know that our house was now occupied by the 82nd Airborne. The garden gate was locked, so he climbed over the fence to get into the house: not a good move under the circumstances. The surprised and alarmed occupants took him into custody and, luckily enough, called for Lieutenant Bentley. Jürgen explained that he was merely trying to get home to his family. The lieutenant was kind enough to give my brother's protestations of innocence sufficient credence to confirm his identity by taking him to us. But he still had a problem: what to do with a deserter from the German Navy who had broken into a US military facility? After his cross-country bicycle ordeal, my brother did not look to be in the best of shape. "I think your brother is a very sick man," Lieutenant Bentley said to me. "I strongly advise you to put him to bed immediately and get a doctor to look after him. I'll come by tomorrow to pick up the doctor's certificate specifying that he is seriously ill."

We got the message. That night, our hastily summoned family doctor certified that Jürgen was indeed suffering from a number of debilitating medical problems. The next evening, Lieutenant Bentley showed up at our quarters and said one word—"certificate"—before disappearing into the night. Jürgen stayed behind under intensive family care. I never met Lieutenant Bentley again and do not know what became of him, but it was another lesson learned and a kindness never forgotten. Jürgen, who recovered speedily from his certified ills, eventually decided to do what I could not: he immigrated to Brazil in 1950 to begin a new—and eventually highly successful—life far away from Germany.

I was eager to get on with my own life, but I remained uncertain as to which direction to take. When the University of Frankfurt reopened soon after the end of the war, I enrolled to study economics and history. However, academic studies did not satisfy my immense curiosity, nor fulfill my desires to establish financial independence (without which I couldn't even begin to think about getting married). The economics courses I took were far too theoretical for a time of extreme scarcity and deprivation. Practical guidance was what I wanted, but did not receive, at the university. The same was true, unfortunately, for the academic approach to history. Above all, we students wanted to learn how Hitler's success had been possible, how he was able to envelop the Germans in politics and policies that led to the catastrophe of a world war and the horrors of the Holocaust. Our teachers, however, were unable or unwilling to confront those questions. Maybe it was too soon for that kind of historical reckoning (which, in fact, would be a long time in coming), or it was too much to ask of an academia that, in far too many instances, had itself easily succumbed to the lures of Nazism. Disappointed and disgusted, I quit my pursuit of academic wisdom after one semester of studies. Instead, I returned to my apprenticeship as an accountant, which I had not properly finished before the end of the war. I had no great fondness for the seemingly mindless number crunching I was again required to do. Once I had my certificate, however, I was able to be properly employed—an important first step toward the fulfillment of my many dreams.

I entered my professional life on a fast track, without knowing it at the time. I had, however, discovered the thrills of high speeds. I managed to obtain a beat-up British military-issue motorbike. I raced it around the countryside, for short periods of time anyway. A good number of hours were spent repairing sundry mechanical problems and fixing flat tires. Some years later, I acquired a top-of-the-line BMW motorbike that I rode well into advanced age. Giving up the sheer excitement of open-road motorbiking was one of the harder decisions of my life. I remain addicted to velocity. Once I could afford to buy cars—after a very early fling with a nearly lame prewar German Ford—I went for the real thing: a Porsche. Twelve Porsches accompanied me through life, with the next always being more exciting than the last.

The biggest speed thrill by far came after I had entered politics and the newly established West German Navy thought it appropriate to give me a commission as an officer in the naval reserves. One of my teenage dreams had finally become a reality in my middle age. Better yet, I was free to choose my annual reserve duty assignments. One summer I did naval aviation. I got to sit in the backseat of an F-104 Starfighter for a total of more than sixty hours of flight time. The Starfighter, its stubby wing-edges razor sharp, was practically a rocket with a pilot. Extremely difficult to fly, and with an unfortunate history of fatal crashes, it came to be known as a "widow-maker." Not only did I survive my confrontation with the Starfighter, but I can also relive with undiminished excitement every minute of flight time to this day. I am proud to say that I was never airsick, despite the best efforts of *Bundesmarine* pilots to shake up that middle-aged member of the German parliament. In later years, I often enjoyed the quite different thrill of supersonic flight in the Concorde during transatlantic crossings.

Back in the early post-war years, my Ariel motorbike offered me not only the excitement of high speeds, but also—and more importantly—the luxury of mobility. I made use of that mobility by going to work (part-time as a trainee) on the production line of Ford

Automobile Works in Cologne. At that time, Ford in Germany was producing only small trucks, at first for sale exclusively to Allied armed forces. As an alternative to number crunching, I found work on the production line to be almost exhilarating. I got to know the real world of manual labor, which, in the political and economic turmoil of post-war Germany, proved to be especially interesting. At one point, Henry Ford II personally had to intervene in order to break the power of the Communist labor union in the Cologne plant. He did so by ordering drastic improvements in the fare offered in the workers' cafeteria. Workers on the production line also received special "heavy work" rations. Enough was left over from these rations to help feed my family members as well as Charlotte and her child.

Toward the end of my stint on the truck production line, Ford management offered me—the trained and now certified *Kaufmannsgehilfe*—a position in the sales department. This is where things really became interesting, and I was extremely lucky. It was 1948. The economic recovery in occupied Germany was sputtering along. The official currency was the old reichsmark, which was worth hardly anything. Germans were forbidden to own any foreign currencies, including the specially issued money of the occupation regime. The unofficial currency for Germans doing serious business was American cigarettes. A carton of Camels fetched about 1,000 reichsmarks. Similar prices prevailed for other luxury items such as a bottle of whiskey or a pair of nylon stockings. These conditions encouraged a burgeoning black market that offered temptations to which I was not entirely immune. It became perfectly obvious that something drastic needed to be done to put Germany's economy on its feet. But what? Some kind of currency reform perhaps? And when would it come?

At the time I was twenty-one, and I decided to take action. I had linked up with family friends who owned a Ford dealership in Frankfurt. Their delivery truck was a prewar model running—if you could call it that—on the infamous *Holzvergaser*: a clunky contraption, usually attached to the outside of the cabin that converted wood into combustible gas. They were desperate for a new truck. Ford in Cologne was manufacturing trucks, and I had a connection to Ford's sales department. A new truck officially cost 9,800 reichsmarks, but a permit was required to obtain a truck, issued by German rationing authorities. In March 1948 I had obtained such a permit, only to see it withdrawn again. I grew frantic, for I knew that currency reform was about to happen.

This is where the worst of times turned into the best of times. US officers lived in our home and its downstairs had been turned into the "Boar's Head Club," so named after the hunting trophy mounted above the fireplace. I had become friends with Sergeant Albert Mulroy, the manager of the club. I was thus able to obtain some cigarettes and whiskey. I traded those in for the truck purchase permit, undoubtedly making some public officials and Ford employees, whom I had been pestering for weeks, quite happy—at least for a few days. On Tuesday, June 15, 1948, I was told by Ford to come and pick up my "goddamn" truck. That Thursday, I drove a shiny new V-8 Ford truck from Cologne to Frankfurt over back roads, since residents of the American zone of occupation were not allowed to enter the French zone of occupation, which stretched along the Rhine River almost all the way to Frankfurt. Like everything else in those days, that simple trip proved to be quite an adventure.

On Friday, June 18, 1948, came the announcement that a *Währungsreform* (monetary reform) would be implemented on Sunday. From one day to the next, the reichsmark became totally worthless and all savings were wiped out. Germans instead got the deutsche mark (DM), and every German was given an initial allocation of DM 40. This currency reform was as brutal in its execution as it was successful, practically overnight. Its originator, Ludwig Erhard—a professor of economics and German director of economics for the American occupation regime—quickly became one of the most popular Germans, known as the father of the *Wirtschaftswunder* (West Germany's economic miracle). That Sunday, as Germans lined up to receive their new money, goods that had been unobtainable for years suddenly appeared again on shop counters and in store windows: from cigarettes and liquor to meat and exotic fresh fruits. And I had a new truck. On Monday morning, the Ford sales department in Cologne informed us by telex that our new truck now officially cost DM 11,000. What a deal! Obviously, we would be much better off selling it than keeping it for our own purposes. A potential buyer emerged quickly. It was a butcher who could now sell his hoarded meat at an incredible profit while satisfying a long, pent-up demand. (Germans went through a number of consumption "waves" after the currency reform; the first one soon came to be known as the *Fresswelle*: the "gorging wave.") But how would he pay for the truck? No problem—in cash, of course, thus confirming why butchers were held in such low esteem at the time. A couple of days later, this butcher showed up with DM 11,000 in cash, almost all shiny new deutsche mark bills in denominations of 10 and 20, with a few DM 5 and 50 bills. It took us a while to count the money, and no time at all to count our blessings.

I was now in business. Better yet, Charlotte was in business with me, too. Together we set up shop at the Frankfurt Ford dealership to buy and sell used cars. The money earned from the truck deal served as our start-up capital. I managed the buying and selling, while Charlotte handled the paperwork. Germans were not yet allowed to drive cars, except where absolutely necessary (doctors, for instance). That meant that there were quite a few cars put away in German garages. Now that money was actually worth something, owners were willing to sell. The only buyers could be non-Germans, however, so our customers were mainly US soldiers, lusting to obtain their own sets of wheels. With eager sellers and buyers, and with me having established excellent lines of communication with the American community in and around Frankfurt, our business was soon booming.

Our American customers quickly grew tired of used German cars. They demanded new American cars, especially since post-war US car production was in full swing and the cars produced in Detroit offered exciting new features and incredible comfort. Operating in an uncertain legal environment of import regulations and currency restrictions, we managed to satisfy our customers' demands by plunging ahead. Ford agreed to supply us with new cars, and they set up special accounts for handling dollar payments. In 1949, our first year in the new car business, we sold more than 350 Ford, Mercury, and Lincoln automobiles. Life was good.

Quite accidentally, if logically, my life took another important, permanent turn. Selling fancy American cars to soldiers flush with cash, but basically bored with their occupation duties, was easy enough. They could drive their new cars without insurance, but obviously they would be better off with some kind of protection. Why not persuade them of the advantages of automobile insurance and offer them a package deal of car and insurance together? German insurance wouldn't offer policies for Allied soldiers, as they drove their private vehicles with license plates issued by their armed forces rather than by the German authorities, so I looked for a way to get into business with an American insurance company. An American acquaintance put me in touch with the Insurance Company of North America (INA), based in Philadelphia. In 1949, I signed a formal agreement with INA to become one of their insurance agents in Germany. Instead of the car business, I found myself in the insurance business, where I would stay for a long part of my life.

Soon after signing on with INA, I was asked to help set up a regional office in Fürth, near Nuremberg—another major concentration of US forces in Germany. Once again, I encountered extremely lucky circumstances. Two years earlier, my father—the erstwhile British citizen—had launched an inquiry regarding some financial holdings in the United Kingdom. For a long time, there was no response. Then one day he was called to the British consulate in Frankfurt. A consular official—with the unforgettable name of Mr. Moneypenny—informed him that, regrettably, his savings were no longer available. His Majesty's Government had taken note of the fact that he had once been a British citizen, however, and it was now prepared to reinstate British citizenship for him and his immediate family. This is how I received a British passport while setting up shop in Fürth. From one day to the next, my life changed dramatically. The minute I received that passport, I bought my first car, a small Ford, since I was now no longer subject to any of the restrictions imposed on ordinary Germans. I received better housing, was able to move into a larger office, had access to all the armed forces facilities, and could throw away my German ration cards. Needless to say, that fortuitous turn of events also improved my business, as I had even better access to potential customers and no longer needed to worry about the finer legal points of import regulations and currency restrictions. Charlotte and I wanted to get married and continue our lives together. The difficult hurdle was Charlotte's father. It was inconceivable that we would get married without his consent. As was still the custom then, I had to formally ask for his daughter's hand in marriage. Charlotte's father, however, was incarcerated as a war criminal. A chemist by training, he had run his family's chemical industry business. In 1925, his company was incorporated into the (later infamous) IG Farben chemical trust. During the Nazi years, he served in top leadership positions of IG Farben. After the war, IG Farben directors were indicted as war criminals for their close cooperation with the Hitler regime. At the Nuremberg trials, Fritz ter Meer was convicted of looting—having played a major role in IG Farben mergers, acquisitions, and construction abroad—and of using slave labor, specifically in a chemical plant located next to the Auschwitz concentration camp. The court sentenced him to seven years behind bars. He was serving his sentence in the Landsberg prison—the very same correctional institution where Hitler had been imprisoned after his failed 1923 putsch. (Hitler had emerged from Landsberg prison "uncorrected," with the finished manuscript of *Mein Kampf* ready to be published.)

I had no choice but to travel to Landsberg in Bavaria for a visit with the father of my bride-to-be. I was completely conflicted. I needed his permission to marry his daughter; if permission was granted, he would become my father-in-law. I knew him fleetingly as the somewhat distant neighbor down the road, who, in fact, had spent the last two years of the war running the IG Farben business in northern Italy. But now he was a convicted war criminal: one of those Germans who presumably had played however small a role in bringing Hitler to power and helping him perpetrate his evil doings. How would I react to him, in a prison environment no less? And how would he react to me—the Kiep kid wanting to marry his precious daughter in her precarious situation? Charlotte joined me for that all-important, yet oh-so-difficult train ride to Landsberg.

It was more than an awkward encounter. I had sent a formal request to the Landsberg prison for a visit with my future father-in-law. I suppose that was a good enough reason, for the commandant of the prison commanded me to appear at a specified time. The setting was surreal and unforgettable. Some twenty prisoners sat in a wire cage—those destined for execution were wearing a red vest. Additional glass plates prevented any physical contact. Obtaining formal permission from the father of one's bride is difficult enough under any circumstances. Under these conditions, it was almost absurd, but we managed it well. I may have impressed him with my determination. He certainly tried to impress upon us the many difficulties we would face, not least our age difference of almost six years, which in his case, he was sure, had led to the breakup of his first marriage. I promised that I would always be there for his daughter and his grandchild. He gave his blessing. I kept my promise.

My father-in-law was released from Landsberg prison in late 1950, one year short of his full sentence and just in time for our wedding. Officially, he was set free for good conduct. In reality, many of those convicted in Nuremberg were now, at the beginning of the Cold War, needed for the speedy political and economic reconstruction of Germany. Besides, significant doubts were being voiced whether justice had truly been served in all cases tried at the Nuremberg Military Tribunal. My own, not entirely unbiased, study of my father-in-law's case convinced me that he was unfairly convicted of what would appear to be, under conditions prevailing at the time, normal business activities. Fritz ter Meer thereafter had a major hand in rebuilding the German chemical industry, eventually serving on the supervisory board of chemical industry giant Bayer AG. But the issue of individual and collective guilt remained a difficult one for me personally, and for Germans in general.

Charlotte and I were married in November 1950. We happily went about establishing our own family. Michael was born in 1951; a second son, Walther, followed two years later. In 1956, we were blessed with our first daughter, Charlotte. In 1962, another daughter, Christiane, was born. Family bliss was complete. Then tragedy struck in 1975.

Michael—a young man of great promise as a journalist—died after a long battle with cancer. We suffered as he suffered, and we were devastated when he was gone. Yet this tragedy brought us even closer together as a family. We vowed never to forget him (a family foundation established in his name awards a fellowship each year on the day of his death to a budding journalist for training and work in the United States). We rededicated ourselves to carrying on in his memory, trying in our own way to make the world a better place. Restless work also helped to dull some of the ever-present pain.

We were, of course, plenty busy back in 1950. Our insurance business was booming. As I traveled around Germany and earned a steady income, I grew restless. I wanted to see more of the world. In 1952 I decided to give in to my wanderlust and make my first trip abroad—to the United States. I had a number of relatives there with whom I could stay, or who could help me to make arrangements, which was not easy in those distant days of unreliable telecommunications, when transatlantic telephone calls cost a fortune and had to be set up way ahead of time through a special operator. A four-week stay in the United States, even if only on the East Coast, required a good deal of planning.

As a child, I had once seen the *Hindenburg* majestically take off from Frankfurt on its slow dirigible way to Lakehurst, near New York. That certainly had whet my appetite for airborne transatlantic travel. In the summer of 1952, I took a Trans World Airlines propeller plane across the Atlantic to New York by way of London, Shannon (Ireland), Gander (Newfoundland), and Boston. I was eager to fully experience this city of my dreams, so I stayed in a downtown hotel, near the action. As it turned out, it also had the advantage of an air-conditioned bar, which I quickly learned to appreciate during that exceptionally hot summer. I took in all the sights, but I also enjoyed what was to me back then the luxurious suburban hospitality of my cousins. America was all that I had expected.

My next stop was Philadelphia. Strangely enough, I had not planned that part of my trip ahead of time; however, once I was in the United States, I thought it would be interesting and appropriate to check in with my employer, even though I was on vacation. So I simply walked into the headquarters of the Insurance Company of North America (a Philadelphia institution since 1792) to say hello, show my face, and get to know some of my colleagues. Everyone was astounded: a young man from Germany was working for us, in Germany? How did that happen? And he had the guts (or the gall) to just walk in and present himself? In good American fashion, surprise and astonishment quickly gave way to curiosity and admiration. This was a guy one had to see, so I was handed up the company personnel ladder until, on the third day of my stay in Philadelphia, I was invited to meet John Diemand, the company president. He took his time to question me about my experiences in post-war Germany and to inquire about my work for his company. I was deeply impressed that he would even speak with a lowly underling like me, and a mere walk-in at that. I liked the American way of dealing with employees!

After Philadelphia I continued my exploration of this fascinating country. In Washington, DC, the still sleepy capital, I experienced both the political splendor of the United States and—especially in the slum areas around the Capitol—its social squalor. If nothing else, it was a country of great contrasts and even greater contradictions. It was a valuable lesson, in that it opened my eyes to some American realities of which I had not fully been aware. I did not turn away from the United States, or, worse yet, begin to harbor anti-American attitudes, as I often saw happening in other such encounters. But somehow it made me appreciate my life in Germany more. It also strengthened my incipient personal commitment to an eventual political engagement that would seek to make a contribution to the firm establishment of democracy—on the basis of social equality—in Germany. If I could help to improve German-American relations in the process, so much the better. I returned to Germany thoroughly excited, but also thoughtfully cautious. I was not yet ready for big-time politics; neither was Germany, with its very limited sovereignty under the occupation regime.

Shortly after arriving back home, I received an invitation from the Insurance Company of North America to return the following year to Philadelphia in order to attend a six-month training course for INA agents. Apparently, I had made quite an impression during my visit at headquarters. INA clearly had bigger plans for that guy with guts and gall from Germany. It was an offer I could not (yet) refuse, so I reported to the Insurance Academy of America in 1954 for the longest stretch of time I would ever spend in the United States. INA went out of its way to make the prolonged visit as attractive as possible for me. Three days after I had arrived, the senior vice president took me aside and informed me that I really needed a car. I certainly did not disagree, but where could I get one for half a year, and could I even afford one? Not to worry, I was told: "We have a car for you!" And what a car it was: a brand-new Chevy, gasoline and maintenance provided for. In Germany, big-sized American cars were popularly known as "street-cruisers," and I felt like a king while cruising through Philadelphia and the surrounding countryside. I made new, lifelong friends among my colleagues. I was invited to parties along Philadelphia's Main Line, and even to a gala event at the DuPonts' estate in Delaware. It was an introduction to America that few, if any, members of my generation experienced. My love affair with America had been thoroughly renewed. To top it all off, INA provided me with the ultimate farewell gift: a first-class ticket on the luxury liner of the day, the *SS Independence*, for my return trip to Germany. I was going home in style.

I was now a fully trained insurance agent clearly destined for more—why else the first-class treatment? INA appointed me their chief representative in Germany at their main office in Frankfurt—a heady position for someone not even thirty years old. The sky seemed the limit, but soon a more immediate limit became apparent. INA let it be known, in unmistakable terms, that any further steps up their career ladder would require moving to the United States. I was more than flattered that they had so much trust in me. The temptation was strong to follow up on my youthful urge to immigrate to the United States, now with a clearly marked career path ahead. But the ties that bound me to Germany were stronger. My family's enthusiasm over such a move was very much restrained. My desire to enter German politics grew stronger in direct relation to the steps that were then being taken on the road to the restoration of (West) Germany's sovereignty. And much as I had grown to like, indeed love, the United States, I did not feel attracted to it strongly enough. Deep down, I was more German, and European (with my British and Turkish background), than American. So we decided to stay.

It was, in the end, not a terribly difficult decision to make. For just as INA was trying to lure me to Philadelphia, I was being tempted by the chief executive of one of Germany's most successful insurance brokerage firms to join his company. If everything worked out as planned, I was promised, I could become a full partner within the next few years. Everything considered, this was an offer I could not refuse. In 1955, I left the Insurance Company of North America and joined Gradmann & Holler. Soon thereafter, I was put in charge of the division handling insurance for Germany's resurgent automobile industry.

It was in 1955 that the Federal Republic of Germany, ten years after the end of the Third Reich, was granted sovereignty (if still somewhat limited) and readmitted into the community of nations. Many in Germany considered the price of admission too steep: the division of Germany into the Federal Republic of Germany and the Communist-controlled German Democratic Republic; the inclusion of each part of Germany in respective military alliances (the North Atlantic Treaty Organization for West Germany, the Warsaw Pact for East Germany); and the rearmament of both parts of Germany, with their troops now facing each other across the Iron Curtain, which ran straight through Germany. The political challenges for West Germany were immense. Never mind that economic reconstruction and democratic reconstitution were not yet fully accomplished. Its leaders now had to deal with many intractable issues relating to the deepening division of Germany, not least the question of how, if ever, to achieve its eventual reunification. It had to manage alliance relations, to which were soon added relations with a growing number of partners in the project of establishing a European Community. And it had to reestablish good relations with the rest of the world. The tasks ahead seemed daunting; to me, they appeared incredibly challenging and inviting. Soon I was to become deeply involved in all of them.

But I was not yet ready for politics. Accepting my new position with Gradmann & Holler in 1955 meant that I had to devote my energy to my expanded responsibilities. My main client was Volkswagen. The car manufacturer founded by Hitler with the socialist goal of making a personal car available to every German—thus the name "people's car"—had survived the war by producing the *Wehrmacht*'s equivalent of the Jeep. After the war, Volkswagen returned to the production of this strange-looking passenger car with a noisy air-cooled engine in the rear and a small trunk under its rounded hood. Living up to its original name, it proved to be highly popular, as economically recovering Germans left the *Fresswelle* behind and started a "car wave." Soon the VW became fondly known as the *Käfer*, since it did in fact resemble a beetle. The Beetle quickly established itself as the symbol, indeed the icon, of Germany's miraculous economic recovery: the widely heralded *Wirtschaftswunder*.

American soldiers stationed in Germany loved the Beetle. Here was a car that they could afford, sturdy and reliable, it was built for bad and narrow German roads, but held its own on Germany's fabled *Autobahn*. It also made for a nice and unique souvenir of their stay in Germany, so they started shipping them back home. Their fellow countrymen took a liking to this strange automotive creature. Owning a Beetle was not only cheap—it was also cool. Volkswagen was ready to supply the vehicles to Beetle enthusiasts. Soon, brand-new VWs arrived in rapidly increasing numbers in American ports. Some Beetles, however, no longer looked brand-new after their transatlantic voyage, having been damaged in transport. We insured against such damage and handled resulting claims. It was a booming business. At its peak, in 1970, Volkswagen shipped nearly 600,000 Beetles to the United States.

I became intimately involved in Volkswagen's American success story. As I had to organize damage inspection and insurance claims facilities in the major ports on both coasts, I got to meet and deal with the importers, distributors, and sellers of Volkswagen products. Some of them became lifelong friends. A few were unforgettable characters. I marveled at the irony that someone who sold a "people's car" could accumulate incredible wealth in the process. Johnny von Neumann was a prime example—and a poster boy for the American dream. He was a Jew from Vienna, forced by the Nazis to immigrate to the United States. He settled in Los Angeles, where eventually he operated a gas station on Sunset Boulevard. When Beetles began to show up on California roads, he recognized their potential as a popular car. He approached Volkswagen with a proposal for a network of California dealerships if he were granted sole import rights. Volkswagen agreed, and Johnny von Neumann had it made. By the 1960s, the former gas station operator was able to buy a villa in Beverly Hills, designed by Frank Lloyd Wright, where he entertained his guests. I was there one evening when he asked me whether I would like to join him for dinner. We climbed into his Rolls

Royce (certainly no "people's car") and headed out. Much to my surprise, we drove up to his Learjet parked at a nearby airport. Forty-five minutes later we were in Palm Springs at a fabulous country club. We enjoyed a fantastic dinner and superb California wine (no beer for us). Three hours later we were back home. Just another day in the lives of a car importer and an insurance broker.

In discussions with American acquaintances and friends, I had made no secret about my interest and ambitions in politics. Many of them were eager to accommodate me by introducing me to political figures of promise and prominence. One of the most helpful was my new friend Arthur Stanton, who had exclusive rights to import Volkswagen automobiles to New York. One evening in the late 1950s, we were on our way to dinner at a neighborhood restaurant. "I'd like you to meet someone," he had said. At the restaurant bar he introduced me to a boyish looking man who was accompanied by a stunningly beautiful woman. It was the newly elected senator from Massachusetts, John F. Kennedy. Stanton knew him from their service in the US Navy during World War II. Kennedy, insiders predicted, was a man to be watched; charismatic, with a stellar war record, and backed by his father's money and influence, he might someday make it to the very top of American politics. I certainly was impressed. Skipping the usual small talk, we immediately engaged in a serious and intensive debate about German and American political developments. He was knowledgeable, an intent listener, and a good debater who quickly and succinctly came to the point. Unfortunately, he did not stay for dinner. I would have loved to continue our conversation with the future president of the United States. I followed his meteoric—but also meticulously executed—rise to the White House closely. If ever my own political ambitions were to come to fruition, I knew I could learn a lot from this dynamic new face and force in American politics.

Nelson Rockefeller, then governor of New York, was another politician whom I admired, especially once I had made his acquaintance and established a friendship of sorts. As governor, this scion of America's plutocracy was extraordinarily successful, and I was impressed by his leadership skills, his political acumen, and his genuine interest in the well-being of those much less fortunate than him. His failures as a presidential candidate (due in part to a messy divorce and hasty remarriage) were less impressive. Maybe he loved life—and women!—too much to succeed in national politics (although Kennedy and, later, Bill Clinton would show how it could be done). We saw each other frequently—even after Rockefeller had become President Ford's vice president—shared many a good laugh, engaged in serious political discussions, and, in short, enjoyed each other's company. He became another important political mentor for me.

By now I was primed for politics. But I needed a primer to take the step into politics. That happened on August 13, 1961. On that day, the East German regime put up a wall between East and West Berlin. Until then, Berlin—still under joint control of the four victorious powers of World War II—had remained the one place where East Germans could cross unimpeded over into West German territory. The Soviet Union, along with its East German puppet regime, had tried for years to change the political status of Berlin, with the ultimate goal of establishing the German Democratic Republic as a fully sovereign nation-state in its own right, thus cementing the division of Germany—and in the process, isolating Berlin as an unsupportable enclave in the middle of East Germany. The Western powers, strongly encouraged by the West German government, had steadfastly refused to give in to Soviet lures or yield to East German threats. But as pressure mounted and the East German regime tightened its Communist rule, more and more East Germans started fleeing to West Germany. Berlin was the place where they could easily do so—if it was ever easy to leave behind everything and walk across the "sector line" with only the few personal belongings that could be carried by one person. The swelling stream of refugees forced the East German regime's hand. It decided to put up a wall in Berlin and reinforce the Iron Curtain elsewhere with minefields and automatic shooting devices. The East German regime justified its actions as "anti-capitalist protection measures." East Germans knew that they were now living in a prison.

Along with many others in West Germany, I was appalled. The Berlin Wall meant that Germany's division was likely to be permanent. That prospect violated my patriotic feelings. However, I also felt strongly that we in the West—blessed as we were by the *Wirtschaftswunder* and the establishment of a functioning democracy—had an obligation to bring these blessings to our fellow countrymen in East Germany. I had no easy or ready-made answers as to what to do. While I was disappointed that our Western allies, above all the United States under the new leadership of President John F. Kennedy, had seemingly stood by and allowed East Germany to put up the Berlin Wall, I also knew that military action—as demanded by some—would make matters only worse. More than anything, however, I was convinced that now was not the time to stand aside and let developments take their course. Active engagement was required: my active engagement.

Easier said than done. Active political engagement under the circumstances required working within the confines of a political party. But I was not sure which party was the right political home for me. Like many in my position, I had voted for the Free Democratic Party (FDP), which basically represented the interests of West Germany's highly educated and well-to-do bourgeois. Germany's much-respected first president, Theodor Heuss, a founding member of the Free Democrats, had been the very embodiment of these virtues. An aunt of mine in Hamburg was a prominent member of the Free Democrats, so it seemed only natural that I should join the FDP. But it was a small party with limited power and an uncertain political profile—since it had to enter into a coalition with another party if it wanted to exercise any influence at all—and therefore not all too attractive for an eager activist like me. Still, I was willing to give it a try. I talked with the local FDP chairman, a friend of mine, about my plans. He arranged a dinner meeting with the national party chairman, Erich Mende. That settled it. Mende was one of the most obnoxious German politicians whom I ever encountered. During the war he had earned the *Ritterkreuz*, the German military's highest decoration for heroism in action. He now insisted, against protocol and postwar custom, to wear this decoration as a civilian. I was completely turned off by this display of obstinacy, insensitivity, and outright nationalism. His rhetoric was not much better, and it frightened me with its militaristic and nationalistic simplicities. A party with a chairman like that was not for me, even if it carried the words "free" and "democratic" in its name.

I basically had no problems with "social" and "democratic" either, but joining the Social Democratic Party (SPD)—the political home of the German labor movement—would have been a big stretch for me. Its chairman was the exact opposite of Erich Mende. Kurt Schumacher, an outspoken opponent of Hitler's grab for power, had spent much of the Nazi years in concentration camps, emerging from this hell unbroken in spirit, but physically handicapped. He fought courageously, if unsuccessfully, for a Germany committed to socialist ideals and pacifist practices. I admired Schumacher personally and respected these convictions, but I found them politically unwise. Germany could recover economically and politically only if it established a market economy and put itself squarely on the side of the Western democracies, even if that meant rearmament, membership in the North Atlantic Treaty Organization (NATO), and temporary acquiescence regarding the division of Germany. Eventually, the SPD would come to embrace these principles, but in 1961, they still had some way to go. At this point, their way was not my way, and I never anticipated that I would support a Social Democrat-led government under Chancellor Willy Brandt in their efforts to achieve an understanding with the Soviet Union, in which self-determination without an exclusion of eventual unification became possible.

That left only one realistic alternative: the Christian Democratic Union (CDU). It was the party of Konrad Adenauer, the Federal Republic's first chancellor. Adenauer, generally known as "Der Alte," was the father of Germany's post-war democracy. He had begun his political career in 1917 as the mayor of Cologne, and he was still mayor of his native city in 1933 when Hitler came to power. Adenauer expressed his disapproval of that turn of events by refusing to meet with the new *Reichskanzler*—a.k.a. *Führer*—and by having swastika flags removed from bridges across the Rhine River. It took the Nazi regime just a few weeks to force Adenauer from office and drive him into hiding. He survived the war years residing in his unpretentious but comfortable house in Rhöndorf, overlooking the Rhine River, near the provincial city of Bonn. After the war, Adenauer was a logical choice (even though British occupation authorities initially did not trust him) to lead Germany's political reconstitution. He played a crucial role in the drafting of the Federal Republic's *Grundgesetz* (Basic Law), helped found the Christian Democratic Party, and led that party—with himself at its head—to victory in West Germany's first federal elections in 1949. At the age of seventy-three (he was, to the day, half a century older than I), Adenauer was elected chancellor of a recently defeated, largely destroyed, and thoroughly demoralized country. If West Germany owed its miraculous emergence from defeat, destruction, and demoralization to any one person, it was Konrad Adenauer.

Adenauer was an extraordinarily crafty politician, whose heart beat for his beloved Rhineland. Thus, the establishment of the Federal Republic as a truncated part—at best, perhaps, a future core—of a larger Germany caused him little heartache. (Asia, he had once remarked, began beyond the Elbe River.) He made sure that the Federal Republic's seat of government would be in the small town of Bonn, and not in Frankfurt, the center of Germany's commercial interests and the headquarters of American occupation forces. Adenauer governed from his provincial home, literally and figuratively speaking. He thereby kept the Federal Republic from policies too ambitious for its own good, but also from interests and influences too far removed. He quietly pursued the challenging goal of reconciliation and restitution with the Jewish community, which resulted in a system of personal restitution payments and massive support for a struggling Israel. He enthusiastically endorsed the project of European unification, at the core of which was reconciliation with France. The German-French Treaty of Friendship, which he concluded with Charles de Gaulle in 1963, was perhaps the culmination of his political life. Realistically and determinedly, but with considerably less emotional commitment, he brought West Germany into the binding ties of NATO. Adenauer knew, though his heart would hurt, that the Federal Republic could only flourish as a functioning democracy right at the Iron Curtain if it maintained the closest of relations with the United States, and that required participation in the North Atlantic Treaty Organization.

By the early 1960s, Adenauer had achieved all he could achieve. His political life had nearly run its course, and now into his late eighties, his real life would not last much longer, either. It was time for a new generation of leadership that would build on his achievements with new energy and drive. I saw my chance. The CDU's program was close to my main political principles, with its emphasis on market economy and close alliance relations, so I decided to become a Christian Democrat and to look for an active role in politics. That momentous step took place in late 1961. I was thirty-five years old and financially well-established enough to enter the less lucrative life of a politician. We had a wonderful house in Kronberg, swimming pool and all, our own private hunting reserve nearby (I had become a licensed hunter and was thus allowed to own firearms), and a vacation home in the Swiss Alps. In short, I had achieved all the dreams of a good life in Germany. In an unguarded moment, I would soon tell an inquisitive reporter that, if need be, I could comfortably live on my investment income. But I wanted more in life, both in terms of responsibility and excitement. Politics was beckoning.

My business partners, of course, did not share my enthusiasm for striking out on new adventures. They were counting on me to continue my highly successful involvement in our firm. It would take a good deal of persuasion, as well as some carefully worked out business arrangements, before they grudgingly accepted my determination to spend a good deal of time and energy on political pursuits. I never left the insurance business entirely, even as my political career advanced. Eventually, I would devote about 60 percent of my professional energy to politics, 40 percent to our insurance business. Luckily, my political activities opened up new business opportunities as well, so that my business partners actually came to appreciate my life in politics. My family was fully supportive of—if not always happy about—late nights, busy weekends, and long absences.

The beginnings of my political life, however, were anything but rapid. At first I became active in county politics. I had some success in organizing the CDU for local elections that saw a significant increase in voter support. The next national elections were scheduled for 1965. I had little hope of getting my party's nomination to stand as its candidate for elections to the *Bundestag* (Germany's parliament that, in turn, elects the chancellor as the head of government). But my luck held. In June 1964, I happened to run into the representative from my district, a member of the CDU, who told me that he would not seek reelection: would I be interested in becoming a candidate? Well, yes, but it wasn't that simple. In the German party system, it is the party members themselves who, in a series of party delegate meetings, nominate not only a candidate for direct election from the district, but also rank-order candidates for party lists from which—under a proportional voting scheme—half of all members of the *Bundestag* are drawn. In a somewhat nerve-racking selection process on the district level, I finally prevailed against my strongest intra-party opponent by only seven delegate votes. I was now a candidate for a seat in the *Bundestag*.

Traditional campaigning in Germany at that time meant mostly speaking at large public gatherings. I was going to do it differently. I had observed how British and American election campaigns were run, with door-to-door canvasing, crisscrossing the district, creating a sense of excitement: a buzz, in modern terminology. That was going to be my style. When the press eventually dubbed me "the German Kennedy," I knew that I was halfway there, not least because being compared to that tragic icon of American vigor and success was itself priceless. So I rented a big modern VW bus, painted "Our man for Bonn: Walther Leisler Kiep—CDU" along its side, hit the road, and started knocking on doors. Untraditionally, I campaigned primarily for myself and not for the party. That was considered almost revolutionary. It was a tough campaign but I enjoyed every minute of it, partly because I found the competition itself invigorating, but mostly because the response among the voters was tremendously encouraging. My district represented a cross-section of Germany, with some of its wealthiest communities, but also with heavy concentrations of workers and farmers. Not once was I met with hostility or resentment. I may not have persuaded everyone to vote for me, but I am sure I convinced many that, twenty years after the end of the Third Reich, democracy in Germany was alive and well, indeed flourishing.

I might have won anyway, but once again a set of unusual circumstances came to my aid. For one, Konrad Adenauer, "the old man," was no longer chancellor. Sensing that he might be a liability rather than an asset in the 1965 elections, the CDU in October 1963 had somewhat unceremoniously replaced him with Ludwig Erhard, the man behind the 1948 currency reform and, as a longtime economics minister, the architect of Germany's *Wirtschaftswunder*. Erhard's standing among the German public was tremendous for that reason alone; however, he was also a folksy character, best known for his ever-present cigar, which contributed to his popularity as well. I personally was less enamored of Erhard, as I saw a distinct lack of leadership that invited constant sniping and snide attacks from his predecessor Adenauer, who proved ever more bitter about his removal from power, as well as from ambitious rivals within the CDU who were all too eager to take over the reins of power. Yet with Erhard running for reelection as chancellor, the CDU seemed primed for success in 1965, which meant that otherwise unknown candidates like me had a good chance of winning. I was willing to ride Ludwig Erhard's coattails.

I had not met Erhard before, but during the summer of 1965, I used a break in campaign activities for a quick business trip to New York. While there, I learned from an article in the newspaper that he would be in town for an official visit. I managed to arrange a meeting with him during a reception at Gracie Mansion, the mayor's residence. We took enough of a liking to each other that I was encouraged to ask him whether he would campaign for me. Erhard spontaneously and enthusiastically agreed to help. And what a show it was! On August 13, 1965, Erhard arrived in my district on his private train from Bonn. He had brought along the chancellor's fanciest limousine, a big Mercedes convertible. We spent the day riding through the district, top down, a box of cigars on the seat between us, enjoying ourselves on a beautiful summer day, addressing a number of huge gatherings, and stopping occasionally for chats with curious onlookers. Now I was not only riding Erhard's figurative coattails, I was riding in his limousine and basking in his glory. The experience only fueled my own political ambitions.

The election was set for September 19. On September 11, one of the candidates in our district, who represented a small right-wing party, committed suicide. Out of respect for this personal tragedy, but also due to requirements for a new ballot, it was decided that the election in our district would be held fourteen days later. This presented a curious situation, but it also opened up new chances for me. On September 19, the CDU won the elections; in a renewed coalition with the FDP, it quickly reelected Ludwig Erhard as chancellor. My two direct opponents in the district had each won a seat in the *Bundestag* through the mechanics of proportional representation. I had not, which encouraged me to strengthen efforts further once campaigning in our district resumed immediately after the election. My opponents felt no such need, and voters knew that the only candidacy really at stake was mine. Just to make sure, Erhard agreed once again to participate in a campaign swing on my behalf. On Sunday, October 3, the battle was finally over. I had won the direct election with a plurality of 6,521 votes. The self-styled "German Kennedy" was now a member of the German parliament. Better yet, and much more importantly, I was a member of the governing party. My political career was set to take off.

It had been a long road from a carefree childhood, a turbulent youth, and a truck purchase leading to a rocket-propelled career. I was ready for a new turn on that road, trusting in my good luck and in my ability to charm people from all walks of life. Of course, I did not know that it would take me from the heights of being a shadow foreign minister to the lows of being a party treasurer accused of corruption. I never dreamed that one day I would find myself naked on the floor of my sauna trying to escape a terrorist's bullets. I could not foresee that I would be asked by a German chancellor to carry suitcases full of cash in a top-secret effort to support democratic movements in Portugal and Spain. I did not anticipate getting engaged in hush-hush mediation efforts involving such figures as a Turkish prime minister, a member of the East German Politburo, a mayor of Shanghai, the leader of a Palestinian terror organization, or the feuding CEOs of the world's largest automobile companies. I did hope that a life in politics would be exciting and rewarding. That expectation was fulfilled, but I also suffered some deep disappointments. This is the story of both, achievements and disappointments—the story of my life in politics.

# Chapter 2

## In Politics

I was a newcomer in Bonn, but I was also a latecomer, having been elected two weeks after everyone else. The new government, which was just the old government with Ludwig Erhard continuing as chancellor, had already been confirmed by the *Bundestag*. The business of politics was in full swing. I did not know my way around and had to learn that business from scratch. I did not get off to a good start. Looking for the room where members of my party were caucusing, I stumbled into a meeting of SPD representatives instead. Due to the peculiarities of my election, my face, at least, was familiar enough even to members of the opposition, who found the situation hilarious. "Come on in and join us," they kidded me, but I beat a hasty retreat amid their laughter and went looking for my real political home.

I had no further difficulties finding CDU meeting places—I am a fast learner. Making the CDU my real political home, however, did prove to be more difficult than I had expected. There were times when my assessments of political necessities were closer to SPD positions than to policies pursued by my party, especially in matters of foreign policy. In that sense, my accidental visit to an SPD caucus was almost symbolic. There were also moments when I despaired over the viciousness of politics, as practiced by prominent leaders of the CDU and its Bavarian counterpart, the Christian Social Union (CSU)—who together formed one *Fraktion* (faction) in the *Bundestag*, and thus one common front in national politics. I realized early on that I needed to develop a thick skin and a great deal of patience if I were to survive, or indeed succeed, in Bonn.

Newcomers face such problems everywhere. Latecomers have a particularly difficult time in German political life, which is dominated by political parties. Unlike in the United States, where access to political office is determined by primary voters and thus open to anyone willing to give it a try (and spend a good deal of money), political offices in Germany are allocated strictly by card-carrying party members, mostly through a series of public delegate meetings (which I had had to face when I was seeking the candidacy in my constituency), but partly through nebulous dealings in back rooms and tit-for-tat deals among party leaders. It is a system that favors party loyalty. You make it to the top only if you begin at the bottom. Latecomers are viewed with suspicion. They have not paid party dues through a lifelong commitment to and work for the party, and thus are seen as seeking rewards that properly belong to party stalwarts. They are also of dubious loyalty—why else would they have waited so long to enter politics? That problem is compounded when the latecomer is not dependent on income and career benefits provided by public office and therefore not subject to party pressure: "Toe the line or else!"

All of these factors applied to me. I had deliberately waited to seek a political career until I was financially independent. I had run my own campaign, new in style and pretty much independent of the party. The party was glad that I had won and welcomed me as a newcomer with fresh ideas, vigorous drive, and strong appeal. But precisely because I was a latecomer—independent in every regard and possessing skills, such as speaking a number of languages fluently, as well as important connections beyond politics that party regulars rarely acquired—I remained somewhat of an outsider. To this day I am convinced (personal considerations aside) that Germany is not well-served by a party system that promotes narrow-minded politicians with more than a touch of provincialism to its leadership positions.

Yes, I was ambitious. Why else enter politics if not to aim for high office and thus the opportunity to make a difference? But I never pursued my ambitions with the ruthless single-mindedness and scheming mentality that is often necessary for ultimate success. In the end, my (never clearly articulated) highest ambitions remained unfulfilled. Yet, during half of a lifetime in politics, with all of its ups and downs, I achieved far more than a quiet existence as a backbencher. I did succeed in making a difference and leaving my imprint on a number of issues and policy areas. What follows in this chapter is an account of my experiences in politics. Detailed descriptions of my involvement in specific policy areas are offered in subsequent chapters.

Throughout my dual careers in private and public life, I have been blessed with good luck. Part of my good luck has involved having the right mentors—people whose advice I could trust and whose support was reliable. One such mentor was Hermann Josef Abs. He was a family friend and a neighbor, having bought my father-in-law's house where I myself had lived for a few weeks at the end of World War II. Abs was one of the most important figures in post-war West Germany, working mostly behind the scenes and succeeding in putting the Federal Republic on the right track toward economic recovery and international acceptance. He was not uncontroversial. He had held high-ranking positions in German business and industry during the Hitler years and, without a doubt, had been aware of—if not directly involved in—the expropriation of Jewish-owned businesses in Germany and in occupied countries. Because of his role as a banker on the executive board of Deutsche Bank and as a businessman—including a position as a supervisory board member of IG Farben, where he had gotten to know my father-in-law—Abs was briefly imprisoned by British occupation authorities after the end of the war. However, as some of his discreet efforts to help disowned and expelled Jewish business owners became better known, and as the demand for his kind of practical economic experience grew immensely when the extent of Germany's economic woes became apparent, Abs was released from prison and hired as an economic adviser to the British occupation regime. Having never been a member of the NSDAP, nor directly implicated in any wrongdoings, Abs was fully exonerated soon thereafter. I had no personal qualms in seeking his counsel and support, and I was especially eager to obtain his advice on how to secure my financial independence while pursuing a career in politics. When it came to dealing with the interrelated issues of power and money, no one in Germany was more qualified than Hermann Josef Abs.

Abs was more than a mentor—he became a role model. Modest in his personal life with no ostentatious displays of power and wealth, he sparkled with wit and impressed with unflappable self-assuredness and supreme self-control. Emotional outbursts of any kind, calculated or not, were alien to him. He enticed his counterparts with rationally precise argumentation and a cool charm that, at appropriate moments, could be superseded by a cunning play on words or an uncannily pertinent—at times even bitingly witty—observation. Of Ludwig Erhard, for instance, he once remarked: "The honorary professor of economics is never happier than when he is addressed by a real professor as *Herr Kollege*." He was able to display his wit and charm in the four foreign languages that he spoke fluently—invaluable skills he had acquired while working as a currency trader in Holland, Great Britain, the United States, and Latin America.

Abs and Konrad Adenauer shared a common background—deep roots in Cologne/Bonn and the Rhineland, a firm commitment to the Catholic faith, and a solid bourgeois lifestyle—that helped cement a relationship of mutual trust, respect, and reliance. Close friends they were not, but they worked in close harmony to put Germany back on its feet. The first major task taken on by Abs was to build up and then head the *Kreditanstalt für Wiederaufbau* (KfW), the German counterpart to the European Recovery Program, more generally known as the Marshall Plan. The KfW's task was to convert Marshall Plan aid into German funds available as credits to reconstruction investors. Abs was the CEO of KfW for four years (1948-52). The incredible success of the Marshall Plan in Germany was based in no small measure on the skill with which Abs guided the KfW through this difficult period. The KfW is still in business today, as the original credits were repaid and the ever-increasing funds made available for new investments, now mostly for projects in developing countries. The KfW's funds, as well as its skills in economic recovery efforts, were much in demand when, after the reunification of Germany, East Germany turned out to be in dire need of both.

There is an important footnote to the Marshall Plan and the KfW. In 1972, twenty-five years after Secretary of State George C. Marshall had outlined the plans for the European Recovery Program during commencement exercises at Harvard University, the West German government under Chancellor Willy Brandt decided to honor the unprecedented success of generous US post-war aid to Germany by setting up a German Marshall Fund of the United States. It was a gift to the people of America, with no strings attached—a foundation (with eventual headquarters in Washington, DC) to be administered by an American board of trustees, dedicated to addressing problems common to industrialized societies. Operating funds were made available in annual installments of $10 million—paid out of KfW funds—and thus not subject to annual budget debates in Germany. When the gift was up for renewal fifteen years later, I was asked by then Chancellor Helmut Kohl to work out the details. It was a task I accepted with great pleasure, for not only was I firmly committed to the idea of demonstrating gratitude for American Marshall Plan aid, but I also could repay, in a manner of speaking, a personal debt of gratitude to Hermann Josef Abs. The German Marshall Fund, in the meantime, has emerged as a major player in transatlantic relations and is heavily engaged in projects helping to rebuild the unfortunate countries that were subject to Soviet domination until the end of the Cold War. It has indeed become a fitting memorial to the generosity of the American people and the wisdom of its leaders during the post-war years.

In 1951 Adenauer appointed Abs as the Federal Republic's chief negotiator for the settlement of German debts. It was an issue with a long history of exceedingly poor management going back to the post-World War I settlement imposed on Germany at Versailles, which had contributed greatly to German miseries and then to Hitler's rise to power. There was, therefore, a strong interest on all sides not to repeat the errors of Versailles; that is, not to force Germany into payment schedules that it could not sustain and that would ruin it economically. On the other hand, West Germany—striving hard, under Adenauer's leadership, to escape the occupation regime and to reestablish its own sovereignty—needed to prove that it was a reliable partner, capable of handling its economic affairs responsibly; that also meant satisfying the justifiable demands of its creditors. In short, Germany needed to become creditworthy again, and Abs was the man to secure that goal. He was not in a good bargaining position between creditors who wanted their money (and investment returns) back, and a debtor who would have preferred to wipe out all debts and to start from scratch—to make use, as it were, of the *Stunde Null*. As Abs later recounted, the German finance minister, when he gave him his instructions, told him half in jest that "if you do this job poorly, you might be hanged from a pear tree; if you do it well, from an apple tree." In the end, he did his job exceedingly well by satisfying both sides with a reasonable compromise. He credited his success to the fact that all negotiating partners in the process—which culminated in the London Debt Conference of 1952-53—were pros, that is, professional bankers: "Everyone knows that boxing matches between pros are much less bloody than fights between bloody amateurs."

Even before going into the negotiations, the Adenauer government had announced that West Germany was prepared in principle to repay debts incurred between the end of World War I and the beginning of World War II. But how was he to calculate those debts, given the uncertainties of exchange rates and fluctuating interest rates, on top of prior debt settlement efforts and the Nazi regime's policy of defaulting on debts? Much of the negotiations involved simply agreeing on proper calculations. Then there was the question of whether West Germany—which generally argued that it alone should represent all of Germany—in this instance could be held accountable for debts incurred by a Germany much larger and therefore economically more powerful (Adenauer's government claimed it could not). Finally, there was the issue of how quickly the debts should be repaid. Both sides agreed in principle that Germany should not be required to pay more than it would be able to earn through its foreign trade, but just how that would work out was, of course, highly uncertain. Moreover, the creditors refused to permit contingency clauses that might enable West Germany to escape debt payments through the manipulation of its economic performance, as had happened during the Weimar Republic with its deliberate inflationary policies.

The London Debt Agreement of 1953 represented a compromise that reflected Abs' negotiating skills on the one side, and a primarily American determination to give the Federal

Republic the benefit of the doubt and to go on establishing West Germany as an economically solid and politically trustworthy country—by now a much-courted future ally in the Cold War against the Soviet Union. Without the settlement of the debt issues, West Germany would not be in a position to join any kind of Western alliance, as was then under discussion. In the end, West Germany was obligated to repay about DM 14 billion in prewar and post-war debt—a sum 50 percent less than a standard calculation of Germany's debt had established. The Federal Republic was given thirty years to make annual payments to pay down that debt—a requirement it fulfilled with ease as the "economic miracle" took hold. Altogether seventy countries received payments from Germany—twenty-six had been directly involved in the London negotiations. Eastern European countries, however, were excluded. In response to the Federal Republic's claim that it should not be held liable for all of prewar Germany's debt, its negotiating partners agreed to suspend part of the back interest due on that debt until the reunification of Germany. When Germany was reunified thirty-six years later, it dutifully began repaying that last remnant of its debt, which amounted to about 100 million euros—a tiny sum compared to the overall cost of reunification.

The London Debt Agreement finally provided for a moratorium on reparations for war-related damages. The German side had claimed that reparations, which included the confiscation of German-owned properties abroad, should be included in an overall financial accounting. "Forget it!" had been the response; if war damages were to be fully taken into account, Germany could only lose. The London Agreement, therefore, specified that no more reparations were to be made until a final peace treaty settled the issue. No such peace treaty was ever concluded. The so-called Treaty on the Final Settlement with Respect to Germany—the "Two-Plus-Four Treaty" that made reunification possible—was concluded in place of a formal peace treaty. The reparations issue thus had been laid to rest in 1953. (When West Germany was granted limited sovereignty in 1955 and joined NATO, Abs successfully negotiated an agreement with the American government that restored some prewar German property rights in the United States.)

Settling Germany's outstanding foreign debt was a difficult enough issue. Settling its debt with the victims of the Holocaust was another—morally much more compelling, yet in practical terms unfathomably more difficult: how can one even begin to think about settling a debt incurred with the murder of six million Jews and the persecution and forced expulsion of many more? Konrad Adenauer knew and felt in his heart that Germany needed to address the issue. Already on November 25, 1949, he had declared in an interview with a Jewish weekly newspaper, *Allgemeine Wochenzeitung der Juden in Deutschland*, that Germany was prepared to provide material help to individual Jews and the newly founded state of Israel: "The German people are willing to make up for the injustice that was done to the Jews in its name by a criminal regime, as much as that is possible after millions of people have been destroyed and will never be brought back to life. We consider such a *Wiedergutmachung* (compensation) our duty." There could never be any doubt, certainly not for me, that Germany needed to provide some kind of restitution to the victims of the Holocaust. Many Germans, however, felt that they themselves had already paid a heavy price for the crimes committed by the Nazi regime: bombed-out cities, thirteen million refugees from what used to be German territories in Eastern Europe, and the general miseries of the immediate post-war years served as proof for such feelings. Accordingly, any offer of restitution was controversial.

Feelings on the Jewish side were equally conflicted. Given the nature of the Holocaust, full restitution was simply not possible; however, anything less than full restitution would be adding insult to injury, while allowing the Germans a sense of exculpation—as *Wiedergutmachung* implied. For many, the mere thought of dealing with Germany, perpetrator of the Holocaust, was painful. In Israel, future Prime Minister Menachem Begin led massive protests against any such deal with Germany. Yet Israel needed all the help it could get. In light of these sensitivities, any negotiations between the state of Israel and Jewish organizations on one side, and the Federal Republic on the other required not only complete confidentiality, but also supreme diplomatic skill. Once again, Hermann Josef Abs was the man Adenauer would rely on. The debt settlement negotiations and the Jewish restitution negotiations were, in any case, closely related, in part because a successful conclusion of both was necessary for the Federal Republic to achieve its goal of regaining sovereignty, but more directly because at the heart of both negotiations was the issue of how much West Germany would be able to pay without risking its economic recovery.

Formal negotiations began in March 1952 in The Hague and ran concurrently with the London debt negotiations. Early on, Abs and Adenauer had a rare disagreement. In preliminary talks, Adenauer, who was also foreign minister at the time, had agreed to a substantial sum suggested by the Jewish side. Abs, the skilled negotiator, worried about his bargaining position in London, where he tried to convince his counterparts that Germany could ill-afford substantial debt repayments; Adenauer's agreement with Jewish demands tended to undermine his arguments. In the end, they achieved a compromise that took account of bargaining necessities and political sensitivities on both sides. Germany agreed to provide Israel—with which it had not yet established full diplomatic relations—goods and services worth DM 3 billion over a period of twelve years. A side agreement specified that the Federal Republic would pay directly for British Oil Company deliveries to Israel. (Only much later did it become known that among the goods provided by West Germany was also military hardware.) By avoiding cash payments, Abs was able to protect his bargaining position regarding Germany's limited capability for transferring funds abroad, while the Israeli government could argue that Germany was not providing "blood money" (as the protesters claimed), but merely material aid to a beleaguered Israel. In addition to the agreement with Israel, the Federal Republic also concluded an agreement with the "Conference on Jewish Material Claims against Germany" under the leadership of Nahum Goldmann, providing for DM 500 million in support of Jews living outside of Israel. Thus Germany had made an important first step in righting some of the injustices of the Hitler regime. Further steps would follow, often unnecessarily grudgingly, as an ever wealthier Germany was asked to compensate victims of the Third Reich. Concluding steps were taken after the fall of the Iron Curtain and the reunification of Germany as East German and East European victims were finally included in restitution and compensation schemes.

I admired Abs for the skill, tenacity, and integrity with which he had brought these extremely difficult negotiations to a successful conclusion. I would later have occasion to remember him as my role model when I became engaged in sensitive negotiation efforts that were not nearly as critical and difficult as the ones with which he had been tasked. I also admired Adenauer for his courage and sense of moral rectitude in pursuing the goals of restitution and German reconstitution. In retrospect, I am much less impressed by the way Adenauer's party, the Christian Democratic Union, behaved when it came time to ratify these agreements. It was only with the full support of the opposition Social Democrats, and against considerable resistance among members of the CDU, that Adenauer was able to secure ratification in the *Bundestag*. It should have served as a warning to me that representatives of my chosen party would not always do what I considered to be morally right and politically the best course.

Abs had reclaimed his position at the head of Deutsche Bank when I entered politics twelve years later. He now stood at the top of Germany's business elite, of which he was the best-known and most influential elder statesman. He arranged for me to meet Adenauer. The former chancellor received me for tea in the office he was allowed to maintain in the *Bundesrat* wing of the parliament. In a number of wide-ranging and lengthy discussions—with me mostly listening—*der Alte* provided lessons in history, offered principles and guidelines, and sought to guide me onto the proper political path. I was not only an eager listener, but also a receptive student. He impressed me with the clarity of his language and the stringency of his arguments. He never lost track of his argumentation, nor did he get lost in mere storytelling (as elderly gentlemen often do). At ninety, his mind was phenomenal, his memory all-encompassing. I owe much to these sessions with the grand old man of German politics, who would die less than two years later.

Adenauer never forgot which powers guaranteed Germany's freedom, democracy, and security. His overarching goal was to firmly anchor this new political entity called the Federal Republic of Germany in the community of Western nations. He was deeply afraid of nationalistic tendencies among his fellow Germans and therefore rejected any policy that might encourage it, or have to rely on it. At the same time, he was unwavering in his pursuit of West Germany's interests, at the top of which had been the end of Allied occupation and the establishment of the Federal Republic as a fully sovereign member state of the community of Western nations. A first severe test of his convictions had occurred in March of 1952, when the Soviet dictator Joseph Stalin sent a note to the three other occupation powers outlining a plan for German unification at the cost of permanent German neutrality. Stalin's proposal aroused a great deal of interest; members of Adenauer's cabinet, along with prominent journalists, pleaded with Adenauer to take it seriously and engage Stalin in negotiations. But Adenauer refused, seeing in Stalin's proposal not a serious solution to the "German Question," but rather a tactical ruse designed to derail the Federal Republic's inclusion in a Western alliance system, and thus a long-term strategic move that was meant to bring a neutral—and therefore powerless—Germany under eventual Soviet control. Stalin had bet on nationalistic desires among Germans to bring about a unified country at almost all costs. Adenauer feared that such a Germany, left adrift without anchor and a sense of direction, would once again succumb to the nationalistic temptations of militarism and revanchism, even if it were able to escape inclusion in the Soviet empire. Aside from being distrustful of his countrymen when it came to nationalism, Adenauer was also not enamored of their political preferences in other regards. He was, in fact, afraid that a reunified Germany would become a "red" Germany—a country dominated by socialists and communists. "In Saxony they always vote red," he confided to me (historically correct, but wrong as a prediction: after reunification, Saxon voters consistently gave the CDU governing majorities).

Adenauer's choice in 1952 was clear, even though it cost him the support of some of his party members. It also proved to be prescient. Thirty-seven years later, German reunification would come about in almost exactly the way Adenauer had predicted: with a highly successful West Germany, embedded in a strong West, exercising such a "magnetic attraction" for East Germans—and to Eastern Europeans more generally—that they would feel encouraged and compelled to overthrow their repressive and underperforming communist regimes and seek inclusion in the West. Adenauer had shown the way, although following it presented enormous difficulties and constant controversies. I would soon find myself in a position to play a role in pursuing Adenauer's policies to their successful conclusion.

Adenauer's heart clearly belonged to France. In our long discussions, he always came back to the overriding importance of close German-French relations for the maintenance of peace in Europe. His perspective spanned a century of German-French enmity and conflicts. Already in 1923, when, as mayor of Cologne and head of the Prussian State Council, he was negotiating with France over the French occupation of the Rhineland, he was pleading for reconciliation between the two archenemies and even flirted with the idea of establishing an independent Rhineland closely linked with France. His efforts then were not crowned with success. Now, with his worst fears justified by yet another German-French war and being in a position of power that allowed him to pursue his convictions with better chances of success, he would not be denied. A first and giant step was taken in 1950, when Adenauer agreed to a proposal by the French foreign minister, Robert Schuman, to subject their countries' coal and steel production to joint control. It was, of course, part of an effort to limit Germany's economic and potential military power. But Adenauer recognized the chance for some degree of Franco-German integration. Out of the European Coal and Steel Community grew a larger European Community and eventually the European Union, with France and Germany at its core and serving as its main engine. German-French rapprochement was Adenauer's lifelong dream and his greatest achievement as chancellor of post-war Germany.

Adenauer's admiration for Charles de Gaulle, the general and statesman, then president of France, knew no bounds. He would describe him in almost hagiographic terms as the great officer of a free France, an unstoppable force for unity and stability—the very personification of French greatness. Adenauer had no cause to be envious of de Gaulle's achievements, though there may have been times when he wished that he had more of a French president's power and stature. In the course of an elaborately staged official visit to France in the summer of 1962—which culminated in an unforgettable ceremony in the cathedral of Reims—he clearly reveled in the ceremony that de Gaulle had laid out for him. Half a year later, after a triumphal return visit by de Gaulle to Germany, the two towering statesmen of Europe concluded a treaty of friendship between France and Germany, which was perhaps more a document of personal friendship than a radically new foundation for German-French relations. Adenauer, however, was firmly convinced that this treaty would one day be recognized as the most important and valuable of all post-war international agreements concluded by the Federal Republic of Germany. He certainly tried to impress me with its importance, obviously displeased with the fact that his successor put less emphasis on close relations with France. He may also have been trying to make me a convert to the priority of German-French relations, for he knew well my record of close relations with everything American. While I never doubted the importance of close cooperation with France, I never became one of its primary preachers or practitioners.

"I am not against America," Adenauer argued, "even though it isn't always easy to deal with them either." He certainly had his share of disagreements with Americans, from the time he had to confront the American High Commissioners for Germany (on one occasion, famously stepping on a carpet that was reserved for the occupation rulers of Germany) to his last years in office when he was faced with an American president almost half his age who insisted on taking America to "New Frontiers." Adenauer had a difficult time with John F. Kennedy, who even insisted that the German ambassador in Washington be replaced. Transatlantic troubles had contributed to Adenauer's fall from power. He continued to insist, however, that the policies he pursued were also in America's interest. This was especially true for solid German-French relations. Without them, Europe could not move forward. And without a strong Europe, American interests would also suffer. Yet he did not hide his thorough dislike for Gerhard Schröder, Erhard's foreign minister (a member of the CDU, who is not to be confused with the younger SPD candidate who would become chancellor in 1998). Schröder was indeed an avowed Atlanticist. Adenauer thought he was anti-French. He once asked de Gaulle, as he told me, to be particularly nice to Schröder at their next get-together. The French president heeded Adenauer's wishes, apparently to no avail. Schröder would not budge from his pro-British and pro-American line. "Heaven forbid that Schröder ever becomes chancellor," Adenauer exclaimed. "That would bring Franco-German friendship to a crashing halt." Neither of these fears ever materialized.

Back in 1946, Adenauer had helped found the Christian Democratic Union. Now he was suffering from the disarray within the party he had led to such extraordinary success. "Purgatory," he once remarked, "is having to attend a party caucus." Not without reason, he saw his party in the doldrums and predicted that it would take a long time and intense efforts to bring it back to the top. My tutorials with him should have prepared me for what lay ahead, but in those heady days of my first exposure to political life in Bonn, I was willing to write off Adenauer's observations and predictions as the complaints of a curmudgeonly old man. He might have sensed my unease over his occasional bitterness and constant skepticism. At the end of our last personal meeting, he patted me on the shoulder in a fatherly manner, told me never to lose faith and courage, and admonished me to always work hard. It was the kind of advice I did not really need, but I took it to heart nevertheless.

As it was, my political career in Bonn had gotten off to a rousing start after the inauspicious beginning of dropping in on the wrong party caucus. Once I had found my way to the right meeting, I was properly—if somewhat too ceremoniously for my taste—welcomed by the leader of the CDU/CSU faction, Rainer Barzel. Barzel was one of those politicians who had worked his way up through various party and government offices. As the caucus leader at the age of forty-one, he had already achieved a powerful position, but he was clearly aiming for even higher office. He was a smooth operator and an even smoother orator, speaking in elaborately constructed sentences with an immediately recognizable oily voice. (Herbert Wehner, his SPD counterpart, best known for his steely exercise of control, but mostly remembered for his biting interjections in *Bundestag* debates, once famously brought a Barzel speech to a raucous halt when he yelled: "Oil change, Dr. Barzel!") One of Barzel's jobs was to assign his party's representatives to committees. I, of course, given my background, interests, and talents, wanted to serve on the foreign affairs committee. I was told that seats on that committee were reserved for more senior members of the *Bundestag*. Instead, I was assigned to the committee with the less prestigious and more onerous task of handling petitions.

But once again my luck held. During that first week in Bonn, I received a summons to see Barzel in his office. Without any further ado he asked me as I walked in, "Are you healthy?" I must have looked somewhat dumbfounded, as I was not prepared for what seemed like an unusual outburst of collegial concern. Not that I had any trouble with answering the question in the positive. After all, I had always taken good care of myself, exercising regularly and staying away from harmful pursuits and substances. Barzel, taking note of my consternation and, perhaps, pleasure in the surprise he was springing on me, quickly explained that he wanted to know whether I could travel, especially in the tropics. I suspect he knew the answer, but I was pleased to tell him that I was indeed fit for the tropics. Well then, would I like to become chairman of the committee for economic development? As it happened, the person slated to be the chairman had taken ill and could no longer serve in that function. I seemed like a good choice to take on that duty on short notice.

I was ecstatic. First-term *Bundestag* members simply do not become committee chairs (in fact, as far as I know, it had never happened before and did not happen again). It catapulted me from the backbenches to the front row. Better yet, as committee chair I received perks that normal representatives could only dream of at that time: my own office, an assistant, and a secretary. I had it made. Or rather, I was now in a position to make my way.

I immersed myself in the tricky details of development aid and politics. Most of it was new to me, the man who had made a successful career in the world of business and high finance. Yet to some extent, Third World problems were not all that different from the problems Germany had faced after the war. I could thus draw on my own experiences and on the lessons Germany had learned in the process of reconstruction and reconstitution. More important yet, I came to this task with a great deal of understanding and a deep sense of empathy for the woes of underdeveloped countries and the problems with which they were faced. Over the course of my political career, the focus of my attention would soon shift back to classical issues of European politics and transatlantic relations, but I never lost my fascination with—and strong commitment to—the Third World and the plight it had to overcome. Whenever I found it necessary and possible, I would remind my interlocutors and audiences not to overlook the problems of the Third World for the seemingly more urgent issues of the day.

We were all well-versed in development aid in the form of the Marshall Plan, which was designed to help war-torn industrialized countries get back on their feet. Development aid for underdeveloped countries was new to us. Many of them had been brutally exploited by colonial powers that dismissed them into independence without the necessary means to establish self-governance or a sustainable economy. In principle, Germany was willing and ready to help. In practice, it was hamstrung by a policy known as the "Hallstein Doctrine" (named after its originator, Walter Hallstein, one of Adenauer's closest foreign policy advisers as state secretary in the chancellor's office and then the foreign ministry). The Federal Republic, insistent that it alone represented Germany as a whole and that the German Democratic Republic (GDR)—formed out of the Soviet zone of occupation in Eastern Germany—was not legitimate, threatened to break off all relations with countries that extended formal recognition to the GDR. It was a rigorous doctrine: member countries of the Soviet bloc, for instance, were soon excused as they, presumably, had no choice but to establish diplomatic relations with the GDR. Elsewhere, however, the Hallstein Doctrine still prevailed, and that applied primarily to Third World countries. In the larger context of the Cold War, they were confronted with a choice of accepting aid from the East or help from the West. Some, of course, opted out of that choice by declaring themselves to be "nonaligned." Because of the East-West competition, foreign aid was actually rather substantial, but it was not an optimal way to help countries in dire need.

I was confronted with all of these complexities when I took on the task of chairing the *Bundestag*'s committee for economic development. I quickly determined that I should try to bring some clarity and cohesion to German development aid. On the one hand, that required close cooperation with other players in the field. That proved to be the easy part. Walter Scheel, the minister for economic cooperation (his ministry had been established in 1961 in a first effort at freeing foreign aid from the competing constraints of economic and political interests), shared my determination. A member of the junior coalition partner, the FDP, Scheel was a man very much to my liking: a sunny disposition, a positive outlook, and a sharp, pragmatic mind. We established a close working relationship and soon struck up a lasting friendship. Together we tried to set German foreign aid on a path of relative independence, oriented more toward the needs of recipient countries than toward the narrow-minded desires of various economic and political interests in Germany.

Before too long, I decided to clarify my thoughts and considerations in a lengthy position paper. The confrontation between the North and the South, I argued, was bound to become the dominant theme in international affairs in the coming years. The threats to peace inherent in that confrontation would one day supplant the conflict between East and West as the main source of international tensions. The only way to prevent such a development was to establish an effective system of international cooperation. That cooperative effort must eventually include not only our current partners in Europe and the world, but also the Soviet Union and Eastern European countries—even the GDR. Many of my colleagues in the faction reacted with livid indignation and outrage. How dare I suggest cooperation with a state that we were determined not to recognize, in favor of countries that many of them could not even locate on a map? They took note of my willingness not only to take on controversial issues, but also to take a stance contrary to prevailing party positions. Along the way, I made long-lasting friends and allies, but also permanent enemies. Eventually, new political constellations in Bonn brought some of my ideas to fruition. The Hallstein Doctrine, for one, was soon quietly set aside. A country striving for recognition as a major economic and political power could not afford to isolate itself with such self-imposed restrictions.

My efforts to contribute to a process of rethinking foreign aid were greatly helped by my American connections. The United States itself, under President Kennedy, had initiated a series of development programs and projects—the most prominent and promising being the Peace Corps. We were now in a position to benefit from American experiences and insights, and to join in the effort. My friend and mentor Averell Harriman put me in touch with American policymakers and members of Congress who were willing to receive a German political newcomer and to help him in his endeavors. Among others, I got to know Senator Edward Kennedy, the president's youngest brother. Soon they would come to Bonn for return visits, where I proudly presented them to their counterparts and other colleagues in the *Bundestag*. I organized international workshops and conferences on development in the Third World, in an ultimately successful effort to bring a touch of progressive thinking to a provincial and, in many ways, Eurocentric Bonn. The high point of my efforts was a visit by Hubert Humphrey, vice president of the United States under President Lyndon B. Johnson. My colleagues were duly impressed, not just by the fact that I had been able to arrange for such a visit, but perhaps even more so by the ease and effectiveness with which they saw me dealing with the vice president. It helped establish my reputation as a skilled and polished player on the international scene. Somewhat to my surprise and certainly to my and my partners' delight and satisfaction, I also noted that this reputation helped me in our business endeavors, as old clients expanded their contacts and new clients came knocking on our doors. My decision to enter politics began to look ever better. The simultaneous pursuit of political goals and business interests was at that time generally considered normal and in no way regarded as unethical, unless there was a direct conflict of interest, which I was always careful to avoid.

As chair of the *Bundestag* committee on economic development, I had occasion for extensive travel to parts of the world that I had never seen before; after all, I had to demonstrate that I was indeed fit for the tropics. Some of these trips were more memorable than others. One trip I never forgot was to newly independent Kenya in April 1966. In the Nairobi "State House"—once the seat of the governor—I was received by Jomo Kenyatta, the courageous fighter for independence from the British Crown. Educated at the London School of Economics and Political Science, he had always been active in attempts to secure basic rights for Africans in general, and for his native Kikuyu tribe in particular, working both in England before and during the war, and then back home in Kenya. He was arrested by British authorities in 1952 because he was allegedly a leading member of the violent Mau-Mau insurgency, a charge he credibly denied. After a highly dubious trial, he was sentenced to seven years in prison. Released from prison in 1960, Kenyatta played a leading role in securing Kenya's independence, which was formally declared in December 1963. In 1964, he became president of his country, and remained until his death in 1978.

There I sat, across from the seventy-year-old Kenyatta—a veritable mountain of a man, both literally and figuratively speaking. He exuded a high degree of self-reliance, a strong sense of realism, and the kind of wisdom befitting his title as "Mzee," the Swahili equivalent of *der Alte*. He also displayed a sharp mind and a biting sense of humor. He took great delight in recounting in derisive detail, accompanied by bitter laughter, the simplistic lectures that he had received from the departing British colonial authorities on how to establish independence and democracy, along the lines of: "We will hand over the government to you. The first thing you have to do is to hold elections. You will form the government. But you must also take care to establish a loyal opposition." At the time, I shared in Kenyatta's bitter amusement over such patronizing lectures from a repressive colonial power. In light of more recent developments in Kenya—including revelations of the kind of corruption Kenyatta had practiced that had made him by far the largest landowner in Kenya—my admiration for Kenyatta's achievements has diminished somewhat. The question of how to establish a reasonably functioning democracy with full protection of human rights under conditions that are not conducive to such an undertaking does, of course, remain one of the most vexing issues bedeviling development aid to this day. We have yet to get it right.

Another memorable trip was to Southeast Asia in May 1968. I was traveling with a group of representatives that included Eugen Gerstenmaier, the president of the *Bundestag*. Gerstenmaier, a Protestant theologian by training, but otherwise an extremely ambitious politician, was not the easiest person to get along with. Particularly irritating was his habit of talking endlessly in well-crafted, yet curiously old-fashioned sentences. This habit might actually have saved his life. A member of the conspiracy of July 20, 1944, which sought to overthrow Hitler, he had been captured—with a pistol in his coat pocket—among those waiting to spring into action in Berlin when the assassination attempt at Hitler's forward headquarters failed. During his subsequent trial before the *Volksgerichtshof*, his way of defending himself—amounting to a form of filibuster—so infuriated and distracted the infamous judge Roland Freisler that in the end he got away with a fifteen-year prison sentence, of which, of course, he only served a few months until the end of the war. His status as a July 20 conspirator furthered his political ambitions.

Another member of the delegation was Alexander Menne of the FDP faction, who at the same time served as a member of the board of directors of Hoechst and as president of the association of German chemical industries. One evening, Gerstenmaier drove Menne into a state of utter disbelief, and me to barely suppressed hilarity, when in his inimitable way and totally without any intended humor he explained to Menne that, since Hoechst had been founded by one of my great-grandfathers, he in reality was just a sous-chef to the Kiep family. Gerstenmaier and Menne had decided to use the occasion to go big-game hunting in Indonesia and were fully prepared with brand-new gear bought for just this purpose from London's finest supplier. Alas, their hunting expedition to a mosquito-infested jungle of Indonesia turned out to be a total failure: Despite the best efforts of their hosts, not a single creature crossed their gun sights during a long night of waiting.

My nightlife could have been more interesting; at least one of my hosts intended it to be so. I had earlier gotten to know the Sultan of Yogyakarta, head of a regional center on the island of Java famous for its exquisite Hindu and Buddhist temples. The Sultan was a member of the royal family who had gained countrywide popularity as a leader of the resistance movement, first against the Japanese during the war, and then against the Dutch when they sought to reclaim Indonesia as their colony. The Indonesian people would probably have preferred the Sultan as their ruler, rather than General Suharto, who had replaced President Sukarno. I visited Sultan Hamengkubuwono IX in his magnificent palace in Yogyakarta, which he showed me with great pride. At the time, he was not only governor for life of his province, but also the head of the Indonesian Secret Service (later he would become finance minister and defense minister). In short, he was a powerful man and tried to be a gracious host. Upon my return to Jakarta, there was a knock one evening on my hotel room door. Two burly gentlemen introduced themselves as messengers of the Sultan. With them was a beautiful girl, perhaps fourteen years old. I realized immediately the purpose of this visit, and it was evident from the girl's behavior that she knew what was expected of her. I invited the three of them into my room and began to chat with the two men about anything that would come to my mind. An hour or so later, as my filibustering efforts ran out of steam, I got up, shook their hands, and bid them a good night. They withdrew, with the girl in tow, probably wondering what was wrong with me. I, in turn, hoped that the Sultan had not found it insulting that I had not availed myself of his "generous" offer of hospitality.

While my traveling companions were out looking to shoot some big game, I decided to do some exploring on my own. First I went to Cambodia, mainly for an unforgettable tour of Angkor Wat, the ancient Khmer temple city. Then I traveled on to Laos. In Vientiane, the capital of Laos, I met with Prince Souvanna Phouma, the country's prime minister. It was an edifying experience. Sitting on the terrace of his residence overlooking the majestic Mekong River, we could hear the constant rumbling of US bombs exploding in the far distance. The war in Vietnam was at its peak, and neighboring Laos—officially neutral—was inexorably drawn into the conflict. Souvanna Phouma sketched out for me a devastating and depressing picture of conditions in Laos. The US Air Force had secretly begun to target presumed enemy forces along the Ho Chi Minh Trail in the "Plain of Jars" on Laotian territory, with quiet approval of the Laotian government. In Laos itself, three factions were now fighting for political control: the Pathet Lao, a Communist movement supported by North Vietnam and led by a half-brother of Souvanna Phouma; the centrist government seeking to protect Laos' neutrality; and a right-wing movement. North Vietnam, the prince argued, was economically and militarily exhausted. South Vietnam lacked unifying leadership at the top. Laos was fighting some 40,000 North Vietnamese troops. It was, said Souvanna Phouma, a "*guerre oubliée*"—a forgotten war about which few seemed to care. He pleaded with me, as the representative of Germany, for economic and political support. American support was crucial, but he was certain that an impatient and dispirited United States would, sooner or later, withdraw from Southeast Asia and leave Laos and other affected countries to their fate. The prince proved prescient. After the United States concluded a ceasefire agreement with North Vietnam in 1973 and then hastily left South Vietnam in 1975, all outside help for Laos ceased as well. The Pathet Lao took control of Laos, which, to this day, remains one of the few countries in the world under Communist rule. (At least Laos did not suffer Cambodia's fate, where the Communist Khmer Rouge, under the leadership of Pol Pot, committed mass murder on the scale of the Holocaust.) I was, and remain, convinced that war can never be a solution to political problems, however, where ghastly crimes against humanity are committed, ways must be found to forestall and prevent them with all means short of war. In Indochina we all failed to live up to this obligation.

While I was busy learning all about international affairs in general, and development issues in particular, I also underwent an intensive learning process in German politics. It wasn't always pretty. In fact, soon after I had arrived in Bonn it became downright ugly. Erhard—*Dr. Wirtschaftswunder*—had won the 1965 election for the CDU/CSU with a comfortable 47.6 percent. That, however, was not enough to govern without a coalition partner, so he was forced to continue the coalition with the FDP (which had received 9.5 percent). One of the perennial problems with such a coalition is that the smaller coalition partner ends up with a share of political power far above its share of votes (in this case, four seats in the cabinet). The coalition is thus under constant strain to reconcile different positions on issues and to satisfy the competing ambitions of powerful individuals. Where positions are not far apart and ambitions modest—as was the case regarding my close cooperation with Walter Scheel, the FDP's minister for economic cooperation—this does not present too much of a problem. All too often, however, the strains are immense. To deal with them effectively requires strong leadership. Erhard, his detractors even within his own party (Adenauer prominently among them) argued, could not and did not offer such leadership. The louder the chorus of dissatisfaction grew, the more it became a self-fulfilling prophecy. Erhard seemed marked for an early exit.

In the end, Erhard stumbled over his own reputation of economic competence. Aside from the "economic miracle," his signature achievement had been the establishment of a "social market economy" in Germany. It sought to combine principles of a market economy with aspirations of social responsibility, from anti-trust regulations to social welfare programs. Needless to say, the specifics of these regulations and programs were often highly controversial. Erhard never tired (even in the occasional conversations I had with him long after his retirement) of explaining that there was nothing dogmatic about his "social market economy" and that constant adjustments had to be made according to the conditions and demands prevailing at the time. Unfortunately for him, economic conditions worsened considerably after his reelection; necessary adjustments were not forthcoming, West Germany experienced its first recession, and unemployment increased drastically. Chancellor Erhard appeared unable to do much about it. His critics decried his incompetence, deliberately stoked a sense of crisis, and thus promoted public panic. Regional elections in 1966 went badly for the CDU. In Hesse, my home state, the recently founded neo-Nazi *Nationaldemokratische Partei Deutschlands* (National Democratic Party of Germany [NPD]) gained 7.9 percent, sending a shockwave through Germany and the Western world. I followed these developments with amazement and an occasional touch of disgust, but as a newcomer, I could not really come to my benefactor's aid.

Erhard was already very much in trouble when he was dealt another blow, this time by the American president. The Johnson administration was dissatisfied with the Erhard government's reluctance to fully live up to its obligations to "offset" the cost of the American troop presence in Germany by purchasing US goods, mostly military equipment. This "offset payment" agreement had been reached after the Federal Republic had been granted sovereignty and was therefore no longer required to pay for the cost of its own occupation by the victorious powers of World War II. But Johnson needed to pay for the rapidly escalating war in Vietnam (his request for more direct German participation was politely but firmly refused by the chancellor). Erhard, in turn, was facing severe economic problems of his own and could ill afford to commit Germany to higher "offset" payments. The American president thought he could put the screws on his most loyal supporter and best friend in Europe. Erhard tried to resist, but by the fall of 1966, he caved. At that point the FDP, still under the control of the nationalistic figures I disliked so much, basically said, "Not with us!"—especially to the necessary adjustments in the budget, namely austerity measures and/or tax increases—and threatened to pull out of the coalition. Erhard tried to rescue the situation by negotiating a compromise with the FDP. However, he was forced by his archenemies within his own party to remain tough and not give in to FDP demands. That meant the end of Erhard as chancellor. In a diary entry for October 27, I noted: "His chancellorship is coming to an end. The Diadochi can smell success and appear—particularly Barzel—very pleased."

I was getting a crash course in power politics on a personal level. On November 2, a visibly embittered Erhard told the CDU/CSU faction that he would not stand in the way of finding a new governing majority in the *Bundestag*. Everyone knew that was his abdication. Rainer Barzel, rarely more "oily" than on this occasion, sanctimoniously praised Erhard for his magnanimous service to his party by stepping aside. For Erhard, I am sure, Barzel's lugubrious farewell salutation felt like nothing short of a slap in his face. What a way to get rid of one of the architects of Germany's miraculous rise from the ashes!

But what now? Who among the contending schemers for power would carry the day? And what kind of coalition could be put together to form a reasonably stable government? These issues were obviously intertwined. The new chancellor, to be nominated by the CDU/CSU faction—with the largest number of seats in the *Bundestag*—would have to be someone able not only to hold the faction together, but also any kind of coalition. After all that had gone on before, this was clearly a difficult task, made no easier by the fact that powerful figures were jostling for positions and, in the process, forming fractions within the faction.

All of the CDU/CSU heavyweights had high hopes. Barzel, faction chairman, who was most responsible for managing Erhard's demise, thought he had his colleagues' support. Gerstenmaier, *Bundestag* president—notorious for his vain insistence that his official limousine's license plate carry the number "1" as the true representative of the people—announced his candidacy. He was convinced that, as the presumably neutral president of parliament, he would be just the right kind of candidate. Gerhard Schröder, the pro-American foreign minister with the cool demeanor presumably typical of Protestant northern Germans, offered himself as the man best-suited for turbulent times. Then there was Franz Josef Strauss, the Bavarian hothead and leader of the CSU in the *Bundestag*, a former defense minister under

Adenauer, who had stumbled badly just four years earlier in what came to be known as the *Spiegel Affair.* (It concerned Strauss's vicious reaction to an article in Germany's primary weekly, *Der Spiegel*, which had exposed a lack of preparation for conventional defense in the case of a Soviet attack, thus making nuclear war seemingly more likely. Strauss, claiming a case of high treason, had the article's author and *Spiegel*'s editor-in-chief—and owner—arrested and the offices closed. Eventually, Strauss was forced out of office because of these transgressions against the principle of freedom of the press, which court proceedings later upheld.) All of these contenders for the chancellorship were men, if not of the *Stunde Null*, then of the "First Hour," having first been elected to the *Bundestag* in 1949. I found none of them very appealing.

Partly because they all came with some heavy baggage, and partly because they were blocking each other, the field was open for an outsider, someone who could not only unite the party, but also gain the support of a coalition partner. That someone, appearing almost out of nowhere, was Kurt Georg Kiesinger, minister-president of Baden-Württemberg. Kiesinger was also a man of the "First Hour." A poet by inclination and a lawyer by training, he had made his reputation as one of the best speakers in the *Bundestag*, where he offered fierce support to Adenauer's policies, especially in the area of foreign policy. He was also a man of compromise, who for many years had chaired the *Vermittlungsausschuss*—the conference committee—whose task it was to reconcile *Bundestag* and *Bundesrat* (representing West Germany's federal states) legislation. When Adenauer refused to appoint him to a cabinet position, a disappointed Kiesinger left the *Bundestag* in 1958 to seek the position of minister-president in his native state. Now he appeared as the ideal compromise candidate for the top position in his country.

There was only one problem: Kiesinger had been a member of the NSDAP, starting in February 1933. Worse yet, he had made a successful career in the foreign ministry's propaganda division during the war. (His defense, that he had sought a position in the foreign ministry in order to avoid military service, while apparently true, did not necessarily please those who felt that they had done their patriotic duty.) Kiesinger was asked to appear before the faction for a job interview of sorts. Particularly its younger members asked intensive, almost inquisitorial questions about his Nazi past. Kiesinger's answers were open and honest, but also—for my taste—too poetically broad and lengthy. That evening I called Aunt Hanna—widow of the July 20 victim Otto Kiep—in Washington, DC, for advice. Amazingly enough at that time, she was serving in the German embassy as the person in charge of women's issues. Could she tell me anything more about Kiesinger's past? Not really. But she confirmed that he had indeed made quite a career as a propagandist for the Nazi regime. How would the Americans react if Kiesinger became chancellor? There would not be much of a reaction. And how would uncle Otto feel about it? He would not be happy. So, what should I do? She left it up to me to decide. In the end, I decided to vote for Kiesinger. I was less appalled about his Nazi past and more impressed by his post-war record and his obvious qualities as a compromise candidate. Besides, I really could not see myself supporting any of the other candidates.

By the time the faction got around to making its decision, the frontlines had become somewhat clearer. Strauss, well-aware of the passions he aroused, had withdrawn his candidacy. Gerstenmaier had incurred the wrath of his colleagues when, as presiding officer of the *Bundestag*, he had allowed a questionable procedural vote (an enraged Barzel told me afterward: "He is gone!" which made me wonder what the excitement was all about). After he clearly lost out in the first round of voting, he threw his support to Kiesinger. With Strauss in the chair, the faction then proceeded to elect Kiesinger as its candidate for chancellor (Kiesinger received 137 votes, Schröder 81 votes, and Barzel—perhaps too closely identified with Erhard's fall—only 26). The CDU/CSU was set to move on under new leadership. But who would be the coalition partner?

Pro forma, Kiesinger negotiated with the FDP. Behind the scenes, he explored the possibilities of a coalition with the major opposition party, the Social Democrats. There were good arguments to be made for such a *Grosse Koalition*—a Grand Coalition (though purists of the English language and skeptical political scientists would prefer that a coalition involving the two major parties be called a big or a huge coalition). The economic recession and the need to adjust West Germany's "social market economy" to accommodate pressing new requirements—consolidating the budget while expanding the net of social support—seemed to call for such painful and controversial measures that only a Grand Coalition would be able to pass and sustain them. Then there was the unique problem of emergency legislation. Until the end of the occupation regime, the occupation powers had claimed emergency rights that could be invoked in the case of public instability in general, and attacks on Allied forces in particular. Once it had regained sovereignty, the Federal Republic needed to reclaim those rights, but that required constitutional changes that were highly controversial—and never more so than in the aftermath of the *Spiegel Affair*. Remembering all too well how the Weimar Republic had come to an end, opponents feared that a government endowed with emergency rights could set aside fundamental rights guaranteed in West Germany's Basic Law. Only a Grand Coalition, it was argued, would find the political will and necessary two-third majority to make the required changes in the Basic Law.

Finally, there was the issue of Germany's voting system itself. As my own experience had demonstrated all too nicely, it was a complicated mix of direct and proportional representation, where half of all representatives were elected directly, but the total number of a party's representation in the *Bundestag* was determined by the so-called second vote for a party. (This could lead to the curious result that a party would seat more representatives than the proportional vote indicated if the number of its directly elected members was larger; such "overhang mandates" would later come to play an important role.) The proportional voting system allowed small parties to be represented in the *Bundestag*, though by law (but not a constitutional requirement) they needed to win at least five percent of the party vote or elect at least three members directly in order to be seated in the *Bundestag*. With its voter support of roughly 10 percent, it was possible for the FDP to play such an otherwise disproportionately important role. Now the NPD was threatening to gain similar support and, perhaps, importance. The CDU/CSU was sick and tired of having to deal with the FDP, and very much afraid that the NPD might encroach on its voter territory. The best way, then, to deal with both issues was to change the voting system to one of direct representation only, such as in the United States and the United Kingdom, which would lead to a traditional two-party system in which the CDU/CSU stood to gain the upper hand. Kiesinger was an outspoken proponent of such a change—and therefore no friend of a continued coalition with the FDP.

The SPD initially was willing to go along with such a change to a direct voting system, if that was the price to pay for a Grand Coalition, for it was almost desperate to get a foothold on power after seventeen years in opposition. In an effort to gain more traction among voters, it had changed itself over the years from a rigidly socialist and rigorously anti-Western (though not pro-Communist) party that appealed mainly to working class voters to a party that embraced the tenets of the "social market economy" and supported the Federal Republic's integration into the Western alliance and the European Community. While that had not brought it overwhelming electoral success, it had made it into a more credible coalition partner. Theoretically, it could even have formed a coalition with the FDP, though given that party's makeup, that simply was not yet possible. A Grand Coalition was the only way it could at least share power and, in the process, prove itself as a party capable of handling the demands and responsibilities of power.

The Grand Coalition thus amounted to a grand bet. The Christian Democrats bet that, with a new voting system, they could eliminate the pesky problem of small parties. Then, after successfully dealing with the important issues of the day, they would emerge as the dominant majority party. The Social Democrats bet that, once they shared power and thus proved their reliability and competence, their social programs would be more appealing and their leadership more attractive. But they also had an important, little noticed, side bet: as they were in a position to thwart CDU/CSU attempts to change the voting system, they could endear themselves enough to the FDP to leave the Grand Coalition behind and continue in power as the stronger partner in a small coalition with the FDP. These bets, and the various political tug-of-wars they entailed, set the stage for the great experiment of the Grand Coalition, which began on December 1, 1966. This is when the *Bundestag*, after the constitutionally mandated "constructive vote of no confidence," replaced Ludwig Erhard with Kurt Georg Kiesinger as chancellor of the Federal Republic of Germany.

The makeup of the government reflected both Germany's tormented past and the incredible nature of the Grand Coalition. At its head was Kiesinger, the former Nazi and Foreign Office propaganda official, who would soon earn the moniker of "Chief Silver Tongue" for his mellifluous voice (with a Swabian touch) and frequent literary allusions. His counterpart from the SPD was Willy Brandt, illegitimate son of a sales clerk, who had refused to reveal his father's name and had him baptized under the mother's name as Herbert Frahm. Already at an early age, Brandt became active for the socialist party and began a writing career as a journalist. In danger of persecution by the Nazi regime, he fled to Norway in 1933 to organize anti-Nazi and pro-socialist activities and to pursue his journalistic ambitions. In order to escape detection by German agents, he changed his name to Willy Brandt. During the Spanish Civil War, he worked there as a war correspondent. In 1938 Germany took away his citizenship; he then was granted Norwegian citizenship. When Germany invaded Norway in 1940, Brandt fled to Stockholm, where he spent the war years as a journalist. After the war, he returned to Germany as a reporter and as press attaché in the Norwegian military mission in Berlin. He quickly became active in Berlin politics. In 1949 he was elected to the *Bundestag*, in 1955 to the Berlin city parliament. In 1957 he became mayor of Berlin, in which function he soon gained national prominence, especially for his handling of various crises involving Soviet and East German attempts to scare the beleaguered city into submission; these culminated with the building of the Wall in Berlin on August 13, 1961. Brandt, who was not averse to being compared with JFK for his youthful vigor and style (at least that much he and I had in common!) stood next to the American president during Kennedy's visit to Berlin in June 1963, when JFK famously, if with some difficulty in pronunciation, declared: "*Ich bin ein Berliner.*"

Twice Brandt had tried to convert his popularity into a chancellorship. In 1961 he had lost to Adenauer, in 1965 to Erhard. The experience had left deep scars, as in both election campaigns the CDU and the CSU had played rough and dirty with his background. Adenauer—in politics not always the gentleman he otherwise was—had repeatedly referred to his opponent as "Herr Brandt alias Frahm" and thus more than hinted at Brandt's illegitimate birth and exile abroad. Franz Josef Strauss, in one of his more vitriolic attacks, challenged Brandt: "What exactly were you doing in those twelve years abroad? We know what we were doing here at home." Others were even more outspoken in questioning Brandt's patriotism and in suggesting treasonous behavior. In light of these scars, it was even more amazing that Brandt was now willing to serve in a Grand Coalition—unless, perhaps, he saw it as his best chance to pay back and get even. As chairman of his party, as vice chancellor and, more importantly, as foreign affairs minister (which Kiesinger had always considered to be his original domain), Brandt was now in an excellent position to pursue his own policies as well as his personal ambitions.

The main protagonists of Erhard's fall from grace and power rewarded themselves generously for their efforts. Strauss enjoyed a rehabilitation of sorts and became finance minister. Schröder, his position as foreign minister now occupied by Brandt, took over the defense ministry instead. Barzel may have appeared as a loser, but he played a crucial role as the leader of the CDU/CSU parliamentary faction. His counterpart for the SPD was Helmut Schmidt, who had gained national fame as the interior minister of Hamburg in 1962, when the city suffered one of the worst floods in its history.

To this day I find it hard to believe that a government composed of such totally different personalities could accomplish anything at all. Never mind the differences between Kiesinger and Brandt. There were Strauss and Wehner, two cholerics of the worst kind, ready to explode at the slightest provocation. Strauss, heavily Bavarian in appearance, language, and orientation, liked to think of himself (not without some justification) as the most brilliant mind at the cabinet table; one of the best students of his time, he considered himself an expert on every subject. He could drive his listeners to distraction and sheer frustration with lengthy historical anecdotes and learned treatises on economic theory. Yet he could also whip his audiences into frenzied excitement with harsh language, sharp attacks on his opponents, and calculated appeals to nationalistic sentiments. Wehner, the power behind the SPD's shift to the middle and mastermind of the Grand Coalition, was anything but a nationalist. A member of the German Communist Party in his youth when he rose to a position in its central committee, he had fled to Moscow in 1935, where he barely escaped Stalin's purges—later there were allegations that he had succeeded in doing so by denouncing other immigrants. In 1941 he was tasked to organize a Communist resistance movement in Germany. On his way there, he was arrested in neutral Sweden and, convicted of being a spy, sentenced to a term in prison. He spent the rest of the war years in Stockholm, where he shed his Communist beliefs and converted to Swedish-style social democracy. Back in West Germany after the war, he helped to reestablish the SPD and was elected to the *Bundestag* in 1949. Strauss and Wehner were both rhetorically brilliant, but they could also be mean and vindictive. Strauss used to joke that he was chairman of the "club for straight talk," but Wehner could lay equal claim to that distinction—his record of admonitions for foul language in the *Bundestag* remains unbroken. I am glad that I never found myself the target of Wehner's biting wit. Over the course of my political career, however, I aroused Strauss's hot temper and provoked his verbal attacks more than once.

The main purpose of the Grand Coalition was to set West Germany's economic house in order. With Strauss as finance minister and Karl Schiller, a prominent economist, as economics minister, it did indeed succeed grandly. Working closely together, they laid the groundwork for long-term budgetary planning, better business-labor relations, and social programs that redefined and were better able to establish the "social market economy." The economy recovered quickly and remained stable.

Political stability was threatened by the Grand Coalition's second important task: to establish emergency powers and legislation. This was an ironic outcome, given the fact that the Federal Republic at that time faced no external or internal threats that would have warranted provisions for emergency regulations. Indeed, at no time since has there been a need to take recourse to such provisions. In a way, it was a testament to the Germans' commitment to their democracy that they so vehemently protested against the Grand Coalition's plans to limit basic rights and to allow the domestic use of its armed forces in the case of emergency situations. Many of the protesters cited the abuse of emergency provisions during the Weimar Republic, which had allowed for the erosion of that fragile democracy and, in the end, Hitler's rise to power.

I shared some of the protesters' concerns. In the course of rebuilding West Germany during the times of the *Wirtschaftswunder*, and then because of the real and alleged challenges of the Cold War, not enough had been done to fully deal with Germany's past and to put its new democracy on a solid foundation. Emergency legislation did nothing to address those issues—quite to the contrary. Much of the resistance to the formation of the Grand Coalition (which had led the novelist Günter Grass, who was later to win the Nobel Prize in Literature, to call it a "dreadful marriage," and the prominent philosopher Karl Jaspers to immigrate to Switzerland) was based on its anti-democratic nature in general—by excluding a strong opposition—and its determination to effect emergency legislation in particular. In that sense, it had seemed a giant step backward, and not a grand move forward. Resistance was especially strong among Germany's students—its future leaders. They eventually came to be known as the "1968 generation" (and their representatives—Gerhard Schröder, Joschka Fischer, and Otto Schily prominent among them—would indeed emerge nearly thirty years later as chancellor, foreign minister, and interior minister, respectively).

The students had rallied under the slogan that academic gowns were covering up the accumulated mustiness of a thousand years (it sounds better in German), focusing their protests both against intolerable conditions at German universities and on the larger political issues of the day. I tended to agree. Many minds were still musty from the mold of a less than fully mastered past.

Some of the protests turned violent, which I found abhorrent. Eventually, the hard core of the protest movement morphed into a terrorist organization—calling itself the "Red Army Faction" (RAF), but known by the names of its principal members as the Baader-Meinhof Gang—which a few years later came to dominate the German political scene with kidnappings and assassinations of prominent business leaders and other public figures, some of whom were my friends and neighbors. The RAF terrorism hit very close to home. In fact, I may have been a target of such an assassination attempt myself. The declared goal of the terrorists was to "unmask" the alleged capitalist and repressive nature of the Federal Republic and thus to gain public support for their political ideals. In this, of course, they failed miserably. They did succeed, unfortunately, in putting tremendous pressure on the Federal Republic, which, at times, felt under siege. In the end, the political system mastered the threats and challenges posed by the RAF quite well—without recourse to the state-of-emergency provisions that had spawned it in the first place.

Another unintended, though certainly predicted, consequence of the Grand Coalition was the general polarization of West German politics. On the right, the neo-Nazi NPD gained support in local and regional elections, raising the specter of a neo-Nazi resurgence on the national level (which, thanks to the 5-percent clause of the election system, never happened). On the left, a new political movement emerged, calling itself the *Ausserparlamentarische Opposition*—APO (Extraparliamentary Opposition). Aiming to be a mass protest movement during the late 1960s, the APO eventually became the breeding ground for a new political party calling itself the "Greens," a party to the left of the SPD with a radical environmental agenda (hence its name), but in reality promoting alternative lifestyles, rigid democratic principles, and strict pacifism. Fifteen years later, the Greens had established themselves as a nagging presence in national politics; another fifteen years later, they became the junior partner in a leftist government. The Grand Coalition's side- and aftereffects finally became visible.

It is, of course, not fair to blame all of these developments on the Grand Coalition. Public unrest over prevailing economic, social, and political conditions was a worldwide phenomenon in 1968. Students seemed to be revolting everywhere, from American university campuses to the streets of Paris (where de Gaulle was later forced to relinquish the presidency) and the streets of Prague (where a promising "political spring" was brutally crushed by Warsaw Pact tanks in August 1968). The late 1960s were turbulent times. The United States was mired in the increasingly brutal war in Vietnam, which provoked protests everywhere (and made Ho Chi Minh an unlikely international hero). The assassinations of Martin Luther King, the Nobel Prize-winning civil rights leader, and soon thereafter of Robert Kennedy, JFK's younger brother and a beacon of hope for the Democratic Party, inflamed passions and raised tensions. In the Middle East, Israel dealt a devastating defeat to the Arab side with its preemptive Six-Day War, setting the stage for future violent conflicts. In China, Mao's Cultural Revolution was in full swing and brought chaos, misery, and death to millions of Chinese; it would subside after four years, but not really come to an end until Mao's death in 1976.

In light of these turbulences on the international scene, it can hardly be surprising that the Grand Coalition's record in foreign affairs was spotty at best. Besides, the policy differences between the main players—Kiesinger and Brandt—were simply too large to be overcome. It was here where Kiesinger resorted to the practice of "bracketing" outstanding issues—postponing them for later decision-making—in an effort to maintain coalition cohesion. Unfortunately, the *Ausklammern* procedure did nothing to enhance his standing as a decisive policymaker, nor did it contribute to the Grand Coalition's self-proclaimed reputation as a device for settling difficult issues. This was the beginning of the end of the Grand Coalition.

Kiesinger and Brandt had set out to seek cooperation instead of confrontation in the Federal Republic's foreign relations. They were off to a good start when West Germany established diplomatic relations with Romania and Yugoslavia and agreed to open trade offices in Czechoslovakia. Kiesinger was encouraged in his new approach by the head of the chancellor's office, Karl Carstens, a seasoned diplomat and public official; however, some members of the faction were less than pleased. Strauss played a leading role in trying to sabotage Kiesinger's cautious *Ostpolitik*, which he thought was influenced too much by Brandt and simply went too far. This led to tumultuous faction meetings. Opening up to Eastern European countries, Strauss and his allies argued, meant an end to the Hallstein Doctrine and thus implied giving up essential positions vis-à-vis East Germany and the Soviet Union. Before too long, the Federal Republic would lose its claim to the sole representation of all of Germany, help to legitimize the East German regime, and thereby contribute to the permanent division of Germany. Kiesinger tried to insist that the Hallstein Doctrine was not written in stone, but should instead be used flexibly and on a case by case basis.

Strangely enough, leaders in East Berlin and Moscow shared some of these concerns, if from the opposite perspective. They feared that East Germany might become isolated even within the Eastern Bloc and that the Federal Republic might ultimately prevail with its claim to sole representation. Their eventual reaction was to insist that no further Eastern European countries could establish diplomatic relations with West Germany unless and until the Federal Republic had extended full international recognition to the German Democratic Republic. The East German leaders themselves sought to move that process along when they sent a letter to the chancellor suggesting direct formal negotiations between the two German states. For Kiesinger and Brandt, the very act of opening that letter proved to be highly controversial, as it could be interpreted as even a slight recognition of the letter writers' legitimacy. When Kiesinger, after some tactical hesitation, replied by suggesting that emissaries might meet to discuss a range of practical problems involving the by now extremely restricted cross-border traffic, East Berlin—under substantial pressure from Moscow—replied that only top-level negotiations were possible after full recognition of the GDR as a sovereign state. That brought an end to the Grand Coalition's efforts to pursue cooperative relations with the Soviet Union and its Eastern European allies. Hard-liners on both sides had prevailed, but the question of a new *Ostpolitk* was only postponed. The next elections would determine whether the hard-line approach—no contact of any kind with East Berlin and no concessions to Moscow—was preferred over the new approach of seeking "change through rapprochement" in the context of a larger détente policy, as proposed by Brandt, and beginning to be pursued by the newly elected Nixon administration in Washington.

For despite hard-line recalcitrance on both sides, the grounds under the East-West conflict had begun to shift. Already the Kremlin had indicated some interest in concluding a non-aggression treaty with West Germany (as had first been proposed during the waning days of the Erhard chancellorship). Discussions on a general conference about security in Europe were far advanced. In June 1968, NATO had agreed to offer the Soviet Union, within the context of such a conference, negotiations about a reduction of conventional forces on both sides of the Iron Curtain, which, of course, would have affected East and West Germany most directly. The Soviet Union and the United States were already exploring the possibility of arms control negotiations regarding nuclear weapons. All of these initiatives would eventually come to fruition.

One arms control agreement already concluded caused the Grand Coalition its biggest problem: the Treaty on the Non-Proliferation of Nuclear Weapons (NPT), which the United States, Great Britain, and the Soviet Union had signed on July 1, 1968. Other countries around the world were invited to join that treaty. It made obvious sense. The Cuban Missile Crisis of 1962 had revealed all too clearly that threatening a nuclear strike need not be confined to the realm of arcane theories. On both sides, voices had been raised calling for a nuclear solution to the problem. In Washington, the notorious chief of staff of the Air Force, Curtis LeMay, suggested "Fry it!"—meaning a nuclear attack on the suspected Soviet nuclear missile installations in Cuba. (Two years later, the brilliant movie director Stanley Kubrick produced a macabre monument to LeMay in his film *Dr. Strangelove, Or: How I Learned to Stop Worrying and Love the Bomb*. It should be mandatory viewing for all those responsible for the use of nuclear weapons.) In Cuba, "Massimo Lider" Fidel Castro exhorted Nikita Khrushchev to use his nuclear weapons to deter the United States from further actions. Khrushchev nearly blew his top and told Castro he must have lost his mind. A nuclear catastrophe was only narrowly avoided. Something needed to be done to prevent another such crisis.

It should have been easy for the Federal Republic to sign on to the NPT. After all, it had already agreed—in the context of joining NATO and the Western European Union in 1955—not to seek access to nuclear weapons of its own. That left open the possibility of gaining access to nuclear weapons under multinational control. To have at least a finger on the trigger—either to keep others from firing, or to fire oneself when others were unwilling—seemed to some a desirable and indeed existentially necessary requirement, given the complexities and uncertainties of nuclear deterrence. At least that was the position taken in 1957 by the defense minister, Franz Josef Strauss. Germany's alliance partners felt differently. They wanted no German finger on anything nuclear (even Germany's civilian nuclear power reactors were under international control exercised by the European Atomic Energy Community). The German public by and large was in favor of joining the NPT, and the allies insisted on it—it should have been a political no-brainer. But the Grand Coalition almost fell apart over it.

What rankled most was the very pressure put on West Germany to join the non-proliferation regime. Some of my conservative colleagues—with Strauss leading the charge—feared nothing more than a permanent discrimination of the Federal Republic. They wanted to secure Germany's place in the sun and were certain that non-nuclear powers would be relegated to second-class status. Unless Germany was granted fully equal status and treatment, it could never reclaim its rightful place among other big powers. Even Konrad Adenauer, ever the sly and suspicious fox, weighed in and heated up the debate, calling Germany's signature under the NPT a "devilish reincarnation of the Morgenthau Plan." (The Morgenthau Plan, quickly shelved for its obvious flaws, had called for the total deindustrialization of Germany after the war.) Strauss, who could never resist an opportunity for one-upmanship, went so far as to call the treaty a "Versailles of cosmic proportions." Unfortunately, he was not totally alone in his display of nationalistic hysteria. Kiesinger, caught between his rebellious faction and an insistent coalition partner, lived up to his reputation as a "walking conference committee," "bracketed" the problem, and played for time, knowing quite well that the next government would have no choice but to sign the treaty. Too bad for him that he lost his credibility in the process. (The Federal Republic signed the NPT in November 1969. When the *Bundestag* finally got around to its ratification five years later, ninety members of my faction still voted against it. Some people simply refuse to see the errors of their ways.)

I had grown rather fond of Kiesinger as chancellor. While I found his occasional excursions into poetic license and literary erudition somewhat tiresome, his nonconfrontational style of governing actually appealed to me. This was especially true of his approach to foreign policy issues. He successfully sought to mend fences with that always difficult alliance partner, France; he practiced comfortable relations with the United States (Aunt Hanna was right—Americans were mostly willing to gloss over his Nazi past); and his openings on *Ostpolitik* were on the mark. I gave him my full support. There were tantalizing hints that my efforts were appreciated. In November 1968, in the days after Nixon's election, I was told by none other than Barzel, the leader of the faction, that the chancellor's office had let it be known that I was being considered for the ambassadorship to Washington. I was flattered but doubtful that anything would come of it, as ambassadorial appointments for non-foreign service officers were unheard of; indeed, the initiative quickly petered out and I heard nothing more about the prospect.

Another opportunity for career advancement presented itself a few months later. In January 1969, Eugen Gerstenmaier was forced to resign as president of the *Bundestag*. His resignation followed revelations that he had received a huge restitution settlement as a victim of the Nazi regime, based on the claim that he had been prevented from becoming a professor at a German university and was therefore owed a lifetime of professorial salaries—as if his pay as a high-ranking member of the *Bundestag* had not more than made up for that alleged shortcoming in lifetime earnings. Neither his colleagues nor the German public at large found the claim convincing and the settlement appropriate. Now a new president had to be elected; as the largest faction, the CDU/CSU had the right to nominate a candidate. I was encouraged by some of my colleagues to seek that nomination. However, when the faction voted, I received only twenty-five votes. I was more disappointed about that low level of support than about the fact that I was not elected, which I realistically had not expected. My disappointment did not abate when I learned later that the SPD had actually planned to vote for me (it then abstained during the *Bundestag* vote, thus allowing the CDU candidate to win). Despite this disappointment, I worked hard for Kiesinger's—and my—reelection in 1969, hoping that a decisive win for the CDU/CSU would strengthen Kiesinger's hand and allow him to pursue those pesky "bracketed" problems with more determination and success during a second term in office.

Alas, Kiesinger tripped up on an issue he had rightly seen as crucial at the beginning of the Grand Coalition, but which he had been unable to bring to a successful conclusion. It was part of the formal coalition agreement between the two major parties that West Germany's election system would be changed from proportional to direct representation, the goal being the elimination of small parties and the establishment of a two-party system. But the SPD leadership—whether by original design or later revelation—had decided against such a change and blocked Kiesinger's efforts. It had come to the conclusion that the chances of the SPD gaining a stronger hold on power with a chancellor of its own were poor in direct competition with the CDU/CSU, and much better in a coalition with another, smaller party—that is, the FDP. Its strategy for electoral success in 1969 was based on that calculation.

The signals for an SPD march to power were set in early 1969. A new president of the Federal Republic of Germany had to be elected. The first president, Theodor Heuss, had been a member of the FDP—much beloved as a folksy, yet intellectually engaged and politically astute figure: just the right kind of highest representative for post-war Germany. The second president, Heinrich Lübke, was a nondescript CDU politician who had served in Adenauer's second cabinet as agriculture minister. Chosen by Adenauer as a president who would not compete with the chancellor for public admiration and political influence (as Heuss had done), Lübke, educated as an agricultural engineer, fully lived up to Adenauer's expectations. By the end of his second term, he had not only become a national joke (famous for his mangled language, especially while traveling abroad), but also an embarrassment when it was revealed that he had been in charge of major military construction projects during the Nazi years—some of which involved slave labor. Now the SPD claimed that it was time for an SPD president—someone who could once again represent the Federal Republic with credibility, dignity, and an unencumbered past.

A German president—an office largely ceremonial and therefore presumably nonpartisan—is elected by the *Bundesversammlung*, a body meeting only for that purpose, composed of all members of the *Bundestag* and an equal number of representatives from the individual states (in proportion to a state's population and the makeup of its parliament). Candidates for president are nominated by the parties. The Grand Coalition could have agreed on a common candidate, but it did not. Instead, the SPD nominated Gustav Heinemann, justice minister in the Grand Coalition. It could hardly have chosen someone more objectionable to the CDU/CSU. A lawyer by training, Heinemann was one of the founders of the CDU after the war and had served in Adenauer's first cabinet as interior minister. He split with Adenauer over the issue of West Germany's rearmament and resigned from his position in 1950. Two years later he went one step further and left the CDU to found his own party, with pacifism and German neutrality as its main goals. Unable to garner much political support for this splinter party, he eventually joined the SPD, which immediately offered him leadership positions. As justice minister he had successfully pursued a broad range of judicial reforms that had gained him widespread public recognition, but also the further enmity of my conservative colleagues. The SPD bet that if Heinemann could be elected as president, he would not only appeal to the "1968 generation" and thus broaden the SPD's base, but would also offer proof that the SPD had indeed matured enough to be entrusted with full political power.

The CDU/CSU had a more difficult time nominating its candidate. Gerhard Schröder, once the controversial foreign minister, now defense minister in the Grand Coalition, was one aspirant to the presidency. But he was not an inspiring personality. An up-and-coming regional party boss and member of the CDU's governing body, Helmut Kohl from Rhineland-Palatinate, suggested Richard von Weizsäcker as a potential candidate. At that time, Weizsäcker was still serving on the board of directors of a pharmaceutical company in Kohl's native state, but he was also—since 1966—a member of the CDU's governing board. The von Weizsäcker name was well-known in Germany. His father had been a state secretary in the German Foreign Office during the Third Reich. After the war, Ernst von Weizsäcker was convicted at the Nuremberg trials and sentenced to a seven-year term in prison. His young son Richard, while still a law school student, had served as an assistant to the lawyer defending his father. His brother Carl Friedrich von Weizsäcker was one of Germany's most famous scientists, and whose role in the potential development of a German nuclear weapon during the war is still highly controversial; he later became an outspoken opponent of nuclear weapons and a prominent proponent of peaceful solutions to world problems. In 1979, Carl Friedrich von Weizsäcker himself would be proposed as a candidate for president, which he refused to accept, not least because there was no majority for him in the *Bundesversammlung*. In 1969, Richard von Weizsäcker lost out against Schröder in the faction vote. The CDU/CSU went for the dull but tested candidate, instead of the more inspiring, but for many too liberal, newcomer. It turned out to be a bad choice.

The *Bundesversammlung* vote was close, but in the end Gustav Heinemann prevailed over Gerhard Schröder with a plurality of six votes. My old friend Walter Scheel had played the decisive role. Newly elected as chairman of the FDP (ousting Erich Mende, who had so turned me off eight years before), Scheel convinced most of his FDP colleagues to vote for the SPD candidate. It was the beginning of a monumental shift in German politics.

The election campaign of 1969 was marked by singularly vicious personal attacks, generally aggressive tendencies among the parties, and an overall heated atmosphere among the electorate. Toward its conclusion, things threatened to get out of hand. Strauss insulted Brandt as a traitor, while his Grand Coalition alter ego, Schiller, attacked Kiesinger because of his Nazi past. Scheel engaged in extraordinary polemics against the CDU and left little doubt that he was campaigning for an eventual coalition with the SPD. It all left a bitter taste.

Personally, I fought my own reelection campaign the best way I knew how: by canvassing throughout my electoral district. On a good day, I managed some 350 to 400 visits with voters. I had a good feeling. Over the course of the past four years, I had established good rapport with the voters I represented in Bonn. My constituency office in Bad Homburg was doing excellent work in helping people deal with unresponsive bureaucracies. I myself held not only regular office hours, in which I had a chance personally to listen to complaints and suggestions, but also met informally with anybody who wanted to join my late Sunday morning *Frühschoppen*—that most German institution of a friendly get-together over wine and beer. The response had been overwhelming; people seemed to enjoy such close contact with a real-life politician who was willing not only to listen to them, but also to do something about their problems, however small or strange they appeared at times. "Kiep fights for you!" was more than a campaign slogan to me. I was firmly convinced that it was the duty of a directly elected representative to serve as an ombudsman for all of his constituents. Such constituent service, together with the national standing I had acquired over the past four years, led me to believe that I had an excellent chance of being reelected. Public opinion survey results seemed to confirm my confidence. That confidence almost tempted me to commit a major blunder. I thought I could win the direct election as before and therefore did not need a "safe" place on the Hesse CDU's list of party candidates. Eventually, I thought better of it and secured such a place, just in case.

What made me change my mind was precisely the sour and aggressive mood prevailing everywhere, even in my district. Chancellor Kiesinger, like Erhard before him, agreed to appear with me for a series of campaign stops. Wherever we went, and whenever he spoke, he was greeted with "*Sieg Heil*" chants and catcalls. In some places, APO activists came prepared to throw all kinds of debris at him, forcing him to speak from the safety of his official limousine. I tried to come to his defense by sharply berating those who were unfairly attacking him, but I had little success. Kiesinger took no public note of such interruptions. In the privacy of the limousine, he complained bitterly that he had to fight this campaign all by himself and that his ministers neither exuded nor aroused much passion. That, he promised, would change in his next administration. I sadly recalled those exciting days of the election four years earlier, when I had crisscrossed my district with Chancellor Erhard. It couldn't have been the fault of the official limousine: Kiesinger and I were touring in the very same Mercedes convertible.

To its very end, the election of September 1969 was marked by the extraordinary uncertainties about post-election coalitions. A continuation of the Grand Coalition was not excluded in principle, but seemed highly unlikely in practice after all the mutual mudslinging. Both CDU/CSU and SPD members were campaigning exclusively for themselves, and not for another Grand Coalition, hoping that they might gain enough votes for an absolute majority. In danger of losing its traditional voters after Scheel's seeming switch from the right to the left, the FDP was fighting desperately not to drop below 5 percent. The NPD, in turn, ran a vigorous campaign in the hopes of making it above 5 percent. The election outcome that would matter could be decided by a few votes for the small parties. Eventually, the NPD received 4.3 percent, the FDP 5.8 percent—for the former its best result, for the latter its worst ever. The CDU/CSU won 46.1 percent, the SPD 42.7 percent. At first sight, early in the evening, it appeared as if we had won the elections. In Washington, President Nixon and his advisers thought so: in one of the more famous diplomatic faux pas of German-American relations, an obviously pleased American president called Kiesinger that evening to congratulate him on his victory.

The victory call was premature. The CDU/CSU had missed an absolute majority. A continuation of the Grand Coalition was ruled out by Willy Brandt. A CDU/CSU coalition with the FDP was refused by Walter Scheel (which was really too bad for me. Had there been such a coalition government, I would likely have become minister for economic cooperation. Another opportunity for career advancement had come and gone). In what was for him an uncharacteristic display of action and determination, Willy Brandt announced immediately after the election results were final that he would seek a coalition with the FDP, even though some of the other SPD stalwarts would have preferred a continuation of the Grand Coalition. Walter Scheel expressed his willingness to take the FDP into such a coalition despite considerable resistance among his colleagues over such a move. Brandt and Scheel prevailed. That meant that the CDU/CSU, for the first time since the founding of the Federal Republic, would find itself in the role of the opposition party, to which it was not accustomed and for which it was totally unprepared. Ours was the largest faction, but we were out of government. It was a deeply disappointing outcome of an election in which we had all fought so hard.

My disappointment was all the more due to my failure to win directly. To be sure, as the CDU candidate, I had garnered 6,250 direct votes more than the voters had given the CDU for its proportional list of candidates—the best such outcome among all CDU representatives. But I could take little comfort from this; I had lost, and the party had lost. After expressing my heartfelt thanks to my tearful election team for their valiant efforts, I—on a perhaps silly impulse that nevertheless reflected my mixed emotions—drove by my constituency office and personally took down the nameplate by the door. I would no longer need that office—let someone else take care of the whims and problems of this constituency's citizens. I was going back to Bonn in a different capacity, no longer directly elected, and now in opposition. I was not looking forward to playing an opposition role; my goals, after all, had been set higher. Would I be able to find and pursue new goals that would satisfy my ambitions?

# Chapter 3

## In the Opposition

The "small coalition" of SPD and FDP had a majority of just twelve seats in the *Bundestag*. This left open the possibility that it might become smaller yet, to the point where it could lose its majority completely. Indeed, Brandt was eventually elected chancellor with only a two-vote majority. For not all FDP representatives in the *Bundestag* were happy with their party's about-face. Even some SPD members openly expressed their dissatisfaction with such a coalition. A few switched sides immediately; others waited for best offers. The CDU/CSU saw its chances and tried especially to lure FDP representatives to its side. It had some success. One of the most prominent party switchers was Erich Mende, that embodiment of German nationalism who had once convinced me that the FDP could not be my political home. In October 1970, he joined the CDU/CSU parliamentary faction. That was adding insult to injury: Mende was now a colleague of mine, in my very own political home. Life in the opposition was going to be very hard indeed.

The social-liberal coalition, as it soon came to be known, formally took office on October 21, 1969, with Willy Brandt as chancellor and Walter Scheel as vice chancellor and, much more important, foreign minister. I had no personal problems with either of them. Scheel was, and continued to be, a good friend whose door was always open to me. I had gotten to know Brandt, then the foreign minister, over the course of the Grand Coalition because of my chairmanship of the *Bundestag* committee for economic development and my broader involvement in foreign policy issues. I found him personally likeable and politically savvy; on many issues we saw eye to eye. These personal relationships and political agreements would make my role as a politician in opposition even more difficult. I now had to find a balance between my personal convictions and my party loyalty, which at times was severely challenged by some of the more obnoxious blockheads in my faction. Fortunately, however, I also found support and friendship among my colleagues. One of my strongest allies was a newly elected member, Richard von Weizsäcker, who shared many of my convictions and concerns. While there were moments when I was less than happy about some of his tactical maneuvers that seemed too clearly and cleverly designed to further his ultimate ambitions (he had not yet given up on becoming *Bundespräsident*), he remained a valuable sounding board, a reliable ally, and always a good friend.

Another potential ally was Helmut Kohl. He had not yet gained prominence on the national scene, but after a picture-book party career in his native Rhineland-Palatinate, he had by then advanced—not yet forty years old—to the positions of a deputy chairman of the CDU and minister-president of his state. He was beginning to pull all kinds of strings behind the scenes (such as nominating Weizsäcker as a candidate for president) and left little doubt that he, too, had far higher ambitions. In his inimitable ways as the underestimated provincial politician, he harbored zero doubts about his ability to outmaneuver everybody else—especially those who doubted his competence. Already Kohl had begun to draw me into his orbit with lavish displays of his provincial empire in Mainz and occasional hints about where my career might take me if only I stayed on his good side. Kohl, not yet a member of the *Bundestag*, professed to share my interests and ideas, but counseled patience and moderation: "Walther, we'll do that once we are in power." I was not one to underestimate Kohl, but I did not have the patience to wait until the CDU would no longer be in opposition. My convictions, as well as my conscience, pushed me into playing an active role in trying to have my faction take what I believed was the right road—right in terms of policies, but right also in regard to politics, for I feared that if we refused to do the right thing, the voters would keep on punishing us. I had far less patience, and perhaps quite a few more scruples, than the scheming minister-president of Rhineland-Palatinate.

Brandt had waged his campaign with the slogan "Let us dare democracy," while Scheel introduced the slogan "We will get rid of old braids" (a German saying, which means removing old practices that are impedimental to progress), thus presenting a more modern FDP. Brandt and Scheel both were committed to a program of wide-ranging reforms in everything from education to social welfare. At that, the social-liberal coalition was quite successful. But for both Brandt and Scheel—passionate as they were about foreign policy—the main emphasis of their government was going to be on foreign affairs in general, and on *Ostpolitik* in particular. For this former mayor of West Berlin, who had experienced not only the crises over the status of this city isolated within the Communist GDR, but also the human misery as a result of the Wall and the Iron Curtain, it was an urgent matter of both head and heart to bring about some peaceful solution to the division of Germany—if not an end, then at least an alleviation of the miseries it was causing. *Ostpolitik* was at the core of the social-liberal coalition's efforts; *Ostpolitik* is what it is best remembered for; and *Ostpolitik* was what tied the opposition in knots.

The details of *Ostpolitik* and my involvement in its conduct—from 1969 to its conclusion with the reunification of Germany twenty years later—are sufficiently complicated as to merit a separate chapter. Here I want to focus primarily on its impact regarding coalition and opposition politics, for never has the Federal Republic experienced more convoluted times and such shameful political behavior. To this day, the full details remain uncertain and unclear, even to those of us who were caught up in the middle of things.

How to overcome the division of Germany? Obviously, there were no good or easy answers. Any reasonable—that is, non-military—approach was fraught with paradoxes and dilemmas. Ever since Adenauer, the main approach had been to insist that, at least in legal terms, Germany as a whole still existed; continued Allied reservations regarding Germany as a whole and its capital Berlin gave credence to that legal construct. For the time being, West Germany claimed to represent all of Germany. Therefore, East Germany as a separate country could and should not be recognized, because to do so would have amounted to a recognition of the finality of the division of Germany. Initially, at least, the East German regime had maintained a similar, if mirror image, position, vying with the Federal Republic over the right to represent Germany as a whole, in the hopes that someday a reunited Germany would be Communist-ruled and join the Soviet Bloc. By now, however, it had shifted to a policy of seeking recognition as a fully sovereign separate state—a goal in which it was supported, indeed to which it was pushed, by the Soviet Union. The Soviet Union's aim was to have the gains it made as the result of World War II and its aftermath fully recognized as legitimate and final. Those aims, of course, ran counter to Western interests in general, and German interests in particular.

Yet to simply do nothing about the division of Germany in the face of these obstacles—to merely wait for a miracle to happen—also appeared to be politically unacceptable. For one, time was not necessarily on the side of the West. The longer the division of Germany lasted, the more likely it was that it could become a matter of fact. Already, family ties were strained and public attitudes seemed to be shifting in the direction of acceptance. The situation of people living in East Germany grew worse as the regime clamped down and severely restricted cross-border contacts. Internationally, support for a hard-line German position was beginning to wane. There was more important business to be conducted (such as arms control negotiations). Clearly, something had to be done. The Grand Coalition, with Brandt as foreign minister, had tried some new steps, without much success. Now Brandt as chancellor was ready to try anew.

Something had to give way somewhere, but what and where? In a clear case of diplomatic give-and-take, West Germany had to meet some East German and Soviet interests, while East Berlin and Moscow had to budge from their extreme positions. Whether the Federal Republic was giving away too much or not receiving enough were the real questions over which *Ostpolitik* was fought. Brandt's basic approach was to open bargaining dialogues with the other side, thus contribute to a relaxation of tensions (or détente, as it would soon be called), and thereby maintain a sense of national cohesion. In regard to East Germany, his goal was to establish procedures for "living side by side" in such a way that, eventually, the two German states could find a way to live together again. After all, Brandt argued, "being a nation means seeing each other." Opening the borders for human contacts would not only help alleviate some miseries, but also maintain a sense of national identity.

Vis-à-vis the Soviet Union, Brandt was willing to negotiate an agreement renouncing the use of force (an idea first launched by the Grand Coalition). After some tough bargaining, such a treaty was signed in August 1970. More important—and therefore much more controversial—than the mutual renunciation of the use of force was a provision that both sides recognized without reservations "the territorial integrity of all states in Europe within their current borders." That was explosive, for it implied a recognition of the division of Germany as final. Brandt, under immense pressure, argued that this provision pertained only to a forceful change of borders, not to peaceful efforts at change. To make that point clearer, he felt compelled to draft a unilateral "letter on Germany unity" in which it was stated that "this treaty is not in contradiction with the political goal of the Federal Republic of Germany to work toward a condition of peace in Europe in which the German people gain their unity through free self-determination." The fact that this letter was delivered, without receipt or later acknowledgment, to a receptionist at the Soviet foreign ministry on the day the treaty was signed in Moscow did little to assuage critics who clamored that Brandt had given up all claims to German unification.

Nearly equally controversial was the inclusion of the Oder-Neisse Line as the border between Poland and East Germany (which East Germany had already recognized as inviolable). That meant giving up claims to formerly German territories beyond the Oder-Neisse Line in what was now Poland and Russia. In December 1970, Brandt concluded a similar treaty with Warsaw during a visit to the Polish capital. (The high point—by now almost iconic—was Brandt's visit to the Warsaw Ghetto Memorial, where, apparently on the spur of the moment and overcome by emotion, Brandt knelt for a long moment of remorse and remembrance. Even that unforgettable gesture was met with stinging criticism back home.) Recognition of the Oder-Neisse Line provoked a fury of opposition, especially among the politically powerful refugee organizations, as this agreement seemed to dash all hopes for the refugees' eventual return to their former homes. Brandt argued that recognition of existing borders did not give anything away that had not already been long lost.

Getting something in return for these concessions proved difficult. By arguing vis-à-vis his domestic critics that these agreements did not really amount to any concessions—that they merely expressed a recognition of long-established post-war realities—Brandt provided an excuse to the Soviet side to ask for more. Ironically, then, the furious criticism unleashed by his opponents actually might have strengthened his bargaining position, as his negotiating partners in Moscow were forced to realize that maybe he was making substantial concessions after all—at some political cost at home. Brandt's double-faced argumentation, whether by clever design or due to political necessities, infuriated his critics at home, who were never quite sure whether he was giving away the store or merely playing his own version of the *Wizard of Oz*. It also made his counterparts highly uneasy. In Washington, Henry Kissinger was forever worried that Brandt and his former Socialist/Communist colleagues might be too eager to seek an agreement with East Germany and the Soviet Union (worries that were fed by Brandt's opponents at home), or that his policies might set free an avalanche of German nationalism—in favor of rapid reunification—that the government might not be able to control (unwittingly, some of our criticism contributed to those worries as well). The Nixon administration was therefore interested in slowing down the momentum of Brandt's *Ostpolitik* and making it an instrumental part of overall détente efforts. Moscow's worries were a mirror image of Washington's. Soviet leaders feared—not without reason, given the "change through rapprochement" rationale offered by Brandt—that *Ostpolitik* was designed to pry East Germany loose from Soviet control, which they felt could happen rather quickly if East Germans were caught up in a nationalist avalanche or lured away by Western ideas of freedom and promises of a better life. Thus, a "go slow" approach was also in their interest. Events in 1989 ending with the fall of the Wall, proved that their fears were justified. All of these factors combined meant that there was an extraordinary amount of speculation, back-channel communication, propagandistic misinformation, and diplomatic negotiation going on at the same time—all of which was highly confusing and did not contribute to a reasonable public debate. My diary entries of that time very much reflect my own personal sense of confusion and frustration.

The concessions Brandt wanted and needed had to come from Berlin, and from East Germany. Early on, Brandt had offered the East German leadership unconditional high-level discussions about the state of relations between East and West Germany. East Berlin responded favorably and suggested that Chancellor Brandt meet GDR Minister-President Willi Stoph, first in East Germany and then in West Germany. The two heads of government had their historic first East German summit in Erfurt on March 19, 1970. Brandt's visit turned out to be a triumphal event when East German onlookers broke through police barriers and chanted "Willy Brandt to the window." Brandt briefly followed this call and tried to dampen an enthusiasm that, in reality, moved him deeply. The East German (and Soviet) leadership was less impressed and decided it could not risk another such demonstration. When Stoph came to Kassel for his return visit on May 21, the atmosphere was decidedly frosty, as Stoph insisted on maximum demands (full recognition of the GDR as the basis for any kind of relations) and rejected outright any discussion of the twenty points offered by Brandt as a possible foundation for East-West German relations below the level of full recognition. It did not help that outside the meeting venue, Communist supporters of Stoph and neo-Nazi demonstrators fought pitched battles that the police were unable to prevent or keep under control. Thereafter, direct intra-German negotiations were put on the backburner.

It was only in conjunction with the Moscow and Warsaw treaties that the Soviet Union finally agreed to an understanding with the other three powers regarding the status of Berlin. In a Four Power Agreement concluded in September 1971, the Soviet Union essentially conceded that West Berlin, though not constitutionally a part of the Federal Republic, could be represented by it abroad. It also agreed to improvements in transit traffic from West Germany to West Berlin, and to improvements in traffic from West Berlin to East Berlin and to the GDR beyond. Finally, it committed itself to seeking general improvements in cross-border communication. The details of these agreements had to be negotiated directly between Bonn and East Berlin. These negotiations were concluded by December 1971 and provided for some marginal, though by no means insignificant, improvements in traffic to and from West Berlin, and from West to East Berlin. Brandt had the concessions he so desperately needed. On December 10, 1971, the West German chancellor—and former citizen of Norway—was grandly honored for his efforts when he received the Nobel Peace Prize in Oslo. This act of international recognition and encouragement did not make the domestic debate any easier.

The first important steps of a new *Ostpolitik* had now been taken. The resulting agreements, in order to become effective, had to be ratified by the *Bundestag*. It was by no means certain that the social-liberal coalition would prevail, given its dwindling margin of support. This is where the opposition came into play. Should it support the government's efforts by ratifying the treaties? Would it allow individual members of the faction to vote their conscience and thus provide a majority? Could it put pressure on the negotiating partners to agree to some last-minute improvements in the overall outcome? The faction went into overdrive trying to stake out its position.

Some of us were pushing for approval; others were pushing back hard. I was perhaps the chief proponent of measured support for Brandt's *Ostpolitik*. Already in January 1970, in the course of a major speech in the *Bundestag*, I had made my position clear. We should not get lost in futile arguments about the past, nor in learned expositions of legal niceties. The German people had a right to expect clear, precise, and understandable language from us when it came to debating the future of Germany. Above all, we should raise neither utopian hopes nor denigrate the seriousness of the situation. Concretely, preventing any kind of formal recognition of the GDR should not be our primary goal. There were other possible solutions to the "German Question" than unification in the guise of a single state. Our strategy should be to press relentlessly for more freedom for the East Germans—up to the point where they would finally be free to decide about their own political future. Obviously, I was not too far from the position taken by Brandt and Scheel.

I had reached my conclusions not least under the influence of policy changes in the United States. In the course of the 1968 election campaign in the United States, which I had closely watched as an official observer of the faction, I had had the chance for extensive talks with the two presidential contenders and their closest foreign policy advisers. Not only had they convinced me of the inherent correctness of a détente approach to the Soviet Union, they had also left no doubt that such a policy would be pursued by either Humphrey or Nixon. In later discussions with Henry Kissinger, Nixon's foreign policy adviser and soon his assistant for national security affairs, I had learned more about the promises and potential pitfalls of détente. There was no way, I had concluded, that the Federal Republic could stand aside, or even actively interfere, while the United States and the Soviet Union were seeking to improve their relations. For that reason, as much as for humanitarian concerns and political calculations regarding eventual reunification, I was pushing for a German policy of détente.

In part to clarify my own thinking, but mostly in order to help shape the public debate, I decided to write my first book, in which I sought to lay out the driving forces in world politics and their impact on the Federal Republic. (Of course, such a book would also help solidify my growing reputation as one of the CDU's more thoughtful foreign policy spokesmen.) The book title reflected my main concern: *Good Bye America: Then What?* (Another book was published two years later under the title *A New Challenge for Western Europe: A View from Bonn*. That title took into account the changes that had taken place in the meantime and accurately depicted another main theme of this book, namely the urgent need for further European integration.) I lauded Brandt's courage in breaking open the frozen frontiers of a divided Europe with his *Ostpolitik*, but I also deplored the haste and carelessness with which it had been done. I also explored the risks Brandt seemed willing to take. The bridge he was trying to build could turn out to become a one-way street for Soviet influence, with the result of an American withdrawal from Europe and significant changes in the Federal Republic's constitutional order. America, I argued, needed to stay in Europe, and especially in Germany: that was the Federal Republic's "second constitution." *Ostpolitik* should not be pursued without a concomitant *Westpolitik* designed to tie the United States to Europe on the one hand, and to tie the Western European countries together as a European power capable of standing up to the Soviet Union on the other. There is no alternative to the Western ideals of liberty, I concluded: "Americans and Europeans cannot politely bow to each other, tip their hats, and say 'good-bye.'"

Along with similar positions I took in countless speeches and interviews, the book was supposed to help shape the public debate in favor of a more realistic *Ostpolitik* and perhaps further my personal ambitions in the foreign policy arena. But even before it was published in spring 1972, my political career took a detour that, in retrospect, turned out to be disastrous. Since 1967 I had served as treasurer of the Hesse CDU. Now Rainer Barzel, at the head of the faction and aiming to become party chairman, urged me to take on the duties of the CDU's national treasurer as well. I refused at first, but then agreed reluctantly. I was well-aware that many of my colleagues viewed me with suspicion, not least because of my deviant opinions about *Ostpolitik*. No party likes a dissenter, not even one who professes to be Christian in orientation. I thought that taking on this additional burden might alleviate some of the suspicion and resentment. Besides, as treasurer, I was elevated to top leadership ranks as a regular member of the party's *Bundespräsidium*, the executive organ of the party. On October 5, 1971, the CDU party convention elected me as *Bundesschatzmeister*, with a very respectable margin of 401 out of 450 votes. I certainly thought, in light of this result, that I had made the right move and that I would now be much better positioned to push my views. Barzel was, at the same time, elected as chairman of the party (against rising star Helmut Kohl as his competitor) and was now the presumptive CDU candidate for chancellor for elections scheduled in 1973. Things looked great for me, I was sure. Ten years after I had joined the party, and six years after I was first elected to the *Bundestag*, I had made it to the top tier. The sky seemed the limit. (The eventual disaster is described in a later chapter.)

The package of treaties generally referred to as *Ostverträge* was scheduled to be debated in both houses of parliament in early spring of 1972; a final vote was set for May 17. Now was the time for its opponents to push back, which they did with a rising chorus of invective and predictions of doom. Franz Josef Strauss led the charge. These treaties, he claimed, were the "can-opener for a Pandora's box" full of political evils (Soviet domination of Europe most of all). He called for an all-out effort to wage a political war against Brandt. It was the first time I heard him make an argument that was to become a stock part of his intraparty rhetoric: "I can only hope that Germany will never be in such bad shape that people will want me to become chancellor." A vain attempt at humor, and what a grandiose conceit: Strauss, the tough guy, as savior of a nation in distress. Then, as well as later on various occasions, Strauss was never far from seeking to create precisely those conditions that would cause a desperate people to call him to the rescue.

In *Bundestag* committee meetings and various faction sessions, I tried to reason with my colleagues, but I faced a wall of opposition. Appeasement, sellout, and treason were some of the kinder accusations with which I was confronted. Representatives of the refugee organizations were particularly vocal. One of their leaders left the SPD and sought political refuge in the CDU, which my faction was all too willing to provide. My position was clear. To be forced out of home and into exile is always a human tragedy. But one tragedy is not alleviated by another, similar tragedy, which would have been the case if refugees were allowed, almost thirty years later, to return and reclaim their homes and properties. We Germans had to be aware at all times that we needed to bear our past the same way children have to deal with their parents' mortgages: by acknowledging responsibility.

The extremists' arguments, or their political power, did not fail to influence even the generally more experienced senior members of the faction. Gerhard Schröder, for instance, haughtily declared that he could easily have achieved such treaties years earlier when he was foreign minister. They would have been no good then, and were not good enough now. Brandt had dared to conduct his *Ostpolitik* without involving the opposition; now, like Schröder, he had to see how he could get the treaties ratified without opposition support. An argument too clever by half, I thought: if the treaties brought some progress, why not say so and act accordingly? Rainer Barzel, leaning toward rejection, announced three conditions under which he—and therefore possibly the faction—would support treaty ratification: Soviet recognition of the European Community, acceptance of the right of national self-determination, and guaranteed approval of steps toward free intra-German travel. Of course, these conditions could not and would not be fully met.

For my taste—or rather, according to my understanding of political realities—the opposition's approach to treaty ratification was clumsy at best, and politically suicidal at worst. Even our own pollsters showed us that German public opinion was generally behind Brandt's *Ostpolitik*. The chancellor's popularity had increased tremendously after he had received the Nobel Peace Prize. There was little to be gained from confrontation and rejection. Besides, once the treaties were ratified and thus in force, even a government under CDU/CSU leadership would have to abide by them—*pacta sunt servanda* is one of the hallowed principles of international law. Faced with these uncomfortable facts, Barzel began to seek a compromise that, to me, represented the worst of all possible worlds: abstention from the ratification vote. I felt that such a display of cowardice and greed would be fatal, and did not tire saying so. Where such fundamental national issues are at stake, an escape into the no-man's land of abstention is simply not acceptable. I was sure that with this tactic we would gain no friends, but rather make additional enemies. Even our oh-so-coddled refugees would, in the end, show little gratitude. Bottom line: the path of abstention meant a prolonged absence from power.

The formal debate over ratification had just about run its course when a chain of events intervened to change the political equations and thus upset all current calculations. On April 23, 1972, the state of Baden-Württemberg held its regional elections. Much to my surprise and the CDU's delight, the CDU won almost 53 percent of the votes, a gain of 8.7 percent since 1968. Never mind that the SPD had also gained 8.6 percent for a total of 37.6 percent (which might have been due to the FDP losing 5.5 percent in its heartland), or that the CDU's gains might have come at the expense of the NPD (which had dropped from 9.8 percent in 1968 to almost zero). The CDU was the clear winner and could claim a mandate for staying its course, even if regional election outcomes do not necessarily reflect national issues and concerns. There had been a good deal of speculation beforehand, some of it unnecessarily public, that the CDU/CSU might use a win in Baden-Württemberg to force a change of government in Bonn, where the social-liberal coalition's majority in the *Bundestag* had just about withered away. I was enough of a party man—and sufficiently convinced of my own arguments that the CDU was in the process of otherwise consigning itself to long-term political exile—that I was in favor of such an attempt. Once back in power, it might even pursue a more realistic *Ostpolitik* of its own.

A change of government without new elections was possible only as the result of a constructive vote of "no confidence." One lesson learned from the failure of the Weimar Republic was that there should not be a vote of "no confidence" without offering a clear alternative at the same time; otherwise, there was the danger of being left without a functioning government. In concrete terms that meant that the *Bundestag* could depose a sitting chancellor either by arranging for new elections (not an easy procedure itself) or by voting in a new chancellor with an absolute majority of all its members; 249 votes were necessary. At the beginning of its term, the SPD/FDP coalition had, on paper at least, a majority of twelve votes; a shift of seven members would create a new majority. Four members had already switched their party affiliations. On the eve of the Baden-Württemberg election, one more FDP representative declared that he was leaving the FDP, while two other FDP members announced that they would no longer vote for Willy Brandt as chancellor. Faction chairman Barzel could be confident that there now was a slim majority for the election of a new chancellor—that is, for him as the CDU/CSU's candidate. With the full support of the party leadership and the faction, Barzel, on April 24, gave the constitutionally required forty-eight-hours of notice for a constructive vote of "no confidence." It was scheduled for April 27.

I was both skeptical and hopeful. I did not quite share Barzel's optimism that he would receive the necessary 249 votes. Initially I thought he might get no more than 248, but I was repeatedly assured by Barzel that he had the necessary votes in his pocket. Even members of the Brandt/Scheel government began to express their conviction that it was all over for them. That stoked the high hopes I had, for Barzel had let me know in no uncertain terms that I would become minister for international cooperation in his cabinet. This was no longer a secret. As the day of the "no confidence" vote neared, I was approached by Erhard and others from the faction, but also by friends from the social-liberal coalition, with requests to consider certain persons for high-ranking positions in the ministry. Even the trusted members of my small staff made preparations for a career move into a federal ministry. Everything was set for after the *Bundestag* vote.

Germans are not necessarily known for their eagerness—much less success—to engage in uprisings, putsches, and revolutions. Lenin had once famously remarked that German revolutionaries would first buy a ticket before storming a railroad station. I was thinking about Lenin's derisive assessment as I sat in the front row of the opposition, wondering whether I would soon sit on one of the cabinet benches. My longtime assistant Peter Radunski compared the effort to overthrow as popular a chancellor as Willy Brandt with an attempt to "spank Mom." Barzel, with all of his "oilyness" and frequent displays of presumed superiority that offended even his close collaborators, hardly appeared the ideal person to get away with beating up on a beloved person, so I had my doubts. Interestingly enough, seemingly confirming Radunski's observation and perhaps disproving Lenin, there was widespread public unrest on the day of the vote. Spontaneous strikes and massive demonstrations hinted at the risks of seeking to overthrow a popular government, even with legitimate constitutional means.

The debate preceding the vote featured the CDU's warhorses, Kiesinger and Schröder, whose speeches were less than inspiring. Brandt, on the other hand, gave a masterly performance such as I had rarely experienced before or after. Once again, he belied the common perception of lethargy and indecisiveness. As I was listening to him, I was forced to change my previously held opinion that he was merely a "do-gooder." At that moment, with everything he stood for on the line, he rose to the occasion with a speech that was rhetorically perfect, rich in substance, full of passion, and deft in its attacks. There were a few hits below the belt, but even I had to admit that they were artfully placed. It was simply a superb farewell performance. My friend Walter Scheel, on the other hand, disappointed me deeply with a hateful tirade that culminated in the accusation that traitors were putting the knife in the back of the government. "Knife-in-the-back" charges have a highly unfortunate history in Germany. Richard von Weizsäcker sought to smooth over some of the passions with a final speech that was calm, reasonable, and appropriate for the occasion. With victory in sight, he could well afford to play the role of the reasoned mediator.

Needless to say, the actual voting and subsequent vote count were extraordinarily tense with excitement and anticipation. The SPD leadership, against good democratic traditions, ordered all its members to abstain from voting and to remain in their seats, thereby trying to make certain—or at least to ascertain—that no contrary votes would be cast. (Only one SPD representative disobeyed that order; soon thereafter, he was forced out of the SPD faction and joined the CSU.) Most members of the FDP cast their votes.

The sensation came at 1:22 in the afternoon: Barzel had received only 247 votes, two fewer than necessary. Tumultuous celebrations erupted on the side of the social-liberal coalition. On our side, nothing but stunned silence and ill-disguised despair. Barzel, showing rare, if stone-faced, class, immediately crossed the aisle to congratulate Brandt on this unexpected turn of events. Something had obviously gone wrong for Barzel and the CDU/CSU: who had voted against—or, by abstention, not for—him? In a faction meeting following the announcement of Brandt's win, tensions were high as this obvious question was raised. Barzel, now showing not only class but also wisdom, put a lid on all speculations by refusing to allow any debate about what had just happened. He did not want the faction as a whole, or the Christian Democratic parties at large, to be engulfed in a crisis that would cause even more damage.

The precise circumstances of Barzel's failed grab for the chancellorship remain unclear to this day. Obviously, all kinds of shenanigans were in play. That became evident to me already on the eve of that historic vote when I interviewed the FDP representative who had just left his party for possible membership in our faction. He revealed himself to be a strange character indeed, full of illusions about his role as a "third force" and decisive player. What fascinated me most, however, were his tales about all the things the SPD and FDP had promised him were he to return into the fold of the social-liberal coalition. Apparently, representatives could be bought, or bribed. We had not been totally innocent in that regard when we lured other FDP representatives to our side with promises of leadership positions and committee assignments. Now it became clear that, when more was at stake, the stakes could be raised. Such corruption did not bode well for West Germany's democracy.

The truth was likely to be even uglier than it appeared at first. In June 1973 Julius Steiner, a CDU representative, revealed that he had abstained from voting for Barzel, thus accounting for one of the two missing votes. His abstention, he claimed, had been bought with DM 50,000 provided by Karl Wienand, Herbert Wehner's right-hand man as whip of the SPD faction. Wienand denied any such bribery, and lengthy *Bundestag* committee hearings into this affair came to no conclusion. Years later, when, after reunification, the files of the East German secret service (*Stasi*) were opened to the public, Wienand was exposed as an East German agent and subsequently sentenced to prison, still protesting his innocence. The files revealed that the *Stasi* had paid DM 50,000 to Steiner and another member of the CDU/CSU faction (thus settling the question of where the second missing vote had come from). To this day it has not been determined whether Steiner received two payments—one directly from the *Stasi*, the other from Wienand—or whether one payment was made through Wienand. Similarly unsettled, but even more unsettling, is the question whether Herbert Wehner, the former communist, had himself been in the employ of the *Stasi*, or at least had willingly done their bidding. I refuse to even consider if Wehner was involved in this Stasi affair. I find it strange that, with all the *Stasi* files now available, more light has not been shed onto this affair and the East German regime's involvement in it. But then, perhaps, it is better that a blanket of discretion and secrecy remains over an episode that, everything considered, was incredibly ugly in its origin and execution, but ultimately entirely beneficial in its result.

After that grotesque interlude, Brandt was still chancellor, but now he had no effective governing majority, which became painfully evident when the *Bundestag*, for the first time, failed to pass the government's budget proposal. Of course, ratification of the *Ostverträge* was also still on the agenda. With much commotion on both sides, it was finally agreed that an effort should be made to come to some common understanding that would make ratification possible. The end result of that effort was a resolution to be approved by the *Bundestag* that once again spelled out German reservations regarding the special nature of intra-German relations, the provisional character of border arrangements until a formal peace treaty was agreed to, and the Germans' right to self-determination. Drafting this resolution proved quite laborious as its language had to be agreeable to the Soviet Union lest it consider it a treaty killer; that required some delicate negotiations involving the Soviet ambassador. He, in turn, made it clear that such a resolution would in no way affect the substance of the treaties themselves. In the end the *Bundestag* passed the resolution nearly unanimously.

We had now agreed to a resolution of reservations, which our leadership had helped negotiate; however, strange as it was, that did not necessarily mean that we were also going to vote for treaty ratification. Faction deliberations were as tumultuous as ever, with Strauss once again leading the charge for a "no" vote and some of the old-timers (especially Hallstein) engaging in endless reminiscences and legal sophistry. Barzel, who for a while seemed willing to support a "yes" vote, eventually caved in and went back to his compromise solution of abstention. I was livid. In my diary I noted that the way the CDU/CSU had acted in this case reminded me of "Cosa Nostra" methods.

The *Ostverträge* votes were set for May 17. During the night I wrote a personal, handwritten letter to Barzel, which I delivered to his apartment early the next morning. I implored him not to have the faction abstain, tried to flatter him with the argument that this was his chance to make himself over from a politician to a statesman, and pointed out that abstention would cause us catastrophic results in the upcoming election. Barzel was unmoved. When we met later that morning, he condescendingly put his hand on my shoulder, thanked me for my letter, and told me: "Nothing doing, Herr Kiep. Abstention it is." It put me in a terrible bind: should I vote my conviction or follow the party line? In a vain attempt to ease my bad conscience, I designed a compromise of my own. If Strauss disregarded party discipline and voted his preferred no, I was going to vote yes. The use of color-coded ballots in an otherwise secret vote allowed me to make that determination, if I stayed close to Strauss, which I managed to do. Strauss abstained, and so did I. Others were less conscientious. There were 12 "no" votes, 236 abstentions, and 248 "yes" votes, which carried the day after all. Ours had been an empty gesture.

I was furious with myself for having lacked the courage to stand by my convictions. The excuses I had—party loyalty, personal loyalty to Barzel, meaningless votes—were no good; deep down, they were less than convincing. If, as I had argued, the party should have taken a clear stand on such a matter of national importance, I certainly should have done so myself. Never again would I succumb to opportunism and make such a mistake, I swore to myself. As for Barzel, whose leadership qualities had been dismal, I decided that I would no longer rely on him, or support him. The faction had shown itself to be bound to the past, unwilling to look forward, and more hard-line than I had been willing to admit up to then. I was going to fight even harder to bring about the changes I deemed necessary.

The next battle was already looming on the horizon. For the initial phase of *Ostpolitik* to be complete, Brandt needed a more encompassing agreement with East Germany (beyond the minor agreements pertaining to Berlin traffic) that would address more pressing humanitarian concerns involving direct personal contacts—everything from mail and telephone service to two-way cross-border travel. The East German side had made it clear that it would not proceed unless its interests regarding formal recognition were met. It wanted a basic agreement on East-West German relations. Such an agreement regarding the bases of relations between the Federal Republic and the German Democratic Republic—known in short as the *Grundlagenvertrag*—was being negotiated after Brandt had survived in office (there was a reason, after all, why the *Stasi* had found it opportune to intervene toward that result). Its outlines became known in the fall of 1972; a final draft was initialed and published on November 8. East and West Germany would recognize each other as fully equal and separate states, yet not as two distinct nation-states under international law—a fine distinction that found its practical expression in the establishment of "permanent representatives" rather than ambassadors in Bonn and East Berlin after the conclusion of the *Grundlagenvertrag*. (Other countries, of course, were free to exchange ambassadors with the GDR and soon did so.) At the same time, the Federal Republic and the GDR would become full members of the

United Nations. Once the basis for relations had been established, East and West Germany would seek agreements pertaining to easier cross-border contacts. They agreed to disagree on the issue of reunification. However, in a letter accompanying the agreement, the Federal Republic once again insisted that it did not preclude working toward a state of affairs in Europe where Germans would be free to exercise their self-determination. For Brandt, the *Grundlagenvertrag* was the capstone of his *Ostpolitik*.

But Brandt had lost his majority in the *Bundestag*. Thus there was little, if any chance for the ratification of the *Grundlagenvertrag*. The way out of this dilemma was to have new elections that would clear the frontlines and give the basic choice to the voters. In a constitutionally questionable maneuver—for the Basic Law was designed to discourage irregular elections—Brandt, on September 20, 1972, asked for a vote of confidence, but instructed the members of his coalition to abstain, thus falling short of the necessary number of votes. Under those circumstances, he could ask the president to call new elections. President Gustav Heinemann reluctantly agreed. The elections were scheduled for Sunday, November 19—Germany's official "Day of Mourning" no less.

We were now faced with just two months of electioneering in the increasingly bad weather of late fall. It was not a pleasant prospect, especially not for me, since, as the party's treasurer, I now had to worry about making sure that our campaign was properly and sufficiently financed. The challenges were significant. Brandt ran a highly emotional and very personalized campaign under the slogan "Willy Brandt must remain chancellor." Our top candidate, Rainer Barzel, could compete neither with Brandt's charisma and rhetorical skills nor with his achievements. We thought our best chance was to focus on economic and social issues, such as a social security reform pursued by the SPD. Karl Schiller, once the SPD's star economist, came to our aid after he had resigned as economics minister and left the SPD. He bargained hard for a leadership position in the CDU, which proved too controversial for us, but eventually he did agree to campaign for our economic policy proposals. The SPD ran primarily on its *Ostpolitik*, which we tried to downplay.

Despite all my doubts, I ran a hard campaign in my own district back home. Given a secure place on our proportional list, my return to the *Bundestag* was not in doubt, but I had higher personal ambitions at stake. I would again be the designated minister for international cooperation if we won. By now I was an old pro at electioneering—it was, after all, my third election campaign in seven years. Rain and snow did not keep me from my usual canvassing. I sought personal contact wherever I could find it—factory gates, shopping malls, market squares—and engaged in many discussions. I was not surprised to learn in the course of these discussions that our stupid rejection of Brandt's *Ostpolitik* had cost us dearly in credibility and voter support. My hopes were not high.

November 19 produced a disaster for us. It was the first—and until 1998 the only—time that the SPD garnered more votes than the CDU (45.8 vs. 44.9 percent). The FDP managed to get 8.4 percent of the votes. The social-liberal coalition had not only survived, it had received a resounding vote of confidence and appeared set for a comfortable and enduring stay in power. We were all deeply disappointed. Barzel was devastated, shutting himself up for days and then hinting that he might step down from all party offices. Clearly the CDU was, before too long, headed for a major shake-up. As far as I was concerned, it could not come soon enough.

But how to proceed in pushing the CDU renewal project along? In long discussions with my family, with assorted friends, and with my staff, I tried to develop a personal strategy. Aim for the CDU chairmanship? That implied aiming for the chancellorship nomination as well, and while I was certainly tempted (and egged on by some of my friends), it seemed a step too far at this point. A more plausible alternative was to be named as the party's official spokesperson for foreign affairs. That would open the path for more national and international recognition and leave the way clear for more lofty ambitions, should the occasion arise. I decided to take an important first step toward forcing a realignment of the CDU, as well as pursuing my personal ambitions, by making myself available for a lengthy interview in Germany's major intellectual (that is, left-leaning) weekly newspaper, *Die ZEIT*. It appeared on December 1 and had the desired effect of a political bombshell.

The *ZEIT* interview had a number of key points. I pleaded for taking our role as the opposition party seriously and not just hoping for an early end of the ruling coalition. That implied the airing of opposing views. Insisting on cohesion and unity was the wrong way to go—down the road of irrelevance. For that reason, I suggested, it might even be a good idea for the CDU and CSU to go their separate ways for a while by each establishing its own faction. In foreign policy, I argued for an acknowledgment of political realities created by the superpowers' détente and Brandt's *Ostpolitik*. Merely posing on a foreign policy "wailing wall" was no longer an option. Importantly, that meant acceptance of the *Grundlagenvertrag*. Whether we wanted it or not, the GDR was going to be internationally recognized. The best we could do was to formalize—not normalize—relations between the two German states and insist on long-term self-determination while working toward short-term solutions to humanitarian problems. Such an overall approach, I concluded, would also have the beneficial effect of keeping the CDU in the political game attractive enough for an eventual reestablishment of a coalition with the FDP. These comments and suggestions, harmless as they appear in retrospect, were meant to cause an uproar in my faction. I was well-aware that I had gone beyond the point of no return with their publication. Criticism (including a reprimanding letter from Barzel) was swift and harsh, and support from my political comrades and friends disappointingly squishy and soft.

The crucial test for my strategy of constructive dissent was going to be the ratification of the *Grundlagenvertrag*. Once again hard-line opponents were ranting against it and criticizing it, on the one hand, as a treaty of permanent division while claiming, on the other hand, that they had it on best authority that the real purpose of the *Grundlagenvertrag* was to bring about an East-West German confederation (albeit on Communist terms) within three years. On the day before the faction debate, there had been another shooting incident on the intra-German border. Passions were high: a party calling itself Christian should never agree to a treaty with a regime that shoots its own people. (Strange, I thought. Anyone in favor of the *Grundlagenvertrag* was therefore not a Christian, and in favor of shooting?) I did not consider the *Grundlagenvertrag* a masterpiece of treaty-making; it had been, I felt, rather sloppily negotiated. But it was an important step in the right direction—a relaxation of tensions in Germany, embedded in the larger process of East-West détente. That's why I was for it, but I also had my own gauge of measuring public opinion in the GDR. Some fifteen years earlier, I had gotten to know Dr. Winfried Müller, a prominent ophthalmologist at the University of Erfurt in the GDR. We quickly established a lifelong friendship. I would call on him to discuss issues of the day. (Meeting him was itself not easy, as he was not allowed to travel to West Germany. We therefore secretly met at rest stops along the highway to Berlin.) He described how much hope the East Germans were placing on improvements in intra-German relations and urged me to vote for the *Grundlagenvertrag*.

Brandt was shrewd enough to link the treaty's ratification with a vote on the Federal Republic's membership in the United Nations (UN), which most everyone supported, thus throwing a deliberate wrench into our debate. I was all in favor of UN membership as a seal of approval for our return to the community of nations. Opponents criticized that the Federal Republic would be a second-class member as Article 53 of the UN Charter allowed for unilateral intervention against former "enemy states" of World War II and had not been lifted. One counterargument was that Japan and Italy had accepted Article 53 when they joined the UN. The other, of course, was that such fears were not only excessively legalistic, but also highly irrelevant. At no time would a well-behaved West Germany be subject to any exercise of Article 53. It was time that Germany played its proper role on the international scene.

Barzel, to his credit, now had come around to supporting ratification because of UN membership. When he asked, after another tumultuous debate, for a final faction vote, 101 were for it and 93 against it. For Barzel it was the end of the line. One day later he resigned as faction and party chairman, less disappointed with the "nay" vote than he was disgusted by the intrigues that had led to it. In his stead, the faction elected Karl Carstens as its chairman—an astonishing development given the fact that he was first elected to the *Bundestag* only eight months earlier. It seemed a hopeful sign: the party was ready for new leadership.

The vote on ratification of the *Grundlagenvertrag* was set for May 11, 1973. The faction would vote against it, but I was determined to vote in favor—and to explain my vote in a speech before the *Bundestag*. I never did get to give my carefully prepared speech, as circumstances (and likely some members of the faction) conspired against me. In the end, I was allowed to submit my speech for the record and permitted to deliver a brief personal statement before the vote was taken. Only three of my faction colleagues joined me in voting yes. That did not speak too well for my powers of persuasion. Not that it mattered as far as the *Grundlagenvertrag* was concerned. It was easily ratified. Even a suit brought by the state of Bavaria in the Federal Constitutional Court, challenging its constitutionality because it allegedly violated the Basic Law's demand for reunification, proved fruitless as the Court ruled in favor of the *Grundlagenvertrag* (admittedly with some convoluted reasoning—but then the whole situation was convoluted to begin with).

I had hoped for quieter times after the turmoil of *Ostpolitik*. It began well. In June 1973, the CDU elected Helmut Kohl, still minister-president in Rhineland-Palatine, as its new chairman. He was now in a position to do more than just pull strings—he could move figures as on a chessboard. I benefited from such a move, I thought, when the party's presidium named me as its chief foreign policy spokesman shortly thereafter. I was confident that the CDU was now on the right track, with fresh leadership and an openness to new ideas.

My optimism had failed to take Franz Josef Strauss into account. The self-styled titan of Bavaria was now vying with Helmut Kohl for the position of chancellor candidate. As head of the Bavaria-only CSU, he had no chance of being elected on his own; he needed to be anointed by the CDU as well. But how was he going to convince the much larger CDU that he should be their candidate for chancellor? This required supporters who believed that he was the best candidate in terms of personality, programs, and overall electability. Additionally, he had to prevail against the competition—above all Helmut Kohl, now CDU chairman. It was fascinating to watch their political wrestling match, but it was not always fun, particularly since I was one of the main targets of Strauss's venom and fury.

Strauss had an uncontrollable temper. Once he got going, he more often than not worked himself into a blind rage, screaming and yelling, accusing everyone in sight of everything from stupidity to treason. Encouraged by excesses of food and alcohol, he would spill out all his animosities and resentments. It was not a pretty sight. On one such occasion soon after we had lost the election, and during a meeting of the presidiums of the two parties that was called to develop strategies for more successful election campaigns in the future, he called Barzel a liar, me a traitor, and the CDU in general a bunch of idiots. The United States, Great Britain, France—they were all crazy, too, hopelessly succumbing to the siren songs of Soviet communism. Brandt was in the Soviets' pockets, the Federal Republic no longer a free country, and so on. There were times when he was able to force his opponents into quiet submission with such sweaty tirades. And, sad to say, not a few of my colleagues shared such sentiments and looked to Strauss as the great rescuer of Germany. I wondered more than once what a CDU/CSU government would have been like under these circumstances.

Ever the master string puller and figure mover, Kohl played Strauss skillfully. As he explained to me on one occasion, there were three faces to Strauss. One was the super ambitious Strauss who wanted to become chancellor, seeing himself as a German Churchill whose dark predictions had all come true, but knowing deep in his heart that this was not going to happen. Then there was the reluctant party loyalist Strauss, willing to support a Kohl candidacy, but expecting to be made vice chancellor and foreign minister (which, of course, would preclude any coalition with the FDP). Finally, there was the rationally realistic Strauss, who wanted nothing more than to become finance minister in a Kohl government. Kohl was sure that he could maneuver Strauss in the right direction by integrating him and thus tying him down. I was doubtful that such an approach of "change through rapprochement" could work with Strauss. I also saw my own chances of occupying an important position in a Kohl government dwindling, all because of Strauss: with him in a leading role, we were not going to win the election; or, the FDP would refuse a coalition; or, he might use his power to keep me in a subordinate position. More reasons to contemplate the options for my political future.

In the midst of our intra-party quarrels, the political landscape had once again shifted quite dramatically. In September 1972, the Olympic Summer Games in Munich had witnessed the terrorist attacks on Israeli athletes; that gruesome event had brought home the dangers of international terrorism. Domestic terrorism had also not abated, even though its originators, Ulrike Meinhof and Andreas Baader, had been captured in June 1972; now their disciples were seeking to gain their release with increased terror tactics. In October 1973, the Yom Kippur War once again engulfed the Middle East in a violent conflict with worldwide repercussions. Oil emerged as a new weapon when Arab oil-producing countries curtailed production and deliveries in an effort to put pressure on countries supporting Israel. West Germany was faced with the issue of allowing US resupply efforts through its ports and airspace (which the Brandt government chose to close, thus risking a nasty confrontation with its main ally). Even so, it could not escape the effects of the oil crisis.

The German government, and Brandt personally, were under extreme pressure to cope with all of these challenges. Brandt was beginning to suffer from poor health, alcohol abuse, and bouts of depression. He carried on gamely, but those close to him—Herbert Wehner especially—began to wonder whether, and how, he should be replaced. Then he was hit by a scandal. In April 1974, one of his closest assistants in the chancellor's office, an otherwise colorless figure by the name of Günther Guillaume, was arrested, together with his wife, as an East German spy. The scandal was not so much that Brandt had been spied on, though Guillaume's arrest did not bode well for further improvements in East-West German relations. More scandalous was the revelation that Guillaume had been under suspicion for more than a year, but was allowed to stay in his job and handle sensitive information so that he could be placed under observation by the Federal Republic's counterintelligence agency. Brandt was not made aware of the situation. Then rumors began to spread that Guillaume was well-aware of Brandt's problems with alcohol and of his dalliances with women (Guillaume allegedly even being the procurer). It was all too much for an already weakened Brandt. He resigned from office on May 7, 1974. The social-liberal coalition elected Helmut Schmidt, its finance minister, as Brandt's successor. Now the man known as the "*Macher*"—who also had a well-deserved reputation as "*Schmidt-Schnauze*" ("Schmidt the Lip")—was chancellor. Undoubtedly, he was going to be a more formidable opponent in the 1976 election than Brandt would have been. It would be hard to run against a Chancellor Schmidt with his hands-on experience, acerbic rhetorical skills, and broad background as interior minister in Hamburg, faction chair in the *Bundestag*, and defense minister and finance minister in Bonn.

Two weeks after Schmidt took over as chancellor, I learned that one of the German Commissioners of the European Community in Brussels was vacating his position. Would I be interested in filling it? I clearly was. Prospects for 1976 did not look good. I was eager for an executive position in government. One alternative frequently considered was serving as economics minister or, better yet, as minister-president in my native Hesse. However, prospects there were hardly any more promising, as a number of potential rivals seemed better positioned (not least because they had not incurred the enmity of Strauss). So I almost jumped at the opportunity to become a commissioner in Brussels, particularly since I was a firm believer in, and supporter of, the project of European integration. Here was a task I could find exciting and rewarding.

I consulted my friend Walter Scheel. He had just left his position of foreign minister as the newly elected next president of the Federal Republic whose term would begin on July 1, 1974. He told me that, while still in office, he and Brandt had agreed that the vacancy in Brussels (to which Germany had a claim) should be filled by the opposition. He was delighted that I was interested and promised to work hard for my appointment—which he did. Unfortunately, it was not his decision to make. Kohl, as opposition leader, had the final word. When I asked him about it, he said it sounded like a good idea, but it would be incompatible with my job as party treasurer. I again weighed all the options, saw few chances for 1976, and decided to go for the opportunity. In the end, however, Kohl refused to let me go to Brussels. He needed me as treasurer, he tried to console me, and he feared such a move might be misunderstood as my leaving a sinking ship. My staff harbored another suspicion: that Kohl did not want to put Strauss off by giving me such a prestigious assignment. I tended to agree that I was a victim of Kohl's "change through rapprochement" policy vis-à-vis Strauss. I was deeply disappointed over once again being deprived of a career option of my choice. At the end of the summer I attended a CDU presidium session in Berlin. My diary entry reflected my state of mind: "After the summer months it is depressing to experience this circle up close again. Such concentrated mediocrity!"

In November 1974, the CSU members of the *Bundestag* met for a closed session in Sonthofen in Bavaria to discuss their party's strategy. Strauss, in his typical fashion, gave a long, ranting presentation about his view of the situation. The gist of his speech quickly leaked. The speech is best remembered for Strauss's "Sonthofen strategy" proposal. In a way, it was not new at all. He restated his old argument that things had to get much worse before they could get better—under CDU/CSU leadership, or best, under his leadership. The opposition should do nothing to help the government out of its current miseries—mostly economic in nature—for to do so would either be a lost effort or, if successful, redound only to the benefit of the social-liberal coalition. In that context he attacked me personally for "suicidal comments" made merely for reasons of "internal enmity" or personal envy. It was par for the course, except for the publicity his attacks now had. It made me wonder whether my own cause had been helped or hindered by Strauss's Sonthofen explosion.

A good deal of the Sonthofen speech dealt with matters of internal security. Baader-Meinhof activities had reached a first peak. A week before, one of the incarcerated terrorists had died as the result of a hunger strike. In response, the president of the Superior Court of Justice was murdered (possibly during a failed kidnapping attempt). Tensions were obviously high.

Strauss accused the government of incompetence in the face of terrorism; worse, he claimed that there was a "bunch" of RAF sympathizers among SPD and FDP representatives in the *Bundestag.* To support his accusation of incompetence, he referred "confidentially" to a letter that had been recently received by the Second Television Network (ZDF), with the demand that ZDF give an hour of airtime to each of the three top RAF "fighters" then under arrest. If that demand was not met by November 22, two leading politicians would be killed. ZDF did not grant free publicity to the terrorists.

In late November, Baader, who had already been convicted and was serving his sentence, was visited in prison by the French philosopher Jean-Paul Sartre—an event that aroused a great deal of public interest (and which was not helpful in terms of disproving allegations regarding sympathy for the terrorists in leftist circles). On November 29, Ulrike Meinhof was sentenced to eight years in prison.

Late November was not a good time for our family. Michael, our son, was suffering from a mysterious illness. Extensive medical examinations proved inconclusive. After one such examination, we were told on Friday, November 29, that at least his problems were not due to a brain tumor. (Later, that diagnosis would turn out to be incorrect.) On Saturday I sought relaxation and comfort in a long walk. In the evening, after a regular massage, I had a sauna in the bathhouse next to the swimming pool. Around seven o'clock in the evening, naked as I was, I wanted to take a plunge in the pool. It was already dark outside, and raining heavily. As I opened the bathhouse door, I noticed a shadowy figure—I am sure it was a man—standing on the other side of the pool. Instinctively I slammed the door shut and threw myself on the floor, when I heard a shot; the bullet went high through the door. Two more shots followed, each lower than the one before—the shooter had obviously anticipated my move. In the meantime, however, I had crawled into the next room; I was not hit.

As I learned later, at the sound of the first shot our dog, a black Labrador, started to bark. Charlotte, not sure what was happening, let the dog out of the house immediately, and the Labrador, all noise and fury, went chasing after the intruder, who obviously thought the better of the situation and disappeared into the rain and darkness. Our brave dog never caught up with him. I, meanwhile, had managed to reach the alarm system installed in the bathhouse, which was connected directly to the police. They quickly showed up in force, looking for the would-be assassin; in the process, they trampled all over any possible evidence that might have provided clues as to the intruder's identity or method of operation.

To this day we do not know for certain whether I was the intended victim of a terrorist attack, or whether I had—with more than good luck—foiled a robbery attempt. Lengthy investigations by the federal criminal police yielded no conclusions (other than the fact, proudly reported to me, that none of the four hundred or so local residents interviewed by the police had said anything even remotely negative about me). The assumption, however, remains that I had indeed escaped a terrorist attack. A few years later, other prominent personalities, many of them good friends and acquaintances, were less lucky, as a second and third generation of terrorists ratcheted up the levels of violence. The climax came in September/October 1977 with the abduction and later murder of Hanns Martin Schleyer (president of the Association of German Industry) and the hijacking of a Lufthansa plane to Mogadishu. When the Schmidt government refused to negotiate for a release of the imprisoned terrorists and German Special Forces successfully stormed the Lufthansa plane and freed its passengers, a number of the top terrorists committed suicide in prison. The remaining terrorists eventually found refuge in East Germany—this was one of the more galling discoveries about the evils of the East German regime after reunification. Almost all of them are now behind bars, some of them already eligible for release or parole, and it remains a highly controversial issue given the nature of their crimes. It seems remarkable that none of them has yet come forward with details about their deeds—including the attack on me.

My presumed exposure to terrorist action had considerable effects on me and my family. We increased security measures around our house. I acquired a Smith & Wesson and a Walther PPK to be able to defend myself at home (fortunately, that never became necessary). I also was provided with a permanent security detail that accompanied me wherever I went. I always appreciated the dedication and professionalism of the young men guarding me while I was in public life. (On one memorable occasion, one of my bodyguards got sick while I was visiting David Rockefeller in his fancy office in New York and threw up right there.) I was very much aware what a burden my hectic political, business, and personal activities imposed on them and how stressful that must have been, but I was not willing to restrict my life; that would have meant that the terrorists had triumphed. Yet being under constant protection did put a crimp in my lifestyle; my motorbike and Porsche excursions, for instance, became much less frequent and enjoyable: who could keep up with me once I got going with lots of horsepower?

1975 was a year of seemingly endless political maneuverings leading toward the elections scheduled for October 3, 1976. Who would be our candidate for chancellor? And should we position ourselves for winning an absolute majority? Or for a coalition with the FDP? There were even plans—top secret at the time—to establish a fourth party to the left of what would then be a more right-leaning CDU/CSU (some of our rightist champions were all for such an attempt). The purpose of a fourth party would have been to draw middle-of-the-road voters away from the FDP and SPD. At one point I was even told that I was slated to found and head such a party. But nothing ever came of these plans, which was just as well. I thought it was a ridiculous idea and no way for us to regain power.

The hot foreign policy issue of the year was the Conference on Security and Cooperation in Europe (CSCE). After years of drawn-out negotiations, an agreement had been reached; this Final Act was formally signed in Helsinki (Finland) on August 1, 1975, in the course of a mammoth summit conference involving thirty-five nations. The "Helsinki Accord" was made up of three "baskets," which represented an overall compromise. The first basket addressed security issues by providing once again for the inviolability of borders and a number of so-called confidence-building measures designed to make military activities such as maneuvers more transparent and therefore potentially less dangerous. (Efforts at reducing the level of conventional arms in Europe were left to a separate series of negotiations programmatically referred to as Mutual and Balanced Force Reductions; these negotiations were stalled at the time and would come to fruition only much later.) A second basket called for increased economic and scientific cooperation among the signatory countries. The third basket contained provisions regarding human rights—that is, not only a commitment to respect human rights, but also practical measures for improving and monitoring them.

Not surprisingly, the CSCE Final Act was highly controversial. Our conservatives claimed that too much was being given away in the first basket and too little given back in the third. They were strictly against expressing support and wanted the faction to clearly say so. I, together with my few like-minded supporters, argued for a qualified "no" that would agree with major provisions but also spell out a number of conditions (keeping the "German Question" open, for instance). In general, I considered the Final Act to be an important step forward. Strauss claimed it was bringing us closer to a final apocalypse. I was going to defend my position in a major speech in the *Bundestag* debate, but once again some dubious machinations kept me from being called to the lectern. So I released the draft of my speech to the press and left the *Bundestag* in a bit of a huff. I was, after all, the CDU's foreign policy spokesman and found it curious, if not downright insulting, that I had been prevented from speaking on a topic as important as the CSCE Final Act. Strauss and his cohorts felt that I had again violated faction discipline and interests and clamored accordingly.

A related foreign policy issue arose later in the fall, when the *Bundestag* was faced with the ratification of a treaty with Poland. It provided for West German financial assistance to Polish citizens with a claim on the German social security system as a first in *Wiedergutmachung* payments to an Eastern European country; in return, Poland would agree to let a certain number of its citizens—namely those who could prove German ancestry—immigrate to the Federal Republic. My position was clear, as was that of the usual *Ostpolitik* opponents who saw no need for any money to go to Poland and who considered the agreed-to number of immigrants to be too low. (Perhaps it might have been more logical for them to refuse any kind of immigration deal, since their opposition was also based on the argument that Germany should not renounce any claims to formerly German territories—what better way to make that claim than to have Germans actually live there?) I would soon play an important role in rescuing this treaty from parliamentary defeat, the details of which are explained later. Suffice it to say here that yet another *Ostpolitik* controversy did nothing to endear me to Strauss and his followers. They missed no chance to tell me so.

Even though the federal election was a year away, this was the time when all the important decisions were to be made. I handily won renomination in my Hesse district. By far my bigger concern was what role I would play in the top team. During the course of the summer, Kohl had prevailed as the CDU/CSU candidate for chancellor. I observed Kohl during the decisive meeting and described him in my diary as a man of "endless patience and calmness, with a soft expression on his face that belies the fact that here is a man of utmost determination who is oh-so-close to achieving his goal." It was the first time, but certainly not the last, that Kohl would deceive his detractors and get his way. Strauss had the reputation of being the ultimate politician (ill deserved, I thought, given his disturbing lack of self-control). Kohl, however, was the consummate politician who used his reputation as a provincial bumpkin to fool others and reach his goals. As the occasional object of his machinations, I resented him for what he was doing, but I certainly came to admire his skills in doing it.

In 1975, looking ahead to 1976, Kohl obviously had a Kiep problem. Strauss wanted me off the team, and Kohl could not risk alienating Strauss too much; there was the constant threat that Strauss might declare the CSU's independence from the CDU, which would have presented a fourth-party problem of a different kind and surely have lost the election for Kohl. However, Kohl also needed me, as treasurer, but also as a representative of the political center who could attract voters that might otherwise fear too much Strauss. It was a delicate problem that Kohl sought to finagle by stringing me along (eventually letting me know that I would be in the shadow cabinet as a likely minister for European affairs—not a dream job for the party's foreign policy spokesman who was hoping for more) and by emphasizing party unity and solidarity above all. In the course of the summer, I lost my official designation as the CDU's foreign policy spokesman when the presidium decided on a different distribution of roles that left none for me. By November I was growing deeply depressed. This was not my party! It would be hard, I noted in my diary, to follow the party line and work to provide the funds for doing so. For the first time I was thinking about quitting.

Then a curious issue arose. In late November I was told that I had been selected as one of three recipients for the 1976 Theodor Heuss Prize—an award established in commemoration of the Federal Republic's first president that honored outstanding civic activities and political courage. Would I accept it? I was more than flattered and thought that I should of course accept such an award, but it wasn't that simple. Heuss had been one of the FDP's founding fathers, and the foundation awarding the prize, while nonpartisan in makeup, was still closely identified with the FDP. Then there was the problem of the other award recipients: Egon Bahr of the SPD (Brandt's chief adviser and negotiator for *Ostpolitik*—the devil incarnate to its opponents) and Burkhard Hirsch (one of the more liberal FDP representatives). That would put me in some pretty awkward company as far as the CDU was concerned—during an election, no less, where I was hoping to be in the top team. On the other hand, I was firmly convinced that our best chance for electoral—and post-electoral—success was to stay open to the FDP and to aim for a coalition with it. Accepting the Heuss Prize might be a welcome signal in that direction. So I faced a peculiar dilemma: should I be politically courageous and accept an award for political courage?

In a telephone call with Kohl, he told me, friendly as always, that he wanted to talk with me about this prize business some more. Yes, it might be a good signal, but he was afraid what it could do to my career. I brashly told him not to worry about my career—I was determined to accept the award. Some of my friends encouraged me, Walter Scheel in particular. Now president and therefore presumably above politics, he nevertheless expressed his conviction that it would indeed be the right signal to the FDP, a necessary signal, he argued, as he was quite skeptical about the political inclinations of his successor as FDP chairman and foreign minister, Hans-Dietrich Genscher. Others whom I consulted advised me to decline the award. If I wanted to play my chosen role as the CDU's dissident with any hope for success, accepting the award would not be helpful—neither in regard to party competitors nor vis-à-vis the voters. It was advice I took to heart.

But the FDP would not leave me alone. Unwittingly, and certainly unintentionally, the Free Democrats shortly thereafter gave my political life a new twist. It happened in faraway Hanover, capital of the state of Lower Saxony. Since 1974, Lower Saxony had been governed by a social-liberal coalition that had a one-vote majority. Its minister-president, in office since 1970, had tired of the resulting political high-wire act, and in January 1976, he decided to step aside in favor of a younger and perhaps more energetic candidate. Alas, neither his handpicked successor nor subsequently another SPD candidate achieved the necessary majority. In that situation the CDU decided to seek the office for one of its candidates. The person chosen was Ernst Albrecht, a prominent member of the *Landtag* with an impressive résumé as a former high-ranking official in the Commission of the European Communities and then as CEO of Bahlsen, a giant in the German cookie business. On February 6, Albrecht was elected as minister-president, though who or which party provided the crucial votes remains unknown. The Lower Saxony FDP, prodded by the FDP leadership in Bonn, refused to enter into a formal coalition with the CDU, but let it be known that it would tolerate a minority government headed by Albrecht. This turn of events in Lower Saxony was nothing short of a sensation and widely seen as the beginning of the end of FDP-SPD cooperation, even in Bonn. Things were looking good for October 1976!

One week later, Carl Horst Hahn, an old friend from my Volkswagen days, invited me to breakfast in his new house. Hahn had been president of Volkswagen of America from 1959-1964, when I was handling the Volkswagen insurance business there. He had been the architect of Volkswagen's incredible success story in the United States. His hopes for becoming CEO of Volkswagen in Germany had apparently run afoul of the incumbent's feudalistic ways of running a modern business: Hahn refused to marry the boss's daughter and instead married a girl from San Francisco, Maria Traina. Her brother John, a shipping executive and art collector, was married to best-selling author Danielle Steel. Hahn was now CEO of Continental, a maker of tires and other automotive products located in Hanover, which he rescued. Also present at this breakfast was Ernst Albrecht—a coup that delighted Carl Horst no end. In the course of our conversation, Albrecht asked for advice as to who might be good candidates for cabinet positions now to be filled in his government. That must have been a leading question, for he went right on to ask me whether I would not be interested in becoming finance and/or economics minister in Hanover.

Not only was I interested, I was thoroughly tempted. But I could not say yes on the spur of the moment; too much was at stake, and too many questions had to be answered first. There followed days of intense discussions with family, staff, business partners, friends, advisers, and the party leadership. Kohl, for one, seemed excited, though I am not quite sure why: because he would be rid of his Kiep problem, or because I would lead an effort to bring the FDP back into the fold of a coalition with the CDU? He assured me that the party would be forever grateful (which I somehow doubted—memories of "a grateful fatherland" from wartime letters of condolence came to mind). He also promised that I would remain part of his team should he win the election—still a highly uncertain prospect. I would, in any case, retain my position as party treasurer (though my active work as treasurer would have to rest while I was occupying a public office).

The temptations were twofold. After ten years of frustrating parliamentary work, mostly in opposition, I could finally prove myself in an executive position. To be sure, Hanover was not Bonn, but given the state of affairs in Lower Saxony as outlined by Albrecht, the challenges concerning budget consolidation and economic stimulation were substantial. I could learn on the job and qualify myself for bigger tasks, should the opportunity ever present itself. Then there was the chance to promote the political change I had so intensively hoped and worked for: to bring the CDU and FDP together again for a solid middle-of-the-road national government.

The downsides of such a lateral move to Lower Saxony, however, were also painfully obvious. First of all, there was the risk of failure. I was confident of my executive abilities, but there was no guarantee that Albrecht's minority government would, in fact, survive for very long. If that were to happen, I would not only be without a job, but also without a political base, because working for the government in Lower Saxony required giving up my *Bundestag* seat. That really hurt, for several reasons. I was fond of my district and enjoyed working for its people, but it was also my home base for an always considered move into the Hesse government, preferably as minister-president. Going to Lower Saxony meant giving up that base, foregoing possible opportunities in my home state, and perhaps being seen as a political refugee from Hesse—none of these being very pleasant prospects. It was, of course, also uncertain whether after a stint in Hanover I could move on to higher callings, or whether that would mark the end of my political career. Finally, my real political love was foreign policy, which I considered my true calling. How long would I enjoy being finance minister in a regional government before I became bored and restless?

Then there were significant personal considerations. Charlotte, always supportive, gently reminded me that a job in Hanover—and no more constituency duties to be performed in my district—meant that I was going to be away from home even more often than was already the case. There was no denying that likelihood. I would also take a big hit financially. A government position required that I end my active participation in our insurance business and become a silent partner instead. A rough calculation suggested that my income might drop to half of what I was then earning. Of course, my business partners were none too happy about the prospect of seeing me give up my active participation completely. Some thought me plain crazy and beseeched me not to accept the offer. There was the problem of a possible conflict of interest, as my firm was doing a lot of business with Volkswagen, and—since VW was still partially owned by the state of Lower Saxony—as finance minister I would sit on VW's board of supervisors. After some intense back and forth, it was agreed that my silent partnership would not constitute a conflict of interest.

In the end, though, the temptations were simply too great, especially when measured against all the frustrations and disappointments I had experienced. To leave Hesse and Bonn behind felt almost like a liberation. Perhaps it was also an escape from the deep sorrow over the death of our son Michael, who had quietly passed away on November 30 after his long and courageous fight against cancer. So I declared myself ready for a new chapter in my life and departed for Hanover.

My move to Lower Saxony had been a closely held secret. When it was announced just nine days after my breakfast meeting with Albrecht, it caused quite a sensation. I went to the *Landtag* for a formal introduction (and promptly walked again into a wrong meeting room). The reception by the legislators was friendly, but not enthusiastic. They were probably wondering about this politician from Bonn whom they knew as a somewhat maverick foreign policy person: this novice to Lower Saxony and to the world of finance and economics was going to be their new minister for finance and economics? But at least they were willing to suspend judgment and give me the benefit of the doubt. Albrecht introduced me and emphasized that I not only had his full support, but also a free hand in running my ministries.

I then had to go through the formalities of giving up a *Bundestag* seat and finding a replacement for my candidacy in the upcoming election. (Until the election, the first person on the previous election's CDU proportional list who had not made it then took over my seat.) I also had to formalize my new status as a silent partner in a firm whose other senior partners were still in a state of shock. To avoid even the slightest appearance of a potential conflict of interest, I prepared a detailed listing of all my properties, business interests, and income; I gave that list to the president of the Lower Saxony parliament with the express permission that, should anyone ever question my integrity in office, he was free to make this list available for further investigation. (I am glad to say that no one ever bothered to request a look at it.)

I was sworn into office on February 25, 1976. In all the excitement, I promptly forgot the standard formula to invoke "God's help," which caused a good deal of consternation about this member of the Christian Democratic Union and required later explanations and corrections of the record. I was now a minister, or rather, a double minister, since I would serve as economics minister until a more permanent replacement for the former FDP incumbent could be found.

From the first day, I had the time of my life. Of course, everything was new, and that in itself was exciting, but I quickly discovered that my subordinates and staff were not only highly competent, but also extremely friendly and helpful. That made work a pleasure. It took a while to learn the ropes, but with a lot of help and plenty of good will on all sides, we were soon off to a splendid start. With two portfolios—that of the finance minister being the more important one, as the real economic decisions were made here—and memberships in a number of supervisory boards, I was busier than ever. In fact, I never worked as hard as I did during that first year in Hanover. I dare say I enjoyed every minute of it.

Another pleasant surprise about working in the province was that it wasn't that provincial after all. As finance minister, for instance, I represented Lower Saxony in the *Bundesrat*, the upper house of parliament, where unelected representatives of the states met to vote on issues that affected state interests. That included such foreign policy issues as the treaty with Poland regarding social security payments in exchange for emigration permits. Just days before, I had voted in the *Bundestag* for ratification of that treaty, as usual against the faction position. Now Lower Saxony had to cast its vote in the *Bundesrat*, where it would, in fact, be decisive, for CDU-governed states now had enough votes in the *Bundesrat* to reject *Bundestag* legislation. I had made it clear to Albrecht that I could not, in good conscience, vote against a treaty in the *Bundesrat* for which I had earlier voted yes in the *Bundestag*. Albrecht agreed with me, but needed some political cover for a decision that ran against a declared CDU position. One such cover was the need to lay the groundwork for an eventual coalition with the FDP, whose foreign minister had, after all, negotiated the treaty. The other was to bring about some presumed improvements in the treaty that would make it more agreeable to the CDU in Lower Saxony. I became the front man for conducting the necessary negotiations with the Polish side. The details of that effort are covered in a later chapter. They were successful and Lower Saxony—together with all other states—cast its vote in favor of an *Ostpolitik* treaty that, for once, was not about basic principles, important though they were, but about direct help for a large number of destitute people. I was proud of my role in helping it pass.

There were other foreign policy activities that kept me busy and involved. Some arose from the commercial nature of my position, which was strongly focused on attracting foreign investments to Lower Saxony. Others evolved in the context of the Hanover *Messe*, Germany's largest and by far most important location for industrial exhibitions, the supervisory board of which I chaired. The various *Messe* events attracted many visitors from abroad, but also visitors from East Germany. This allowed for the occasional informal discussion of sensitive issues. Finally, while I was in Hanover—perhaps even because I was there—I was called upon to conduct critical and sensitive international missions, such as a financial rescue effort for Turkey. All of these activities are described in greater detail in later chapters.

I also had more time to attend international meetings and conferences of all kinds. Among the more interesting were the annual Bilderberg Conferences, convened and chaired by Prince Bernhard of the Netherlands, which brought together a highly select group of international businessmen, politicians, and foreign policy experts. It was there that I first met such up-and-coming political leaders as Donald Rumsfeld (then chief of staff in the Ford White House) and Margaret Thatcher ("a resolute, very blond woman," I noted in a diary entry about the future prime minister, "who is very sharp and articulate in her formulations—extremely right wing"). Discussions at these conferences were broad, frank, and far-reaching. Relaxation at the carefully chosen conference sites was equally impressive: some of us would meet regularly in the sauna—it was quite a sight, and perhaps some photojournalist's dream picture, to see the rich and powerful of this world (from the Agnellis to the Rockefellers, Rothschilds, and Wallenbergs) sweating it out together.

In 1977 the Bilderberg Conference took place in beautifully located Torquay on the British Channel coast. Helmut Schmidt, the chancellor, honored the meeting with his presence. My main task in Hanover, of course, was to put Lower Saxony back on a sound economic footing. In this I was highly successful. Part of my success was due to some fortunate personnel decisions. Early on I needed to find a new director for the NordLB, Lower Saxony's "central" bank. A friend of mine, Ludwig Poullain, was director of the WestLB in North Rhine-Westphalia. I asked him for advice. Yes, he indicated, he had a suitable candidate among his directors. Would I want to come by and interview him? I did, but then this person wanted to know what guarantees there were that the Albrecht government would last and that he would keep his job. I was forced to admit there were none. He then politely declined any further discussions. But I had done my homework and mentioned the name of another promising candidate on his staff. Poullain flat out told me that it was out of the question—the young man, Adolf Kracht, was being groomed as his successor. I insisted that I at least wanted to talk to him. Kracht and I hit it off, and he agreed on the spot to what was, for him, a fantastic career move. The problem was, I needed to take him to Hanover right away and introduce him as the NordLB's new director. Thoroughly flabbergasted, Poullain finally relented and even let us use his bank's business jet to fly back to Hanover. Once we were airborne, one of the pilots came into the cabin with a bottle of Dom Pérignon champagne: "With best regards and wishes from Mr. Poullain!" I was similarly, if not quite as dramatically, lucky in luring away the director of the Düsseldorf *Messe* to become the director of the Hanover *Messe*. Both turned out to be inspired choices and proved instrumental in furthering Lower Saxony's economic development.

A coup of a different kind was my effort to extract more money from Lower Saxony's oil and gas producers (Lower Saxony being one of the few places in Germany where oil and gas can be pumped from the ground). The state had a long-term agreement with the producers providing for a fixed-sum payment on 5 percent of total production. But as energy prices had increased dramatically since 1973, I thought it was time to tap into the producers' windfall profits. It took a while, and some serious negotiations, to convince the producers to increase their annual contributions to the state coffers. By 1980, that amounted to ten times more than what they had paid in 1976. Lower Saxony's budget was well-served by this increase. (Not so my personal budget: at the conclusion of the negotiations, I invited the heads of the oil and gas companies to a very elaborate dinner in Hanover's fanciest restaurant. When I presented the bill to my office for reimbursement, I was told by a crestfallen assistant that my predecessor had already used up all appropriated representation funds; using other funds would strictly violate all rules established by the finance ministry. So I ended up being stuck with the bill. Another lesson learned.)

Economic growth required new investments and new business opportunities. So I approached some 1,500 directors of German and international companies, pointing out that Lower Saxony was perfectly situated for industry (including excellent port facilities) and now, with a new government, had a superb business climate. My approach proved successful. Soon some forty-five companies were considering setting up business in Lower Saxony; eventually, we saw new investments amounting to DM 10 billion, providing some 20,000 new jobs. These included nuclear processing and storage facilities (that before too long became the source of considerable controversy and many disruptive demonstrations). Another major new project was a chemical plant put up by the British industry giant ICI. The personal connections I made in the course of that project would later lead to a seat on ICI's international board of advisers and then to an appointment as Commander of the Order of the British Empire (a story of its own to be told later). Who would have thought of that in 1976?

My thoughts in 1976 were focused mostly on the tasks at hand in Lower Saxony, but I was still national treasurer of the CDU and a member of its governing board, the presidium. By necessity, therefore, I had to also think about the ongoing election process. I was committed to Hanover, but I was serving in a minority government and had to consider fallback positions. One such position was that of minister-president in Hesse, my old dream. At one point, Helmut Kohl told me that if he won the election, the leading candidate for a CDU-run at the Hesse government (then in the hands of the SPD) would likely join his government in Bonn; in that case, the road would be clear for me. That produced mixed emotions. I detested Alfred Dregger for his right-wing radicalism and nationalism (which made him an ally of Strauss); getting him out of Hesse would be great, but seeing him in a Kohl government would be disastrous. My trusted staff and I once again weighed all the options. Polls in Hesse looked encouraging for me; national polls did not look so good for the CDU. In August, Kohl introduced the members of his shadow cabinet. I was not included, which was okay by me as I wanted to focus on my tasks in Hanover and not be distracted by a national campaign (for which I would have had to secure a candidacy for the *Bundestag*—another potential distraction). Just in case, though, I did let Kohl know that I wanted to be considered for a second-tier position. He readily agreed to do so.

The election results on October 3, 1976, put an end to all such maneuverings and speculations. The CDU and the CSU won the most votes, but fell short of an absolute majority. The FDP easily overcame the 5 percent hurdle and remained committed to a coalition with the SPD. That confirmed Helmut Schmidt as chancellor, though with a majority of eight seats, his government rested on shaky foundations. This narrow margin again left open hopes for an early end to the social-liberal coalition, which in turn opened the door wide for renewed and continuous jockeying over who would lead the opposition and what efforts should be made to turn the FDP around. Expectations were muted, aspirations were high, and the prospects for more all-around unpleasantness discouraging. (Strauss proved that point when, shortly after the election, he publicly blamed those "northern German assholes" for the CDU/CSU's loss.) I was sad about the election outcome, but glad to be in northern Germany, far enough away from this circus's center ring.

The failure to win in Bonn made it all the more important to secure our foothold in Hanover and to show the way forward. On the eve of the national election, Albrecht issued an invitation to the Lower Saxony FDP to enter into formal negotiations, working toward the establishment of a CDU/FDP coalition in Hanover. To nudge the regional FDP to agree to such negotiations—and then to bring them to a successful conclusion—required extensive discussions in both Hanover and Bonn, a lot of persuasion involving reluctant FDP members of the Lower Saxony parliament (who, after all, had promised their voters that they would not seek a coalition with the CDU), and a good deal of hand-holding up to the very end. I was intimately involved in all of these efforts. Bringing about such a coalition had been one of the primary reasons for my move to Hanover, so I had a strong personal interest. I also had a significant stake in a successful outcome, as it would help cement my reputation as a man of the middle who could attract support from the left side of the political spectrum and thereby change the political landscape. In fact, both Strauss and Brandt—that is, the representatives of both ends of the political spectrum—actively worked to undermine our efforts: Strauss, because he feared it would invalidate his strategy of open confrontation; Brandt, no longer chancellor but still head of the SPD, because it could prove to be the beginning of the end of the social-liberal coalition in Bonn, which, of course, was exactly our ultimate goal.

Opposition by Strauss and Brandt became one of our best selling points in Hanover: if they were against it, surely the FDP was doing something right! By late November 1976, we had reached agreement in principle. The details of the coalition agreement—specifying not only who would get what job, but also which policies should be pursued—were nailed down by early December. On January 19, 1977, the first CDU/FDP coalition government since 1966 was formally established when the new ministers were sworn into office. It was that great day for which I had gone to Hanover, I wrote in my diary. I also noted, however, that "my principal task here in Hanover is now finished."

I was, in fact, looking ahead to what should come next. Being finance minister in Lower Saxony was fun, but not my ultimate political ambition. I had always considered it a stepping stone; now I had to think about what step to take next—and where, and when, and how. Ernst Albrecht—well-aware of my situation and anticipating my musings—strongly encouraged me to stay in Lower Saxony, run for a seat in its *Landtag* in the 1978 election, and at some point become his successor. He also agreed, however, that should opportunities present themselves in Bonn or Hesse, I was, of course, free—indeed obligated—to pursue them. I very much appreciated his friendly openness and candor at that point. Later, unfortunately, we grew somewhat distant as our paths began to diverge. That, in turn, increased my desire to move on.

Hesse was still beckoning. I saw a chance to run for minister-president there, but my trusted staff saw it differently and succeeded in talking me out of it. That meant that I decided to follow Albrecht's advice to stay in Lower Saxony for a while and await those better chances. In June 1978, I won election to the Lower Saxony parliament, which ensconced me more firmly there. The overall election result, however, was bittersweet for me. With Albrecht in the lead, the CDU won an absolute majority! The voters had rewarded us for our resounding successes. Almost overnight, Albrecht became one of the leading CDU candidates for chancellor. That would have opened the way for me to succeed him, but it would also block me from being nominated as candidate for chancellor—something I had begun to think about more openly as a long-term perspective. Then there was the problem of the FDP losing in the election, indeed not making it above the 5-percent hurdle. For them, our grand demonstration project of a middle-of-the-road coalition had proved fatal. From now on, the FDP would look long and hard at CDU coalition offers, making that path toward electoral success in Bonn or elsewhere that much harder. It seemed I might be stuck in Hanover for a while longer. That was not too bad. I now had time for occasional excursions into the somewhat secret world of diplomacy (to be discussed later), which brought me great personal satisfaction and more public recognition, but also a good deal of griping from people, like Strauss, who did not necessarily agree with what I was doing. But in a way, that merely increased the itch to leave Hanover behind.

The next big occasion to scratch that itch presented itself with the federal election of October 1980. Realistically, I had no chance under ordinary circumstances to compete for the nomination of my party; but the question was whether circumstances would be ordinary.

Helmut Kohl had had his chance in 1976, and it was unlikely that he could win the nomination again. Ernst Albrecht was the clear favorite of party members and the public at large. Franz Josef Strauss thought his time had come and launched a massive campaign to secure the nomination, against considerable resistance based on his abrasive personality, controversial policies, and uncertain electability. Election prospects for the CDU were not that good. Chancellor Schmidt had just lived up to his *Macher* image during the "German autumn" in 1977 when the terrorist attacks had reached their peak; to defeat him at the height of his newly gained popularity would be very difficult. And the FDP was not yet fully convinced that it was time to switch sides and align itself once again with the CDU (the Lower Saxony experience served as a deterrent).

Albrecht hesitated, for reasons I never quite understood, perhaps because he figured his chances were not too good. I finally challenged him in a cabinet meeting: shouldn't we discuss your candidacy and how to win your election? It became apparent that he did not quite have the necessary fire in his belly. The nomination was his for the asking, but he did not want to ask for it. He would accept the nomination if it were offered on a silver platter, but he refused to actively campaign for it. "I don't jump when Kohl whistles," he told me. That left the field to Strauss, who played his trump card: if he was not nominated as chancellor of the Christian Democrats, he threatened to cancel his cooperation with the CDU and establish the CSU as a national party. The CDU was not unprepared for such a move, and we even had some money set aside to expand the CDU into Bavaria—the CSU's exclusive territory. But in light of Schmidt's strength, Albrecht's hesitation, and the highly unpredictable consequences of an open split between CDU and CSU, the CDU finally caved in. On July 2, 1979—more than a year before the election—the faction voted in favor of Strauss. After that vote, his actual nomination by the party convention would be a mere formality. And with that vote, the election campaign for 1980 began in earnest.

The bind I was in had now gotten worse. I was basically determined to leave Lower Saxony behind. I had achieved what I had set out to do, and I felt I had learned about as much about finance and economics as I needed to, or cared to. Staying on the job for another four years (that is, until Albrecht would try again in a more determined fashion to become chancellor) and then taking over as minister-president in Lower Saxony hardly seemed attractive. I now had my own "Goal 1" (as I called it): become chancellor myself. That made me a competitor of Albrecht, and thus not a good subordinate finance minister. I wanted and needed to get back onto the national, indeed international, stage, but my party's candidate for chancellor was more than just someone with whom I had been fighting over policy issues for so many years.

Family, friends, and advisers helped me work through these problems and find a way out of my dilemma. The focal point for our deliberations was "Goal 1"—how to become chancellor. That goal seemed within reach. A number of public opinion polls listed me as one of the most popular politicians in Germany and among the top four contenders for the chancellorship; however, it was a goal that could realistically only be achieved if I had a prominent role in Bonn, or if I was minister-president in a federal state. The time horizon for Lower Saxony was too far off. Hesse remained a dream, in the dual meaning of the word: I would have loved to become its minister-president, but all avenues appeared closed off. Another possibility might have been North Rhine-Westphalia with upcoming elections and a shifting political landscape, but that seemed a stretch, as I had absolutely no political connections in that state, West Germany's largest. In the middle of these deliberations, I was approached by the chairman of the opposition CDU faction in the Hamburg city parliament (*Bürgerschaft*): might I be interested in running for mayor in 1982? The city of Hamburg (which is also a state, its mayor therefore equivalent to a minister-president) was attractive enough; after all, I was born and raised there. But at that point, the prospect was too uncertain, the date too far off. Another temptation that came my way was the position of NATO Secretary General. I expressed my interest, but nothing ever came of it as the incumbent stayed on for another four years.

I seriously considered leaving politics altogether, but in the end I was persuaded to stay and fight. "Goal 1" was not yet out of sight, and certainly not out of mind. I decided to return to Bonn by seeking a seat in the *Bundestag*. In order to keep all options open, however, I did not yet relinquish my position as finance minister. The Lower Saxony CDU put me on the top of their proportional list of *Bundestag* candidates; my election was therefore guaranteed. Should things not work out in Bonn—that is, were I to find myself in the role of a mere backbencher, rather than in some leadership position—I would stay in Hanover and relinquish my *Bundestag* seat.

I was still left, however, with the awkward problem of how to deal with Franz Josef Strauss. Two factors combined to ease my conscience and make subordinate cooperation more palatable. For one, Strauss began to show moderation and reasonable behavior once his nomination was certain. Maybe he would live up to the demands and expectations of the position and adopt a different personality and style. The other factor concerned consistent rumors—first mentioned to me by Chancellor Schmidt, of all people—that Strauss would select me as his shadow foreign minister. Were that to become true, I would, of course, put aside most of my scruples, since I would then be in a position to influence Strauss directly and to stake out my own policies. Besides, if Strauss really had it in him to make me—who had been such a thorn in his side—a member of his top team and prospective foreign minister, I would be forced to see him in a different light. Conversely, if Strauss felt compelled (not least by CDU chairman Kohl) to put me on his team merely to have a prominent northern German help balance the ticket and thereby increase his chances, that would give me added influence and allow me to play an important role in the party. On balance, then, I convinced myself that being on Strauss's top team had sufficient enough advantages to outweigh any scruples and hesitations. So I swallowed my pride and vowed to be a loyal member of the team.

It wasn't easy. Strauss was slow in making any official announcement as to who would be in his shadow cabinet. He was also testing me, perhaps even teasing me. We met a number of times for pleasant enough conversations without him extending a formal invitation. I was asked to speak to a CSU leadership meeting, but not necessarily about foreign policy issues, rather, about how to run (and finance) election campaigns. In early spring 1980,

Strauss informed me that he was planning a trip to the United States. I succeeded in persuading him that it might be a good idea if I went with him.

These were difficult times for the United States. In Teheran, radical Muslims still held American embassy employees hostage (and would continue to do so until the day President Carter left office in January 1981). In Afghanistan, the Soviet Union was engaged in a brutal campaign to subdue this neighboring country (where, ironically, the United States would later provide support to radical Muslims fighting Soviet troops). And in the Persian Gulf, Saddam Hussein in Iraq and Ayatollah Khomeini in Iran were ratcheting up their hostile rhetoric (which eventually led to an Iraqi attack on Iran in September 1980—a move that the Carter administration quietly encouraged). World politics were obviously in a complex and potentially dangerous phase in which, much to my dismay, the Schmidt government had not taken what I considered to be the necessary steps to protect Germany's interests—at the top of which was showing support for the United States. I thought I could be of help to Strauss in traversing this tricky terrain and was glad that he agreed to let me join him for this by now traditional excursion to Washington of a German candidate for chancellor.

The trip was a balancing act, during which I tried my best to show loyalty while maintaining a proper distance as the not-yet-anointed shadow foreign minister. I traveled separately, for instance, and not as a member of his delegation, and I abstained from any media contacts that might have upstaged Strauss. He had a difficult time, mostly because of language problems. His attempts at humor fell flat, while his heavy Bavarian accent and non-idiomatic English made him appear almost like a caricature of a German provincial politician. It did not help that he tried to compensate for his flaws with loud and aggressive-sounding deliveries. But Strauss also revealed a problematic lack of understanding for American sensitivities. He nearly insulted a group of presidents of American Jewish organizations when he admonished them to tell "their prime minister" to do something about the Palestinian problem. The delicate situation was barely rescued when it was pointed out to him that, as American Jews, they owed allegiance only to the president in Washington and not to a prime minister in Israel.

In Washington we were received first by Secretary of State Cyrus Vance (who, as it turned out, would soon leave office in protest over the bungled effort by US Special Forces to rescue the American hostages in Teheran). Vance complained bitterly about a lack of transatlantic cooperation, especially regarding trade and economic issues, but also about the hesitation of the Schmidt government to join the United States in a boycott of the Olympic Summer Games in Moscow. Strauss certainly got an earful.

Next we went to the White House to see President Carter, who immediately recognized me and kindly praised my efforts regarding Turkey. Carter then asked to talk to Strauss privately (an unusual privilege granted to a foreign candidate for public office). The president used the occasion—as Strauss later told us—to complain about Chancellor Schmidt and to set the record straight regarding the neutron weapon controversy. This proved to be a clever move on Carter's part, for by taking Strauss into his confidence, he converted him almost on the spot from the Gaullist Strauss usually was into an Atlanticist fully supporting close relations with the United States. All in all, Strauss's US visit in March 1980 was neither a total disaster nor a triumphant success. Strauss and I got along well, sharing some lighter moments, but also engaging in serious discussions. Strauss could be charming and his intellect, when properly restrained, was never in doubt. I saw his best sides during that trip, and now felt confident that I should, and would, be on his team.

I also managed to arrange a pre-election visit by Strauss to Number 10 Downing Street. It was quite an event to see the Iron Lady and the Bavarian Lion interact. In fact, Strauss had decided to present Prime Minister Margaret Thatcher with a Bavarian Lion as a personal gift. He carried the somewhat oversized porcelain figurine (from the Nymphenburg Porcelain Manufactory, of course) on his shoulder, sweating profusely, as we stood in front of that famous door waiting to be admitted. Thatcher was at her charming best. She took an immediate liking to Strauss, who was equally fascinated by that icon of British resolve and toughness. They shared a similar life history in that they had both risen from simple family backgrounds to positions of power through extraordinary intelligence and steely determination. Now Strauss was trying to achieve what Thatcher had already accomplished. Here, too, they shared a common bond, with Dennis Thatcher looking on with barely concealed amusement, Thatcher and Strauss engaged in an open political flirt, sharing their fascination with power, exchanging views on world politics, and trying to convince each other of the correctness of their views regarding European integration (Strauss being all for it, Thatcher insisting on the special role and sovereignty of the United Kingdom). When we left, Strauss was high.

As the election campaign heated up, I did not hesitate to make my views known in media interviews and public speeches. My views were clear: the most likely way to win the election was to appeal to FDP voters, both directly and indirectly (by keeping open the option of a coalition government right of center). Even Strauss had at one point indicated as much. I was therefore all the more surprised, indeed stunned, when, in early May, I received a five-page letter from Strauss, addressed as personal and private, in which he berated me for these views and accused me of disloyalty and disrespect. Strauss had sent copies of this letter to others (including Helmut Kohl), which made it anything but personal and private. Strauss called my behavior "parasitic publicity," characterized more by personal ambition and a desire for making a name for myself than by a willingness to serve a common cause: strong stuff indeed. He also referred to earlier "escapades and solo rides" that had left his supporters both embittered and disgusted. They would not understand if I was now rewarded with a position of responsibility on his team, unless I was willing to change my ways and toe the line. Kohl added to my surprise, discomfort, and disgust when he wrote me a letter a few days later (copy to Strauss!), in which he claimed he was spending a good deal of his time cleaning up the mess I had left behind with my public comments. "I understand your political calculations and intentions less and less," he wrote. "Maybe it makes sense to you. I can only see that your way is leading straight into a cul-de-sac."

I understood that there were some games being played, between Kohl and Strauss for sure, but also between me and the party leadership in an obvious effort to rein me in, perhaps even to put me in my place and demote me—Strauss had indicated as much in the conclusion of his letter. But obviously this double-barreled attack meant the end of my hopes for inclusion in the 1980 CDU/CSU top team. I resigned myself to that fact, even told myself that it was better that way if I wanted to be able to look at myself in the mirror and not lose face in public by changing my views. After a suitable waiting period of a week, while I was mulling things over and trying to calm down, I carefully drafted a reply to Strauss, as "personal" as his letter to me had been. I once again explained why I thought my strategy of reaching out to the FDP was the most promising path toward a return to power. I pleaded for a plurality of opinions even within the party and told Strauss that his attempt to enforce a single message per order from above would not yield the desired results. Subordination no, solidarity yes: that was my offer to Strauss. I was sure that would be the end of it.

It was not—much to my surprise again. Apparently Kohl's ploy had worked, and perhaps my protestations, too. Strauss finally relented and agreed to the formation of a top team. Its composition was announced on June 6—and I was included as shadow foreign minister. There was a good deal of astonishment all around, not least among political observers who rightly wondered how Walther Leisler Kiep would get along with his foreign policy nemesis Franz Josef Strauss. I was willing to give it a try, swallowing some of my pride, but also determined to stick to my principles and to uphold my views. Deep down, however, I remained skeptical that we would actually prevail with Strauss at the top. I practiced solidarity with little expectation of immediate success, but with long-term hopes of political rewards.

Getting the election campaign organized proved to be quite a struggle. It also revealed the value of having a team that could restrain the candidate from following his lesser instincts. Strauss was determined to run a personal campaign against Schmidt, his erstwhile colleague in the Grand Coalition, heaping all kinds of invectives on him (dumb, no sense of history, a willing tool of the Left, the destroyer of Germany . . . ) and seeking to offer himself as far more qualified to be chancellor. CSU headquarters suggested a suitable slogan for such a campaign: "Moscow wants Schmidt. Germany elects Strauss." The team was terrified. In meetings with Strauss and his staff, we tried to talk him out of his attacks on Schmidt. He grew so frustrated with us that at one point he came close to quitting altogether. Kohl had a hard time calming him down. "What do you want," Strauss bellowed, "that I praise Schmidt to high heaven?" "Exactly, Herr Strauss," I quickly jumped in. "Find some good words for Schmidt, but damn his party as unworthy of its faithful servant." Strauss looked at me incredulously, but then laughed: "Herr Kiep, that will be the most boring speech of my life." We managed to tone Strauss down. We also agreed on a different campaign slogan: "Peace and liberty. With Franz Josef Strauss for Germany." Not brilliant, but at least not offensive.

My own campaign slogan was "Fight with Kiep and win with Strauss" (reflecting more hope than conviction). Nevertheless, as the top candidate in Lower Saxony, I was determined as ever to give the campaign my best effort. In Lower Saxony alone I spoke at seventy major campaign events, traveling more than ten thousand kilometers in my now traditional "Kiep bus." I also put in appearances elsewhere, not least in Bavaria, where I spoke mostly in places known for their liberal leanings. I stayed true to my principles, not launching personal attacks on our opponents in the firm belief that such attacks were not only counterproductive, but also detrimental to a democratic political culture. One of my colleagues in Lower Saxony once said about me: "His opponents fear him, the people love him, and he has no enemies." That was perhaps too flattering; after all, I did want to get elected, and I wanted my party to win.

We lost, yet could have won. The CDU/CSU received 44.5 percent—4 percent less than in 1976. The SPD remained the same, with 42.9 percent. But the FDP gained almost 3 percent with 10.6 percent overall: the party's best result in a long time. I figured that my strategy had essentially proved correct, but for Franz Josef Strauss. The CDU/CSU could easily have formed a coalition with the FDP. In fact, I am quite sure that the FDP's additional voters had hoped for precisely such an outcome. But Strauss was simply a too controversial figure to head a CDU/CSU/FDP coalition. And he was not magnanimous enough to set his own ambitions aside and let such a coalition be formed with someone else as chancellor. Strauss's main competitors were quietly satisfied—Kohl above all. They knew from their own intimate contacts with the FDP leadership that the social-liberal coalition would fall apart before too long, and certainly not survive the next election. Strauss had had his chance and would not be around for a second try. Now it was going to be someone else's turn. Kohl as CDU chairman and the leader of its faction in the *Bundestag* was in the best position, even though he, too, had already lost an election in 1976. No wonder he felt smug about his chances, and was ready to take on future challengers, like Ernst Albrecht or even me. It appeared that he had outmaneuvered us all.

All of which made my life no easier. I had decided for Bonn, but kept open the option for Hanover. Now I had to make up my mind. I was still torn. "Goal 1" would be hard to reach under the circumstances, but it would be practically out of reach if I stayed in Hanover, where I could become minister-president only if Albrecht moved on to become chancellor in Bonn. That was not a prospect I found promising or rewarding. I tried to sound out Kohl about possibilities for a leadership position in the faction, but he was coyly noncommittal. Hamburg remained a possibility two years down the road. Another option was, once again, a move to Brussels as a Commissioner of the European Community. But this time I declined without hesitation; by and large, a seat on the Commission was for political has-beens, not for the politically ambitious. So I decided to stay in Bonn, knowing that I had strong support elsewhere in the party, including that of Albrecht, who, after he finally accepted that he could not keep me in Hanover, was gracious enough to lobby on my behalf. On October 28, 1980, I relinquished my position as finance minister in Hanover, proud of my accomplishments and eager to move on.

It felt good to be back in the middle of things in Bonn. I was no longer bound by requirements of cabinet discipline or restrained by party solidarity. It felt even better when Kohl, out of the blue but in his typical manipulative style, informed me rather casually—in early November in the course of the *Bundestag* session that reelected Schmidt as chancellor—that he would nominate me as a deputy faction chairman responsible for economic issues. I was elated, even though I had hoped for a leadership position where I could exercise my expertise in foreign affairs. On second thought, though, I was pleased that Kohl, and with him the faction, recognized my newly gained economic expertise, and I felt confident that it would sharpen my political profile for a future pursuit of "Goal 1." My first major speech in the *Bundestag* on economic issues only a few weeks later was very well received and proved a resounding success. It heightened my desire for more and better things to come. I had every reason to believe that I was on the right track.

But soon the track signals became quite confusing again. Stories appeared with increasing frequency that mentioned me as one, if not the, leading candidate for the 1984 election. That certainly indicated the right direction and was not entirely unwelcome. But by putting me in the spotlight, these stories also tended to alarm potential rivals and spur them to take defensive countermeasures. To help defuse that situation, I eventually decided to invite my main rivals for a friendly chat behind closed doors (German style, that is, for coffee and cake at home), to sound them out and to see where we stood. My three guests were Ernst Albrecht, minister-president of Lower Saxony; Gerhard Stoltenberg, minister-president of Schleswig-Holstein; and Richard von Weizsäcker, newly elected mayor of West Berlin. I came away with the impression that Stoltenberg was determined to seek the nomination, Albrecht was interested, but not yet fully engaged, and Weizsäcker had not yet made up his mind, perhaps because he lacked an ultimate drive for power. In any case, we agreed that we would not campaign against each other, but rather await a decision by the party and then fully support the nominated candidate. We were also unanimous in our assessment that, should the social-liberal coalition collapse early, Kohl could not be denied the chancellorship. In that case, however, we would support each other for prominent representation in a Kohl government.

I had not invited Kohl to our meeting, partly for personal reasons, but mostly because we all thought that he was not really a credible candidate for the 1984 election. Kohl, of course, had other ideas; however, he also knew that his best chance was, in fact, an early end of the Schmidt government. He was clearly working toward that goal and already scheming to push his rivals out of the way. I bore the brunt of these efforts.

Kohl's lever for ever so gently shoving me to the sidelines was Hamburg. I had already been approached regarding a run for mayor of Hamburg in 1982, but I postponed a decision until after the *Bundestag* election. Now I had to make a decision. All the uncertainties were still there. Hamburg, with one brief exception in the 1950s, had always been governed by the SPD; were the chances now better for a CDU mayor? Maybe, because the incumbent had just been forced out of office as the result of a personal scandal. But his successor, Klaus von Dohnanyi, was a formidable candidate ("a man of the Left who hides his ideology underneath a cloak of aristocratic manners and proffers his attacks in the guise of feudal poses," I noted in my diary). There was no guarantee that I would win outright, or bring the FDP along for a governing coalition, though a repetition of that feat was certainly our hope. If I won, would that bring me closer to "Goal 1"? If I lost, could I go back to Bonn, even as damaged goods? Or would that be the end of all my dreams? Once again, we went back and forth discussing all options and scenarios, trying to figure out how best to keep me on track.

There were times when I was leaning toward accepting the Hamburg offer. Finally, the temptation to run a campaign entirely on my own and then to prove myself in a top executive position was hard to resist. At other times I was inclined to reject it, as I saw the dangers of losing it all in Hamburg and contemplated—even if I were to win—the disadvantages of yet another stint in the province, far away from the excitement in Bonn and the pleasures of involvement in world affairs. It was primarily Kohl who egged me on, arguing that I needed to do it for the good of Hamburg and for the benefit of the CDU. He even told me that, of course, a Mayor Kiep would be a natural candidate for chancellor in 1984. At the same time, frequently right after I had talked to Kohl, there were newspaper stories that I would, in fact, be the CDU candidate in Hamburg, and that Kohl was trying to get me out of the way as a possible rival for 1984. I might have been warned, but I saw these stories as a challenge: now I had to do it. Kohl had pushed the right buttons: directly with me, but also behind the scenes.

At the last possible moment, in late June 1981, I decided to go for it. The challenges, as well as the possible rewards, were too tempting. Kohl assured me that, should there be an early change in government and he were to become chancellor, I would of course be considered for a top position regardless of the outcome in Hamburg. He also supported me in my position that I was competing in Hamburg in order to become mayor, not to serve as leader of the opposition. Until the election outcome was clear, I would keep my seat in the *Bundestag*; in case of a loss, I would not take up my seat in the Hamburg parliament. I felt confident that I had covered all bases and secured sufficient fallback positions. Hamburg was a risk—that was half of the challenge. Prudence, however, suggested that I minimize the risk.

The formal announcement of my candidacy for First Mayor in Hamburg took place in late August 1981; the nomination process was to be concluded in October, the election itself set for June 1982. There was some controversy over my decision not to stay in Hamburg in case of a loss; some argued that I would be cheating my potential voters, perhaps even keep some from voting for me. I countered that Hamburg needed a new First Mayor, not a new leader of the opposition (which I did not need either, but I left that unsaid, though understood). Besides, Dohnanyi had done exactly the same thing a few years earlier when he had run for minister-president of Rhineland-Palatinate (against Helmut Kohl), so I saw no problem fending off SPD attacks against my decision to stay in Bonn in case of a loss. Given Dohnanyi's background, I also felt quite immune against any charges that I was an outsider—a "reimported Hamburger," as some wit put it. I offered myself as a politician born and raised in Hamburg who wanted to bring a "liberal renewal" to his native city. The Hamburg CDU responded with overwhelming approval to this message with its evident overtones.

Then a bombshell hit. On August 29, a Saturday, a Düsseldorf newspaper reported that the state prosecutor there had opened criminal investigations for tax evasion against me and thirty-nine other prominent members of the CDU. Allegedly, we had collected tax-deductible contributions for nonpartisan organizations, but diverted the funds directly—and therefore illegally—to the CDU. For the investigations to go forward, the prosecutor had requested that my immunity as a member of the *Bundestag* be lifted. I was stunned. As treasurer of the party, I had been aware of irregularities in collecting funds, indeed had worked hard to correct them. I was also familiar with investigations involving one of my deputies as well as financing officers of other parties. But I had no clue that I myself was about to become a target of investigations, nor had I any reason to fear any such investigation, for I was sure that I had never done anything illegal. The state prosecutor's office had not informed me about its pending investigations. To read about it in a newspaper did little to increase my respect for the German judicial system. And to this day, I wonder whether that leak was purposefully timed to coincide with the beginning of my campaign in Hamburg. (The details of my struggle with party financing laws and practices are the subject of a later chapter.)

I now had a weekend to ponder the ramifications of this development, without being able to learn any more specific details. I knew that the investigations and any resulting legal proceedings could drag on for a long time (though I never expected them to last as long as they eventually did). With that cloud hanging over me, should I step back from my Hamburg efforts, which undoubtedly would be affected by such a scandal? Or should I press on, confident that my innocence was going to prevail? I received little encouragement from the CDU's chairman. Kohl called me that evening at home, talking endlessly about his problems, but never once mentioning mine. I couldn't believe it. Was he just insensitive or cruelly calculating? Still, I decided to fight it out. Resignation now might not only give my opponents too much comfort, it could also be wrongly interpreted as an admission of guilt. Later I found solace and strength in the support of the Hamburg CDU. I offered to withdraw my candidacy, but was beseeched not to do so. In October the party convention formally nominated me nearly unanimously as their candidate for First Mayor of Hamburg.

I entered the campaign with my usual verve and energy—it was the first time I was at the top of a ticket! I did not underestimate my opponent, a seasoned campaigner himself. We fought a tough but fair fight, always the "gentlemen" that the both of us were. (In fact, we shared an eerily similar background. Dohnanyi's father had also been involved in the July 20, 1944 assassination attempt against Hitler; like my uncle Otto Kiep, he was sentenced to death and brutally executed. Klaus von Dohnanyi's brother, by the way, was the world-renowned conductor Christoph von Dohnányi.) Of course, Dohnanyi tried to exploit the party financing affair—politics is not an exercise in good manners—but I had to admit that he did so in a tolerable way, never gleefully insulting me. Others were less considerate. At one event, I had just climbed up to the podium when I noticed a man sitting in the front row, wearing prison stripes, with a placard dangling from his neck that read: "I am a tax evader." I was, of course, taken aback and had to struggle to regain my composure. It is moments like these, thankfully rare, that make a politician's life less than pleasant on occasion.

In general, I enjoyed the campaign. Since I was not running in a constituency, I did less canvassing and more public speaking. I found "taking a bath in the crowd"—in market squares or shopping malls—both challenging and invigorating. I had to be on my toes at all times, ready to answer all kinds of questions clearly and precisely, prepared for displays of hostility and good will, required to stay nice and calm. It was not always easy, but it was fun. By April 1982 I felt at home again in Hamburg, personally and politically. My campaign was going well and had indeed created a groundswell of sympathy and support. I wanted to repay the trust I met with trust of my own, obviously also hoping that I might be able to draw some undecided voters to our side, so I changed my mind and decided to stay in Hamburg, come what may. On April 26 I formally relinquished my seat in the *Bundestag*. I was now on my own—a high-wire act without a safety net. Helmut Kohl congratulated me on my decision. "You have done the party a great service," he told me. I was too caught up in my campaign and the excitement of the moment to give much thought to the deeper meaning of Kohl's comments.

June 6, 1982, was a day of triumph and tragedy. We won the most votes—43.2 percent. That was 4.6 percent more than in 1978. The SPD lost almost 9 percent and thus its absolute majority, reaching only 42.7 percent. A new radical party on the left, the Green-Alternatives, won 7.7 percent (foreshadowing future shifts of Germany's political landscape). The tragedy (for us, anyway) was the FDP: 4.9 percent meant that it failed to clear the 5-percent hurdle by a measly 0.1 percent. The coalition partner I had counted on was not available. We had one more seat than the SPD and therefore could rightly claim that we should be allowed to try and form a new government. But the SPD—itself caught in a bind over the issue of forming a coalition with the hated Greens—refused to let the government resign, or to vote for its dismissal in the *Bürgerschaft*. I was playing for an eventual Grand Coalition, under my leadership, of course. The SPD was playing for time, hoping that it could either solve its problems with the Greens or prevail in new elections; in the meantime, it retained its hold on power.

In the middle of these complex calculations and machinations in Hamburg, dramatic events were taking place in Bonn. Chancellor Schmidt had been fighting a losing battle with his own party over the issue of new intermediate-range nuclear forces (INF) to be stationed in Germany. He had provoked that issue himself in October 1977 when he pointed out the new threat posed by Soviet intermediate-range missiles (SS-20) targeted at Europe and requested that Germany's alliance partners do something to meet that threat. Ideally, this could be achieved by convincing the Soviet Union to dismantle its INF systems. Otherwise, the West would have to install INF systems of its own in order to maintain a desirable balance of nuclear forces in Europe. Eventually, the translation of these two approaches into diplomatic reality came to be known as the "dual-track": negotiating for zero deployment while preparing for the stationing of INF systems—Pershing rockets and cruise missiles—in Western Europe.

The Carter administration at first was reluctant to react to Schmidt's concerns, not wanting to install new weapons systems at a time when it was negotiating the removal of longer-range strategic nuclear weapons, and fearing that INF negotiations would further complicate the ongoing Strategic Arms Limitation Talks (SALT). Eventually, it acceded to the German chancellor's wishes in the hopes that INF might actually become a bargaining chip in US-Soviet negotiations. Later the Reagan administration, less interested in détente and more strongly committed to a restoration of American strength, endorsed the INF proposal much more enthusiastically, thus putting Schmidt into a bind. His party wanted to have nothing to do with new nuclear weapons on German soil, especially not in the face of large-scale public resistance, nor with the new party on the left that made opposition to INF deployment one of its core issues. Schmidt, of course, could hardly back down, though he fervently hoped that the INF problem might be solved with an agreement to do away with all intermediate nuclear weapons systems (which at that point neither Washington nor Moscow appeared willing to do). Schmidt had campaigned hard in Hamburg, trying to make a local election a referendum on national policies. The Hamburg election outcome was widely interpreted as a rejection of Schmidt and his approach.

Long unhappy with Schmidt's style of governance, but also in disagreement with SPD economic policies, the FDP had been waiting for a propitious moment to call an end to the social-liberal coalition. Behind the scenes, it was already negotiating the terms for joining a coalition with the CDU/CSU. This was, of course, what I had been working toward for a long time. Given Schmidt's troubles with his own party, and after the Hamburg election results that were so disastrous for the SPD and FDP, the FDP leadership decided that the time had come to switch sides. In September it pulled out of the coalition. Schmidt tried to hang on by forming a minority government, but that proved futile. On October 1, 1982, the CDU/CSU forced a constructive vote of "no confidence," with Helmut Kohl as candidate for chancellor. He won with a majority of seven votes, thereby bringing thirteen years of social-liberal governments to an end. Few of us expected that Kohl himself would last sixteen years in office.

I was not in Bonn for that momentous development. I was in Hamburg, desperately trying to rescue a seemingly hopeless situation. There the SPD had finally agreed to dissolve the *Bürgerschaft* and to have new elections on December 19. Now I was tied down, confronted with the task of running yet another election. I don't know whether Kohl ever remembered his promise to give me a top-tier appointment in Bonn once he became chancellor. He certainly never asked me. And since I was engaged in Hamburg, I would have had a hard time saying yes in any case. So his government was formed without me, which was hard to observe from distant Hamburg. I soldiered on and, in fact, threw myself into the election campaign with renewed determination, for this was my last chance at political success; however, I was also painfully aware that with Kohl's accession to the chancellorship, the bottom had basically dropped out of my own strategy for "Goal 1." Even if successful, 1982 would not lead to 1984. In fact, Kohl, rightfully eager to cement his hold on power, had already announced that he would seek new elections for spring 1983. If he won those, who knew when anyone else would have a chance to become chancellor. Things looked bleak in late fall of 1982.

My last opportunity vanished five days before Christmas. Some thought that Hamburg voters expressed their dissatisfaction with the turbulent turn of events in Bonn (Schmidt, after all, was a favorite son of the city). Perhaps voters were tired of the stalemate we had been unable to resolve. Maybe they did not relish the prospect of a Grand Coalition. It is possible that I had failed to present myself and the CDU's programs as the best alternatives for the city. Whatever the reason, we were clobbered. On December 19 the SPD won 51.3 percent of the votes, gaining an absolute majority. We came in with 38.6 percent. The FDP dropped to 2.6 percent, while the Greens held a respectable 6.8 percent. Not only could we not form a government, even our role as opposition would be irrelevant under those circumstances.

My business partners were ecstatic that I finally returned as a full—and fully active—partner. In fact, from a strictly financial point of view, leaving politics largely behind turned out to be quite rewarding. That helped mollify some of my disappointment. From my Lower Saxony days, I had retained membership on the supervisory board of Volkswagen. I now was invited to join other supervisory and advisory boards. Soon I was engaged in a broad range of activities where I could bring my talents in business and politics to bear, including occasional forays into the worlds of big business and high politics.

In addition to all my other political activities both on the national and international level, I was national treasurer of the CDU from 1971 to 1992. Over a period of twenty-two years, I was involved in a variety of legal proceedings. My task was to provide the party with the financial means it required to fulfill its aspirations and obligations, in particular, financing federal elections, which I successfully fulfilled. From the beginning, I was aware of the constant conflict between legal requirements—especially maintaining transparency and avoiding inappropriate influence peddling—and the realities of a democratic system that cannot function other than through parties, which face a steadily growing need for adequate funding. As treasurer I was walking a fine line in a decidedly gray zone.

Throughout my trials and travails, I insisted on one central point: throughout the time I was CDU treasurer and when Helmut Kohl was chancellor, there was never the slightest evidence that a donation to the party had ever been directly repaid with any kind of political favors. The *Bundestag*'s investigative committee confirmed that point. The Kohl government was not, and could not, be bought.

Upon more sober reflection, I realized that my life in politics was not entirely without some "tracks in the snow." I had left many marks, from constituency service in Hesse to business promotion in Lower Saxony, from pushing *Ostpolitik* in the right direction to helping rearrange Germany's political landscape, from strengthening transatlantic ties to securing Turkey's economic survival. I had fun and made an impact. Not everything I had done was for naught, as the following chapters should demonstrate.

# Chapter 4

## Ostpolitik

The building of the Berlin Wall in August 1961 was the event that had triggered my decision to go into politics. I wanted to do something about the division of Germany that now seemed to be cemented in such an ugly, cruel, and potentially dangerous way. Over the course of the next decade, I established my reputation as a proponent of an *Ostpolitik* that would create a modus vivendi between East and West in general, and East and West Germany in particular—a form of peaceful coexistence that would keep open the possibility of eventual reunification while helping to lessen some of the worst problems created by the Wall and the Iron Curtain. Of course, I was not the originator of that kind of *Ostpolitik*; the party I had chosen to join was, in fact, dead set against it. My reputation, therefore, was more of the dissident within his own party than of an original foreign policy thinker. Once *Ostpolitik* became the law of the land, however, I was well-positioned as a man of the political middle who was not afraid to pursue policies contrary to the party line, even if that meant cooperating with presumed political enemies.

Initiated in earnest by the social-liberal coalition under Chancellor Willy Brandt after it had gained power in 1969, the first phase of *Ostpolitik* had laid the foundations for a policy of détente and a regulated modus vivendi between the Federal Republic of Germany and the German Democratic Republic. The big—and therefore exceedingly controversial—steps in *Ostpolitik* were the series of treaties concluded with the Soviet Union, Eastern European countries, and East Germany. They had recognized post-war borders and states, but reserved the possibility that borders could be changed peacefully and that states could decide their own fate through the free exercise of self-determination. The *Ostpolitik* treaties thus constituted a grand compromise, but also a huge gamble, with the Soviet Union and her allies betting that the status quo, now legally recognized, would remain firm and unchallenged, while the West was betting on change through rapprochement—change that might ultimately overturn the status quo.

What these original treaties had not provided for were the specifics of the modus vivendi, that is, the details that would actually make the daily lives of people affected by the Wall and the Iron Curtain less onerous and more tolerable. Small steps were now called for: the more the better. Given the nature of the grand bet, even small steps were never perceived as innocuous, since they might lead to big results. Negotiating them was therefore a laborious process on tricky terrain. Most of the negotiating took place through the official channels, particularly through the offices of the "permanent representatives." But a good deal of informal sounding out, raising of issues, laying of groundwork, and asking for help regarding very specific humanitarian concerns took place outside the formal channels. That's where I became personally involved. For me, *Ostpolitik* had never been primarily about legal principles or grand political theories. I wanted to see concrete results for the people most directly affected. When the chance arose, I was therefore more than eager to be of help and play the role of the back-channel facilitator. Perhaps my business background made this my preferred modus operandi. In any case, it proved to be highly rewarding.

I was somewhat familiar with the GDR. Over the years, I had used the few opportunities available to West Germans without family ties in East Germany—industrial fairs and exhibitions—to travel to East Germany and look around. On one such occasion, as described earlier, I met and developed a close friendship with an Erfurt eye doctor, Winfried Müller, who became my best source on public attitudes and sentiments in the GDR. It was with him that I enjoyed a long conversation in the days before ratification of the *Grundlagenvertrag* in order to get a better understanding of how East Germans viewed the importance of that treaty. We were forced at times by travel restrictions to meet at rest stops along the transit routes to West Berlin, but I had no illusions that we were closely watched by the East German regime's police apparatus. Since I was now a prominent figure in West German politics, I had to assume that leaders in East Berlin were well-aware of my abiding interest in everything East German.

In late November 1973, I attended a conference of the *Bergedorfer Gesprächskreis* in Vienna. (The *Bergedorfer Gesprächskreis* was a series of conferences begun in 1961 by the Körber Foundation in Hamburg-Bergedorf. Its purpose was to bring together, in an informal setting, representatives from the East and West for discussions of topics of the day. The Vienna meeting focused on the question of neutrality.) One of the conference participants was the director of the East German Institute for International Affairs, which undoubtedly had close connections with the East German leadership. His attendance symbolized the small steps now possible under *Ostpolitik*. I used the occasion of small talk during a conference break to let him know that I personally and the CDU as the opposition party were strongly interested in establishing a dialogue with the East German leadership. My initiative was grounded in the firm belief that such a dialogue was urgently needed, especially if—and when—the CDU should become the governing party and then have to deal with the consequences of the *Grundlagenvertrag*.

I later learned that my small talk initiative caused quite a stir. Under direct instructions from Erich Honecker, East Germany's supreme leader since 1971, Wolfgang Vogel, his emissary for delicate missions to West Germany (mostly having to do with the hush-hush business of arranging for the release of imprisoned East Germans to West Germany in return for quite substantial cash payments), approached Herbert Wehner, chairman of the SPD faction, to ask what the Brandt government thought about such contacts with the CDU. Not surprisingly, Wehner was livid, telling Vogel that he wouldn't dare give the East Germans advice on how to deal with a party that had rejected all *Ostpolitik* treaties. The matter rested there. Eventually, though, both sides had to confront the importance of such contacts. And since I had supported Brandt's *Ostpolitik*, I must have appeared to be an ideal candidate for opening the East German leadership's dialogue with the CDU.

It took a while and some doings to arrange the first meeting. I had to make sure that I had the backing of Helmut Kohl and Kurt Biedenkopf (the CDU's general secretary, who was not without ambitions of his own). Given the constant sniping from within the party (and from Bavaria) against anything having to do with *Ostpolitik*—and against having anything to do with East German leaders—that was not a simple proposition. But eventually I got the green light, provided that proper cover and discretion were maintained. My East German counterpart was to be Herbert Häber, who, since September 1973, had been in charge of the Communist Party Central Committee's directorate for relations with the West. Häber was eager to make the most of his new position in an effort to win the East German bet: establish the GDR as an equal partner of the Federal Republic and thus cement the status quo. However, he faced opposition within the Communist Party, where some feared that contacts with the West would contaminate the East, and he needed to get his own green light from the Soviet Union, which watched everything that East Germany was doing abroad. This he achieved in March 1974 after lengthy consultations with his counterpart in Moscow, Vadim Zagladin. Zagladin essentially agreed that too little was known about the CDU and that it would be good if contacts could be established with a view toward better information and eventual dealings with a CDU government.

Now it became interesting. For more than two years I had been in touch with the Soviet Ambassador in Bonn, Valentin Falin, about an invitation for a visit to Moscow. Somehow we had not been able to work it out. Now I learned that Moscow would be pleased to receive me for informal talks. My dialogue partner would be Vadim Zagladin, deputy director of the Central Committee's directorate for international relations. I was intrigued and, of course, eager to go.

Everything happened in January and February of 1975. The East German contacts and I had agreed that we would meet, innocuously enough, in the course of a trip to East Germany. Günter Gaus, the newly installed "Director of the Permanent Representation of the Federal Republic of Germany to the GDR" (which was his official title; unofficially he considered himself to be an "ambassador of the reformation to the Vatican"), was going to arrange a visit for me in his office and then invite me and some East German guests for dinner in his residence. The highest ranking guest would be Herbert Häber. It was the first time that Gaus had hosted such a prominent group. Everything worked out as planned (although, as I learned later, one of the members of the Politburo tried to prevent the meeting at the last moment—he was overruled by Honecker himself). Over the course of six hours (until two in the morning), we covered just about every conceivable political topic. I emphasized the importance of humanitarian concessions; the East German side insisted on continued *Abgrenzung* (formal distance), but indicated some interest in improved economic relations. At one point I had a chance to speak with Häber privately. I assured him that the

CDU leadership was seriously interested in a useful dialogue, with me as the main contact person. I offered to convene a small group of leading CDU politicians for confidential discussions with him during his next visit to West Germany.

Häber wrote lengthy summaries of our discussions after each of our meetings (some twenty altogether). I reported to Kohl and Biedenkopf only orally, though they might have made notes that are not available to me; only my diary entries help me to refresh my memory. Häber's minutes, however, surfaced in East German archives after reunification and were painstakingly put together in a publication appropriately titled *Die Häber-Protokolle.* These protocols provide a comprehensive, if obviously one-sided, record of our conversations and offer fascinating insights into the mind-sets and inner workings of the East German leadership. They also allow for some interesting comparisons between what I was trying to convey and what Häber chose to report.

My emphasis on humanitarian concessions, for instance, was mentioned only briefly in Häber's summary with reference to the issue of the mandatory currency exchange. West German visitors to East Germany had to exchange a fixed amount of (hard and valuable) deutsche marks for an equal amount of East German marks, for which they could buy little in East Germany and which they could not exchange for deutsche marks upon their return. This imposed a significant hardship on Western visitors, with the (for East Germany not unwelcome) result of limiting the number of such visits. Only pensioners were exempted from the currency exchange requirement. I proposed that children up to the age of eighteen also be exempt, which would have been a very small but not insignificant step. At this point, Häber's summary refers to Gaus' "energetic" defense of the GDR's policy and quotes Gaus as complaining about the CDU/CSU's constant efforts to raise that issue, thus interfering with the "normalization of relations." In my diary I noted that Häber had termed a recent doubling of the mandatory exchange a "mistake," while I called it a violation of treaty obligations. I also referred critically to "all too evident" efforts by Gaus to seek short-term spectacular concessions from the GDR before the 1976 election. We all had our agendas.

Others had their agendas as well. The following day Gaus released a list of his dinner guests to the press; together we provided some background information. That evening, on the way to see my friend Dr. Müller in Erfurt, I learned from the evening news that some of my radically conservative CDU colleagues were demanding my resignation because of my "secret" contacts with the enemy. It was unbelievable and inexplicable, as I had fully cleared my visit with the CDU leadership (including a four-hour preparatory meeting with Biedenkopf). The news did little to cheer up my friend, who was ill and under none too subtle observation and "protection" by the police. There followed a peculiar charade with Kohl and Biedenkopf, who were reluctant to offer me public support. We then agreed, somewhat to my chagrin, that I would admit to a "wrong assessment" of the possible consequences of the meeting in East Berlin and accept a rebuke for failure to coordinate with the leadership. I, in turn, insisted in party meetings and in public statements that there was an eminent need for such meetings with East German counterparts and that I would not exclude the possibility of future meetings involving me or others. That helped to dampen the uproar, but it also left a bitter taste.

While I was in the GDR, I used the occasion for a nostalgic side trip to the small town in the Harz Mountains where my grandparents had lived and where I had spent many happy fall vacations during my childhood. Time had stood still in Ballenstedt, as it had in so much of rural East Germany (a cause of nostalgia for many West German visitors who felt that East Germany had remained truly German, while West Germany had become modernized, perhaps even Americanized. East Germans seemed less enamored by the backwardness of their countryside). My grandparents' house with its magical garden was still standing. I paid a visit to their graves. To my great delight, I met an elderly lady who had known my grandparents well. It was a strange experience revisiting a place of childhood happiness that now stood in an almost foreign country. Stranger yet, but also very touching, was the feeling of walking down the street in front of their house, once Louisenstrasse, now renamed Otto-Kiep-Strasse. The dictatorial East German regime had thus honored my beloved godfather for his heroism in resisting the Nazi regime: weird, and explicable only in terms of the Communist regime's claim to be the true inheritor of anti-Nazi resistance in Germany.

A few years later, the topic of *Vergangenheitsbewältigung*—mastering the past—came up in one of my discussions with Häber. I complained about the fact that the GDR was claiming everything positive in Germany's past as its own historical legacy, while consigning the Nazi era to the Federal Republic. In typical Häber fashion, he had a stinging reply ready: we can't help it that you've got problems with Germany's past, evident in the reemergence of reactionary traditions—after all, the GDR didn't select the names for *Bundeswehr* bases (some of which had been named for *Wehrmacht* generals). We did not explore this issue any further, though it had significant practical implications for the GDR. By refusing to accept any historical responsibility, East Germany could also reject any demands for *Wiedergutmachung*—restitution: it was, by definition, inapplicable to the country's situation. Already at that time, the issue presented a major obstacle to a normalization of relations between the GDR and the United States, where refugees from the Nazi regime and survivors of the Holocaust put pressure on the US government to extract restitution concessions from the East German regime. By the late 1980s, after Honecker had grown almost desperate to crown his foreign policy achievements with a visit to the United States, East Germany was negotiating with the United States over the modalities of a restitution package that would include East German demands for most-favored-nation treatment of its exports to the United States. An agreement could not be reached before the collapse of the GDR due to the clumsiness of its negotiators and the untenability of its proposals. One of the results of reunification was the late inclusion of East Germany in *Wiedergutmachung*: an agreement for restitution payments was reached with the Jewish Claims Conference in 1992.

In the course of my discussion with Häber that day, I mentioned that, as far as I knew, the person who had denounced Otto Kiep and who was therefore responsible for his execution now lived in the GDR and was still practicing medicine. How did that square with the GDR's anti-fascist protestations? Obviously, I was not interested in personal restitution, but cared strongly about justice; scoring a debating point may also have played a role. Sure enough, Häber asked me to provide him with all of the details at my disposal and promised to look into the matter. It turned out that my information was indeed correct. Dr. Paul Reckzeh was a physician at the famed Charité Hospital in Berlin, but had also been a *Gestapo* agent who, under the guise of being a Swiss citizen, infiltrated the resistance movement (which was interested in Swiss connections in order to broaden its reach). His denunciations and later witness statements in the *Volksgerichtshof* trials led to the incarceration and execution of numerous victims. In 1945 some of his victims filed formal accusations. He was arrested by Soviet occupation authorities and held in prison (including former concentration camps). In 1950 he was sentenced to fifteen years in prison as a former *Gestapo* agent. A general amnesty in 1952 set him free, and he went to West Berlin. When investigations into his past were opened there, he fled back to the GDR to escape a pending arrest. Granted asylum in the GDR, he was allowed to work as a physician, with the argument that he had suffered enough for his transgressions during seven years of brutal imprisonment. After reunification, criminal proceedings were opened again but eventually closed because the statute of limitations for his crimes had run out. Reckzeh, eighty-two years old, died in Hamburg in 1996. His fate is a textbook example of the extraordinary complexities and difficulties of *Vergangenheitsbewältigung* in Germany in general, and in the context of East-West German relations in particular. Here the Otto-Kiep-Strasse, there his denunciator as a practicing physician: a sad situation all around.

After my memorable trip through East Germany, I was already looking forward to what promised to be another significant journey—my first trip to Moscow. The Central Committee of the Communist Party of the Soviet Union had invited a German delegation of the *Bergedorfer Gesprächskreis* for a meeting; the event itself was organized by a Soviet Peace Committee. It served as a cover of sorts for a get-together with Zagladin, the details of which, however, were unclear until the very last moment. The Soviets liked to keep such things under a veil of secrecy and suspense. It was only in the late morning of our second day in Moscow that I was told to prepare myself for a one-on-one meeting with Zagladin that afternoon.

The first evening after our arrival in Moscow on February 4, a few of us made use of some free time for an informal tour of the Soviet capital, accompanied only by a senior member of the embassy staff. It was both instructive and disorienting. We explored old Moscow: wooden houses full of life in late evening. Then we went to a railroad station where throngs of people stood, sat, and lay in the waiting rooms. Others pushed onto an already overcrowded train, carrying an unfathomable amount of luggage. We played with a railroad timetable, a mechanical system where, with the push of a button listing a destination, a metal strip would pop up specifying departure and arrival times. It all seemed to work, but it hardly appeared indicative of a self-proclaimed superpower with the most modern weapons and the first man in orbit. These contrasts could not have been more startling or disconcerting. I went to bed full of wonder and questions.

The next day was reserved for conference activities. Over lunch I had a private meeting with our ambassador in order to feel out the political terrain. He was marginally helpful and even admitted that he had little contact with the Soviet leadership and felt thoroughly frustrated because of his lack of operative involvement. It seemed that my planned meeting with Zagladin might be even more important than I had at first assumed. But before I finally met with him, we had to endure a visit to the Kremlin, where the president of the Soviet of Nationalities lectured us endlessly and shamelessly about the wonders of parliamentary democracy in the Soviet Union. "The president of the High Council of eunuchs is talking about group sex," I wrote on a sheet of paper and passed on to my equally bored colleagues. They could barely conceal their laughter.

Around lunchtime I was driven to the guesthouse of the Central Committee, which was a kind of hotel—without any identification—where a suite had been reserved for us. After some obligatory vodka and the usual exchange of pleasantries, Zagladin and I got down to business over a fancy lunch. For more than four hours we talked about everything from German politics in particular to international relations in general. A member of Zagladin's staff was also present as note taker, as well as a young interpreter whose help was infrequently required as Zagladin understood my German and spoke a reasonably understandable German himself. I expressed my opinions and assessments openly, without holding back. I came away from the meeting with the strong impression that my counterpart appreciated such openness, that I had actually helped to clear up some misunderstandings and uncertainties, and that dialogues of this kind ought to be continued.

As usual, I made extensive notes about our discussion in my diary. Zagladin, following his own routine, prepared a much more detailed report for his superiors. That report was translated into German and provided to the East German leadership. Amazingly enough, Erich Honecker himself read it and then passed it on to Willi Stoph, among whose files it was discovered almost twenty years later. Published in the *Häber-Protokolle*, it, too, is an invaluable document allowing fascinating insights into differences of emphasis and perception.

In my diary, for instance, I merely mentioned a "Strauss trip to China" as one of the topics and then concluded with the observation that the Soviets' fear of China appeared to be genuine. The Zagladin summary begins with my assessment of the political situation in the Federal Republic (I claimed the CDU/CSU had a good chance of winning the 1976 election and taking over power) and the CDU/CSU's struggle over nominating a candidate for chancellor. I am quoted as arguing that Kohl had the best chance, but that Stoltenberg and Carstens were serious competitors—in my diary I noted that Zagladin thought Carstens would end up being our choice. Then the Zagladin minutes continue with a long discussion of Strauss. According to me, Strauss was a great politician, perhaps the Christian Democrats' best since Adenauer. Unfortunately, his energy and analytical brilliance were too often accompanied by "extremist statements and actions surpassing the boundaries of political usefulness." As an example, I referred to Strauss's recent visit to China, where he was seen by Mao Zedong and Zhou Enlai, but where he also made the grave mistake of visiting military units and speculating about German-Chinese military cooperation.

The China visit by Strauss, along with an earlier visit by Kohl, did, in fact, provoke great interest and consternation in both the Soviet Union and the GDR. For a while, it was the most pressing topic in every discussion I had. Perhaps this was understandable; after all, President Nixon had opened relations with China a few years earlier, precisely with the intent of putting strategic pressure on the Soviet Union. Now there was concern that this might become a concerted action among Western powers with the goal of increasing that pressure to the point of isolating the Soviet Union even more. I tried to argue against any such interpretation. Kohl and Strauss were not (yet) the German government, and their visits served no larger strategic purposes; they reflected curiosity, an interest in expanding economic relations, and, of course, the desire to create publicity for electoral gains. (Very privately I thought that Strauss was inordinately fascinated by men in—and of—power; in his darkest dreams he probably wished he could be like Mao.) So I defended Strauss, highlighting some of his more conciliatory statements and arguing that Strauss in power would be quite different from Strauss the campaigner. I also pointed out that right-wing "cold warriors" in our party were gradually being replaced by younger politicians with more reasonable perspectives who had no interest in conflicts or confrontations with the Soviet Union. The Soviet leadership should therefore make every effort to establish contacts with them and to seek mutually productive dialogues.

Another interesting difference between my recollection and Zagladin's interpretation pertained to the issue of German reunification. Following the official *Ostpolitik* line, I claimed that Germany was one nation split into two states, and I conceded that reunification of the two states was extremely unlikely for the next century or two, not least because neither the East nor the West had any inclination to permit it to happen. In my diary I noted that Zagladin gave an evasive answer when I asked about the possibility of German reunification under a socialist regime, something the GDR had at times advocated as its own version of keeping the "German Question open." The Zagladin summary, however, quotes me with the argument that there were now two nations developing in Germany and that East Germany was increasingly distancing itself from everything German—that we had, for all intents and purposes, already accepted an "Austrian solution" to the "German Question": two separate nation-states with a common language and culture. These were fine, but in the context of the discourse about German identity, they were highly important distinctions. Different interpretations may have been due to the translation to some extent, but they certainly reflected different presumptions and outlooks regarding the question of how to deal with the issue of German unification.

Other important topics covered that day were the Conference on Security and Cooperation in Europe (CSCE) negotiations—then in their final stage in Geneva—and the Mutual and Balanced Force Reductions (MBFR) negotiations in Vienna, which at that point were going nowhere. I pleaded for pragmatic step-by-step approaches, rather than engaging in futile searches for grand solutions. I made similar arguments regarding the status of West Berlin, which was one of the main issues raised by Zagladin. But because of the extremely sensitive nature of everything having to do with Berlin, every small step could be interpreted as a giant stride toward undermining the city's status. Zagladin, for instance, complained bitterly that passport visa stamps specified "valid for entry into the Federal Republic of Germany, including the state of Berlin," whereas according to the Berlin Agreement, West Berlin was technically not a state—that is, a constituent part—of the Federal

Republic. I promised that I would bring this "stupidity" (as Zagladin quoted me) to the attention of policymakers in Bonn. Another source of complaint was the recent relocation of a federal office for environmental protection to West Berlin, as well the introduction of an adult education center by the European Community. Such were the minute maneuverings causing major problems—hard to believe in retrospect.

At the end of our meeting, I mentioned that there was a good deal of concern about the stability and continuity of Soviet politics due to the prolonged absence of Leonid Brezhnev from the political scene. Would it be correct and agreeable if, upon my return home, I issued a public statement saying that there was no reason for any such concern? Zagladin indicated that I could make such a statement "without reservation."

I met the first deputy secretary of the International Department of the Central Committee of the Communist Party of the Soviet Union a few more times over the course of the next decade. The pattern of our conversations remained the same: open and frank discussions of the main issues of the day, exchange of information about the political goings-on in our respective capitals, but no formal negotiations or specific requests for help. I know our conversations were extremely valuable for me personally, and for promoting a better understanding of Soviet points of view within my party. I can only assume that they proved similarly beneficial to Zagladin and his superiors. It is worth noting, however, that after 1988 Zagladin became one of the key advisers to Mikhail Gorbachev and played a prominent role in pushing the new Soviet leader's reform policies of *glasnost* and *perestroika*. I like to think that our conversations made an ever-so-small contribution to Zagladin's conviction that openness and political restructuring could and should be pursued not only in the interest of the Soviet Union, but also to the benefit of better relations with the Soviet Union's European neighbors and its rival across the Atlantic.

I met Herbert Häber again in late June 1975, this time in my office in Bonn. We now felt more comfortable dealing with each other, a fact reflected in our language and in the issues we raised. In his obligatory summary, he duly—perhaps even slyly—noted that I termed Strauss's late 1974 Sonthofen speech as "that earlier shit" that had actually redounded to Kohl's benefit. He also reported correctly my faint attempt at ice-breaking humor when I told Häber at the beginning of our conversation that we could talk openly—no secret recording equipment was being used, though one could not be entirely certain these days given recent revelations about East German spying activities. (I do not recall his reaction; his *Protokoll* does not refer to his reply.) Toward the end of our talk, I asked how things were going for the two "permanent representations." Häber recorded this dry replay: "I said one difference is the fact that no West German flags had yet been burned outside the FRG representation in Berlin" (such an incident had just occurred in Bonn). These were friendly little jabs. Häber was entirely correct in his overall assessment of our conversation: "It took place in a very open and friendly atmosphere without any provocative barbs."

The main points of interest were the upcoming election campaign, the role of reunification in that campaign, and the seeming stagnation in East-West German relations. I tried to convince him not to take campaign rhetoric, including references to reunification, too seriously; a CDU/CSU government (which, however, I thought unlikely) would be surprisingly reasonable—in fact, it would pursue a better *Ostpolitik* than the social-liberal coalition under Schmidt. Things were bound to improve, particularly once Kohl had visited Moscow—a trip scheduled for that summer—and after Schmidt and Honecker had finally had their first face-to-face meeting, which was tentatively set to take place in the course of the Helsinki CSCE Final Act ceremony.

But in the spirit of our informal discussions, I also pointed out some stumbling blocks erected by the GDR. Negotiations over the actual border along the Elbe River—the middle of the river, as demanded by the GDR, or its eastern bank, as claimed by the Federal Republic—were at an impasse. A West German project to build a nuclear reactor in Kaliningrad, Russia, which would mainly produce electricity for West Berlin, was stymied by an East German veto. Blatant efforts by the Soviet Union and its allies to support the buildup of a Communist regime in Portugal were crass violations of one of the basic tenets of détente, namely that each side should refrain from interfering in the internal political developments of the other side. In fact, I told Häber that East German support for the Communist Party in West Germany was equally problematic. I had heard rumors that evidence was about to be presented showing that East Berlin had funneled some DM 100 million to its paltry sister party. If that were true, it would turn into a massive scandal. Häber correctly concluded in his report that I had given him a big hint that Bonn knew what was going on and that East Berlin should practice restraint in order to avoid additional pressures on East-West German relations.

Later that summer, my family and I made a private trip to the GDR (so private, in fact, that the original plan for yet another meeting with Häber did not succeed). We spent a good deal of time visiting with the Müllers in Erfurt. Soon thereafter I learned that, in typical *Stasi* fashion, Winfried Müller's brother had been called in by the *Stasi* in Berlin and subjected to extensive questioning about the Müllers' contact with me. Apparently the lines of communication between Häber and the Service for the Security of the State had not yet been established well enough to prevent this form of harassment. I could understand, though, that the East German authorities in general, and the *Stasi* in particular, had a difficult time trying to figure out just who I was and what I was doing. Was I a future candidate for chancellor looking to enlarge my political profile? Or was I just another typical representative of big-time capitalism and thus an archenemy of the East German state? As far as Winfried was concerned, the *Stasi* let him know that it thought he was preparing to "flee the republic," which it preferred not to see happen. In reality, Winfried never seriously considered leaving the GDR behind; he was much too involved in his medical research and practice and had too many strong roots in his native East Germany; however, the *Stasi*'s clumsy approach presented the opportunity for me to seek short-term travel permits for Winfried, which we thought would be more easily granted if they were based on my invitation and if it was clear that he would return. Our calculations eventually turned out to be correct: Winfried was allowed to visit me on a number of occasions. I arranged for him to meet with some of my high-ranking friends and colleagues, including Richard von Weizsäcker, then president of the Federal Republic, and Helmut Kohl when he was chancellor. These contacts provided additional cover and protection for Winfried and his family, who remained largely untouched by the East German state security apparatus.

My immediate involvement in *Ostpolitik* took a new direction after I became finance minister in Lower Saxony in February 1976. At issue was the ratification of a treaty with Poland providing for West German financial aid in return for Polish permission to let ethnic Germans emigrate. As already described in the previous chapter, I had fought hard while still a member of the *Bundestag* for a "yes" vote by the CDU/CSU faction. In the middle of preparations for the crucial debate in the *Bundestag*, I met with a special emissary from the Polish government, who made it clear that Warsaw had reached the limits of its willingness to accede to further demands by the German side regarding changes in the treaty text. But as a gesture of good will, the Polish government would shortly present a memorandum outlining some clarifications and affirmations. I thought that was exactly the wrong thing to do; such a memorandum—dropped like a hot potato into the *Bundestag* debate—would do more harm than good. I implored the emissary to tell his foreign minister to withhold that memorandum until after the *Bundestag* vote. He did, with the desired result. Not a single syllable leaked. The faction voted no, I voted yes, and the treaty was approved by the *Bundestag* with the majority of SPD and FDP votes.

The critical hurdle for final approval of the treaty with Poland was now the *Bundesrat*, where the CDU had a blocking majority. However, if Lower Saxony and the Saarland voted for ratification, the treaty would be ratified. I had made it clear to Minister-President Albrecht that I could not in good conscience vote against the treaty as a member of the Lower Saxony government after I had expended a good deal of political capital with a "yes" vote in the *Bundestag*. While I never issued a formal threat to resign if forced to vote no, that implication was very much on the table. Albrecht understood and agreed to work toward a "yes" vote together with the minister-president of the Saarland if some improvements in the treaty text could be achieved; he needed that much political cover.

I immediately set out to work toward those changes by conducting some behind-the-scenes diplomacy on my own, though I did keep Foreign Minister Hans-Dietrich Genscher of the FDP informed about my efforts. I invited Poland's Ambassador in Bonn, Wacław Piątkowski, for a weekend meeting in my home in Kronberg with Ernst Albrecht and his Saarland counterpart Franz-Josef Röder. Piątkowski explained that the German side had indeed made a mistake back in 1970, when the treaty was first negotiated, by not including provisions about consular representation, as suggested by the Polish side. That allowed imprecision about implementation provisions to creep into the text; it also made it possible for local bureaucrats to handle emigration requests much more restrictively than originally envisioned. But, as we read in a surprise announcement, the Polish government was about to send yet a second memorandum of clarification to Bonn. That announcement immediately raised another red flag: if it were made public before March 12, the day of the *Bundesrat* vote, it could throw a wrench into the proceedings. Every word and every number was of critical importance. The memorandum needed to be vetted first before we could agree to its language and support treaty ratification.

In the meantime I had learned that the East German leaders were considering retaliatory measures should the treaty with Poland fail in Bonn; specifically, they threatened to reduce the number of East Germans permitted to leave for West Germany under an agreement providing for "family reunification"—at 5,000 per year, that number was already small enough. Getting the treaty with Poland ratified now appeared even more important.

I met again with Piątkowski, who informed me that a memorandum, not yet fully cleared by the Polish foreign minister, had been forwarded to Genscher. I succeeded in persuading him to share a copy with me; without it I could not push our *Bundesrat* deliberations forward. I then contacted a somewhat disgruntled Genscher, who indicated that the clarifications contained in the memorandum did not go far enough to satisfy his concerns. Now what? Albrecht called a cabinet meeting in Hanover, where we discussed how to proceed. It was agreed that we should give the negotiating track another try. Again I invited Piątkowski for a "private" meeting to hash out the details. It basically came down to substituting the word "can"—pertaining to the issuance of future emigration permits and the role Red Cross representatives would play in the process—with the word "will." Piątkowski claimed the Polish side had already made more than enough concessions, but finally relented and agreed to forward our request to Warsaw. For two days we were biting our nails. Then, on the night before the vote, we were told that First Secretary Edward Gierek himself had approved the requested changes in the treaty text. We had accomplished what we had set out to do, and more. The following day, the *Bundesrat* vote was unanimous; that is, all CDU-governed states, including even Bavaria, followed our lead and voted for ratification of the treaty with Poland.

We were exhilarated. Not only had we rescued a treaty of great importance, even though it only specified a number of small steps, but we had also shown that a CDU government could work closely with the FDP in matters of foreign policy. We were instilled with the hope of effecting larger changes in West Germany's political landscape before too long. For me personally it was a triumph, quietly achieved behind the scenes. I could hardly have imagined a better beginning for my work in Hanover. Ironically enough, that excursion into the world of personal diplomacy also reinforced my desire not to get bogged down in regional politics. The stage for my political performances needed to be larger than what was offered in Hanover.

Three days after the Poland treaty triumph, I was in Leipzig representing Lower Saxony at the largest East German industrial fair. West German industries were traditionally well-represented there. Equally traditional were carefully choreographed visits by the top East German leaders who would tour the exhibition and, depending on the overall quality of East-West German relations, "honor" a major West German exhibitor with a stop and a friendly chat. It was on those occasions that I first met, briefly and quite informally, the major figures—from Honecker on down.

East-West German relations were not good during the March 1976 Leipzig Fair. East Berlin had refused to let three West German journalists travel to Leipzig. We official representatives already in Leipzig decided to stage a protest and walk out. To some extent this was literal: The West German economics minister, the permanent representative, and I took a walk on a busy street—protected by police, filmed by TV crews, and gawked at by curious onlookers—to discuss the situation out of reach of any possible *Stasi*-snooping equipment. After further consultations with Bonn (Chancellor Schmidt gave his personal okay), we agreed that we had no choice but to pack up and go back home—after we had explained the situation on live TV.

But before I left, I had another "private" meeting with Häber in my hotel room. I raised the issue of the journalists' visa refusal, which led Häber to complain about the role of government-sponsored media like the *Deutschlandfunk* and Radio Free Europe. Mostly, we talked about the upcoming election. I pointed out that the CDU/CSU was going to campaign on the issue of national security, positioning itself as the party that would be less tolerant of Communist subversion attempts in places ranging from Angola to Portugal and Spain—an open reference to our continued dissatisfaction in that regard. I also explained the significance of the Poland treaty vote and talked about my role in Lower Saxony as a "utility" minister, pointing out that, unfortunately, the state did not have a foreign minister, but that I would continue to be active in foreign affairs whenever and wherever possible. It was a typical discussion with Häber, covering issues of immediate concern in East-West German relations, developments in West German politics, larger international problems, and some personal perspectives.

We had agreed in Leipzig that we would meet again later that year at the Hanover Fair, but it took another year before we could get together; the election campaign kept us too busy. But then the pace of our conversations picked up considerably. In 1977 alone, we met five times on various occasions and in different locations to analyze post-election developments, to confer about that strange phenomenon called the Carter administration, and to discuss some immediate concerns. For instance, the *Autobahn* issue concerning a new transit road to be built partially through Lower Saxony remained a constant topic. The agreement to build it was finally concluded in November 1978, along with an agreement to open existing canals for barge traffic to West Berlin. In return (though it was not formally specified), West Germany agreed to significantly higher lump-sum payments for the use of the transit routes to West Berlin. It was all about small steps.

In the course of one of our meetings in East Berlin, at a dinner hosted by the permanent representative, I met Alexander Schalck-Golodkowski, probably the most colorful figure in the panoply of East German leaders. Formally employed by the ministry for external trade, he was also—as came to light only much later—a member of the *Stasi*, in which he eventually reached the rank of general. His job was to provide the GDR with hard currency, which made him the ultimate pragmatist. Some of his methods were less than honorable, for instance, cheaply acquiring valuable belongings of persons imprisoned or expelled by the regime and then selling them on Western markets for going rates. Other methods, by any other definition and under normal circumstances, could be called highly corrupt. But he was the main go-between for any kind of commercial deals. Whereas Häber, at times dourly, pushed the party line, Schalck-Golodkowski took delight in being nonideological. In the course of that dinner, he must have been particularly provocative, causing Häber to be even more rigorously ideological than was normally the case. It was quite a performance for both of them.

One sign of the kind of progress we were looking for was the GDR's purchase of 10,000 VW Golf passenger cars in 1977. It was a good deal for the GDR as it alleviated some of the public pressure for more modern means of transportation, but it was, of course, also a good deal for us in Lower Saxony, home of VW. It made me wonder about the possibility for more East-West German cooperation in car production, a topic I first raised with Häber in a meeting in December 1977. Earlier, I had asked Schalck-Golodkowski for help in establishing contacts between the Lower Saxony "central bank" (NordLB) and the East German *Staatsbank*, hoping for an easing of money transfer restrictions. By late 1977 he had come through, not in a big way (East-West German money matters remained problematic throughout), but with some helpful small steps.

1977 was the height of the terrorism campaign in Germany. Since that mysterious shooting incident in my home in November 1974, I had been considered a prime target for another terrorist attack and therefore was under especially heavy protection. Häber would report time and again, with obvious amazement and occasional amusement, that I was accompanied by heavily armed policemen, fingers always on the trigger, even in my anonymously acquired new apartment in Bonn. (On one such occasion he was surprised when I drove up for a meeting in a Bonn hotel in an armored Mercedes limousine, but was picked up afterward by a young lady in a VW Golf—though accompanied by a police detail). Police protection in East Germany was different. Since there was no agreement with East Germany in providing for West German security personnel to accompany people like me, I had to leave my security detail behind every time I went into East Germany. I raised that problem with Häber, who in his report only noted my wife's reaction: "At last I can move around freely for a few days, without constantly having to face people with loaded machine guns around me."

I suppose my request for "technical cooperation" between security agencies on both sides of the Iron Curtain for the protection of high-level politicians like me must have struck Häber as more than odd. Surely we never moved around in East Germany without being under constant observation, which would have allowed a fairly instantaneous reaction in case of an immediate threat. In fact, at times it appeared that it wasn't just East German agencies that were interested in my activities. There were occasional reports in the West German press about yet another "conspiratorial" meeting between Kiep and Häber, reports which were probably based on leaks from West German intelligence agencies and usually combined with vehement attacks by my conservative party "friends." On one occasion, Strauss himself let it be known that he had been made aware of one of my meetings through a report from a "friendly agency"—presumably the CIA. In that case, however, the report proved to be wrong; no such meeting had taken place at the time and in the place specified by Strauss. I nearly told Strauss to mind his own business, as all of my meetings were cleared with the CDU leadership and often with the chancellor's office as well. In fact, at one point Schmidt specifically asked me to convey his personal dissatisfaction with continued East German spying activities, which could only undermine mutual trust. Jokes about being overheard and taped were a constant in my conversations with Häber.

So I had a pretty good idea of what was going on, but by and large, I thought *Stasi* interest in me was fairly limited. Only once, as far as I know, was there an attempt to spring a "honey trap" on me, when two beautiful young ladies showed up at my Berlin hotel room door one evening and explained that they had observed how lonely I seemed. I sent them on their way with assurances that I did not suffer from loneliness. Thus, I was all the more surprised when I had a chance to examine my 3,000 or so pages of *Stasi* files soon after reunification. Every one of our meetings was meticulously documented. Worse yet, every chance encounter I had with East Germans on the streets or in hotel lobbies was recorded, with photographs attached. The poor people were thoroughly questioned afterward, their statements duly written down. I was relieved to learn, upon reviewing them, that I had never encouraged provocative or incendiary remarks that could have gotten them into trouble. And, of course, I was never caught in any other kind of compromising situation. My driver at the time was not quite that lucky. He had proven quite susceptible to various "honey traps." His trysts were meticulously recorded. These recordings showed him endlessly talking about me, but never in any abusive or disloyal fashion; he certainly spilled no secrets. I remain grateful for both his loyalty and his discretion, and I felt sorry for all of the *Stasi* agents who engaged in such activities, listening to reels of tapes and evaluating reams of paper. What a dreadful waste of time, energy, and resources.

The *Stasi* collected an incredible amount of information; the system probably choked on it, if it did not outright drown in it. To what extent these files should be open to the interested public—beyond those persons immediately affected—is a difficult public policy issue, where privacy considerations clash with scholarly interests regarding historical accuracy and the general public's curiosity. By and large, personal files remain closed, as do files about all public figures. Some public figures took more radical precautions. Franz Josef Strauss, it is reported, used his connections with various intelligence agencies and quickly acquired the 20,000 pages of files the *Stasi* had collected about him. They were, presumably, destroyed.

The *Stasi* remains the signature characteristic of the GDR as a dictatorial state. Another, far less insidious characteristic of authoritarian regimes is their leaders' willingness to respond to direct appeals. Elsewhere, the rule of law and bureaucratic prerogatives would prevail; here, a leader could act quickly, if at times capriciously. I learned to exploit that. As word about my role as an informal go-between spread, I became a go-to person for human hardship cases. Through my contacts with Häber and other GDR officials, I was able to quietly resolve a number of such problems behind the scenes. The one I remember best, because it affected me personally and gave me the most satisfaction, involved a typical hardship situation. A West German man wrote to me asking for help: his wife, an East German, had been prevented from joining him in the West. In desperation, she had turned to a professional human smuggling operation, was caught, and put in prison. I knew her, the man pointed out, because she was a professional masseuse and had once given me a massage in a hotel where I was staying. I wrote a personal letter to Erich Honecker in which I explained the situation, conceded that under East German law she had done something illegal, but asked him in this case to show mercy—to let the illegal prevail over the law. I must have pushed the right button, or perhaps we were just lucky, but not a week later she was united with her husband in West Germany.

Over the course of the years, my underlying approach to *Ostpolitik* transformed ever so slightly from one of small steps designed to help individual people into one of bigger steps intended to undermine the regime. A number of factors contributed to that shift. There was the Reagan administration in Washington, set on pursuing a tougher line vis-à-vis the Soviet Union. (I spent a good deal of my time in conversations with Häber trying to explain what that might portend for East-West relations.) When Kohl took over in Bonn in 1982, we were under some pressure to follow the Reagan approach; for instance, not to finance and build a gas pipeline from the Soviet Union to West Germany (I personally was very much in favor of that project). German domestic opinion was overwhelmingly opposed to Reagan. It was partly in order to placate the domestic mood that the Kohl government was interested in pursuing other cooperative arrangements with the GDR and Eastern European countries.

Then there was Poland. The labor movement *Solidarnosz* under the leadership of Lech Wałęsa had almost brought the Polish government to its knees. Poland seemed on the way to a significant degree of liberalization when General Wojciech Jaruzelski declared martial law in December 1981, claiming that order needed to be restored (and forever defending his action with the argument that otherwise the Soviet Union would have intervened directly). Events in Poland had a considerable impact on East-West relations, raising hopes for peaceful revolutions, but also stiffening a resolve to confront the Soviet Union more harshly. Chancellor Schmidt got caught up in these events as he was finally meeting with Erich Honecker in East Germany in December 1981. His refusal to cancel that summit meeting, along with some conciliatory remarks about the need to maintain order in Poland, was widely criticized and contributed to the erosion of his support in an already wobbly coalition. There was no easy way out of his dilemma: détente now more than ever versus a show of strength, resolve, and disgust. But what Poland appeared to signal was that a Communist system could indeed be undermined from outside, as the Gierek government had previously received substantial Western help, not least through the German-Polish agreements concluded less than five years before. Some of us took note.

Finally, of course, better economic relations were advantageous to both sides. East Germans could get more—and more attractive—consumer goods, like 10,000 VW Golf cars, while West German firms could produce more of them at a neat profit. It looked like a clear win-win situation. A classic case for this began to take shape in the early 1980s. My old friend Carl Horst Hahn, now CEO of VW, and I had been in South Korea exploring the possibility of joint automobile productions with Kia in order to lower VW production costs. The visit was memorable for the lavish entertainment the Kia directors laid on for us (and for themselves: I never forgot how one of them was lovingly fed while his head rested in the lap of a gorgeous young lady). But otherwise it was a bust. At that point, Kia could not meet VW requirements, both in terms of cost and quality. On the flight home I remembered my previous speculations about cooperation with the GDR. Labor costs there were low as well, transportation costs would be minimal, and quality control could be exercised more readily. Besides, it would make a positive contribution to East-West German relations. Hahn looked at me somewhat incredulously as I developed these ideas, but he promised to look into it from the VW point of view. I told him I would explore the idea from a GDR perspective through my contacts with Häber.

A few weeks later, Hahn informed me that my idea might just work out. VW had a now superfluous production line for four-cylinder engines. It could be installed in an East German factory, which would then produce engines for the "upper class" Wartburg line of East German automobiles as well as the "lower class" Trabant line, both with their stinking two-stroke motorcycle engines dating from the late 1920s. Average East German buyers had to wait for more than fifteen years to receive delivery. The "Trabi" was an icon of East German backwardness, but later became a similar icon of *Ostalgie*: nostalgia for everything East German. The VW-designed engine was not only more powerful, it also used less gasoline and met the stringent West German and European emission standards. To make the deal even more attractive, VW would agree to buy some of the engines so that the GDR need not worry about a deficit in its hard currency balance.

My explorations with Häber had been similarly successful. By June 1982 Hahn and the East German state secretary for foreign trade, Gerhard Beil, agreed to strike the deal during a meeting arranged by me. It ended up being the only formal joint venture involving major East and West German industries. After lengthy negotiations, the agreement between VW and the *Automobilwerke Eisenach* was concluded in late 1984. Engine production did not begin until August 1988—a year before the collapse of the GDR. Meanwhile, the budget of the engine project had exploded from 3.7 bn to 9.7 bn mark of the GDR. Realistically, this particular project ultimately had little impact on the GDR in terms of providing consumer goods and thus helping to undermine the East German regime, except at the very end. In other ways, however, the repercussions of the deal were huge. For Volkswagen, the GDR engine capacity was a godsend, reducing the capacity shortages after the reunion.

The surprise came from where we had least expected it: from Franz Josef Strauss. The Bavarian minister-president (since 1978) had never given up his hope for a major political role in Bonn, especially that of foreign minister. But Kohl (not least because of coalition requirements) had refused to award that position to him when he took over as chancellor in 1982. Strauss won a *Bundestag* seat in the March 1983 election just so that he would be eligible for a minister position, but Kohl again passed him over. A clearly disgruntled Strauss renounced his *Bundestag* seat and stayed in Munich as minister-president. He also let it be known that he nevertheless intended to leave his mark on the Federal Republic's foreign policy. And so he did, in a spectacular fashion.

The GDR at that time found itself in ever more dire financial straits. Its foreign exchange earnings, not very impressive to begin with, were no longer sufficient to meet regular interest payments and to pay down its debts. Schalck-Golodkowski's increasingly inventive (and corrupt) efforts to extract hard currencies wherever possible did not yield enough to make up the difference. The GDR desperately needed new credits to tide it over—credits that could be had only from the West. As it became known only much later, the Schmidt government and the Honecker regime began exploring some extremely big steps in order to find a solution to the GDR's problems. I was not aware of these very secretive explorations, and I am not sure that Häber was familiar with them either. Our discussions never touched on really big steps; in fact, we agreed that it was useless to even think about them, since they involved impossible linkages. Middle-size steps, like joint ventures, seemed more promising to me.

Big steps aimed at linking the big issues: these were well-known, and raised repeatedly in my conversations with Häber. The Federal Republic wanted a lifting of all kinds of restrictions (travel and communication above all) right up to the tearing down of the Wall. The GDR wanted the Federal Republic to fully recognize it as a separate state. One of the last hurdles to that goal was Bonn's refusal to recognize a separate East German citizenship. According to West Germany's Basic Law, all Germans were (West) German citizens. Thus East Germans, if they could make it across the border, were automatically accepted as West German citizens—obviously a huge incentive. Conversely, if West Germany recognized a separate East German citizenship, not only would that incentive disappear, but the Federal Republic might also be obligated to return any—then illegal—immigrants. In practical terms, recognition of a separate citizenship would have sealed the permanent division of Germany. This was something East Berlin strongly desired and Bonn simply could not accept. A subset of the citizenship issue—and a constant source of irritation to East Berlin—was a West German agency located in the West German city of Salzgitter established for the investigation and registration of criminal acts by individuals acting on behalf of the East German regime, especially along the border. If East Germans had their own citizenship, West Germany could no longer consider East German activities in their own country as crimes under West German law and prepare to bring the perpetrators to justice. East German leaders, including Häber in discussions with me, never tired of demanding that "Salzgitter" be dismantled as an illegal interference in the domestic affairs of a sovereign GDR.

These, then, were the main building blocks for grand solutions. Apparently, two such big steps were under discussion in the early 1980s. One was known as the "Zurich model," which in fact was promoted with the help of a Zurich banker who had long been involved in East German financial dealings. The idea was to establish a bank in Zurich to be jointly owned by Schalck-Golodkowski's organization and the West German *Kreditanstalt für Wiederaufbau* (KfW—that remnant of the Marshall Plan). KfW would then extend credits to the Zurich bank in return for specific East German concessions. The first big step envisaged a DM 4 billion credit, in return for which East Germany would lower the age of people allowed to travel to the West by four years, thus enabling people other than pensioners, whom the GDR was basically happy to get rid of, to leave the GDR. A far more nebulous—and at that point much less advanced—scheme foresaw West German recognition of East German citizenship in return for dismantling the Wall. With the Schmidt government nearing its end, however, and facing likely objections by Moscow, the East German leadership determined that it could not agree to such deals. In particular, it was unwilling to accept any formal linkages between credits—which, after all, might be considered just a normal business transaction—and humanitarian concessions. The deal was dead. But the GDR still needed money.

By now, prospects had seemingly gotten much worse for any major East-West German deal. The "dual-track" issue impeded improvements in East-West relations: the East Germans had warned that West Germany would face a "fence of rockets" if it moved ahead with INF stationing. East German humanitarian concessions were either refused outright, or extremely slow in coming. In spring of 1983, a West German traveler to East Berlin had suffered a heart attack while undergoing harsh questioning by East German border guards. Strauss himself had termed that "murder" and called for consequences. A long-planned visit by Erich Honecker to West Germany had to be canceled as a result.

Franz Josef Strauss and Schalck-Golodkowski somehow met and started talking about a major credit deal. Their intermediary was Josef März, the owner of a Bavarian meatpacking firm with well-established business contacts in the GDR (it bought East German cattle for meat distribution in the West). The East German leadership was desperate enough to deal with one of its archenemies. Perhaps it also figured that under the circumstances, Strauss would be the least controversial and, therefore, the most reliable business partner. Strauss, of course, had his own motives. He saw a chance to enhance his reputation as a political genius willing to take big risks for big gains. Better yet, here was a wonderful opportunity to upstage the new chancellor after having been so grossly slighted by Kohl, who had just refused to offer him a major post in his government. Strauss's official explanation for seeking to conclude this deal was that he considered an adequate East German standard of living a necessary condition for sustainable détente in Europe, as any social unrest in East Germany would have unpredictable consequences—which, of course, was what those of us in support of *Ostpolitik* had argued all along, against his vitriolic opposition. From any perspective, his role in providing a huge chunk of cash to a desperate East German regime represented a stunning turnaround for Franz Josef Strauss.

I had to admire Strauss's political chutzpah. It was a personal coup—he had come around to our position, and he had done it right. Instead of forcing East Berlin into an unpalatable contractually formulated linkage between credits and humanitarian concessions, Strauss was satisfied with merely expressing his "expectations" that East Germany would ease its many restrictions. But in order to give those expectations some weight, the credits—DM 1 billion in 1983, another DM 1 billion in 1984—were not paid out in full at once; that allowed for close observation of the quid pro quo provisions. In his negotiations with Schalck-Golodkowski (which took place in the idyllically located guest house of Strauss's friend, the meat packer), Strauss had obtained these "promises" from the East Germans: less onerous border-crossing formalities, dismantling of automatic shooting devices along the border, elimination of the mandatory currency exchange for children under fourteen, as well as a reduction of the total amount for pensioners, and more travel permits for East-West German family members in emergency situations. In and of themselves, these were small steps; collectively they amounted to a major concession. Even before the credit deal was publicly announced in late June 1983, travelers to and through East Germany noticed a veritable charm offensive by East German border personnel. Thereafter, step by step, the GDR implemented the agreed-upon provisions. Honecker lived up to Strauss's "expectations."

Of course, Strauss took care of his side of the business as well. The credits, at normal rates and conditions to be repaid after five years, were provided by a consortium of public and private banks under the leadership of the Bavarian state bank. They were guaranteed by the federal government, and secured by an East German commitment to forego annual lump-sum transit traffic payments in case of a default on the loans. Some of the hard currency thus gained was later used by the East German airline Interflug to buy three longer-range Airbus passenger planes—Strauss was then serving as chairman of the Airbus supervisory board.

Strauss basked in the glory of his conversion to *Ostpolitik*. In July 1983 he went on a "private" trip to some Eastern European countries, the main purpose of which, however, was to visit the GDR. He was received by Honecker in what, for all intents and purposes, amounted to a state visit—the meeting site being the very same *Schloss Hubertusstock* where Honecker had received Chancellor Schmidt two years earlier. The East German leader demonstrated his gratitude in other ways as well. He allowed Strauss's private plane to be flown to the *Werbellinsee* so that Strauss, a passionate hobby pilot, could fly his own plane back to Munich—the first time ever that a private plane had been permitted to cross the East-West German border.

Back home, Strauss found himself in a less welcoming situation. Many of his erstwhile supporters in the CSU were aghast over their chief's sudden Saul to Paul conversion. Some of them left the CSU to form a new party of the right, which they called *Die Republikaner*. Unwittingly, Strauss had now contributed to the creation of a "fourth" (or rather, with the Greens now on the scene, a "fifth") party that he had so often threatened to establish himself. The *Republikaner* succeeded in creating quite a stir for a while, raising fears of a strengthening of the right in Germany, but they eventually faded from the scene.

The real winner in this episode, however, may well have been Helmut Kohl. Strauss had kept him informed about his dealings with Schalck-Golodkowski and Kohl let him proceed. He coolly calculated that it was to his advantage if Strauss took the political heat for a deal that he supported, but which would cause considerable controversy so early in his chancellorship. If everything worked out, Kohl could reap some of the credit for continuing his predecessor's *Ostpolitik*; if it did not, Strauss would be stuck with all of the blame. If Strauss had hoped to establish his foreign policy credentials as a rival to Kohl, he was wrong. Once again, Kohl had outmaneuvered one of his main competitors. Until his death in 1988 (from a heart attack while on a hunting trip), Strauss played an increasingly marginal role in German politics, while Kohl rose to almost Olympic heights as the eventual unifier of Germany.

East-West German relations had reached a new level of quality with these deals. Critics in the West claimed that we were too accommodating to an evil and corrupt regime; that we were in fact helping to prop them up. To some extent that was precisely the aim. A sudden collapse of these systems carried the danger that the resulting debris would rain down on all of us in Western Europe (as I told Herbert Häber at one point in our discussions). But such fears as well as more immediate humanitarian considerations aside, we had no interest in propping up the GDR forever. Rather, we wanted to corrupt it even more, to the point where it would one day quietly collapse under the weight of its inherent inefficiencies and contradictions. Egon Bahr of "change through rapprochement" fame later felicitously called

*Walther Leisler Kiep with US Senator Edward M. Kennedy*

*Walther enjoys a new Porsche (Image courtesy of J. H. Darchinger/Friedrich-Ebert-Stiftung)*

*Walther's favorite motorbike, a BMW*

*Walther sits with US Vice President Nelson Rockefeller*

*Walther runs for a seat in the German Parliament (Photo: Arbogast)*

*Walther with German Chancellor Ludwig Erhard and Walther's wife Charlotte*

*Walther visits his sons Edmund, Walther, Jr., and Michael, who were enlisted in the German Navy and Air Force*

*Walther speaks with German Chancellor Helmut Kohl*

*Walther shakes the hand of US Senator Edward M. Kennedy*

*Walther in action*

*Walther listens to Richard von Weizsäcker, who later became President of Germany*

*Walther speaks with Rainer Barzel, the leader of the opposition in the German Parliament*

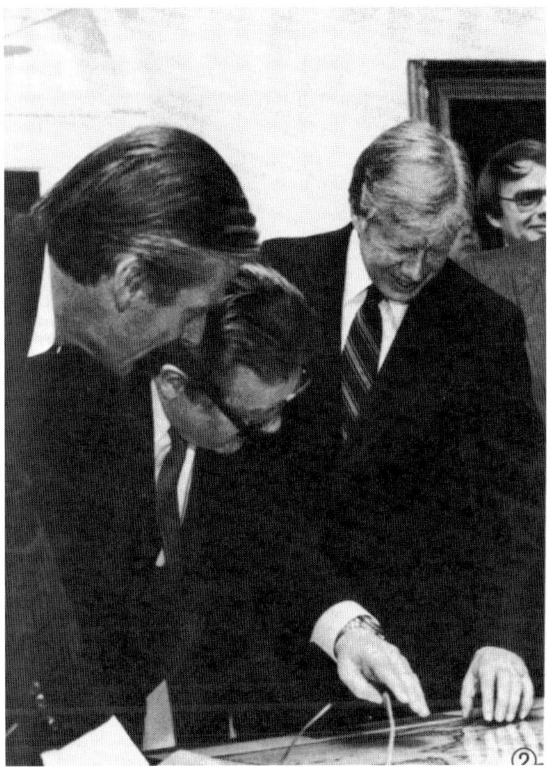

*Walther with US President Jimmy Carter and CSU Chairman Franz Josef Strauss*

*Walther with German Minister of Defense Helmut Schmidt, who later became Chancellor of Germany*

*Walther with US National Security Advisor to President Jimmy Carter, Zbigniew Brzezinski*

*Walther speaks with US Senator Charles "Mac" Mathias*

*Walther shakes the hand of US Vice President George H. W. Bush*

*Walther looks on as US Ambassador to Germany Vernon A. Walters greets Beate Lindemann, executive vice-chairman of Atlantik-Brücke*

*Walther with Guido Goldman of Harvard University*

*Walther speaks with US Ambassador to Germany Arthur F. Burns*

*Walther poses with the head of the Palestinian Liberation Organization (PLO) Yasser Arafat*

*Walther with former German President Karl Carstens (right) and US Ambassador to Germany Richard R. Burt (left)*

*Walther poses with US Senator Richard G. Lugar (right) and former chairman of NATO Military Committee General Franz-Joseph Schulze (left)*

*Walther embraces the founder of Atlantik-Brücke, Eric M. Warburg*

*Walther presents the Eric M. Warburg Prize of Atlantik-Brücke to Henry A. Kissinger, former US Secretary of State*

*Walther with CEO of Volkswagen Carl H. Hahn (left) and head of government of the German Democratic Republic Erich Honecker (right), during his first and only state visit to the Federal Republic of Germany in 1987*

*Walther poses with US Ambassador to Germany Robert M. Kimmitt (right) and editor in chief of the weekly* Die Zeit *Theo Sommer (left)*

*Walther with US Ambassador to Germany John C. Kornblum*

*Walther with historian Fritz Stern (right) and US Ambassador to Germany Richard Holbrooke (middle)*

Walther speaks with German President Roman Herzog (left), Beate Lindemann, and John W. Kluge (right)

*Walther with Governor of Texas George W. Bush*

*Walther with former German President Richard von Weizsäcker and German Chancellor Gerhard Schröder*

*Walther socializes with former German President Walter Scheel (right) and Egon Bahr (left), former foreign policy advisor to German Chancellor Willy Brandt*

Walther enjoys his Chinese "godchild" Xuelian (front right) and her family

Walther embraces kids at HOKISA Home in Masiphumelele, South Africa

*Walther poses with chairman of the Chinese People's Institute of Foreign Affairs, Beijing, Ambassador Yang Wenchang*

*Walther enjoys an afternoon with former US President George H. W. Bush at Kennebunkport, Maine, on the President's seventy-seventh birthday*

*Walther embraces chairman of Russian trade union movement Mikhail Shmakov*

*Walther with Ratan N. Tata in Mumbai, India*

*Walther speaks with Turkish Foreign Minister Abdullah Gül*

*Walther with Chinese Deputy Foreign Minister Fu Ying in Berlin*

*Walther shakes the hand of German Chancellor Angela Merkel in Washington, DC*

*Two former chairmen of Atlantik-Brücke, Arend Oetker and Walther Leisler Kiep, shake hands*

*Walther poses with Jürgen Grossmann, leading figure in German business*

*On the occasion of awarding the 2007 Eric M. Warburg Prize of Atlantik-Brücke to US Secretary of State Condoleezza Rice in Potsdam, Germany, Walther poses with Thomas Enders, Beate Lindemann, and Helmut Kohl*

*Walther speaks with US Vice President Joseph ("Joe") R. Biden*

*Walther with Chinese Ambassador to the United States Zhang Yesui, Washington, DC*

*On the occasion of awarding the 2009 Eric M. Warburg Prize of Atlantik-Brücke to German Chancellor Angela Merkel at the Library of Congress in Washington, DC, Walther poses with Thomas Enders, US Senator Chuck Hagel, and Beate Lindemann*

*Walther at the twentieth Enchanted Holiday Evening of the Youth for Understanding Foundation in New York, December 2011*

that approach an "aggression on felt slippers." We talked about it—only among ourselves, never publicly, and of course never in our conversations with Häber or other East German interlocutors—as the "corruption strategy." The GDR could be corrupted, we thought, in a number of ways: by making it ever more dependent on us, thus restricting its freedom of maneuver; by familiarizing its population with the blessings of a Western lifestyle, thereby increasing domestic pressures on the regime; and, finally, by exposing its corruptness at the core, where its leadership was willing to make concessions in return for hard cash from the West. Many small steps, each carefully taken, would eventually lead to big results that needed to be managed just as carefully. Of course, we never dared hope that our strategy would yield the biggest result of all within a mere decade.

In my conversations with Häber, I continued to push for more and bigger joint venture projects. In July 1984, after Häber had just been installed as a member of the Politburo and had now reached the zenith of his career, I mentioned how satisfied I was that the VW engine production agreement had finally been concluded. Why not go further, I suggested. VW had gained a leading position in the design, construction, and employment of robots (primarily for use on production lines). The GDR was trying hard to establish itself as a producer of advanced industrial robots. Maybe there was room for cooperation? I was at that time a member of the international board of directors of ICI, Great Britain's largest chemical firm (which had built a major plant in Lower Saxony). Maybe ICI could get into business with the GDR? The East German communication infrastructure was in bad shape, certainly not worthy of a country claiming to be the world's tenth biggest economic power. The West German electronics giant Siemens once had had production facilities in East Germany, now nationalized by the Communist regime. Maybe Siemens could be persuaded to move back into East Germany and help bring the GDR's telecommunication system up to international standards? In the end, none of these ideas came to fruition (though in the Siemens case, high-level discussions were actually fairly advanced when the collapse of the GDR made them moot). But they captured the attention of an eager East German leadership.

The GDR's exposure to West German credits and business deals also captured the attention of the Soviet leadership. In early October 1983, Häber himself was asked by his counterpart in Moscow, Vadim Zagladin, to come and explain what was going on. In his report about this meeting, Häber merely mentioned that with regard to Honecker's talks with West German politicians and the line that was pursued, "I presented point by point our line of argumentation. The comrades from the Communist Party of the Soviet Union (CPSU) took extensive notes." Perhaps the comrades in Moscow were satisfied (Häber noted that the atmosphere of the talks was "characterized by great cordiality" and that Zagladin expressed "great satisfaction" with the course of their discussion). The rest of the memo dealt with deliberations as to how the anti-INF "peace movements" in West Germany could be strengthened, and what might be done should the INF negotiations in Geneva fail.

In February 1984, on my way to China via the Trans-Siberian Railway, I met Valentin Falin, the former Soviet ambassador to Bonn, who was then working as a journalist, having been forced out as director of the Central Committee's international affairs division after a conflict with General Secretary Yuri Andropov. Falin, always somewhat moody, was gloomier than I had ever experienced him before—almost nihilistic, as I recorded in my diary. War was virtually inevitable, he argued, given the growing East-West tensions over such Western projects as INF deployment and SDI "Star Wars." I told Häber about my discussions with Falin when we met in July, and how concerned I was about the mood of desperation seemingly prevailing in Moscow. I don't recall his immediate reaction (if any), but surely my impressions could not have been news to him.

After the second "billion-mark credit" was announced in early 1984, and as Honecker was entering into final negotiations with Bonn over the precise details of his official visit to the Federal Republic now planned for later that year, the leadership in Moscow grew ever more concerned about a course of events that did not favor Soviet interests. In the course of a Council for Mutual Economic Assistance summit meeting in Moscow in June 1984, newly installed (and visibly ill) General Secretary Konstantin Chernenko pulled Honecker aside and told him that the GDR was too conciliatory toward the Federal Republic. More pressure was needed to bring about a reversal of Western policies, especially in regard to INF stationing in Europe. Apparently, Honecker did not quite get the message. In August, the Kremlin leaders practically ordered Honecker and other members of his Politburo to come to Moscow and explain themselves. Häber, though a member of the Politburo and chief architect of Honecker's *Westpolitik*, was not included in the delegation that traveled to Moscow for the August 17, 1984, meeting—perhaps it was better not to have that lightning rod present. He was, however, asked by Honecker to prepare a memorandum outlining the GDR's approach to the Federal Republic (drawing on the points he had presented to Zagladin nine months before). The text of Häber's memorandum was verbally presented in its entirety during the course of this bilateral Politburo summit meeting.

The transcript of this meeting, as prepared by the East German side, was found in East German archives (and later published in the *Häber-Protokolle*). It offers stunning insights into East German-Soviet relations at the highest level at a time when the Soviet Union and its "allies" found themselves challenged on almost all fronts. It is a document depicting the desperate and ruthless attempts by the Soviet leadership to rein in a recalcitrant satellite country in order to protect the Soviet empire from crumbling. As such, it portends the end of the Soviet Union. It also explains, on a much more personal level, the cruel end of Häber's career as the GDR's front man for dealing with the West.

The main defense of the GDR leadership against the Kremlin's accusations of being too accommodating to West Germany was captured in two slogans: "damage limitation" and "coalition of reason." With the "dual-track" negotiations apparently headed for failure—that is, for Western implementation of the INF deployment track—the likely damage to East-West relations needed to be limited. East and West Germany, Honecker argued, had entered into a "coalition of reason" that was designed precisely to yield such damage limitations. He strenuously tried to convince his Soviet Politburo colleagues that all of this was in the GDR's—and therefore the Soviet Union's—interest, because the GDR had much more influence on the Federal Republic (as evidenced in the strength of the "peace movement") than the Federal Republic had on East Germany. It was the right-wing extremists in West Germany—the "revanchists" in East German political propaganda—who actually wanted to cut off all relations with East Germany, implying that the Soviet leadership and West German right-wingers (Strauss now prominently excluded) were pursuing the same goals; everyone else was falling for the East German line. Even the big-time capitalists in West Germany were so greatly interested in pursuing their business deals that they supported improved relations with East Germany. For instance, Honecker declared, the CDU politician Kiep, a member of the presidium and the party's treasurer, but also a major stockholder in Hoechst AG, has been a longtime supporter of close East-West relations. Without making the point outright, Honecker seemed to refer to Lenin's (alleged) dictum that the capitalists would gladly sell the Communists the rope by which they would be hanged.

The Soviet leadership was not persuaded. They claimed that things had gotten worse, not better—the Soviet Union's position in West Germany had clearly eroded over the previous years. Mikhail Gorbachev pointed out that the Soviet Union had warned the West that the stationing of new rockets in Western Europe would have consequences—things could not go on as before. But now that new missiles were being deployed, the GDR was intensifying relations with West Germany, making new credit deals, and preparing for a Honecker visit: "This does not comport with our stated position." Conversely, the Kremlin leaders argued, the stranglehold West Germany had on the GDR had obviously increased to dangerous levels. With arguments uncannily similar to the main points of our "corruption strategy" (or had the Soviets listened in on our discussions?), they charged that the GDR was systematically being undermined—in fact, that it was coming close to the situation in Poland a few years earlier, the lessons of which we always ought to keep in mind. The GDR was making all of the concessions, including an easing of travel restrictions. The more West Germans come to East Germany, Defense Minister Marshal Dmitry Ustinov told his counterparts, the greater the danger of espionage and the more likely of a negative impact on the morale of the soldiers. Meanwhile the main East German interests—above all recognition of full sovereignty as a separate nation-state—were no closer to realization.

An already tense discussion grew contentious when the GDR was compared to Poland. Don't lecture us on Poland, Honecker replied. We tried our level best, at great cost, to keep the situation in Poland from deteriorating. It was not the GDR's fault that Poland almost went down the drain, and in no way was the GDR comparable to Poland. The basics of its political and economic condition were sound, despite much more serious challenges from the West than ever existed in Poland. No doubt, Honecker claimed, the GDR was stable. Erich Mielke, the infamous head of East Germany's security apparatus, chimed in: "In the course of my career I've had to deal with twelve Polish ministers in my area of responsibility. We've been telling them for thirty years to pay more attention to the problem of political and ideological subversion. But they did not do it. We have experiences that tell us unequivocally that there will be no subversion of socialism in the GDR." Mielke was clearly convinced—five years before the fall of the Wall.

The whole point of the Politburo summit was to force the GDR to change its course regarding its *Westpolitik*, or, more specifically, to keep Honecker from visiting West Germany. Chernenko told Honecker that it was, of course, his decision, but that Chernenko believed he ought to reconsider it in light of Soviet concerns: "We would like to tell you that the Soviet Communists would take it positively if, in this situation, you were to step back from such a visit." Honecker vehemently defended his interests in making such a trip, as well as the advantages it would bring (not least West German recognition of East German sovereignty); he also denied that there was any kind of linkage between credit deals and humanitarian concessions. (Never mind that what looked like concessions represented no danger to the GDR; children under the age of fourteen were not going to harm the GDR in any way, he claimed.) But in the end, Honecker agreed, of course, to keep Soviet objections in mind before making a final decision. Two weeks later, he canceled the visit, claiming that he and the GDR had been insulted by my old Hesse nemesis, Alfred Dregger, now chairman of the CDU/CSU faction, who had stated (correctly, but certainly not diplomatically) that "our future does not depend on whether Mr. Honecker grants us the honor of his visit." Honecker was left to continue dreaming about his triumphant visit to the Federal Republic.

Somebody else's dreams, however, were about to be shattered. Somebody had to take the fall for Honecker's embarrassments to Moscow and serve as the sacrificial lamb for the restoration of good relations with the Kremlin. The obvious scapegoat was Herbert Häber, the man with the Western connections and the wordsmith for Honecker's *Westpolitik*. Immediately after his return from Moscow, *Stasi* chief Mielke went to work, ordering a compilation of "operative information" about Häber that might serve to discredit him. Reaching deep down into the past and into databanks of "friendly services," the *Stasi* came up with such nuggets of information as his father's alleged participation in a *Wehrmacht* execution commando in the Balkans during World War II or the allegation that his name was listed in the databanks of Western intelligence agencies. This led the *Stasi* to conclude that there was a "hostile interest" in his person and that he could possibly be used as part of a smear campaign against the party leadership. The report from October 15, 1984, issued by Mielke's ministry for state security (retrieved among *Stasi* files and reprinted in the *Häber-Protokolle*) meant the end of Häber's career.

Häber had an inkling that his days on the Politburo might be numbered. Not long after Honecker's Moscow debacle, Häber was making a minor point about a rather unimportant issue in the course of a regular Politburo meeting when he was interrupted by Honecker and basically told to shut up. Given the byzantine ways of the Politburo, where everyone tried to impress the general secretary while seeking to position himself as his potential successor, that rude interruption clearly indicated that Häber was now out of favor. As Häber reported much later, from that moment on he was isolated in the Politburo, cut by his colleagues, and cut off from routine information and invitations. Party protocol required that he could not be fired outright, as that would have meant an unacceptable admission of party fallibility in that an unqualified person had been elevated to Politburo rank. So Häber felt relatively safe, if under extreme pressure.

Häber carried on for a while, meeting with his West German interlocutors (now only in East Germany, as his status as a member of the Politburo prevented him from traveling abroad) and pushing the party line more strenuously than ever. I met him for the last time in January 1985, totally unaware of his difficulties. Häber reported in his *Protokoll* of that meeting that I had just come back from a trip to the United States and that I was glad to be able to report that US policies vis-à-vis the GDR were undergoing significant changes, evident not least in the appointment of a high-ranking State Department official as ambassador to East Berlin. I took some credit for having brought about these changes (and in reporting that, Häber might have offered some justification for his efforts in dealing with me). But then Häber demanded that I explain to him with all due honesty how to interpret the anti-GDR comments and activities coming from CDU/CSU leaders. I conceded the point, but expressed my conviction that things were about to get better, partly because of likely election results favoring moderate forces, but mostly because of an apparent thaw in US-Soviet relations. Häber concluded our discussion with an exhortation to stop talking about a "new European order" and to recognize instead the realities of the present order, including the existence of the German Democratic Republic as a fully sovereign state.

I was scheduled to meet Häber again on June 5, 1985, but he could not make it for our lunch and sent someone else instead. The Politburo intrigues had finally caught up with him. Häber fell seriously ill in August 1985, apparently the result of a nervous breakdown. He was admitted to a hospital reserved for high-ranking officials, where he was given psychopharmacological drugs, which—according to Häber—did little to improve his condition and probably made it worse. In September Erich Honecker himself stopped by. Häber expressed his pleasure; Honecker replied that he had no reason to be pleased. It had come to his attention, Honecker explained, that Häber had divulged confidential Politburo information (in chatting with a member of the hospital staff, he had apparently talked about political differences between the GDR and Gorbachev's Soviet Union). Therefore, Häber was no longer tolerable as a member of the Politburo. Honecker requested that he submit his resignation, effective immediately, due to his illness. Häber had no choice but to comply.

The Politburo formally accepted Häber's "resignation" by late November, at which point he was also deprived of all of his Politburo perks such as a house in the leadership's gated community, his office, a Volvo with driver, a protective detail, a housekeeper provided by the *Stasi*, and a *Stasi*-issued pistol. He was assigned a new office, but no duties, in the GDR's Academy of Social Sciences. He reported there on January 3, 1986, but was immediately requested by Honecker to go to the government hospital for further checkups. He was held there incommunicado for three days and then sent to a psychiatric hospital for additional observation and "treatment." He was finally released three months later—a broken man, and all because he had run afoul of the pitfalls of East-West relations at the time of the Cold War.

I learned of Häber's illness—though not his ultimate fate—when I met his successor as director of the international department in the Central Committee in late November 1985 during a lunch meeting at the Permanent Representation in East Berlin. Gunter Rettner explained, quite credibly, that Häber had suffered a near total collapse of his circulatory and nervous system, which had left him unable to function—he could not even read (Häber later claimed that he was deliberately deprived of all reading materials). But, according to Rettner, Häber would be back at work soon, though with a reduced workload. In the meantime, Rettner would maintain Häber's Western contacts. I did not see Häber again until after the fall of the Wall, when we met for a friendly review of old times and he told me the gruesome details of his fall from grace.

I continued my regular contacts with Rettner and other high-ranking East German officials, especially Günter Mittag—the man in charge of the East German economy and a member of the Politburo since 1966—and Gerhard Beil, foreign trade minister since 1986. Little came of these contacts, as the investment projects we pursued did not reach fruition before the collapse of the East German regime, but they were helpful in more personal matters. In particular, they made it possible for my Erfurt friends, the Müllers, to be allowed to travel west. On one memorable occasion, they joined me for a birthday party given in my honor by Richard von Weizsäcker, now president of the Federal Republic. Winfried Müller, needless to say, was overwhelmed to meet my friend, the very popular president, and used the occasion of a late-night fireside chat in the president's residence for a lengthy and detailed discussion of just about every political issue under the sun. A year later, Winfried received an offer (arranged by me) to spend a year at Johns Hopkins University in Baltimore to pursue his ophthalmological studies. The rector of his university bluntly told him there was no way he could go. After I interceded on his behalf with Rettner, the very same rector called Müller in and heaped praise on him for having received such a distinguished invitation, which reflected so gloriously on his university—of course he was free to travel and the university would be honored to provide his travel expenses. That's how the system worked, and that's how I was able to exploit it.

The GDR's "chairman of the State Council" and first secretary of its ruling party, Erich Honecker, finally saw his dream come true when he visited the Federal Republic in mid-September 1987. Dramatic changes had been taking place in Moscow after Gorbachev's ascension to power in March 1985. All of us had a hard time believing that Gorbachev was for real—that he was truly interested in reform, and not engaged in some devious acts of deception that would lull us into a potentially dangerous state of complacency. Chancellor Kohl, in an October 1986 newspaper interview, went so far as to liken Gorbachev's public relations skills to those of Nazi propaganda minister Joseph Goebbels—a comparison that did not go over well in Moscow. It took a while for the wounds created by this ill-timed and poorly worded comment to heal.

I began convincing myself that, just maybe, Gorbachev's reform efforts were genuine and presented us with unforeseen opportunities that we should explore. Certainly Honecker seemed willing to explore them. No longer faced with a Soviet counterpart who told him to stay away from those dangerous liaisons with West Germany, the East German leader now felt free to travel there (after Gorbachev had received President von Weizsäcker in Moscow in July 1987, thus emphasizing Soviet priorities). Honecker could now bask in the glory of what was officially termed a "working visit," but which in reality amounted to a state visit. Honecker's visit did not deliver much substance; no far-reaching agreements were concluded in its wake. That made its symbolism all the more evident and important, from receptions in Bonn by Chancellor Kohl and President von Weizsäcker to almost triumphant visits in his native Saarland (where he took delight in speaking the local dialect) and in his main benefactor's Bavaria.

Symbolism can be tricky. This was clearly the case when Honecker visited Essen in the heart of the Ruhr area, once Germany's economic core. As a young man and devoted member of the Communist Party, Honecker had worked in Essen and engaged in anti-Nazi activities, which eventually got him arrested (he spent ten of the twelve years of the Third Reich in prison). But when he returned to Essen fifty-three years later, the main purpose of his visit was a glittering reception in the *Villa Hügel*—once the palatial home of the Krupp dynasty, now a museum and cultural center under the control of the Krupp Foundation. The CEO of Krupp industries and head of its foundation was Berthold Beitz, one of West Germany's most prominent capitalists. Beitz had played an important, if not always visible, role in promoting better East-West relations. In the process, he had become personally acquainted with Honecker, who used Beitz as his own direct link to the world of high capitalism. Now Beitz could show off the incredible progress in East German relations by hosting the arch-Communist Honecker in the former home of the arch-capitalist Krupp, in the presence of the Federal Republic's business elite.

I was among the guests in the *Villa Hügel* that day, marveling about the strange symbolism of seeing Honecker mingle with his "class enemies" in the obscenely ostentatious main hall of the Krupp family's erstwhile residence. In the course of the evening, Honecker, much to my surprise, asked Carl Horst Hahn (CEO of VW) and me to join him at his table. I had met Honecker a number of times before during his visits to the Leipzig Fair, but had never exchanged more than a few pleasantries with him. My repeated requests (through Häber) for a more personal meeting under less restrictive circumstances had proven unsuccessful. So I was pleasantly surprised when Honecker greeted me effusively, almost as an old acquaintance. He brought up the subject of VW's projects in the GDR, about which he seemed fully informed. Then, out of the blue, he asked me what I thought about his visit here. I expressed my deep satisfaction and then joked: "What do you think would be happening here if we had an SPD-led government in Bonn—most of us would be standing outside demonstrating against you." Honecker laughed and agreed: "I can well imagine that."

Compared to when I first met him, Honecker's demeanor had changed incredibly for the better. Back then he had seemed uncertain in his behavior, incapable of speaking without notes, awkward, indeed almost doltish. Now he acted self-assured, clearly relishing the fact that he received equal treatment and extraordinary attention, fully comfortable in his role as the leader of that other German state, which had now arrived on the international scene. If he was at all aware that the GDR might be crumbling under his feet while he lived it up with its "class enemies," he certainly did not show it that evening. Quite to the contrary, he gave every appearance of enjoying the symbolism as he likely perceived it—capitalists eager to bestow legitimacy and the blessings of their capital on a true believer in the cause of Communism and a genuine representative of the "worker and peasant state" that the GDR claimed to be. I must admit that I was so sufficiently caught up in the excitement of the moment and taken in by the charm Honecker exuded that evening that I did not step back enough to reflect on the fact that he also represented a highly repressive regime. I rather thought it a culmination of *Ostpolitik* and thus proof of the validity of my personal efforts.

As if he sensed my feelings, Honecker all of a sudden asked me what I thought about twinning programs, where two cities in different countries agree to become "sister cities" and engage in direct relations on a local—that is, highly personal—level. The establishment of such twinning projects had long been a goal of West German policies, but was viewed very skeptically by the East German leadership. Now Honecker was getting involved directly? I told him it was a great idea in principle, but best practiced between smaller communities, as personal interest in direct exchanges was much greater there than in bigger cities where people lived more anonymously and local governments had more pressing concerns. Honecker nodded, thought for a moment, and then asked me if I had two such places in mind. Yes, I did, I replied without hesitation: Kronberg and Ballenstedt—smaller cities each, spectacularly located in medium-size mountain ranges, well-known for their historical appeal, and cherished as quiet retreats from the hurly-burly world of big cities. Besides, Kronberg was my hometown and Ballenstedt had been my grandparents' home.

A few weeks later I received an urgent phone call from the mayor of Kronberg, who was almost beside himself with excitement. The government of the GDR, he told me, had asked whether Kronberg might be interested in establishing a "sister city" relationship with Ballenstedt. Apparently Honecker, who had taken no notes as far as I could remember, had made this a project of personal interest and thus of highest importance. Did I have anything to do with that, the mayor wanted to know. I admitted that I had indeed, and urged him to pursue the project expeditiously. Soon thereafter Kronberg and Ballenstedt initiated their "sister city" activities. After reunification, the relationships established through this program assumed immense importance, as Kronberg (obviously one of the wealthier communities in West Germany) was able to help Ballenstedt recover quickly from the ravages of Communist rule and socialist neglect. That was not exactly what Honecker might have had in mind that evening in Essen's *Villa Hügel*. For my part, I remain proud of this contribution to later East-West German mutual understanding and help.

Honecker's tour through West Germany in September 1987 marked the high point of his career. In retrospect, it may also have signaled the beginning of the end of the German Democratic Republic. For Honecker, it represented proof that the GDR was now recognized as a separate German state (with such small details as the establishment of embassies and the recognition of a separate citizenship presumably being close to resolution). Among the East German people, however, it raised expectations that the regime could not possibly meet. The GDR thus became like a pressure cooker that would either explode if unattended or render its contents properly prepared in record time. Arguably, the latter happened in the GDR.

The factor that contributed most to increase the domestic pressures in the GDR was a curious reversal of poles and roles, where the Soviet Union under Mikhail Gorbachev was pushing for decisive internal reforms and a determined effort at détente with the United States and the West, while the East German leadership was clinging to party orthodoxy and resisting calls for reform and greater openness. That was not only in contradiction to the implied promises of Honecker's opening to the West, it also offered the East Germans a new role model, indeed a new hero. They could now demand that East Berlin follow Moscow's lead. They also realized that the Kremlin would not necessarily come to the aid of a tottering regime, which increased their courage and hope. Elsewhere in Eastern Europe, some regimes went right along with Gorbachev; Hungary and Czechoslovakia, for instance, opened holes in the Iron Curtain that were quickly exploited by eager East Germans seeking to escape to the West. East Berlin was unable to stem the increasing flow of refugees or to quash the rising resistance to the socialist regime, all too evident in nightly demonstrations throughout the GDR. Gorbachev, who visited East Germany in early October 1989 on the occasion of the GDR's fortieth anniversary, reminded Honecker and his minions that "those who are late will be punished by life itself." That slogan (which apparently did not literally originate from Gorbachev himself, but rather was coined by his spokesperson) gave additional impetus and verbal ammunition to the resistance movement.

Gorbachev's history lesson was driven home a few days later. In a desperate attempt to hold on to power, the Communist leadership finally dumped Honecker (again for reasons of "ill health") and instituted a government that pledged reforms and an easing of restrictions. After a Politburo meeting on November 9, 1989, one of its members told the press that some travel restrictions would be lifted. Did that include Berlin, he was asked. Yes, it did, he replied, and that was the end. As word of this announcement spread, crowds began to gather at the Wall in the middle of the night, demanding to be let through to West Berlin. Border guards lost control of the situation and yielded to the crowd's demands. Not a shot was fired as ever more East Germans streamed through the few border crossings, but also across death strips and over the Wall. It did not take long before the delirious crowd began tearing holes in the Wall, blow by blow, piece by piece, section by section. By the morning of November 10, the Wall was essentially history.

The Communist reform regime tried to make the best of the situation, but its primary goal was, of course, to remain in power. The Kohl government—totally surprised by this development and now scrambling to figure out how best to respond—was willing to go along. Instinctively, it wanted neither an escalation of the situation that might result in total chaos, nor to consider the possibility of immediate reunification, which it thought was not really supported by the Germans themselves, and more importantly, would surely be resisted not only by the Soviet Union, but also by the Federal Republic's allies in the West. Chancellor Kohl announced in November that a German confederation might be a long-term objective; until then, the Federal Republic would help East Germany maintain stability by putting it back on its own feet. It was in pursuit of those objectives that I met one last time with my East German interlocutor, Gunter Rettner, to explore possibilities for economic cooperation, with the Siemens project for the resuscitation of the East German communications infrastructure now being of primary importance. But events rolled right over our plans.

The last remnants of the socialist regime were soon swept aside, replaced by a grassroots movement with revolutionary ambitions. Relying on the slogan of the day "We are the people"—that is, claiming the right of the East Germans to democratic self-determination—it set to work in trying to establish the GDR as precisely that: a genuine German Democratic

Republic, a separate country living up to its own best socialist ideals and traditions, neither subservient nor beholden to West Germany. Its dreams faltered on the realities of East Germany's miserable conditions that could be alleviated only by a rapid and complete merger with West Germany; that, at least, was the conclusion drawn by ever more East Germans as they traveled West, recognized what they had been deprived of, and realized that there was no way that they could ever make it on their own.

"We are the people" quickly changed to "We are one people." East German elections in March 1990 gave political legitimacy to these voices calling for reunification. Economic unity was achieved in July 1990—not least under the entirely credible threat that "if the *Deutschmark* does not come to us, we will go to the *Deutschmark*," as another East German slogan put it. After an astounding flurry of negotiations between the two German governments over the incredibly complex details of reunification, and among the two German states and the four victorious powers of World War II who had retained all rights pertaining to Berlin and Germany as a whole, reunification finally took place on October 3, 1990. At that point I was a bystander, no longer involved in any of the proceedings. (Kohl did not even bother to keep the CDU presidium informed, much less involved.) Nevertheless, I was an extremely happy bystander. I watched the TV in awe as that historical moment unfolded.

During those heady days I had always argued—in fact, warned—that talk about reunification was wrong and potentially dangerous. There was no "re" in reunification. The two German states that were about to merge did not represent Germany as it had existed before the end of the Third Reich (which is why the issue of the border between Germany and Poland was so controversial). Nor were East and West Germany similar enough to allow an easy and meaningful "re"-unification. After more than forty years of division, they had grown incredibly far apart—politically, economically, socially—each having gone their separate and at times totally opposite ways. I thought "unification" would have been a more appropriate term to use under those circumstances. But "reunification" prevailed.

Real reunification took a lot longer than originally thought; in many ways, it is not yet complete. The two German states were too different to simply be reunified. The easy way to reunification under Article 23 of West Germany's Basic Law—according to which East Germany, in the shape of five new states, joined the Federal Republic as constituent parts—carried not only a legitimacy deficit (no referendum was ever held), but also the heavy weight of a straightforward takeover of East Germany by West Germany. East Germans had hoped that the best features of their system (where the state had presumably taken care of everybody from the cradle to the grave) could be retained. They were thoroughly disappointed as their system was completely dismantled from one day to the next—by administrators imported from West Germany. West Germans expected that there would be few, if any, costs, and that reunification would practically pay for itself, through the privatization of East German state-owned industries and properties, for instance. Their expectations were quickly dashed. Instead of yielding a surplus, privatization efforts ended with a huge contribution to public debt. There was probably no other or better way, but the unification process turned out to be much more difficult and costly than most anybody had anticipated. Early on, Chancellor Kohl had promised that East Germany would turn into a "flourishing landscape" within five years. Almost twenty years later, that promise still remains elusive.

I tried to be of help as much as I could. I offered advice, where it seemed welcome and appropriate, drawing on my prior experiences in preparing for joint ventures and promoting investment opportunities. I helped in establishing contacts among those in the East and West who now needed to get to know each other. In the course of my international travels, I never ceased talking about the marvels and challenges of reunification, asking for involvement and support. But I am most proud of initiatives developed by Atlantik-Brücke, where I was chairman at the time. Atlantik-Brücke is a membership organization devoted to building and maintaining bridges across the Atlantic. Founded after the end of World War II, its immediate goal was twofold: to help with the reconstruction of Germany and to bring Germany and the United States closer together. Those goals were now essential with regard to East Germany. We focused on two projects. One was to promote youth exchange activities so that young people could get to know each other. We founded the Youth for Understanding Foundation, which proved hugely successful, with funds raised primarily through an annual "Enchanted Holiday Evening" gala event in New York to bring East German high school students to America. The other project was to help rebuild the Technical University of Freiberg. We offered assistance in many ways, not least through moving some of our conference and seminar activities to Freiberg. It was a proud and very emotional moment for me when the Freiberg Technical University awarded me a doctorate *honoris causa* in honor of my efforts.

Herbert Häber, my erstwhile East German co-conspirator, was far less lucky. His trials and tribulations were not over yet. Understandably enough, reunification required another attempt at *Vergangenheitsbewältigung*—East Germany's, that is. Clearly those responsible for the injustices committed by the regime needed to be brought to justice. That proved to be highly difficult, however, as those in a position of responsibility could only be tried for transgressions that were illegal under East German law at the time. Laws passed retroactively, or the application of West German laws (though conceivable under West Germany's claim to represent all of Germany), would themselves have violated every tenet of proper justice. Bärbel Bohley, one of the charismatic leaders of the resistance movement, expressed the resulting dilemma, and her disappointment, best: "We thought we were getting justice, but we only got the rule of law."

The results arising from this dilemma were indeed often absurd. Mielke, for instance, the most evil of East German leaders as head of "state security," could only be tried for the murder of two policemen back in 1931. Then, in 1993, he was sentenced to six years in prison, of which he served only two because of poor health and advanced age. His East German spies went scot-free, whereas West Germans in his employment were hit with the full force of the law. Schalck-Golodkowski apparently squirreled away some of the ill-gotten gains of his hard-currency deals, moved to Bavaria, spilled some beans to Western intelligence agencies, and settled down comfortably in a fancy villa on the *Tegernsee*, one of Germany's most beautiful spots. He was later indicted, tried, and convicted for illegal arms sales and embargo violations, but he was put on probation and never had to serve his sixteen-month prison term.

Honecker himself avoided an early trial by his successors when he fled to Moscow, where he found refuge in the Chilean embassy. Two years later, he was finally turned over to the authorities of reunited Germany. He was indicted on forty-nine cases of second-degree murder, the result of shoot-to-kill orders for which he was allegedly responsible. In a separate case, he was also accused of squandering public funds. Already severely ill with liver cancer, Honecker prevailed with the argument that his cases should not be brought to trial due to his illness. He was then allowed to go live with his daughter in Chile, where he died in 1994 at the age of eighty-two. Most other members of the Politburo also escaped trial and punishment because of poor health and/or advanced age. It was all unsavory and did little to satisfy the demands of—and for—justice.

Herbert Häber, neither of advanced age nor in poor health, was less lucky (or savvy) as he got caught up in the effort to bring East German leaders to justice. He was indicted as an accomplice to murder for his failure to have the shoot-to-kill orders overturned during his brief tenure as a member of the Politburo. The prosecutors claimed, strangely enough, that the Politburo was a semi-democratic institution where every member could speak freely and without fear of retribution and therefore had no excuse for failing to do so. Häber's failure to speak up against the shoot-to-kill orders thus made him culpable. His case came to trial only in the year 2000 (until then he was under travel restrictions and had to report regularly to the local police). The trial court ruled him innocent of the charges under GDR law then prevailing. The prosecution appealed that verdict. The appeals court set aside the original ruling and ordered a retrial. In May 2004 Häber was convicted as an accomplice to second-degree murder, but he was spared any punishment as the court ruled that Häber had, in fact, tried to lessen the severity of the shoot-to-kill orders—as evidenced not least by his many meetings with me, in the course of which he had tried to bring about humanitarian concessions.

I found the way Häber was treated by the German legal system appalling, beginning with the initial indictment and ending more than a dozen years later with his conviction. It seemed to me that, even if he might be held responsible as a member of the Politburo, his brief tenure—and, even more so, the way he was unceremoniously removed and then subjected to demeaning "treatment" in psychiatric institutions—should have been exculpatory enough. An early showing of mercy might have been more appropriate than lengthy proceedings and repeated efforts to secure a conviction. There was little I could do to help Häber while he was under indictment and then on trial. After the conclusion of his ordeal, however, some of his other former interlocutors and I agreed to help him by paying for his legal costs. It was the least we thought we could do for someone who had pleaded for a "coalition of reason" and had suffered because of it—even if he had also been a staunch defender of a repressive regime.

Both Richard von Weizsäcker and I had our own experiences with legal efforts at *Vergangenheitsbewältigung*—Weizsäcker with his father, I with my father-in-law, both convicted as war criminals by the Nuremberg Military Tribunal. We knew that responsibility and guilt were problematic categories under conditions arising in dictatorial regimes, and we agreed that the past can sometimes be mastered better with reconciliation and forgiveness than with tribunals and retribution.

Other than those brave East Germans who dared to demonstrate against their regime and eventually brought it to its knees, the real heroes of reunification were George H. W. Bush, the American president, and Mikhail Gorbachev, the Soviet leader. Gorbachev's reform efforts had set in motion the series of events that led to the collapse of the GDR and, soon thereafter, the Soviet Union itself. He did not stand in the way of reunification, but rather agreed to negotiate the terms under which it could take place. That included a rapid withdrawal of all Soviet forces—for which Germany paid a significant amount of money—and united Germany's continued membership in NATO, with the provision, however, that no foreign NATO forces could be stationed on the territory of the former GDR, which thus became a nuclear-free zone, since Germany also renewed its commitment not to acquire nuclear weapons of its own. For his immeasurable contributions to the peaceful resolution of the Cold War, Gorbachev was rightly awarded the Nobel Peace Prize in October 1990. His countrymen, unfortunately, were less impressed by these achievements. Economic reforms at home had proved disastrous; political reforms strengthened internal independence. A coup by hard-liners in August 1991 sought to restore strict Communist rule, but failed when Boris Yeltsin rallied forces to defend the new order. By the end of the year, Gorbachev was left without any real power and forced to resign. Communist rule and the Soviet Union itself had come to an end. Gorbachev returned to private life (no effort at *Vergangenheitsbewältigung* there), despised at home but revered abroad.

I experienced Gorbachev's immense popular appeal in Germany when, some years after he had left office, he came to visit Volkswagen in Wolfsburg. Practically all of VW's employees turned out to greet him and to applaud him, with an exuberance such as I have never seen before or since. Later that evening, I had the privilege of joining VW's leadership for dinner with the guest of honor. Gorbachev, clearly reveling in the attention and adoration he received, was obviously much in demand that evening, but I had the chance for a brief discussion with him (hampered by the need for translation). I was most impressed by his description of how the Politburo had functioned. Military matters, for instance, were rarely, if ever, discussed. The issue of SS-20s—leading to the INF-deployment problem—had come to his attention only in 1983, after it had become the subject of intense posturing and negotiations. (Gorbachev, of course, had eventually motioned to solve the problem by agreeing to the "zero solution" of dismantling all intermediate nuclear weapons systems.) I was fascinated by the man and his stories—a truly unforgettable moment.

President Bush had been instrumental in bringing about reunification in other ways. Where Kohl was hesitant, Bush urged him on, pointing out that reunification was only natural and would be fully supported by the United States (against quite different sentiments expressed in London and Paris, where Prime Minister Thatcher and President Mitterrand harbored hopes of preventing the creation of a unified Germany, which they feared might become too dominant and potentially dangerous). When Kohl claimed that Germany could not accept the Oder-Neisse Line as the final border between a reunified Germany and Poland, President Bush invited him to Camp David and convinced him that he had little choice in the matter. In the end, it was Bush's friendly persuasion and hard-nosed diplomatic skills that made reunification possible. The German people, as well as Helmut Kohl personally, were forever grateful to "Bush 41" for his crucial role, masterfully performed.

In April 2002, President George H. W. Bush received the Atlantik-Brücke's Eric M. Warburg Prize for his extraordinary contributions to German-American relations. It was a wonderfully festive occasion in Berlin's historic Charlottenburg Palace. Helmut Kohl introduced the guest of honor and gave a touching speech about his friend, the former American president, confirming once again his crucial role in the unification process. It was a fitting tribute to Bush by Germany's premier transatlantic organization, Atlantik-Brücke, of which I had been chairman from 1984 until 2000. As I took in the splendor of the venue and reveled in the glory of the occasion, I reflected on my own small role in *Ostpolitik*. It had been a long and at times difficult journey from my decision to enter politics after the Wall went up in August 1961 to the Wall coming down in November 1989. But what a glorious ending! I was proud of my contributions, and so happy for my country.

# Chapter 5

## Special Missions

It was sometime in early spring 1975. I was sitting in the *Bundestag* minding my own business (that is, half-listening to a speech while doing some paperwork), when I was approached by one of the fancily dressed ushers: "Chancellor Schmidt would like to confer with you." Of course I interrupted my business; one does not leave a chancellor waiting, even if one is a member of the not-so-loyal opposition. I caught up with Helmut Schmidt in the lobby outside the chamber. He pulled me aside and told me that he needed my help, urgently. Thus began my introduction into the world of special missions performed on behalf of the German government.

These were turbulent times. Never mind our own conflicts over *Ostpolitik* and détente, which presented enough problems. Elsewhere, the world seemed on fire. The Middle East was recovering from the Yom Kippur War of 1973; Henry Kissinger's "shuttle diplomacy" came to a successful conclusion only by September 1975 with an Egyptian-Israeli disengagement agreement (which eventually opened the way for a more far-reaching peace accord between Israel and Egypt). In Cyprus, the Turkish army had occupied the northern part of the island in July 1974 in an alleged effort to protect its Turkish minority from attacks by the Greek military government. One year later, Cyprus was formally divided into two separately governed territories, leaving behind yet another legacy of division and international efforts at (re)unification. The only silver lining of this development was the collapse of the dictatorial colonels' regime in Greece.

In Vietnam, the cease-fire agreement of 1972 had long ago broken down. The Vietcong and North Vietnamese units were advancing rapidly on Saigon, encouraged by domestic political developments in the United States, where President Nixon had been forced to resign in August 1974 as a result of the Watergate Scandal; a rebellious Congress—strengthened in its antiwar resolve by the November 1974 elections—refused to allow any further US involvement in support of the South Vietnamese regime. Nixon's successor, President Gerald Ford, declared an end to the Vietnam War on April 23, 1975. One week later, the last US personnel—along with a few lucky Vietnamese—beat a hasty and inglorious retreat by helicopter from the roof of the US embassy in Saigon. America had suffered a crushing and humiliating defeat.

Vietnam was not the only place where the Communists appeared to be on the march. The specter of "Eurocommunism" was haunting Europe. Communist parties seemed to be making significant electoral strides throughout southern Europe: from Greece and Italy to France. Nowhere was the danger of a communist takeover more imminent, however, than in Portugal and Spain. The fascist regimes in these countries were exhausted and on the point of collapse, threatening to create the kind of political chaos from which Communist movements could benefit. Portugal was the more problematic case, not only because it was a member of NATO and therefore of special importance, but also because the revolutionary fervor in Portugal was particularly pronounced. Unlike in Spain, where democratic forces could rally around the King as a stabilizing core, Portugal lacked such a unifying force. Developments in Portugal were therefore much less certain, and that much more critical.

Portugal had been governed since 1932 by the former finance minister António de Oliveira Salazar, who established an autocratic system (called the "New State") based on economic corporatism, conservative Catholic principles, and a strong anticommunism (for this reason Portugal was deemed acceptable as a member of NATO despite its dictatorial regime). Portugal was also a colonial power, with possessions primarily in Africa (Angola, Mozambique, Guinea-Bissau, and the Cape Verde islands) and in Asia (East Timor). Anticolonial resistance movements were active in all of Portugal's colonies. Efforts by the Salazar regime to hold on to its colonies were becoming increasingly expensive in terms of blood and treasure. The usually gentle Portuguese found themselves fighting ever more brutal wars in faraway places, at a time when colonialism was coming to an end everywhere else. The people grew tired of seeing their young soldiers being killed in hopeless efforts to maintain a colonial empire. Salazar suffered a debilitating stroke in 1968 and died in 1970. Hopes for a change of course under his successor, Marcelo Caetano, unfortunately proved ill-founded. The situation deteriorated steadily at home and abroad, as the political leadership gradually lost control despite increasingly repressive measures.

Dissent grew even within the ranks of the military. By February 1974, a group of young military officers, many of them with leftist political leanings (most likely acquired while fighting similarly oriented revolutionaries in the colonies), decided they had had enough. They formed an "Armed Forces Movement" and organized a coup that was executed in delightful Portuguese style. Late in the evening of April 24, 1975, the state-owned radio played a song that had previously served as the Portuguese entry in the wildly popular Eurovision song contest; it was the signal to stand by for the coup to begin. A little while later, just after midnight, another song was played, this time a protest song by a popular (but publicly banned) Portuguese folk singer. Now the troops moved out to occupy the key positions for any successful effort to overthrow a government: government offices and communication centers. In the morning, the Portuguese people streamed into the streets to show their support for the coup. In the Lisbon flower market, they took the carnations then in season and stuck them into the soldiers' rifle barrels. The "carnation revolution" had its name, its symbol, and its success. The "New State" regime was history.

What followed was a chaotic jockeying for power—accompanied by increasingly violent attacks and counterattacks—among different military and political groupings, with leftist forces seemingly gaining an upper hand in a succession of further coups and shifting provisional governments. The situation appeared critical in March 1975, when a coup attempt by right-wing military units barely failed, but as a consequence the more moderate

"National Junta of Salvation" was replaced by a "Revolutionary Council" made up of 240 strongly leftist military leaders. Portugal threatened to slide into yet another dictatorship, this time one of the left. The only (small) hope for avoiding such a development was to be found in elections for a constitutional assembly, originally to be held in March, but now rescheduled for late April. This is when Chancellor Schmidt—of *Macher* fame—went into action.

That the future paths of Portugal and Spain were of extreme importance to NATO and the West was beyond any doubt. The question was how to set and guide these two countries on the right paths. In Washington, Secretary of State Henry Kissinger—whose plate at that time was more than full—professed to be deeply skeptical that anything short of direct intervention could be done to prevent Portugal from becoming a Eurocommunist state. Once that happened, he believed, NATO would experience a "Euro-domino" effect, with the demise of the alliance its ultimate outcome. Therefore, he was prepared to apply outside pressure in order to keep Portugal from going Communist, beginning, perhaps, with a blockade of Portuguese ports. The American embassy in Lisbon was much less skeptical and worked hard to convince the secretary of state that less drastic measures might help to prevent Portugal from turning into an American nightmare.

Schmidt and his Social Democrats neither shared Kissinger's skepticism (almost amounting to fatalism) nor thought much of his more heavy-handed approach. What might turn the tide in the West's favor, they thought, was a concerted effort at "state-building" by means of well-targeted support for middle-of-the-road political parties. The SPD had already begun such an effort (in cooperation with other Western European social democratic parties) through the Friedrich Ebert Foundation, a political foundation supposedly free of direct connections with the SPD, but in reality—as was true for all other such political foundations in West Germany—closely aligned with the party. The mission of these foundations was to promote political awareness at home and abroad, or in more modern terms, to help in the formation of "civil societies."

In March and April 1975 Schmidt must have realized that these efforts were not sufficient; "civil society"-building required the establishment of more than one party. Perhaps he also wanted to take the SPD out of a potential line of fire by getting other parties involved. Additionally, maybe he wanted to show the Americans that Europeans were quite capable of taking care of their own affairs, in their preferred way. And undoubtedly time was of the essence: with elections about to be held, the moderate parties in Portugal needed help and support. So Schmidt decided that the Federal Republic should provide such support—massively, expeditiously, and of course, secretly.

The secrecy part was critical. At the beginning of my conversation with Schmidt that day in the *Bundestag* lobby, he swore me to absolute secrecy concerning what he was about to tell me. He then explained that developments in Portugal were reaching a critical stage, that something needed to be done to help a NATO partner and future member of the European Community, and that he was thinking of providing financial aid to moderate parties in Portugal that were struggling to gain a foothold in an increasingly chaotic political landscape. Would I be willing to help out by personally delivering some cash to a Portuguese party of the CDU's choice? He informed me that he was also asking high-ranking representatives of the other parties—including Franz Josef Strauss of the CSU—for similar favors.

I agreed immediately to Schmidt's request. I thought it was the right thing to do, I was flattered that he had asked me to do it, and I welcomed the chance to do something both important and slightly risky. The appreciative chancellor asked me to arrange the details with his chief of staff, secured my word of honor not to tell anybody about our agreement, and sealed the deal with a handshake. I was off on my first special mission.

When I met with the state secretary in the chancellery soon thereafter, he offered me a cup of coffee—along with a shot of brandy. He must have anticipated that I could use some alcoholic reinforcement, for he pulled a suitcase out of his safe, handed it over to me, and said: "Careful now—there are more than a million US dollars in this suitcase." He explained that the money had been provided through the West German Federal Intelligence Service, the *Bundesnachrichtendienst* (BND), and that it was to be delivered in person to the chairman of our partner party in Portugal. I signed a receipt (without counting the money) and was told that I needed to obtain a receipt from my counterpart in Portugal as well. Then I took the suitcase full of cash and went on my way, more glad than ever that I was under heavy security protection. At least I did not have to worry about keeping the money safe.

But at that point I did not really know what to do with the money: who was going to receive it when, where, and how? Since I was sworn to absolute secrecy, finding reasonable answers to these questions was anything but easy. So I went to the CDU's political foundation, the Konrad Adenauer Foundation, to get a briefing on the political situation in Portugal in preparation for a "fact-finding" trip. That at least gave me an idea as to which might be our counterpart party and whom to approach there for delivery of the money. I also had to confer with Strauss about which party the CSU was thinking of supporting; it would have made little sense to go after the same target. Finally, once I had made my choice, I had to make travel arrangements and set up an innocuous appointment—using the services of the BND and the German embassy—with my putative counterpart in Lisbon as well as with other political figures in order to disguise the real purpose of my trip.

I almost did not make it in time. In late March I joined the family for our annual Easter vacation in Lenzerheide, our vacation home in the Swiss Alps. I was going to fly directly from Zurich to Lisbon. But on the morning of April 4, Lenzerheide was covered with more than a foot of snow. The car of my security detail got stuck in the snow and could not be moved. So we tried it in my VW and, with the help of family and neighbors, finally broke through the massive drifts of snow, barely making it to the airport. Accompanied by one of my "protectors" (and feeling even somewhat more protected by the Smith & Wesson revolver I had packed in one of my suitcases), I got on the plane to Lisbon. Since I was traveling with a diplomatic passport, I did not need to worry about my luggage being subject to any kind of search. Money and gun seemed safe.

On the way from the airport to the hotel in Lisbon, I had second thoughts about just how safe we were. Police were visible everywhere, but their presence did not instill a sense of security. The city's nervousness was palpable. Every conceivable space was covered with posters and slogans, the Communist Party's emblems clearly dominating. Roving groups of demonstrators with their ubiquitous loudspeakers competed for space and attention. The revolution had been mostly peaceful so far, but everyone knew that yet another coup might happen at any moment. So I decided to change our plans and asked the driver of our car to take us directly to the German embassy, where I deposited the moneybag in a safe place. I then went back to the hotel to change for my formal visits and a dinner planned for that evening at the embassy. When I returned to the hotel later that night, I found my room in a total mess. Someone had broken in and rifled through my suitcase. Shoes, shirts, and suits were strewn all over the room. Nothing was missing, except for my gun. Had the thieves been looking for more? I wanted to report the break-in and theft to the police, but the hotel staff persuaded me not to. It would only cause me more trouble and the perpetrators would never be found.

The following day I delivered the money in the course of visiting different political party headquarters (all of which had been ransacked in previous days and weeks). Maintaining secrecy about my real mission was not easy, as I was accompanied by German media representatives, but I managed with a certain degree of stealth and sleight of hand. I even succeeded in obtaining a receipt from the general secretary of the Central Democratic Party. And after what I had seen and heard, I was more convinced than ever that we were doing exactly the right thing in supporting the build-up of democratic parties in Portugal. For that I gladly sacrificed my Smith & Wesson (which I soon replaced).

After my return to Bonn, I reported back to the chancellor's office and turned in my receipt to a visibly relieved state secretary. Strauss, I learned, had been less punctilious and failed to return with a receipt. Not much later I went on a similar mission to Spain that proved much less dramatic or exciting. That marked the end of my direct involvement with these special missions to Portugal and Spain. I remained engaged, however, in discussions—especially with the ever volatile Strauss—about the proper timing and right recipients of such additional help, which the Schmidt government continued to make available until its end in 1982.

History shows that Chancellor Schmidt must have had the right idea. Both Portugal and Spain emerged from their periods of intense political struggles with strong democratic systems. Eurocommunism did not prevail and "dominoes" did not fall. Spain joined NATO in 1982. Portugal and Spain became member countries of the European Community on January 1, 1986. (Sad to say, though, Portugal's former colonies fared less well. Angola, Mozambique, and East Timor were racked—and wrecked—by intense civil wars that lasted more than two decades.)

The Schmidt government, of course, could take no credit for its earlier contributions to the stabilization of Portugal and Spain. Everyone involved kept silent, as promised. Word about these activities leaked only in the early 1990s in the context of legal investigations into party financing in Germany, when prosecutors came across evidence of otherwise unreported financial transactions and suspected that the parties had kept the money for themselves, rather than pass it on to the intended recipients. According to newspaper reports, the Schmidt government, through its BND funds, allegedly provided some DM 40 million in the years between 1974 and 1982 for party activities in Portugal and Spain. I have no way of verifying these figures, but I do know that all the money I ever received, or became aware of, was promptly delivered to our counterparts in Portugal and Spain. The methods may have been unusual, and perhaps not always applicable elsewhere, but given the circumstances and the times, they were entirely appropriate. In light of the highly favorable outcomes, I remain proud of my special missions to Portugal and Spain.

The specter of Eurocommunism haunted not only Spain and Portugal, but also Italy. Here the Communist Party had long found its own way to accommodate itself to capitalist practices and the Catholic faith (a process funnily and lovingly depicted in the "Don Camillo and Peppone" books and movies that were immensely popular throughout Europe during the 1950s and 1960s). From farther away, however, the rising popularity and influence of leftist parties in Italy (symbolized by the election of Alessandro Pertini of the Italian Socialist Party as president of Italy in 1978) seemed less amusing and more foreboding. The Christian Democratic Party had dominated Italian politics since the end of World War II. Its rule now appeared threatened, especially since a rising wave of terrorism by the Red Brigades put additional pressure on the Italian political system. The Christian Democratic Union in Germany, which had long practiced close relations with its counterpart in Italy, was greatly concerned. It looked for ways to help the *Democrazia Cristiana* (Christian Democrats, DC) survive. I got to play a very minor role in that effort.

As it happened, I had excellent personal contacts in Italy. One of my childhood playmates was Moritz von Hessen, whose grandmother, the *Landgräfin* of Hesse, resided in Kronberg, where, at the end of the war, she was forced to room with our family for a few weeks. Moritz's mother was a daughter of the last king of Italy. From his father's side, he was related to the German emperors as well as to Queen Victoria. Born in Italy, he maintained lavish residences in Rome, where I joined him occasionally for all kinds of festivities, which involved Italian high society. On one such occasion I made the acquaintance of Umberto Agnelli, a member of the family who owned and ran FIAT industries of Turin. In the late 1970s, Umberto Agnelli became a senator and was now a fellow politician. I maintained contact with him, and we had many stimulating discussions about political developments in our countries.

As Eurocommunism became a hot topic, I asked Umberto whether it might be possible for him to arrange a meeting with some leaders of the Communist Party. He seemed more than happy to oblige, inviting not only the complete leadership of the party, but also the president of Italy for dinner in his residence in Rome. It was a memorable event, and not only because it was remarkable how easily Italy's Communist leaders mingled with Italy's top capitalist. I came to appreciate that evening that Italy's Communists were indeed a different breed, in no way comparable to the East German and Russian Communists I had gotten to know over the years. They were eager to impress me with the argument that they represented no threat to Italian democracy and thus to the rest of Europe, pointing out that they had repeatedly staked out anti-Soviet positions (when they denounced the Warsaw Pact intervention in Prague in 1968, for instance). I reported my impressions back to Helmut Kohl, the leader of the CDU.

I am not sure that Kohl was strongly impressed by the Italian Communists' arguments and my observations, for soon after he had become chancellor in November 1982, he asked me to carry out a special mission to Rome as his personal and private envoy. Kohl claimed to be very much concerned over the decreasing distance between the DC and the Communists (a potentially critical problem as NATO was agonizing over the dual-track INF issue). He wanted his concerns to be conveyed to Italy's prime minister outside the usual diplomatic channels, in order to give them more weight, as he told me. So through my Italian connections, I approached Amintore Fanfani, who at that point was prime minister for the fourth time since 1954, and asked to see him privately. He invited me for breakfast early one morning in his splendid Roman home high above the city. I told him why I had come to see him. He looked at me kindly, pointed at the city below him, and said: "I am Italian, but I am also a Roman. You are familiar with Rome's history going back more than 2,500 years. In the larger scheme of things, the development of the Communist Party of Italy is highly negligible. Tell your chancellor not to worry." He also pointed out what we had heard before, but found a bit hard to believe—namely that the Italian Communists were trying very hard to be unlike any other Communist party. I agreed that his points were well-taken and promised to inform Chancellor Kohl accordingly.

Kohl had asked me to do another little favor for him while I was in Rome. It was even more secretive; not even I was fully in the picture. It involved the Vatican. Kohl had claimed that he needed to return a favor to the *Democrazia Cristiana.* Through his Vatican channels, he had learned that a specific DC politician needed financial help, not least in order to better deal with a Communist challenger. Now he asked me to deliver a sizable amount of money (a quarter million deutsche marks or so) from the CDU's account to this person. The conduit was to be the cardinal of Florence, to be met in the Vatican. I was instructed to report to a back entrance, where I was met by an unobtrusive Swiss guard, who then spirited me through back hallways and a rear door into the cardinal's office. After some polite conversation, I handed over an envelope containing the money and bid farewell. Then came the embarrassing part. I was guided to leave through the office's front door. Outside in the reception room, I ran into the German ambassador to the Holy See. We were both equally astonished to see each other. He asked me what I, a member of the *Bundestag* and not known for being a Catholic, was doing in the Vatican. Somewhat sheepishly, I said something about taking care of some urgent private business and rushed on. I am not aware that my brief encounter with German officialdom while on a secret mission to the Vatican had any further consequences. I also cannot say whether my mission itself yielded the desired results. I heard no more about it, neither from Chancellor Kohl nor from my Italian contacts. In the end, though, Fanfani's broadly historic perspective proved correct. Eurocommunism in general, and the Italian Communist Party in particular, soon ceased to be of any concern.

Helmut Schmidt seemed to like these kinds of surprises. This time it was a Saturday evening, March 10, 1979. I was relaxing at home in Kronberg when the phone rang. In his usual no-nonsense style, Schmidt came right to the point. As you well know, he said, Turkey is in dire financial straits and requires urgent help; the West simply cannot afford to let its exposed NATO partner straddling Europe and Asia go down the drain. What is needed is a speedy infusion of funds to prevent Turkey's imminent economic collapse. "You are familiar with Turkey. You have excellent connections in the United States. I would like to ask you to organize an international rescue effort—as soon as possible."

Once again, I was surprised, flattered, and pleased that Schmidt had asked me to carry out such an important mission. But while I was eager to do it, and told the chancellor so, I also knew well enough that I could not simply accept without clearing it first with my (very few) superiors. I might have been the best man for the job—and was self-assured enough not to doubt that—but I also had to consider the political angles. Why would Schmidt want to ask a prominent member of the opposition to conduct a mission that could just as easily—as well as eagerly—be performed by someone in the chancellor's office or, even more logically, by the Foreign Office, perhaps even by Foreign Minister Genscher himself, who was always prickly when someone else threatened to encroach on his turf? Clearly Schmidt was also looking for some political cover, as well as future political support when it came time to actually provide the money, for which reason he preferred a front man from the opposition. I was happy to be that man, as I firmly believed that a successful conclusion of the Turkey rescue mission would not only benefit Turkey, NATO, and the West, but also help improve our party's standing. Beyond these political calculations, I also felt a strong personal motivation to accede to Schmidt's wishes. I was still fond of Turkey, where I had spent carefree childhood years. Turkey had opened its arms to many refugees as the rest of Europe was engulfed in the Holocaust and war. The Turkish people had shown themselves to be tolerant and friendly as Europe was sinking into flagrant barbarism. Turkey had developed a reasonably democratic political system with a free press and a functioning parliament. We owed it to Turkey and its people to come to its aid and not let it be threatened by poverty and anarchy.

Still, I had to make sure that my party's leaders shared my assessments and my interests. First, I got in touch with Ernst Albrecht. Without the minister-president's permission, Lower Saxony's finance minister obviously could not absent himself from his duties for a prolonged period of time. Albrecht immediately encouraged me to do it. He knew that I had an excellent deputy in the finance ministry who could capably run the ministry's affairs in my absence. He was also well-aware that there were times when I was less than fulfilled with my work in Hanover and therefore itching to take on more challenging tasks. By letting me go, he made sure that I would stay.

Next I talked with Helmut Kohl, chairman of the CDU and thus leader of the opposition. He saw no problems and agreed that this was a mission I simply had to perform. That left Franz Josef Strauss, leader of the sister opposition party, the CSU, minister-president of Bavaria, and at that point the CDU/CSU's likely candidate for chancellor in the 1980 elections. Since I had high hopes of being included in his top team, I needed to touch base with him. His initial reaction was typical. After some hemming and hawing, he burst out: "Don't they have someone else to do this?" At the end of that highly charged weekend, I informed Chancellor Schmidt of my decision to undertake the Turkey mission. He told me that I would be his personal representative and that his office would handle all administrative details, thereby assuring my high-level entry with foreign governments. The costs of my efforts would be reimbursed by the Foreign Office. The chancellor's office also cleared the formalities of my leave of absence from the Lower Saxony state government, carrying the costs of my salary, as well as that of one assistant, while I was acting as the chancellor's representative. It all sounded almost too good to be true. Soon I was off and running—or rather, flying high.

Turkey's problems were not entirely new. When Chancellor Schmidt had visited Turkey in 1976, his (not very diplomatically voiced) overall impression was: "a pigsty." Turkey's efforts to go its own way economically with a massive industrial development effort had faltered in the aftermath of the 1973 energy crisis, but there was little inclination to offer concerted help. After all, Turkey, under then Prime Minister Bülent Ecevit, had angered its allies in July 1974 when it occupied Northern Cyprus; "Let Turkey suffer the consequences" was the prevailing mood in the West. When Turkey began to run short of money, it took recourse to short-term credits to tide it over and to avoid the hard choices necessary to put its economy and finances back on a sound footing. In the course of these developments, the Turkish government cut off all contacts with international lending institutions—the International Monetary Fund (IMF) above all—as it saw their seemingly harsh demands for a restructuring of Turkey's economy and finances as patronizing and demeaning, as well as politically unacceptable.

Turkey's problems began to reach crisis proportions by late 1977. Its foreign debts amounted to some $19 billion ($12 billion of which were high-interest short-term loans), which it was unable to service or repay. In March 1979, the Turkish central bank announced that it would cease all currency transactions. The inflation rate rose above 70 percent; the unemployment rate reached more than 20 percent. Remittances from Turkish "guest workers" abroad (mostly in Germany) decreased by 35 percent, as a worldwide economic downturn began to hit home. In the spring of 1979, Turkey found itself without the cash reserves necessary to buy the oil and machinery it would require to bring in the annual harvest. Turkey needed money—fast.

What might have saved Turkey at that point were developments in neighboring Iran. Ruled by Mohammad Reza Shah Pahlavi, Iran was a key US ally in the Middle East. Not least under the influence of President Carter's human rights policies, the Shah began to face increasing domestic dissent by 1978. His regime began to crumble. In January 1979 he was forced to leave the country, setting in motion a series of events with far-reaching consequences. Of immediate importance was the emergence of Ayatollah Khomeini as the new leader of Iran, who began to institute a religious dictatorship. The United States had now lost its key ally in the region. It also lost access to military installations from which it could monitor Soviet missile firings; that loss threatened the verification procedures vital to the SALT agreements with the Soviet Union. The United States now needed alternative verification sites. It also could not afford to lose yet another ally in the region. Turkey's survival was of critical importance. A mortally "sick man on the Bosporus" would not do.

In Brussels, General Alexander Haig, the Supreme Allied Commander Europe (SACEUR), had grown increasingly alarmed about the looming disaster in Turkey. A Turkey caught up in chaos and turmoil would no longer be a reliable NATO partner. As conditions worsened in and around Turkey, Haig finally prevailed upon the Carter administration to do something. NATO itself, much to Haig's dismay, proved unable to be of help, partly because economic rescue efforts do not constitute NATO's main mission, but mostly because Greece and its friends (France prominently among them) were able to block any such effort. Turkey itself proved no easy partner in this situation. The Turkish government, undoubtedly following the lead of public opinion, resented that offers of help appeared to be based more on cool calculations regarding the strategic importance of Turkey (with concomitant expectations regarding Turkish behavior and concessions) than on a heartfelt desire to come to the aid of a trusted friend in need.

In January 1979 President Carter, Chancellor Schmidt, President Valéry Giscard d'Estaing of France, and Prime Minister James Callaghan of Great Britian met in the idyllic Caribbean setting of Guadeloupe. The four leaders had decided to meet among themselves in order to allow as open and informal discussions as possible. That meant that the leaders of other countries, such as Japan, Canada, and Italy, as well as the head of the European Commission, were excluded. Four years earlier, when Giscard and Schmidt had launched a different summit effort along the same lines, the excluded leaders had protested vehemently and succeeded in being included in what turned into an annual G-7 summit—a massive and formal event that no longer reflected the original intent of openness and informality. In Guadeloupe they tried to resurrect the original format, which produced the same result: distrust and protest among the excluded. Ostensibly the purpose of the meeting in Guadeloupe—and the reason for the exclusion of other countries—was to discuss ways to deal with the threat of Soviet intermediate-range missiles in Europe. The main result of that meeting was, in fact, the "dual-track" decision, but other topics came up as well.

Early on, Carter (properly briefed by Haig) brought up the issue of Turkey. The European Community could not help, NATO would not help—perhaps now was the time for the Organization for Economic Co-operation and Development (OECD) in Paris to jump in. Would Germany be willing to head such an effort? Schmidt at first declined. For one, he really disliked "that peanut farmer" and "Baptist preacher" Carter, whom he considered a naïve and amateurish "do-gooder" doing less good and much more harm with his ill-conceived human rights campaigns and arms-control initiatives. For that reason alone, Schmidt was disinclined to do the American president's bidding. Conversely, he was totally enamored of Giscard d'Estaing, the elegant and worldly French aristocrat with his technocratic brilliance and persuasive realism. And the president of France was opposed to a concerted rescue effort for Turkey. But beyond those more personal reactions, the German chancellor also hesitated to accept a leading role that would single out Germany and cause unease and resentment among its European partners. If that were to happen, he argued, the Turkey rescue mission itself might become endangered. Finally, he was also afraid that if Germany led the effort, Germany would be expected to provide most of the funds, and that was out of the question. The American president, however, was insistent: Turkey needed help, and Germany was in the best position to organize it. Germany, after all, was Turkey's most important trading partner; shouldn't it have an interest in propping up the Turkish economy? Schmidt finally relented, with one stipulation: whatever the final agreement, the German contribution had to be less than the American one.

Yet little happened after the Guadeloupe summit. It took the pressure of events in Iran and the rapid deterioration of Turkey's financial situation to spur the Western leaders into final action. I have reason to believe that it was Robert McNamara, the unfortunate American secretary of defense responsible for the mishandling of the Vietnam War and now president of the World Bank, who convinced Schmidt in the course of a visit to Bonn on March 7 that a Turkey rescue effort was overdue. McNamara had undergone a remarkable transformation at the World Bank. The former head of the Ford Motor Company and then chief architect of a "rational" approach to the use of military power—which had failed so miserably in Vietnam—was now a firm believer in the responsible use of economic power to alleviate the world's ills. I had gotten to know McNamara while he was in the Pentagon and maintained contact with him after his shift to the World Bank. McNamara told Schmidt that I would be an ideal candidate to organize an international money-collection effort on behalf of Turkey: familiar with the country, acceptable to both the Carter administration and the international financial institutions, and unaffected by existing animosities. So Schmidt called me that Saturday evening, after he had cleared my prospective role with the Carter administration and within his own coalition.

According to IMF estimates, Turkey was facing a current account deficit of $1.9 billion for 1979 that needed to be bridged. When I began my efforts, the OECD had pledges for $215 million ($100 million each from the United States and Germany, $15 million from Great Britain). Experts in the German Foreign Office thought I might be lucky if I could raise a total of $600 million. I set my own goal higher: I wanted to collect $800 million in new pledges. My approach to achieve that goal was two-pronged. First I needed to get the IMF involved again. Without some kind of IMF approval—based on a yet-to-be-concluded agreement with the Turkish government—other countries would not agree to release funds to the Turkish rescue effort. Then I had to go begging for those funds from as many foreign governments as possible. Neither task was easy. The IMF and Turkey were not on speaking terms. And all of the countries that had not been present in Guadeloupe and resented their exclusion needed to be persuaded that it was nevertheless in their interest to chip in and help out.

In a first round of talks, I covered many bases. I needed to sound out how much willingness there was to move forward. I was also aware that not all the organizations involved in this effort regarded my activities with unadulterated delight, viewing me instead as a possible intruder on their turf and as a potential nuisance rather than as a welcome mediator. In high-level meetings at NATO, the OECD, the World Bank, and the IMF, I tried to alleviate such concerns and reassure the skeptics and doubters that my role was that of a facilitator who would not step on toes or usurp the prerogatives of others. I was reasonably successful in that effort. Of special importance was the fact that the managing director of the International Monetary Fund, Jacques de Larosière, agreed in principle to meet with Turkish counterparts in order to find ways for a reopening of Turkish relations with the IMF.

Next I had to convince the Turkish government that it had no choice but to deal with the IMF. That proved to be even more difficult than I had anticipated. Turkey not only hated the IMF for its alleged disrespect, unreasonable demands, and severe interference in its domestic affairs, it even resented my efforts on its behalf as an exercise in begging that was deemed unworthy of a great and proud nation. I realized I was walking through a political minefield of considerable dimensions. I began to remember stories my father had told me long ago about how to deal with Turkish counterparts: proceed carefully, practice all courtesies, know when to pull back, and always leave room for face-saving. Above all, keep in mind that insults can be perceived easily and grudges can be carried forever. But if you show respect, and if you can demonstrate that you are a friend and on their side, you will be successful. I had plenty of occasions to heed that advice.

By early April I was ready to go to Ankara to meet with the Turkish government. After an early breakfast meeting with the American ambassador—I made it a point to keep the American side informed at all times and to solicit its advice—I met with the Turkish finance minister. He was the one person most responsible for the breakdown of relations with the IMF. An irascible character whose mastery of the English language, unfortunately, was not quite adequate for his position, he took a hard line and insisted that Turkey could not agree to any kind of IMF conditions and would have to try and find its own way out of its difficulties. I listened patiently, knowing that the hard decisions were up to the prime minister, whom I was scheduled to see next.

Bülent Ecevit had been returned to power as prime minister the year before and was therefore not immediately responsible for Turkey's economic problems. His predecessor Süleyman Demirel was carping from the political sidelines, making fun of that "cashier" from Lower Saxony who was trying to save Turkey. A real solution to Turkey's problems, he let it be known, would only be achieved once he had replaced Ecevit as prime minister. (In fact, Ecevit and Demirel were playing a political tag game of sorts, repeatedly replacing each other as prime minister, with Ecevit serving four times and Demirel five times.) I had gotten to know Ecevit in the course of a Bilderberg Meeting a few years earlier, so there was already a modicum of trust and understanding between us. It served us well that day. I explained my mission to him, placing particular emphasis on the importance of Turkish-German relations (as evidenced by my role) and on the fact that we were acting in our own "enlightened" self-interest and not out of pity for Turkey. I then went on to point out how crucial it was that the IMF be involved, not only as the provider of a seal of approval for short-term financial aid, but, even more important, as an indispensable partner for medium- and long-term solutions to Turkey's economic problems. The finance minister once again reacted with misgivings about the role of the IMF, especially if IMF representatives were to come to Turkey and their presence to become public knowledge. I then suggested that I might be able to arrange a secret meeting on neutral ground between the finance minister and the IMF managing director. Ecevit immediately accepted this suggestion; the finance minister had no choice but to follow suit. Thus the most delicate part of my mission to Turkey had been achieved.

After our formal discussions, Ecevit had arranged an informal dinner with members of his cabinet. He had warned me beforehand that I needed to be careful in my remarks, as his cabinet represented an odd assortment of political persuasions, from extreme left to extreme right: "What can I do? Every time there is a government crisis or a parliamentary crisis, I have to enlarge my cabinet, and that means having to buy yet another vote . . ." I was mindful of this warning when my time came to offer some after-dinner remarks. Instead of talking about the debt issue, I reflected on my personal experiences as a child growing up in Turkey. I even managed to resurrect some Turkish phrases I thought I had long forgotten.

One of them was "German and Turks are friends." Another, no longer appropriate phrase was "I am a little German boy" (which had come in handy when I needed to defend myself on the playing fields of my Turkish childhood). Now it allowed me to segue into a story about how I, just a little German boy, had watched with great fascination and deep admiration the funeral procession in Istanbul of Kemal Atatürk, the revered founder of modern Turkey. My listeners were duly impressed. I am sure that I won them over that day, as I was able to convince these members of the Turkish government that it was not a sign of shame but rather a symbol of friendship to accept outside help. I left Ankara later that evening (on a chartered private jet) full of optimism that my mission would meet with success.

Success, however, depended on Turkey and the IMF actually patching up their differences. I knew that the right setting for such delicate endeavors is always crucial, so I chose Switzerland as the neutral ground for the meeting agreed to in Ankara, and I chose Zurich's best-known and fanciest hotel, The Dolder Grand, as the proper venue. The Turkish delegation, headed by the finance minister, arrived on April 12. Their trip to Zurich was entirely secret; had the Turkish press gotten wind of the trip and its purpose, anguished cries of "treason" would have been the result. I met with the delegation that evening to impress upon this group of financial experts once again the importance of dealing with the IMF. IMF Managing Director Jacques de Larosière arrived the following morning—on Good Friday—by Concorde from Washington. I very much appreciated the fact that he had agreed to interrupt his Easter vacation to meet with his Turkish counterparts. I introduced him to the Turkish side and then left them alone. All I could do was build the bridge; it was up to them to cross it.

Turkey and the IMF did manage to cross their divide that day, over the bridge I had provided. When I met with the group for tea that afternoon, they were able to report an agreement in principle to restart negotiations at the expert level on a "standby" accord. We then proceeded to celebrate that agreement in a relaxed and friendly atmosphere. As I told the press later, we had provided the food, while they had to swallow it. (As it turned out, they took in an awful lot of food and drink in The Dolder over the two-day meeting. To this day, the German Foreign Office—which had to foot the bill—maintains that the reimbursement request that I presented later is still the largest such bill it ever had to pay. I find that hard to believe, but even if it were true, it was well worth it.)

After The Dolder exertions in Zurich, I took a brief Easter vacation myself in our vacation home in the nearby Alps. But soon I set out again, visiting a number of the smaller prospective donor countries, such as Austria and Belgium. With success looming on the horizon, I found it much easier to convince foreign governments to contribute to the Turkey rescue effort. Later in April, I went to Paris to consult with Emile van Lennep, general secretary of the OECD. The disbursement of the funds I was going to gather was ultimately to be administered by the OECD. It was important, therefore, that the OECD be kept appraised of developments. I also discovered again that van Lennep required reassurances that my mission did not in any way reflect German and/or American distrust of the OECD and its general secretary. There was, however, a sore point. The OECD had approached Turkey with the idea of establishing some council of elders, or wise men, who would supervise Turkey's use of its funds. The Turkish government had made it clear in the course of my discussions in Ankara that it found that proposal highly insulting. The establishment of a special OECD "supervisory board" strictly for Turkey was unacceptable, and no Turkish government would long survive if it agreed to it. I now had to convince van Lennep to drop that idea. Eventually, and reluctantly, he agreed to do so.

When I returned to Bonn to give Chancellor Schmidt and his finance minister an interim report, a new issue had arisen. The Carter administration, I was informed, had in the meantime decided to increase its contribution to my collection efforts. I was highly pleased and felt that perhaps it could be interpreted as an expression of confidence in the ultimate success of my mission. The chancellor, of course, was not unhappy either, especially since it met his priority of Germany not carrying more of the burden than the United States. However, I now found myself in a curious position. As the chancellor's personal representative, charged with raising as much money as possible (and now charged up with determination to achieve my goal), I sought to convince the chancellor that Germany had no choice but to increase its own contribution if it wanted to be a credible partner of the United States in that effort. Carter had raised the ante; Schmidt, with some hesitation, eventually followed suit. Not a bad moment for a loyal member of his opposition.

In addition to obtaining an increase in the German contribution, I also sought a commitment by the European Community for a significant amount of financial aid. In early May I went to Brussels to sound out what might be possible. The figures mentioned were between $100 million and $300 million. I, of course, pleaded for the larger sum, but I ran into a hot political issue. Since 1964, Turkey had had an "association agreement" with the European Community (the goal being a gradual integration of Turkey to the point of eventual full membership in the EC). One provision of that agreement allowed the free movement of labor after 1986. In the meantime, however, Turkish "guest workers" had streamed into Germany even without that provision in force, causing considerable social, economic, and political strains in the Federal Republic. German diplomacy now saw a chance to link the financial rescue effort with attempts to restrict further Turkish labor coming to Germany. The formal place to effect such a linkage was Brussels. If Turkey was to receive more money from the EC, it should agree to drop the 1986 deadline for the free movement of labor. I was not too happy about that roadblock in my efforts, and neither were the Turks. The EC contribution remained open for the time being.

While I was dealing with the EC, I also met Prime Minister Ecevit again. He had come to Strasbourg to give a speech at the Council of Europe, where he was going to plead his case for Turkey's inclusion in Europe and the help it would need to get there. We had agreed to meet at his hotel at eight o'clock that evening. I arrived ten minutes early, found him already there, and launched into an explanation why I was early. He smiled at me and gently informed me that he had been waiting for me for almost an hour. It turned out that France had already switched to summer time, and I was running on German time, unaware—and uninformed—about the time difference. I was flabbergasted about my faux pas and began apologizing in earnest. but Ecevit interrupted me and told me not to worry: "I know you and was sure you would show up eventually." We met privately and I brought him up to date on my efforts, emphasized again the importance of Turkish-IMF negotiations, and encouraged him to mention the OECD rescue effort prominently in his speech. Then eight of us retired to an informal dinner in an Alsatian country inn, where the discussion was as free-flowing as the excellent local wine. Ecevit and I were well on the way to forming a close personal friendship, as well as a political relationship based on mutual trust and understanding. (How much that was lacking in a larger political context became evident the following day, when Ecevit faced a quite hostile reception at the Council of Europe, where Greek representatives in particular confronted him over the Cyprus issue.)

Immediately after the Strasbourg meeting, I set off for the most challenging part of my mission. At Guadaloupe, Japan—which was not present—had been an afterthought. I determined that a more deliberate attempt should be made to include Japan in the Turkey rescue effort. I was well-aware of the difficulties. Tokyo felt slighted because of Guadeloupe and had little incentive to contribute funds to help a country that barely showed up on its radar screen, but I convinced Chancellor Schmidt that we should give it a try. He wrote a note to the Japanese prime minister introducing me as his personal emissary. That was good enough to get me appointments, on very short notice, with the prime minister, the foreign minister, and the finance minister. So off I went on a very long flight, halfway around the world (with the then still necessary stopover in Anchorage, Alaska). What I was doing was, to some extent, sensational: a German going to Tokyo to ask for money in support of Turkey. Germany and Japan had come a long way since the end of World War II.

In one way, my visit to Japan was a complete success. To be sure, as had been predicted by the German embassy, my Japanese interlocutors all insisted that "Turkey is very far away"; however, they also showed themselves to be remarkably well-informed about all aspects of the Turkish crisis. They agreed that Turkey was like a sinking ship that required immediate help. Japan, they indicated, was willing to contribute $70 million to the effort, a good deal more than I had dared to hope for. That issue having been settled, our talks turned to other matters. The Japanese leaders made it clear that their real concerns were closer to home: developments in China. China, they argued, should not be encouraged to modernize too fast. The best way to achieve that goal would be a coordinated approach by the United States, the European Community, and Japan. No formal linkage was established, but it seemed evident—and understandable—that Japan expected Europe and the United States to heed its concerns while Japan helped meet our interests.

In a different way, however, my Tokyo trip almost turned into a disaster. At the end of that day, I was informed by the German embassy that I should expect a phone call from the Turkish government during the night. I feared the worst. Sure enough, the Turkish finance minister reached me in my hotel room to tell me that the negotiations with the IMF were close to failing. Turkey simply could not accept IMF demands for a devaluation of the Turkish currency and cuts in its budget. The situation was made worse by the fact that Ecevit had apparently decided to go campaigning (for elections to the Senate) rather than meet with the IMF representative, Sir Alan Whittome, to settle the issue. A few hours later, now early in the morning in Tokyo, Ecevit called to report that he had, in the meantime, talked with Whittome, but had also been unable to reach an agreement. Whittome had rejected Ecevit's proposal for a "gentlemen's agreement," whereby Turkey would undertake some financial reforms, which the IMF could monitor with a view toward an eventual agreement. Until then, Germany and the United States could make their pledged funds available to Turkey. That was not good enough. In order for the funds that I was collecting to be released to Turkey, a "green light" was required from the IMF that negotiations were either successfully concluded or at least on track. Failure in Ankara meant failure of my mission. Ecevit was well-aware of that. He was almost despondent, suggesting that perhaps he should just throw in the towel and resign. I urged him not to do anything rash, to hang in there, and to ignore the chaos around him. My mission was running well, I told him, and should not be aborted. I tried to assure him and said we should carry on and pretend that everything was okay—and that it would be okay. Ecevit agreed to think it over and call back later.

I thought of trying to reach the IMF person on the ground in Turkey for a firsthand report, but realized that was nearly impossible. I called IMF headquarters in Washington instead, where I was told that Whittome had not reported any failure and was still engaged in his negotiation efforts. Some time later Whittome himself called me to confirm that he was still active. Details of his activities would be sent to the German embassy; I should not do anything further until I had taken notice of them. Then Ecevit called again, indicating his willingness to carry on. I implored him to consider at least some concession (perhaps a formal state guarantee to back up the loans) that would allow the negotiations to go forward; he agreed to do so. I also asked him to keep mum about all of this—any leak to the ever-suspicious Turkish press could mean an end to our efforts. Ecevit concurred. That brought a sleepless night of long-distance mediation to a hopeful end.

What followed was the longest day of my life. I flew directly (via Anchorage) to New York and on to Washington. In New York I was met by a State Department officer with the hot news that the negotiations in Ankara had collapsed. I could not believe it. Had all my efforts been for naught after all? When I probed for details, it turned out that Washington was not up to date (literally: time and dateline differences between Japan, Turkey, and the United States had apparently led to some confusion as to the state of affairs in Ankara). I was able to confirm that the IMF and Turkey were still negotiating, not least due to my all-night mediation efforts. We all breathed a big sigh of relief.

The following day I met with Deputy Secretary of State Warren Christopher and his staff. We reviewed the state of my mission. Christopher expressed both his satisfaction and appreciation for what I had achieved so far. He himself had been to Ankara a couple of times to prevail upon the Turkish government to let the United States establish military bases in Turkey. He had met with limited success, as Turkey resented the seemingly singular American focus on strategic aspects. That was not quite justified, as my mission—initiated by President Carter himself—should have made clear. Christopher was all the more pleased, therefore, that the Turkish rescue mission appeared close to a successful conclusion. We agreed that the formal end of my efforts—a donors' pledging conference that would nail down the individual contributions—should take place at the OECD in Paris on May 30, 1979—that is, in just about two weeks. That date was confirmed by the IMF, where I stopped by after my visit to the State Department. This was all the more remarkable since it was clear that the IMF would not be in a position to provide a "green light" statement by then. But the IMF and Turkey's commitment to continue negotiating should provide sufficient cover for the funds to be made available to Turkey. Everybody agreed to that solution. We had just about reached the finish line.

When Christopher (who later became secretary of state in the first Clinton administration) asked me to confer with him after my trip to Tokyo, he had an ulterior motive in mind. "Foreign entanglements" of any kind are never without some kind of domestic repercussions in the United States (as President George Washington had already discovered more than two hundred years earlier). One of the Carter administration's main headaches regarding its cooperation with Turkey was the strong opposition of Greek interest groups. Some three million voters of Greek descent carried a good deal of political weight, especially since they were quite successful in electing their representatives to Congress. So Christopher asked me to sit down with members of the Greek caucus in Congress to explain to them why it was important that Turkey be provided with help, and describe the exact conditions for such aid. It was not a pleasant experience. Arguments against helping Turkey ranged from condemnation of its occupation of Northern Cyprus to fears that the United States, with its emphasis on the strategic importance of Turkey, was about to become embroiled in another Vietnam. I had a hard time keeping my patience—and, at times, a straight face—over such intense animosity and decided lack of understanding. But I knew how important it was that Congressional opposition be at least taken into consideration, if not completely mollified, so I persevered. I owed that much to my American counterparts—and to the ultimate success of my mission. In the end, the Carter administration was able to uphold its side of the bargain I had put together during those frantic weeks.

My mission was now completed, though not yet fully accomplished. President Carter had his National Security Advisor Zbigniew Brzezinski call me that last evening in Washington to convey his sincere gratitude. Upon my return to Germany, Chancellor Schmidt wrote me a formal letter of thanks. I returned to Hanover to pick up my duties as finance minister of Lower Saxony and as a member of its parliament. It was, admittedly, anticlimactic. Instead of conferencing with foreign governments, I was now back to the realities of provincial politics. (That June, as a *Spiegel* article about my Turkey mission somewhat cynically noted, I gave talks at the Lower Saxony association of sugar beet growers and at the one hundred fiftieth anniversary of a local People's Bank. As described in a previous chapter, this experience reinforced my determination to leave Lower Saxony behind and reenter national politics in Bonn.) The donors' conference in Paris on May 30 took place without me. I was specifically excluded, since it involved only government experts. The German representative was a Foreign Office official who had served as one of my aides and accompanied me on most of my trips. Elevated to the rank of ambassador specifically for this conference, he represented us well. He also kept me informed, so I was not completely out of the loop.

As expected, Turkey and the IMF had not reached a final agreement. The donors' conference took place nevertheless, though now under the cloud that Turkey might be dissatisfied with both the overall level of support and the lack of short-term loans, which in turn might cause some donor countries to renege on their commitments. Fortunately enough, that did not happen. At the end of the day, the overall result was announced: $910 million. To be sure, there was some creative accounting involved; not all of the aid pledged was entirely new, nor without some stringent conditions. Still, it was much more than I had imagined in my wildest dreams when I took on the mission. I was overwhelmed, in faraway Hanover. Only now could I truly claim: mission accomplished!

Turkey had survived its financial crisis; politically it did less well. Half a year after the successful conclusion of our rescue effort, Ecevit was replaced as prime minister by Süleyman Demirel, his perennial rival. Demirel himself lasted less than a year in office. In September 1980 Turkey's military—considering itself to be the protector of the state and claiming a need to reestablish stability in the tradition of Kemal Atatürk—took over power in a relatively bloodless coup d'état. Thus began a three-year period of military rule that saw many human rights violations, but ended with the passage of a new constitution that reintroduced a semblance of civilian government. The military rulers banned all political parties and excluded leading political figures from any political activities. Some, Ecevit prominently among them, were at first incarcerated and then held under house arrest. This was not necessarily the political outcome I had expected as the result of my rescue mission.

Not long after the military had taken over power, I received a request from Turkey's de facto ruler, General Kenan Evren (who would later be elected president and served a full term until 1989), to come to Ankara for a consultation about what had transpired during my rescue mission and how it might still impact Turkey. I saw little reason to refuse the general's request and set off for Ankara. We had a long talk, in the course of which I tried to make clear that putsches and military rule were, by and large, not viewed favorably by international financial institutions; if Turkey expected future international support, a return to civilian rule would be absolutely necessary. General Evren, who, I must admit, impressed me greatly with his personality as well as with his command of the situation, sought to explain how Turkey's civilian rulers had almost run their country into the ground and why military rule seemed a short-term necessity. I saw his point, though I did not express any agreement.

After I had left General Evren, I told the German ambassador who had accompanied me that I wanted to visit my good friend Ecevit. The ambassador was horrified. Such contacts with politicians under house arrest would not be appreciated by the military rulers and could cause all kinds of diplomatic trouble. Besides, Ecevit lived on the other side of town and would be hard to reach. I told him bluntly that I could not care less about diplomatic niceties or traffic difficulties—I wanted to see Ecevit. I was determined to do so because I had grown fond of Ecevit, not only the politician, but also the man who had aspired to become a poet and an artist and who was simply fun to spend time with. I also figured that a show of support for the former prime minister might help him personally, as well as impress upon the junta that not every foreign visitor was happy about their rule.

Ecevit and his lovely wife lived in a small apartment in a dreary building in a less than fancy part of town. When I rang his doorbell, he opened the door and then broke into tears. Visitors were rare, and he was more than delighted to see me. We spent a long time reminiscing about old days, reviewing present developments, and speculating about what the future might hold. Ecevit always wanted to see Turkey on the side of the West and fully integrated into Europe. Would it ever get there? Conditions seemed bleak then, but Ecevit was full of optimism. I left him in high spirits, fully convinced that I had done the right thing, personally and politically. As it turned out, I was right. My visit had no ill consequences, neither for Ecevit nor for German-Turkish relations.

My next memorable encounter with the vagaries of Turkish politics and German-Turkish relations took place more than ten years later. In 1993, Tansu Çiller became prime minister—an American-trained economist (with a PhD from the University of Connecticut) and, more importantly, the first and, so far, only female in that office. A stunningly beautiful and reputedly very wealthy woman, Çiller proved to be a controversial prime minister, mostly due to various corruption charges. One of her major achievements in office was the conclusion of a customs union agreement with the European Union that went into effect on January 1, 1996. Turkey had formally applied for membership in what was then the European Community in 1987, but consideration of that application had been postponed time and again, because Europe was preoccupied with the fall of the Wall and its aftermath, including the deepening and widening of the European Community into the European Union. There was also a good deal of hesitation to make Turkey a full member of the European Union, given Turkey's record of political and economic instability. The customs union agreement served as an interim step, meant both to mollify Turkey and to prepare it for eventual full membership in the European Union.

It was in the course of that process that Chancellor Helmut Kohl asked me to travel to Ankara to sound out Prime Minister Çiller about how things were going. Of course, the fact that he thought it necessary to send me as his special emissary indicated that Turkey's relations with Germany and the European Union were not as strong as both sides might have wished. When I met with Çiller and introduced myself as the chancellor's personal envoy, she was furious. "I don't want to hear his name," she launched into me. I tried to calm her down, pointing out that for all I knew, Kohl greatly admired her. No, she replied, she used to admire him—in fact adored him as a second Ludwig Erhard; however, now Kohl had betrayed her with what she saw as shady maneuverings regarding Turkey's application for EU membership. I never did find out from her how exactly the German chancellor had betrayed the Turkish prime minister. When I reported back to Kohl, he professed not to know what he might have done to invite Çiller's fury. But it was no secret that Kohl was reluctant to give Turkey full EU membership, as he had little sympathy for, or understanding of, Turkey. It was only later, after one of his sons had long courted and married a Turkish woman in 2001 that Kohl became more appreciative of Turkey, and more supportive of Turkish aspirations. By then, however, Çiller had been forced out of office (in 1996) and Kohl had lost an election (in 1998).

The man who beat Kohl—the longest serving chancellor in German history—was Gerhard Schröder. I had known Schröder for a long time, going back to my days in Lower Saxony, where Schröder was earning his political wings at the time as leader of the Young Socialists. In 1980, he was elected on the SPD ticket to the *Bundestag* as the representative from Hanover, while I reentered the *Bundestag* as the CDU's top candidate. We were far apart politically, but we saw eye to eye on many issues and therefore got along well. In 1990, Schröder became minister-president of Lower Saxony, succeeding Ernst Albrecht, my former boss when I was finance minister there. Since I was still very active on the supervisory board of Volkswagen, Schröder and I had quite a few dealings with each other, as the minister-president of Lower Saxony is an *ex officio* member of the VW supervisory board. Along the way, we formed some close bonds.

The question of Turkish membership in the European Union was still unsettled when Schröder became chancellor. It was now his problem, especially after Germany took over the presidency of the European Union in January 1999. The European Union had told Turkey in 1997 that it could be considered for full membership. In 1998, however, the European Union decided to open formal accession negotiations with a number of Eastern European countries—but not with Turkey. Prime Minister Mesut Yilmaz of Turkey rightly felt that his country had been slighted and angrily called off any further talks with the European Union. That did not necessarily help his political standing at home, however. In January 1999, he was replaced as prime minister by none other than my old friend Bülent Ecevit, who had diligently worked his way back into positions of political power. The question now was whether Ecevit would forego his predecessor's rejection of EU overtures and return to the negotiating table. Schröder certainly was eager for Turkey to do so.

This is where I came into play again. In a now familiar pattern, the chancellor called me one day in early 1999 to ask whether I would serve as his personal envoy to promote Turkey's membership in the European Union. Of course I agreed immediately—my sense of duty, my passion for these kinds of missions, my love for Turkey, and my fondness for Ecevit had not changed one bit since my rescue effort twenty years earlier. So off I went again. The first stop was Ankara, where the prime minister needed to be convinced to set aside Turkish anger and frustrations over EU foot-dragging regarding Turkey's accession to the European Union. Chancellor Schröder drafted a four-page letter to his colleague in the Turkish capital, which he asked me to deliver personally. I was more than happy to do so.

Ecevit received me like the old friend that I was. He had aged visibly and seemed much frailer. I handed over Schröder's letter, which was written in German. A translation into Turkish had, unfortunately, not been provided. I proceeded to translate it into English. Ecevit listened without interrupting me. After I had finished, but before we sat down for business, he took me aside and said: "I've got to ask you something, just out of curiosity, are you still a member of the CDU?" I looked somewhat startled, which must have been the desired effect, for Ecevit then explained with a twinkle in his eyes: "In 1979 you traveled around the world on our behalf as a personal emissary of Chancellor Schmidt. Today you are bringing me a letter from Chancellor Schröder. Both are SPD. I was just wondering . . ." I assured Ecevit that I had indeed not changed my party affiliation (though there had been times when I had questioned it myself).

Schröder's letter implored the Turkish prime minister to agree to reopen Turkey's bid for full EU membership. A formal decision by the European Union was to be taken at the end of the year at a regular EU summit meeting, but that decision would only be made if Turkey signaled its readiness. Ecevit settled back in his chair, looked at me with resignation, and told me that he was sick and tired of this EU business. It was much too complicated, would take far too long, and surpassed Turkey's capabilities. He saw no reason to even attempt it. Instead, he proposed, let Turkey and the European Union enter into a special relationship of sorts, where both sides could pursue their interests as they saw fit, rather than have both sides pressed into the straitjacket of the European Union's *acquis communitaire*—that voluminous body of rules and regulations binding all EU members.

I can't say that I was shocked. Ecevit's points were understandable, given the long, unfortunate history of Turkish-EU relations. But I was dismayed, for I was firmly convinced that Turkey needed to be in the European Union, to the benefit of both sides. I explained to my weary friend that he might have misunderstood the chancellor's opening. Germany was not trying to promote Turkish membership in the European Union out of the goodness of its heart, simply to do Turkey a favor. Turkish membership was in Germany's original interest. Turkey had stood faithfully by the side of the West throughout the Cold War. Now that the Cold War was over, and the focus of international conflicts was on the Middle East, the West needed Turkey more than ever. What better way to tie Turkey to the West than to have it become a full member of the European Union? The Cold War had left a lot of unfinished business behind. There was a lot of urgent business to be done—with Turkey, and with the help of Turkey.

Ecevit had listened to me patiently. We then went back and forth. Finally the prime minister said: "Okay, you have convinced me." He acknowledged that Germany, and I personally, had done a lot for Turkey in the past. He did not want to be ungrateful. So he was willing to give it yet another try, fully aware that it was not going to be easy. I thanked my old friend profusely, promised him I would do everything in my (admittedly limited) power to help make it happen, and went on my way. Back home, Chancellor Schröder was astonished and delighted over what had transpired in Ankara. He had been pessimistic regarding the outcome of his initiative. I was glad that I had been able to help dispel his pessimism.

But my job was not yet quite done. Not all member states of the European Union were supportive of a Turkish candidacy for membership. Greece—Turkey's ancient enemy—was understandably less than enthusiastic. Italy, too, proved reluctant, especially its foreign minister, Lamberto Dini. What could be done to change their minds? I was not unaware that economic interests can play an important role in politics. Maybe they could be brought into play here? I decided to give it a try, relying on some personal relations and contacts. First, I called on my friend Max M. Warburg, head of the Warburg banking family, to get his ideas about what might be done. Together we came up with a plan to put some pressure on the Greek government with the help of one of Greece's most important industries: shipping. We extended an invitation to the most important and influential ship owners for a fancy dinner in London. Much to our surprise and delight (but also as proof of the pull of the Warburg name), some fifty Greek shipping magnates accepted our invitation. It was a splendid evening. I can't say for sure that we changed many minds, or succeeded in putting pressure on the Greek government, but we certainly tried hard to weave the importance of Turkish EU membership—especially its importance to other EU members—into our dinner conversations. The Greek government, it turned out, eventually did not seek to block Turkey's candidacy.

Many roads lead to Rome. One of them leads through Turin, where an old friend of mine lived. Gianni Agnelli was the head of a family that controlled a good portion of Italy's industry through its ownership of the automobile giant FIAT in Turin. I called him up while I was vacationing in Switzerland and arranged to have lunch with him the following day in St. Moritz. In the course of a delicious lunch and a friendly conversation, I brought up the topic of Turkey, pointing out how much I liked Turkey, and how important I thought its membership in the European Union was. Could he explain to me why Foreign Minister Dini of Italy was opposed to Turkey's candidacy? Agnelli (whose sister Susanna had preceded Dini as Italy's foreign minister—ample proof of the importance of the Agnelli family) expressed his surprise and astonishment: "I can't believe that. We've got a 30-percent market share in Turkey . . ." I changed the subject, having made my point. At eight o'clock the next morning, my phone rang. It was Gianni Agnelli, telling me briefly and to the point that Foreign Minister Dini always was and still is in favor of Turkish EU membership. Agnelli—known throughout Italy as "*avvocato*," the fixer—had come through for me, or rather, for Turkey. It made my vacation.

Turkey's candidacy for membership in the European Union was formally accepted at the EU summit meeting in December 1999. Given the European Union's (never mind Turkey's) byzantine ways, this did not, however, mean that negotiations over the details of Turkey's membership began right away. Rather, Turkey was reminded that it needed to fulfill a range of criteria pertaining to democratic governance and market economy, as well as adapt to EU rules and regulations, before one could even think about entering into negotiations. The most complicating factors were Turkish control over Northern Cyprus and its treatment of the Kurdish minority. The important aspect of the 1999 decision, however, was that the European Union offered Turkey extensive help toward meeting its membership criteria. In that sense, it was a huge step forward. Ecevit, who lasted as prime minister until November 2002, and I agreed that we would stay alive until we could witness the accession of Turkey to the European Union. Since we were both nearing the age of eighty, our compact was an expression of optimism, both in regard to our life expectancies as well as the political processes of Turkey and the European Union.

Unfortunately, Ecevit's optimism turned out to be ill-founded, on both accounts. The European Union announced in 2002 that it would decide in December 2004 whether formal accession negotiations could begin. Turkey, in turn, made significant efforts to meet EU preconditions and requirements. In December 2004, the European Union declared itself satisfied with the progress of Turkey's reform efforts and set October 3, 2005, as the starting date for negotiations. That date was met, after some internal EU controversies over the desirability and conditions of moving ahead. Since then, the negotiations have moved along at a snail's pace—deliberately so, as the European Union made it clear in October 2005 that it would take at least ten to fifteen years before they could be concluded and that, until then, Turkey must complete the necessary reforms. Reacting to many concerns raised by individual member countries, the European Union also explicitly reserved the right to examine at the conclusion of the negotiations whether Turkish membership could, in fact, be tolerated by the Union, both politically and economically. Turkey's relations with the European Union have already followed a long and tortuous road. That road, unfortunately, will remain long and tortuous, with no clear end in sight.

Bülent Ecevit died in November 2006 after suffering a massive stroke a few months earlier. He was eighty-one years old (a few months older than I). His state funeral took place in Ankara on November 11. Chancellor Angela Merkel of the CDU, who had replaced Gerhard Schröder as a result of early elections in September 2005, which led to the formation of a second Grand Coalition, asked me to represent the German government at Ecevit's funeral. It gave me great personal satisfaction to do so, even though it was also an occasion that filled me with considerable sadness. As fate would have it, however, it also offered me an opportunity for yet another special mission.

My deep concerns over the lack of progress regarding Turkey's membership in the European Union had caused me to look for ways that might help speed up the process. One of the main stumbling blocks was the still unresolved Cyprus issue. As a result of heavy Greek pressure that amounted to political blackmail, Cyprus had been admitted to the European Union in May 2004 (Greece had threatened to veto EU membership of Eastern European countries unless the internationally recognized Greek part of Cyprus was admitted at the same time). That led to the curious result that formally all of Cyprus was now a member of the European Union, whose writ, however, extended only to the demarcation line between the two parts of Cyprus. The European Union was confident that this issue might be resolved with what came to be known as the Annan Plan (named after UN Secretary General Kofi Annan), which proposed a loose confederation between the Greek and Turkish parts of Cyprus. The Annan Plan was put to a referendum in both parts of Cyprus just a week before Cyprus joined the European Union. Much to everyone's surprise, the Turkish Cypriots voted for it, while the Greek Cypriots—who knew that they would become EU members regardless of the outcome of the referendum—rejected it. The European Union, to put it bluntly, had been duped by the Greeks. Turkey, in turn, was not too happy about this turn of events. Even though Cyprus was now a member of the European Union, Turkey refused to include Cyprus in its custom union arrangements with the European Union (for instance, by not permitting Greek Cypriot ships to sail into Turkish ports). The European Union, not surprisingly, interpreted that Turkish refusal as a serious violation of the conditions it had laid down. Things did not look good.

I thought I might be able to play a mediating role between the Greeks and Turks in order to help resolve the issue. I was going to do this entirely on my own, though I kept the German Foreign Office informed and received some support in return. After delving into the history of the Cyprus conflict and informing myself about the realities on the ground, I was just about set to begin my mediation efforts when Ecevit died. The state funeral—however sad an occasion it was otherwise—all of a sudden appeared to present an excellent, if totally unexpected, opportunity to approach some of the main players and to plead my case.

But then another issue intervened. In April 2005, German Cardinal Joseph Ratzinger had been elected Pope. Benedict XVI was eager to present himself to his flock, and to the world. The Vatican arranged for him to visit Turkey in late November 2006—obviously a highly important visit by the head of the Catholic Church to Islamic Turkey. This put the Turkish prime minister on the spot. Recep Tayyip Erdoğan had become prime minister in March 2003 after a career in politics that had seen him as a highly successful mayor of Istanbul, but also seen him in jail a few months for allegedly inciting "religious hatred" with his outspoken Islamist sympathies. Erdoğan was, in fact, skirting Turkey's rigidly secular restrictions on Islamic political activities. Yet he was also a firm supporter of Turkey's membership in the European Union. Caught between his Islamist convictions and his political interests, Erdoğan let it be known that prior commitments—namely, attending a NATO summit meeting in Riga—would not allow him to meet with the Pope. The prime minister absenting himself from a meeting with the Pope, who is also the head of state of the Vatican, was widely interpreted as a highly unfortunate symbolic gesture with grave political consequences.

The Ecevit funeral took place less than three weeks before Pope Benedict was scheduled to arrive in Ankara. As I was representing the government of Germany, I had the good fortune to be placed right next to Prime Minister Erdoğan during the ceremonies. We struck up an easy relationship, though the funeral did not allow the time and was not the proper place for more serious political exchanges; however, the prime minister invited me for dinner that evening. Now I had a choice to make: bring up the Cyprus issue or weigh in on behalf of the Pope (with whom I had no prior or later contact). For that matter, should I be a respectful guest and abstain from any political interference at all? I decided that the Pope's visit was too important an issue not to raise. When the chance presented itself, I told Erdoğan as diplomatically but also as firmly as I could that he really ought to meet with Pope Benedict. The prime minister took refuge to the argument that he was committed to attending the NATO meeting in Riga. I replied, with all due respect, that surely he could miss NATO—and NATO him—for half a day or so. Not to receive a German Pope would send a spectacularly bad message to the German people; worse, it would also create precisely the wrong impression for the Turkish people. At a time when Turkey's membership in the European Union was critically at stake, the prime minister of Turkey simply could not afford the symbolism of refusing to meet with a German Pope on his first visit to Turkey. Erdoğan seemed impressed by my passionate plea and promised to think it over.

The following morning, I flew to Istanbul where I met with Foreign Minister Abdullah Gül (who became president in August 2007). Much to my surprise and satisfaction, Gül informed me that Erdoğan would indeed meet with Pope Benedict upon his arrival in Ankara. For once I was pleasantly surprised about the speedy coordination between the prime minister and his foreign minister. A potentially bad situation had been averted. When Erdoğan and Pope Benedict met immediately upon the Pope's arrival in Turkey, the Pope told him that he fully supported Turkey's membership in the European Union. This was an important statement, since some of the reluctance to admit Turkey to the European Union was (and is) based on the argument that a Muslim country has no place in a Christian Europe. The Pope's visit to Turkey—which turned into an unanticipated triumph—helped to defuse that argument.

Turkey has a long way to go before it will become a full member of the European Union. I am afraid that I, like my friend Bülent Ecevit, will not live long enough to see it happen. Some of the stumbling blocks remain (not least the Cyprus issue, to which I did not return). But I have high hopes that it will happen eventually. In the meantime, I take a good deal of pride and satisfaction in my contributions to making that road a little bit less rocky and tortuous.

Turkey was as close to the Middle East as I ever wanted to get. I was, of course, generally interested in Middle Eastern affairs and had traveled there on a few occasions, but both in terms of business and political interests, I never really got involved. My priorities were focused elsewhere. The special problems of the Middle East—at the heart of which are, of course, Israel and its relations with its Arab neighbors—require much more intensive background knowledge and constant efforts to stay informed and in touch than I was prepared to acquire and to expend. This made it all the more surprising that one of my special missions was to serve as a mediator between the Israeli government and Yasser Arafat, the undisputed leader of the Palestinian liberation movement.

It began with the sudden death of Franz Josef Strauss, minister-president of Bavaria, while he was on a hunting excursion in the Bavarian forests on October 3, 1988. I was abroad at the time, but hurried back to attend his funeral on October 7. I owed that much to a person whom I never considered a friend or a political ally, but who had done much to shape post-war Germany in his towering, if always controversial, political figure. Besides, I had once served as his "shadow" foreign minister when he ran, unsuccessfully, for chancellor in 1980. His funeral brought together luminaries from around the world who testified to his importance and to the broad swath he had cut in his dealings with world leaders. Strauss had never fulfilled his burning political ambitions, but he left behind a legacy of considerable achievements.

The day after the funeral, I happened to meet with Dieter Holzer, a businessman of wide and varied interests and connections. Holzer had long been a member of Strauss's inner circle and had probably been involved in any number of intrigues and shady dealings (which eventually caught up with him when he was convicted for helping another member of that circle—who had been indicted for corruption in office—escape from German justice). Holzer's main business dealings were in the Arab world. His wife, from one of Lebanon's more prominent families, played a leading role in his efforts there. In the course of our conversation that day, Holzer told me that Strauss had been in the process of arranging a meeting with Yasser Arafat, the purpose of which was to seek an end to the violent Palestinian uprising against the Israeli occupation regime—the (first) Intifada that had erupted spontaneously the year before.

I am not quite sure who got the ball rolling in this effort to bring about some kind of understanding between the Israeli government and the Palestinian leadership in order to end an uprising that was proving costly to both sides. Holzer had his connections in the Arab world. Strauss, in turn, was close to Shimon Peres. The two had been working together ever since they were the political rising stars in their countries in the 1950s. Strauss, as defense minister, had been instrumental in arranging for the highly secret transfer of arms to the beleaguered Israel. His counterpart was Shimon Peres, then still in his twenties, who served as director general in the Israeli defense ministry, in charge of weapons acquisition. Even though they represented different political orientations—Peres was a social democrat—they formed a close bond that lasted through the ups and downs of both of their political careers. He and fellow Social Democrat Yitzhak Rabin vied for the leadership of their party (which over the years presented itself in different guises). Rabin was first in making it to the position of prime minister, in 1974. After Rabin was forced to resign in the wake of a scandal, Peres became leader of their party, but failed to win in a series of elections. In 1984, he again lost narrowly. However, in a unique version of Israeli grand-coalition building, the two leading (and opposing) parties agreed to a power-sharing arrangement where Peres would serve half of the term as prime minister and then step back to become foreign minister while Yitzhak Shamir (of the rightist Likud Party) took over the prime minister's office. The next round of elections was scheduled for November 1, 1988. Peres was now foreign minister, and had every interest in winning these elections against the Likud party (while prevailing over his rival Rabin). To achieve that goal, however, he needed all the help he could get.

Arafat was in a position to provide such help. If he could persuade the large number of Arab-Israeli citizens to vote for the Social Democrats, Peres just might be able to prevail. The two leaders could then go ahead to work out the details of some Israeli-Palestinian reconciliation scheme. That, of course, was Arafat's primary motive: to advance the cause of the Palestinians and to achieve the establishment of a separate Palestinian state. But he also had short-term goals. The Intifada threatened Arafat's leadership and the Palestine Liberation Organization's (PLO) control of the Palestinian resistance movement. If he could succeed in dampening the Intifada (with Israel's help), he would protect his and the PLO's primacy among the Palestinians. It was this convergence of interests that led to the idea of trying to seek an Arafat-Peres understanding. The problem was, however, that Peres and Arafat, for legal and political reasons, could not negotiate directly with each other. Some intermediary was required. Franz Josef Strauss had offered to play that role, but now he was dead. Time was running out, as a deal had to be struck before the November 1 elections. So Holzer approached me: would I be willing to serve as a mediator between Peres and Arafat? I immediately agreed—this was the kind of challenge that I simply could not turn down, for its importance as well as for its excitement. However, I needed to make sure that the two sides were, in fact, willing to engage in such an effort and prepared to carry out any resulting agreements—and, of course, agreeable to my playing a role originally envisaged by, and for, Franz Josef Strauss.

Holzer and I sprang into action. First we arranged a meeting with the Israeli ambassador in Bonn. He agreed to see me for breakfast on October 13 in his heavily guarded residence. Ben Ari had been born in Vienna and retained much of that city's cultured openness and easygoing charm. Yet he was also an extremely perspicacious person and thus a highly effective ambassador; behind his charm was hidden a steely determination to do whatever was best for his country. I put him in a difficult position. The suggestion that Peres and Arafat try to seek some kind of arrangement seemed news to him, though I assumed that Strauss had been in touch with his friend Peres about it. He now had to weigh whether to get involved in a conspiracy of sorts with his foreign minister, while keeping his prime minister out of the loop (who stood to lose if the conspiracy was successful). I had little doubt that Ben Ari would successfully navigate these treacherous political waters. He promised that he would see what he could do.

Ben Ari did well. Four days later he came to see me while I was in the middle of a CDU presidium meeting. We both acted as if it was entirely normal that an Israeli ambassador would call a member of the presidium out of a meeting for a private consultation. We retired to a quiet corner, where Ben Ari told me about the results of his talks with Foreign Minister Peres. Peres, I was informed, would indeed be most grateful if I were to confer with Arafat—without letting anybody else know, of course, that Peres was in any way involved. Arafat should be told that Peres was asking for an end to Intifada violence; that such a cessation could conceivably help him in his election bid, and that, once elected, he might be in a better position to conduct further negotiations. I was now set for my special mission.

The meeting with Arafat was arranged for October 21, 1988, to take place in Holzer's vacation home in the Austrian Alps. I had originally agreed to participate in an important conference in Toronto beginning on that day. In order to protect the secrecy of my mission, I did not cancel my participation in Toronto entirely, but I did book a Concorde flight from London to New York (with a connecting flight to Toronto) for the following day. I explained this slight change in my travel plans with a special mission to Turkey that had unexpectedly become necessary. It wasn't a total lie. . . .

On Friday, October 21, I flew to Zurich, where I was taken to the Holzer home in Vorarlberg in a limousine provided by The Dolder Grand. Mrs. Holzer received me warmly and told me Arafat would arrive shortly. Dieter Holzer was to meet the PLO leader—who was traveling in his own private jet—at the airport in Innsbruck, where he would bring him to his home. But Arafat kept all of us waiting. Around six o'clock that evening, Holzer called from the airport to inform us that Arafat had changed his travel plans: instead of coming to Austria he was now on his way to Morocco for an urgent meeting with King Hassan, who wanted to confer with the Palestinian leader about an upcoming Arab League summit meeting. (Since Arafat was extremely security conscious and never even slept in the same bed on consecutive nights, I suspect that this change of plans had less to do with the Moroccan King and more with his usual security precautions.) Holzer urged me to agree to a meeting with Arafat later that night in Rabat. Holzer's own jet would take us there from the nearest airfield, Friedrichshafen on Lake Constance. So The Dolder limousine rushed Mrs. Holzer and me to Friedrichshafen, where the jet was already waiting for us, with Dieter Holzer and a PLO representative from Athens on board. We immediately took off for a three-hour flight to the Moroccan capital, enjoying dinner on board and then a quite spectacular view of northern Africa on a moonlit night.

On the way to Rabat, the PLO representative explained the situation to us. The PLO wanted to make use of the special conditions that had arisen after a year of Intifada, with a growing interest on both sides to bring the escalating violence to an end. The recent improvement in East-West relations seemed to offer a chance for a settlement of the Arab-Israeli conflict. The upcoming elections in Israel held out the prospect of a change in government that might lead to an Israeli willingness to negotiate such a settlement. Conversely, if Yitzhak Shamir were to win, Israeli recalcitrance might only get worse. In this situation the PLO, together with other Arab states, was considering an appeal to the voters of Israel (that is, to its Arab voters) to support the forces of peace in Israel, presumably represented by Peres. Arafat was eager to hear how Peres might react to such an opening.

But when we arrived in Rabat, Arafat was not there. We were instructed to continue on to Fes, where Arafat was (allegedly) preparing himself for the meeting with King Hassan. We jetted on to Fes, another half hour of flight, where a convoy of cars whisked us to a secluded hotel. Finally, around midnight, I got to meet the legendary and controversial leader of the Palestinians. He displayed little of the ferocious image he usually cultivated in public (such as addressing the UN General Assembly with a sidearm strapped to his waist). Instead, he talked at length—and it was mostly he who talked—in a quiet voice, relying mostly on his halting English, but resorting occasionally to interpretation help provided by either his PLO representative or Mrs. Holzer, about his personal life, his struggles on behalf of the Palestinian people, and his political dreams for them. I found Arafat to be personally unassuming and was quite taken in by him. I was well-aware of his terrorist background, his poor public image, and the many rumors about the corruption surrounding him. But as I listened to him, I began to understand how and why he had risen to be the leader of the Palestinian people.

Then we got down to specifics. I conveyed the message Shimon Peres had asked me to deliver, which boiled down to the quid pro quo of a halt in the Intifada for future negotiations—provided Peres was in a position of power to conduct such negotiations. I was not authorized to offer more; I was playing the role of a mediator, not a negotiator. Arafat's reply was more detailed. He admitted (or made the argument as a bargaining ploy) that his leadership position was in danger, as the Intifada threatened to spiral out of control and brought more radical elements to the forefront. If there was an interest in Israel in seeking a negotiated solution to the conflict, then Israel should deal with him, the more moderate Palestinian leader, thereby helping him to stay in power. In fact, he would appreciate any support, including especially that of the German government, which is why he had agreed to meet with Strauss and now me.

Arafat's long-term goal was to convene an international conference where the Israeli-Palestinian issues could be resolved. He declared his willingness to fully recognize UN General Assembly Resolution 181 of 1947 and UN Security Council Resolution 242 of 1967 in order for such a conference to become possible. Palestinian refusal to accept these resolutions, which implied recognition of Israel as a legitimate state living within secure borders, had so far been a major obstacle to any Israeli-Palestinian agreement. In turn, however, he insisted that Israel abide by the provisions of these resolutions, which called for "withdrawal of Israeli armed forces from territories occupied in the recent conflict," a "just settlement of the refugee problem," and the establishment of a homeland for the Palestinians. While resolution 242 had deliberately left the all-important details open (Must Israel withdraw from all territories it had occupied? Should refugees be allowed to settle in their former homes in Israel? What should be the boundaries of a Palestinian homeland?), an agreement to begin negotiations over them would have meant a significant first step forward. In that sense Arafat was offering a major concession. He also indicated that he would try to stop any violent Palestinian reactions to the Israeli use of force until the Israeli elections, which amounted to a one-sided cease-fire promise. Finally, he offered to issue an appeal to Arab-Israeli citizens to vote for peace-loving parties. All Arafat expected in return was a willingness on the Israeli side to enter into negotiations with him after the elections.

By three o'clock in the morning, our conversation had come to an end. I expressed my gratitude to the PLO leader for having received me and promised that I would convey his remarks promptly and accurately. Then Arafat called in a photographer, which made me none too happy, as I was afraid that any picture-taking might compromise the utter confidentiality of our meeting. The picture shows me, arms crossed defensively, sitting on a couch listening to Arafat; it reflects my dismay over the photographer's presence, not my feelings toward Arafat. I finally got to go to bed, dead tired after an exceedingly long day, but satisfied with the outcome of our conversation.

Two hours of sleep was all I got that night in Fes. I was up again at five o'clock, and back in the air by seven, as the sun was rising spectacularly over the Atlas Mountains. While in the air, Ambassador Ben Ari reached me by radio phone to inquire (as circumspectly as possible under the circumstances) about the outcome of my mission. He also told me that Hezbollah had exploded a car bomb that morning in South Lebanon, with Israelis among the victims. He asked me to report that the PLO was not involved, and that Israeli retaliation strikes should not target the PLO. It was a grim reminder of the situation's fragile and explosive status.

We were headed for London when word reached us that the Concorde flight from London to New York would be delayed, making it impossible for me to get to Toronto in time. Instead, I secured a seat on the Air France Concorde flight from Paris instead. I finally made it to Toronto, without some of my luggage, which had been stranded in London. It seemed a fitting end to an extraordinary excursion into the turbulent waters of the Middle East conflict.

Given the convoluted nature of the Israeli-Palestinian conflict and the "peace process" designed to bring it to an end, it is not easy to assess whether the effort started by Strauss and concluded by me yielded any results. The course of events, however, suggests that it may at least have been helpful, if not indeed the decisive beginning of a process that eventually led to considerable progress. Arafat did try to dampen the Intifada before the November 1, 1988, elections in Israel (for which, of course, Peres could not publicly claim any credit). Peres narrowly lost by 1.1 percent and lacked two seats to form a government of his own. He agreed to enter into another "national unity" government with the Likud, ceding the position of prime minister for the entire period to Shamir; Peres took on the positions of vice premier and finance minister when the new government began its work on December 22. He was now out of the foreign policy loop. In the meantime, however, Arafat had gone through the symbolic motions of declaring an independent state of Palestine. Of far more importance was Arafat's acknowledgment of Israel's right to exist when, on December 13, he announced that the PLO accepted UN Security Council Resolution 242. He also repudiated terrorism "in all its forms." Arafat appeared to stick to his "quid," even though Peres seemed in no position to offer a "quo."

But behind the scenes, Peres worked hard to fulfill his end of the bargain. In early 1990, the American Secretary of State James Baker suggested that the Israeli government begin negotiations with a delegation of deported Palestinians (though not with Arafat himself). Judging from my own experience with secret background talks, I can only assume that Baker's initiative had met with the prior approval of Peres, for the vice premier demanded that the prime minister accept the Baker proposal, threatening to leave the government should Shamir refuse. Under pressure from his party, Shamir did refuse. Peres then tried to engineer a change of government that would have put him at the top of a government made up of a number of leftist splinter parties and ultraorthodox parties. That effort failed and became known as the "dirty trick" because of its seemingly corrupt machinations. In June 1990, Shamir formed a cabinet made up of rightist forces. Politically speaking, Peres was not only out of the loop, but also out in the cold. In 1992, his party deposed him as its leader, choosing Yitzhak Rabin instead, who then went on to win the elections and become prime minister. That put Peres back into a position of power, as Rabin was magnanimous enough to make Peres Israel's foreign minister once again.

In the meantime, the idea of an international conference dealing with Middle Eastern issues had come to fruition, made possible not least by the end of the Cold War and the outcome of the 1991 Gulf War. The United States and the Soviet Union jointly invited Israel and a number of Arab countries to a conference in Madrid in October 1991. Though they were not members of the PLO leadership, Palestinian delegates were officially part of the Jordanian delegation. The purpose of the conference was to serve as an opening for a series of bilateral and multilateral negotiations. In that regard, the Madrid Conference proved to be a disappointment as little progress was achieved in those channels. Informally, however, the groundwork was laid in Madrid for one of the major advances in the peace process—the Oslo Accords. It was in the context of Madrid Conference follow-up meetings a year later, in December 1992 during a negotiating session held in London, that a Norwegian Middle Eastern expert and the Israeli vice minister of foreign affairs brought together a PLO representative and an Israeli history professor. That initial meeting, arranged so as to see if they could develop some common ground, blossomed into a series of intense and highly secret follow-up meetings held at a research institute in Oslo. Eventually, the Norwegian foreign minister, Johan Holst, and the Israeli foreign minister, Shimon Peres, got involved. The result was an agreement, which at its core established Palestinian self-rule (under PLO leadership) and provided recognition by the PLO of Israel as a legitimate state. In September 1993, Prime Minister Rabin and Yasser Arafat formally signed the agreement on the lawn of the White House in Washington. One year later, Arafat, Peres, and Rabin were awarded the Nobel Peace Prize for this historic achievement.

In essence, the Oslo Accords fulfilled the bargain outlined that night in Fez. I can only claim that I was present at the creation, not that I created it—if, that is, Fez was indeed the first step on the way to Oslo. Perhaps Israelis and the Palestinians would have reached some such agreement without our initial efforts; they certainly should have. But it seems to me that what transpired between Arafat and Peres in the run-up to the 1988 elections in Israel helped pave the way, as it established a minimum of trust and understanding between the two leaders. Full credit belongs to Franz Josef Strauss and Dieter Holzer, who saw—or were offered—an opportunity and made the best of it. Strauss's untimely death brought me into play on short notice for yet another special mission. I am glad that I was able to be of help. And I fervently hope that all of the unfulfilled and sometimes broken promises of the Oslo Accords will yet be met—the sooner the better, for all concerned.

# Chapter 6

## Business, Politics, and Personalities

My adult life began in the world of business, as a salesman of cars and car insurance to American GIs in post-war Germany. I achieved success and prosperity in the insurance business as managing partner of an insurance brokerage firm. That allowed me to enter the world of politics in middle age, at which time I experienced the ups and downs described in previous chapters. Politics also introduced me to the world of big-time business, where I discovered—and practiced—business politics. Along the way, I dealt with some fascinating personalities, as colorful in their characters as they were outsized in their influence. Most of my experiences had to do with the automobile industry, taking me from Wolfsburg in Lower Saxony to Changchun in China and then to Detroit, Michigan, with an important intermediate step in London. It was quite a journey.

The story actually begins in Wilhelmshaven and has its start with the chemical industry. In 1976, I had become finance minister and economics minister in the government of Lower Saxony. One of my tasks in those positions was to secure business investments in a state that desperately needed new industries to provide additional jobs. Wilhelmshaven, on the North Sea coast, had traditionally been a naval port—its very name deriving from the German emperor who sought to establish Germany as a naval power. After World War II, Wilhelmshaven no longer hosted major naval installations, as the Federal Republic's navy had been dramatically downsized. In an effort to attract other business, Lower Saxony initiated a program of developing Wilhelmshaven as a deep-sea port, second only to Rotterdam in terms of capacity. When I arrived in Hanover, that project had reached completion; now Wilhelmshaven needed industry to make use of the port's capacities.

It was well-known in business circles at the time that Great Britain's industrial giant ICI—Imperial Chemical Industries—was considering building a huge new chemical plant for its rapidly expanding plastics business. So I got in touch with ICI to see whether it might be lured to Wilhelmshaven. That's when I first met Sir John Harvey-Jones, then ICI's territorial director for Continental Western Europe and soon thereafter (1978) its deputy chairman. I quickly realized that we had lucked out. Harvey-Jones was an extraordinarily colorful figure (even literally: he was famous for his outrageously colorful ties that earned him the "Great Britons' Tie Award" of the Guild of British Tiemakers). A student at the Royal Naval College in Dartmouth, he entered naval service in 1940 at the age of sixteen and saw immediate combat duty. After two destroyers he served on were sunk in the Mediterranean, he decided to become a hunter rather than be hunted and joined the submarine force. After the war, the Royal Navy sent him to Cambridge University for half a year of German and Russian studies, destined for a career in intelligence. Soon thereafter he was sent to Germany, mostly to run secret patrol boat missions in the Baltic to spy on the Russians, but partly also to oversee the dismantling of the port facilities in Wilhelmshaven by German and Russian workers for shipment to Russia. One can only imagine how difficult a job it must have been for a twenty-two-year-old British naval officer to supervise the destruction of a port that deprived German workers of their long-term employment and enabled Russia to take home some heavy-duty loot and thus increase its economic and military power. Harvey-Jones stayed in the Royal Navy until family circumstances (his daughter had come down with polio) forced him to look for civilian employment that allowed him more family time. He joined ICI as a junior training manager in 1956 and rapidly worked his way up into leading management positions, even though he was neither a chemist by training nor had he earned any university degree. Along the way, he gained a reputation as a troubleshooter; in later years, he became well-known to a larger public as host of a BBC television show called "Troubleshooter."

Harvey-Jones and I hit it off immediately. We obviously had a lot in common: he the teenaged naval war fighter and I who had so desperately wanted to be one (following the examples of my two brothers, both submariners, one killed in action when his submarine disappeared in the Atlantic off Newfoundland). He had spent his boyhood years with his parents in India, I with mine in Turkey. He had built up ICI as a giant in the chemical industry; my grandparents, as well as my father-in-law, had been leaders in the German chemical industry. Then there was the fact that he was quite familiar with northern Germany in general, and with Wilhelmshaven in particular. Harvey-Jones may well have felt a sense of responsibility and remorse over what had happened to Wilhelmshaven after the war under his supervision. He was, in any case, familiar with the location and immediately taken by the prospect of ICI building a chemical plant there. We quickly reached an agreement that eventually saw the investment of more than DM 1 billion by ICI in Wilhelmshaven. Getting ICI to Wilhelmshaven was one of my major successes as a member of the Lower Saxony government; it also was the beginning of a lifelong friendship with Sir John Harvey-Jones.

Harvey-Jones became chief executive officer and chairman of the board of directors of ICI in April 1982. He immediately asked me whether I would like to join the ICI board as a nonexecutive director—its first foreign member (well, sort of: I do have dual German and British citizenship). Even though I was at that point still hoping to become mayor of Hamburg (which never came to fruition), I was delighted to accept that invitation. I joined ICI's board in July 1982, and I remained a member until 1993 (beginning in 1985, I also served as chairman of the supervisory board of Deutsche ICI). Harvey-Jones retired from ICI in 1987, at the height of ICI's economic success—evident in the fact that ICI became the first British firm to make an annual profit of more than £1 billion. In later years, following the fashion of the times that emphasized maximizing short-term shareholder value, ICI began to pursue a different business model. In 1993, for instance, it spun off its highly successful pharmaceutical and agrochemical businesses when it formed ZENECA (from 1993 until 1998 I served as chairman of the supervisory board of ZENECA's German affiliate). Thereafter, ICI fell on hard times, mainly because it accumulated too much debt in the acquisition of eventually unprofitable businesses, until it was finally taken over by the Dutch chemical giant Akzo Nobel in January 2008—two days before Harvey-Jones died after a long illness.

I owe Harvey-Jones and ICI a lot. Not only did they introduce me to the world of big international business and thus open new doors for me, but they also brought me back in touch with the country of my father's birth. I learned to appreciate the British way of doing business, just as I came to appreciate British life and culture. Unlike German supervisory boards, ICI's board was actively involved in major decision-making processes. That brought me to London on a regular basis, and often for days on end. Through ICI's board activities, I made many new friends and acquaintances whose help proved critical on certain occasions in my other political and business pursuits.

I suppose it stands to reason that my service on the board of ICI eventually qualified me to become a Commander of the British Empire (CBE). No doubt due to Harvey-Jones' influence—who in 1985 was made a Knight Bachelor and was known thereafter as Sir John—I was offered membership in the Most Excellent Order of the British Empire with the rank of Commander, which, alas, did not make me a knight and therefore does not allow me to be called Sir. I proudly accepted the offer and gladly went through the pomp and circumstance affiliated with the occasion. I was given a choice for the formal induction ceremony: come to Buckingham Palace, where I would be joined by many others as Her Majesty the Queen performed a mass ceremony, or accept an invitation by Her Majesty's ambassador in Bonn for a far more intimate event that would include my family and friends of my choosing. Of course, I opted for the latter. It was indeed a memorable occasion, the high point of which came when the Ambassador Sir Nigel Broomfield, decked out in full regalia, touched me, kneeling in front of him, on my shoulders with his ceremonial sword and declared me to be a Commander of the British Empire. Family and other guests were duly impressed.

All members of the Most Excellent Order of the British Empire—of which there are five classes, the CBE being the middle one—are occasionally invited to a formal gathering in St. Paul's Cathedral in London, hosted by the Order's Grand Master, Prince Philip, Duke of Edinburgh (and husband of Queen Elizabeth, who is the Order's Sovereign). It is a festive event and one of the few occasions when members get to wear the full splendor of their Order attire. After one such event, I returned to my hotel and ran into one of the best-known people on the planet at the time, Larry Hagman, a.k.a. J. R. Ewing, star of the TV series *Dallas*. Hagman, on seeing me in my sartorial splendor, did a double take (as did I, facing one of the most nefarious characters in TV land). "What is this?" he wanted to know, so I explained that I had just come from a meeting of the Order of the British Empire. "What does one have to do to become a member?" "Well," I told him, "you must serve the British empire." Even though Queen Elizabeth was reputed to be a devoted *Dallas* watcher, I doubt that Hagman ever fulfilled the qualifications for serving the British empire to become a Commander of it.

I had the pleasure of meeting Queen Elizabeth and Prince Philip on a number of occasions, mostly in the course of state visits to Germany. The Queen, who is three months younger than I, has always struck me as an extremely gracious person who would make a point of recognizing me in the usually large crowd of people waiting to greet her and say "how nice to see you again." In smaller settings, she would inquire about political issues of the day, displaying a broad range of interests and knowledge. She always impressed me. Prince Philip I got to know as his usual self, well-aware of his role as the Queen's consort, but also taking a certain degree of delight in being brusque and contrary. The first time we met was at a small gathering, where champagne was being offered. "You shouldn't drink champagne," he told me as I approached him for some small talk, "it's not good for you." I was taken aback and inquired as to what kind of drink I should prefer. "Gin, of course," was his succinct reply. It was advice I did not take to heart.

The royal family's great tragedy was, of course, Princess Diana, the beautiful (first) wife of Prince Charles, heir to the throne. Prince Charles' fate of having to wait out his mother's seemingly endless reign is not without its own tragic elements. The few times I met him, he seemed nice enough, but without much self-assurance, as if living in the shadow of his mother took too much out of him. Perhaps he was trying to escape that shadow when he married Lady Di, but the subsequent worldwide adoration of Princess Diana must have imposed yet another shadow on him—a shadow from which neither he nor his wife could ultimately escape.

I met Princess Diana only once, but it remains an unforgettable event. The German ambassador in London had invited a group of about thirty guests for a candlelight dinner, with Prince Charles and his wife as the guests of honor. Ambassador Rüdiger von Wechmar, a good friend of mine going back to the days when we jointly fought for *Ostpolitik* (Wechmar was then Chancellor Brandt's press spokesperson), had struck up a good relationship with the young royal couple. Now he honored me by seating me next to Princess Diana. I was overwhelmed by two things: her incredibly deep eyes and her stunning figure. So here I was, a (relatively) old man—I was just over sixty at the time—and a beautiful young woman in an exalted position, possibly the best-known and most admired woman in the world. I normally have no difficulty striking up a conversation in situations like these, but with Princess Diana I had a most difficult time. Her replies to the subjects I raised were nearly monosyllabic, from political issues (which she showed little inclination to discuss) to people both of us might know (yes, she knew my old friend Moritz, pretender to the Italian throne, because he was a frequent guest of the royal family). She ventured some observations about Germany that were nothing but banal. At one point she asked whether I had children. Told that I did indeed, she asked whether I was not worried about the kind of world our children would inherit, but she had no interest in pursuing that subject any further. I was beginning to resign myself to the prospect of a long and dreary dinner.

Then somehow the topic of cars came up. What kind of car do I drive? she wanted to know. A Porsche, I told her. All of a sudden her eyes lit up: "Really? A Porsche? That's my dream car!" She got excited, wanting to know what it was like to drive a Porsche. Our conversation became even more lively when I mentioned that I also rode a BMW motorcycle whenever I had a chance. Was it difficult, she wanted to know? No, I replied, but quite dangerous. Two speed aficionados had discovered something to talk about. The rest of the evening was thoroughly delightful. Princess Diana shed her usual reserve and opened up to me. She admitted that she absolutely loved fast cars, but for safety and security reasons was rarely allowed to drive herself, and never fast. The idea of riding a motorcycle intrigued her even more; she was fascinated by the exhilaration and feeling of freedom that driving a fast car or motorbike provides, at least as I described it. Here I was, the old man doing something that she, the thoroughly modern young woman, could only dream about. I was happy that I was able to help her dream a bit and lighten the load of her daily life, if only for a brief moment. Princess Diana was gracious enough to thank the ambassador afterward for providing her with such a charming dinner companion. "What in the world were you talking about?" Wechmar wanted to know. Oh, cars and motorbikes . . . I was deeply moved when, ten years later, Diana, Princess of Wales, now divorced and in frantic search of the happiness that had eluded her before, met a tragic early death in a high-speed automobile accident.

China has always been a country inviting extraordinary fascination as well as irrational fear. Back in the 1960s, when I entered German politics, then Chancellor Kiesinger had famously warned: "All I can say is: China, China, China." In the early 1970s, the United States, under President Nixon, opened relations with the mysterious Communist-ruled country. German politicians—Franz Josef Strauss prominently among them—began to pay visits to China and its dictatorial leaders, provoking much (intended) angst and anguish in Moscow, thereby putting Germany's relations with the Soviet Union at risk. It seemed like everybody of any importance was going to Beijing. But I had never been there, and that gap in my international travel experiences became an increasing source of frustration. Going to China became a must.

My luck changed in 1983. Bruno Heck, the head of the Konrad Adenauer Foundation, invited me to a symposium on Confucius. Heck himself was a profound student of Confucian philosophy. In the course of a visit to China, he had met a similarly interested Chinese politician who was deputy head of the party's Economic Planning Commission and a member of the Chinese Communist Party's leadership. Heck invited Ma Yi to Germany for a public discussion of the teachings of Confucius. It was there that I first met Ma Yi. Even though I am not a Confucianist, nor am I very familiar with his philosophy, Ma Yi and I took an instant liking to each other when we engaged in a spirited—though, because of interpretation requirements, somewhat limited—debate over dinner. Perhaps he also saw in me someone whose expertise in the world of business might be valuable to China—or at least to an economic planner like him—as China struggled to emerge from the disaster of the Cultural Revolution and sought to catch up with the industrialized world. In any case, he invited me on the spot to visit him in China and to tour China for a firsthand look at its development. A few weeks later, the Economic Planning Commission extended a formal and very official invitation for a lengthy stay in China, which I was happy to accept. Such invitations were still rare at the time, and therefore much treasured; tourist travel was not yet possible. The Konrad Adenauer Foundation helped with the details of my travel plans. My business partners—glad that I was finally back full-time after my excursion into the world of politics, which had ended with my electoral defeat in Hamburg—swallowed hard but finally agreed to raise no objections to another prolonged absence of their managing partner.

I decided to make my first trip to China a real adventure. Instead of flying I would go by train, via Siberia. Such a Trans-Siberian Railway trip had long been a dream of mine; now was the chance to make it come true. I invited my brother Jürgen to leave Brazil behind for a few weeks and join me for the adventure in the middle of winter, to which he readily agreed. We decided to fly to Moscow, buy most of the provisions we needed for the trip there (we did not want to rely on the on-board offerings, having heard that the Soviet-style dining car was dreadful), and then begin our six-day, 7,865-km trip on the Beijing Express.

After a memorable meeting in Moscow with Valentin Falin, the former ambassador to Bonn, who described the Reagan administration's secret plans to control the world and trigger the demise of the Soviet Union, Jürgen and I set off on the evening of February 28, 1984 for our adventure. It was an experience as impressive as it was strange. Fortified by our ample supply of French bread, cheese, and wine, we felt like we were in a cocoon as the snowy and icy Russian landscape rushed past our windows, interrupted only occasionally by gray and anonymous-looking cities. Every now and then the train would stop, allowing us to sample the Siberian cold and to inspect life on Russian station platforms. To us, Siberia lived up to its reputation, which was none too good—gulag and all. The train ride was fascinating, but we were glad to finally reach our destination.

Our Chinese hosts had asked us to be prepared for a formal reception at the Chinese border, where the railroad cars were reconfigured for normal-gauge tracks and the diesel engines replaced by steam engines. It was three o'clock in the morning when we stumbled off the train and were guided to a reception room for a meeting with three officials in Mao suits. It was the first time that I experienced that ritual of Chinese officialdom, where the guest of honor and his host are seated in oversized chairs (carefully protected by lace doilies) with a low table between them supporting a huge bouquet of flowers, behind which the translator can hide. We were formally welcomed to China, plied with tea, and given the astounding message that German unity achieved in peace and by self-determination had the full support of the Chinese people and the Chinese government. We were then brought back to the train to continue our journey to Beijing (and catch up on some missed sleep).

Late the next morning, we reached the outskirts of Beijing. There I had my first impressions of China: innumerable small houses, masses of people, then the first industrial plants and taller buildings. Everything looked poor and primitive, but much more orderly than in Russia. We rolled into the Beijing train station, where we were met by the German Ambassador Per Fischer (who gratefully pointed out that I was the first German official to arrive by train, thus sparing him the difficult ride to the airport). Also present was a representative of the Economic Planning Commission, who guided us outside and to a "Red Flag" official limousine that was reserved for our use while we were in Beijing. We went to our hotel, freshened up, and then proceeded to the German embassy for an introductory briefing. The main event that evening, however, was a carnival party at the embassy: it was Fat Tuesday, the high point of the carnival season (which Germans take very seriously). We did not escape having to put on disguises (like a bulbous nose) and willy-nilly joined the merriment, which included circus-style artistic performances and some pretty wild dancing. It was a surreal introduction to an equally surreal visit. Marco Polo might have appreciated it.

The following morning, the official part of our visit to China began. We were introduced to our travel guide, a professor at a Beijing university, who would serve as translator, facilitator, and general expert in everything Chinese. He became an invaluable and trusted companion, who fulfilled his official obligations flawlessly, but also offered us much background information and many insights over the course of countless hours spent on noisy trains and in crowded waiting lounges. We were valuable to him as well, as it turned out. By traveling with us, he was able to supplement his meager income as a professor, since intellectuals, he told us, were still suffering from the aftermath of the Cultural Revolution. He also took note of—and then conveyed to other officials—our impressions of China as an investment location and tourist destination. How could hotel service be improved? (Well, better bed linens might help, toilets should meet Western standards, and you really ought to train hotel service personnel before you let them loose on hotel guests.) At times I had the impression that we were useful guinea pigs of sorts: upper-class Westerners testing the adequacy of China's tourist infrastructure. I can't claim any credit, but I can testify to the fact that, over the next twenty-five years, China made tremendous progress. The "first-class" hotels of yesteryear that had left much to be desired have long been replaced by hotels of the highest international standards. The hotel on the top floors of the Jin Mao Tower in Shanghai, for example, (until 2007 the tallest building in China, surpassed only by a skyscraper built right next to it) is breathtaking in terms of luxury and location.

That China was on the verge of a truly great leap forward was evident to me as I traveled around the country in 1984. I saw many of the problems that would have to be overcome, especially the grinding poverty in the countryside and the massive inefficiencies in huge state-owned industries. In Wuhan, for instance, we toured what was originally a Russian-built steel plant that employed about 140,000 workers—more than half of whom, we were told, were poorly trained relicts of the Cultural Revolution who could not (yet) be laid off. It was there, too, that our hosts took us to the home of a worker's family—undoubtedly carefully selected—for a simple meal and an extended discussion of their situation. While some of it may have been staged, our overall impression still proved accurate: the Chinese people were eager to get on with their lives according to Deng Xiaoping's guiding motto: "Enrich yourselves!" We were impressed as much by their determination to doing it and get it right as by the dignity and pride with which we were received by these still very poor people.

What struck us on a personal level was reinforced at the official level. Throughout our trip we met with high-ranking officials who explained to us how China was planning to proceed. Above all, China wanted to avoid the mistakes made by other developing countries (and later by that constantly looming neighbor Russia): too much indebtedness in an effort to grow too fast. Ma Yi explained to us on that first morning in Beijing that China had internal debts of some $4 billion, an external debt of perhaps $3 billion, but foreign exchange reserves amounting to $17 billion. They were determined to keep it that way, and they did: by 2007, China held foreign exchange reserves of almost $2 trillion, with the United States as its biggest debtor.

One of the ways China intended to grow economically was to invite foreign investors. The Chinese leadership was well-aware that it could not go it alone; if nothing else, the miserable failures of the Great Leap Forward and the Cultural Revolution had taught it that much. Under no circumstances should these nightmares of Chinese history be repeated. But China, still smarting from a "hundred years of humiliation," also was determined to avoid any kind of reliance on foreign help that would lead to renewed subordination and further humiliation. It laid down two basic principles for achieving that goal. For one, foreign investments could only take place in the form of joint ventures, where the Chinese side retained ultimate control (and would be able to acquire the know-how for eventual independent production). Secondly, the sources of investment needed to be as diversified as possible; no single country should be the primary source. That point was emphasized time and again.

And I got it: it was one, if not the most important, reason why I was treated so graciously by my Chinese hosts. Japan and the United States, they explained, were poised to jump in and make use of investment opportunities. But China still had not reconciled itself with Japan and was reluctant to let Japan achieve now what it had almost achieved forty years earlier in the guise of a "Greater East Asia Co-Prosperity Sphere." America—where by now an ever-increasing number of students were sent to learn all about modern science, engineering, and government—would have been more welcome, except that the Chinese leadership was afraid of replacing the predominance of one superpower with that of another. Europe in general, and Germany in particular, appeared much less threatening and in many ways far more promising as an investment partner than the old enemy Japan and the ideological and looming military rival, the United States. The message to me was clear, if never expressed directly: your help in securing investments would be much appreciated.

As it happened, I was able to be of some help. Since my days as finance and economics minister in Lower Saxony, I had been a member of the Volkswagen supervisory board, first representing the state of Lower Saxony (still a major shareholder) and later the federal government (also a shareholder) and later shareholders at large. Ordinarily, supervisory board members do not play an active role in company affairs, and I had little intention of doing so. But in the case of Volkswagen, I had the lucky fortune of getting involved almost involuntarily.

Under the energetic leadership of my old friend Carl Horst Hahn, who, since his days as VW's head manager in North America, was determined to make VW a global player in the automobile business, Volkswagen in the early 1980s had begun to look to China in order to gain a foothold there. Prospects were not promising, as China was not prepared to allow direct investments, nor was there really a market for automobiles. Only officials were allowed to have cars, and the official cars, made in China, were of the "Red Flag" variety—modeled after Russian cars, which, in turn, were knockoffs of 1950s-style American cars. But as China was opening up, officials not only wanted better cars, but they also realized that a more modern society (and economy) required at least a taxi fleet in order to permit a minimum of personal mobility. Thus a demand for more and better cars arose, which could not be met by the few outmoded and outdated Chinese production facilities. Having been made aware of this shift in Chinese perspectives, Hahn succeeded in 1982 in reaching a general agreement with Shanghai Automotive Industry Corporation to form a joint venture—eventually known as Shanghai Volkswagen Automotive Corporation—for the production of what was then VW's biggest and most modern passenger car: the Santana.

When I came to Shanghai in March 1984 at the end of our China tour, I was eager to get a firsthand impression of VW's China project, with which I was, of course, broadly familiar from supervisory board presentations. A VW advance team happened to be in town in order to finalize the arrangements and determine the specific requirements for a joint venture production. I linked up with the VW team and thus had a chance to inspect the planned production facilities (which looked pretty dreadful) and meet some of the decision-makers on the Chinese side. Obviously these were representatives of the city of Shanghai, the Communist Party's leading figures there. They not only had de facto control of the city's industries, but they also determined just how many cars would be produced, and who would receive them. It was an instant and impressive lesson in the peculiar, often unsuccessful practices of a planned economy, which China was ultimately intent on overcoming. I got to know some of these powerful figures well and maintained close contact over the years.

Ultimately, the most important among them was Zhu Rongji, who served as a high-ranking member of the State Economic Commission in the 1980s. In that position, Zhu was intimately involved in the decision to have Volkswagen form a joint venture in Shanghai. From 1989 until 1991, he was a highly successful mayor of Shanghai, under whose leadership it developed into the ultra-modern city that we know today. Zhu's leadership qualities propelled him to the vice premiership and then, in 1998, to the position of premier of the State Council of the People's Republic of China. Throughout these years, I found him to be an exceedingly open and gracious interlocutor when I came to visit; he never hesitated to give me his frank assessments of Chinese developments. After the spring 1989 uprisings, which led to the Tiananmen Square massacre in Beijing on June 4, 1989, Zhu explained to me how the Shanghai leadership had avoided a similar bloodbath there. In Beijing, the political leadership looked primarily to military force for a resolution of the conflict, though it took a long time to find military units it could trust to put down the uprising, rather than join it. In Shanghai, the use of military force was rejected outright, against the preferences of local commanders. Instead, Zhu and other leaders went on the recently installed regional television network and called on workers loyal to the Communist Party to come to the city and remove the barriers put up by the protesters. This they did, with minimal bloodshed, thus averting a major crisis in Shanghai. Zhu readily admitted to me that China was—and is—engaged in an experiment of historic proportion and importance, trying to fundamentally change the world's largest country while seeking to hold it together in the face of severe centrifugal forces. He put the chances for success at fifty-fifty at best. Not least due to his own contributions, the Chinese experiment so far has proved to be highly successful.

In October 1984, Volkswagen (literally "people's car," a name that must have appealed to Communist Chinese sensitivities, though its Nazi Germany origins probably did not) succeeded in finalizing the deal with the Shanghai authorities. Production of the Santana began in 1985. It became the car of choice not only for Chinese officialdom and for many taxi fleets, but also for private car buyers once an automobile market was allowed to open up. It helped to establish Volkswagen as the by far largest foreign carmaker in China. Over the years, Volkswagen profited handsomely from its engagement in China, even though it was fully aware that eventually China would seek to build up its own automobile industry—on the basis of the know-how gained from its joint ventures—and compete with Volkswagen at home and abroad. Volkswagen and its suppliers actually had to build the entire infrastructure for an automobile industry, eventually to the delight of its competition many years later. Volkswagen's benefit: the VW investments were financed entirely out of cash flow, as VW just also confirmed for the years to come.

Not long after VW had agreed to its joint venture in China, I met with Dr. Shoichiro Toyoda, son of the founder of Toyota and the driving force behind Toyota's rise to automotive preeminence. Toyoda expressed his interest in what VW was up to in China, but told me flatly: "You are crazy." The Chinese, he explained, were only interested in exploiting Western companies and stealing their technologies—which is why they only allowed joint ventures. Toyota would not join most automobile manufacturers in the rush to China until the end of the twentieth century. Today, Toyota is producing cars in China as well, having been forced to admit that, despite all the obvious problems, there simply is no alternative to joint ventures Chinese-style, if their products are to be present on the Chinese market.

The Shanghai joint venture was only the beginning of VW's engagement in China. The second major step took place in the late 1980s, with some unintended help from me. I visited China in 1988. In the course of my usual round of talks with high-ranking officials, I learned that Chinese authorities were about to conclude yet another deal for a joint venture for automobile production. The candidate on the Chinese side was First Automobile Works (FAW) in Changchun in distant Manchuria. I had never heard of First Automobile Works, which turned out to be the world's largest manufacturer of trucks—with production facilities of breathtaking antiquity at the time, as I eventually saw firsthand. FAW was close to signing an agreement with the American carmaker Chrysler, famous for its jeeps, but the party bureaucrats in Beijing were not pleased with that proposal. For reasons I am not aware of (which I can only guess have to do with political issues at the time, or with fears of potential sanction pressures by the US government), they felt that a joint venture with Chrysler was not a good idea. So I was asked directly: would Volkswagen be interested in a second joint venture? If so, time was of the essence. The deal with Chrysler could not be postponed much longer. Apparently, Beijing's reach into Manchuria was not strong enough to prevent an FAW-Chrysler deal without presenting an alternative.

I agreed to explore the Chinese proposal, which I personally felt was an exciting one. I immediately contacted Carl Hahn, who agreed with my assessment and rushed himself with a small team to Changchun to see if FAW might be an appropriate partner for VW. The two sides quickly came to a preliminary understanding and initialed an agreement calling for the local assembly of Audi 100 car kits in the world's largest truck factory. The first Audi thus assembled rolled off the production line in August 1989. Soon thereafter, FAW expressed an interest in establishing an original production line that would produce VW cars from scratch. The VW supervisory board approved this expansion of VW's Chinese exposure in the course of its November 1990 meeting. In February 1991, FAW-Volkswagen Automotive Company was formally founded as a second effort by VW to increase its share of the Chinese automobile market, which all analysts agreed was about to take off like a rocket once private car purchases were officially allowed. FAW-VW was set to produce VW's smaller cars, thought to be ideal for middle-class consumers in China.

In a curious, indeed ironic, twist of fate, VW in its new venture in Changchun was able to make the best of a VW disaster. In the 1970s, VW had found itself under pressure in the American market. The Beetle had run its course; a new model was needed for American consumers. Currency fluctuations made business in the United States increasingly difficult. Protectionism loomed on the horizon, not least because of the inroads Japanese carmakers were making, which also threatened VW. Given these challenges, VW decided to open a production line for its highly successful Beetle successor car—the Golf—in the United States, and call it the VW Rabbit. Availing itself of a number of incentives offered by the state of Pennsylvania (worth almost $100 million), VW opened a plant in 1978 in Westmoreland County, in a facility originally built, but then abandoned, by Chrysler. But VW's engagement in the United States—which I had supported—turned out to be less than fortuitous. Labor problems caused constant interruptions and contributed to quality issues that would plague the Rabbit throughout its short run. American management, hired from Detroit, insisted that the US version of the Golf be adjusted to presumed American consumer preferences, particularly in regard to the softness of seats and suspension. That turned out to be a mistake, as American VW-lovers looked for a genuine European car and then turned away in disappointment when they were offered an American car. Carl Hahn, who had become VW's CEO in 1982, test-drove the Rabbit at one point and agreed with dissatisfied US drivers: "It felt like a Chevrolet," he complained. "If you want a Chevrolet, you should go to General Motors." The competition, especially from Japan, offered cars similar to the Rabbit at lower cost, better quality, and eventually with a more modern design. As Rabbit sales lagged and the Westmoreland plant produced far below capacity, VW finally decided to cut its losses—then about $120 million per year—and call an end to its US manufacturing venture. The last Rabbit rolled off the production line in July 1988.

But now VW had a complete and unproductive production line on its hands. That's where FAW-VW came to the rescue. As part of its deal with FAW, VW agreed to ship its entire Westmoreland plant to Changchun. A team of Chinese workers came to Pennsylvania to dismantle the production line and prepare it for shipment to Changchun. When I visited Changchun in the winter of 1991, I saw huge crates sitting out in the ice and snow, marked with the VW logo. How in the world could their contents ever be put together again? I wondered aloud. Not to worry, I was told, everything was perfectly packed and clearly marked for reassembly. And so it was. Before too long, the production line was up and running—and is still running today. Its installation and startup were greatly helped by Dr. Wenpo Lee, a German-trained engineer whom I eventually helped to become a German citizen. I had gotten to know him at VW in Germany, where he worked in engine development with a number of patents to his credit. As the FAW-VW deal was concluded, I mentioned to Carl Hahn that VW had in its employ a highly competent Chinese engineer who might be of help in Changchun. Lee readily and successfully took on the task of getting FAW-VW underway. He has since become a dear friend.

FAW-VW made rapid progress in manufacturing a broad range of VW products. An entirely new production line built in 2004 is now the most modern among all VW plants. It is here that some of the most advanced Audis—designed specifically for the Chinese market—are being produced. VW's engagement in China has not always been easy, not least because its cars are being produced by two competing joint ventures with separate marketing and service chains. Maintaining an element of central control has proved to be challenging. In addition, VW's partners have seen fit to take in competing carmakers in other joint ventures (such as Toyota in Changchun and General Motors in Shanghai), which raises obvious problems ranging from the protection of trade secrets to brand establishment and marketing priorities. In the meantime, Chinese competition has indeed strengthened. I saw firsthand how an energetic local politician—enamored of everything having to do with German car technology—was able to establish a modern car factory in 1997 and a few years later put out highly competitive cars with their own design (of somewhat dubious originality, however). Lee, who accompanied me on this visit, pointed out that the layout of the production line at Chery Automobiles in Wuhu looked exactly like the VW production line he had helped to install in Changchun fifteen years earlier. The competitive climate in China is rough. But VW, precisely because it had an early start, remains well-positioned to maintain a strong hold on the Chinese market that it helped define. The decisions made in the 1980s have served VW very well indeed.

Under the leadership of Winfried Vahland, executive vice president of Volkswagen Group, and president and CEO of Volkswagen (China) Investment Company from 2005 to 2010, China became the biggest market for VW in the world. After this great achievement Vahland is now the Chairman of the Board of Directors of Škoda Auto in the Czech Republic, a subsidiary of Volkswagen.

I remain impressed by the tremendous progress China has achieved ever since my first exposure in 1984 to this strange and fascinating country. I am well-aware of the political issues arising from the still-authoritarian Communist Party rule. Yet here, too, I have witnessed significant changes for the better over the years, which leave me optimistic that China will continue to master its incredible challenges reasonably well. I am convinced that economic progress is the best instrument for promoting democracy. As we have already seen in Taiwan and South Korea, China, too, will eventually embrace greater political freedom as economic liberties expand under the pressures of domestic growth and globalization. But the final outcome is unlikely to be a democracy along Western lines. China is too large, too tradition-bound, and too self-reliant simply to adopt Western approaches and models. Instead, China will develop a system based on a synthesis of Western-style freedom and traditional Chinese forms of hierarchical order.

Today, China can neither be ignored nor in any way isolated; it has become far too important and powerful for any such effort to succeed. In recognition of that fact, Atlantik-Brücke—an organization originally founded to promote better transatlantic relations—has initiated a program that seeks to involve Chinese and American counterparts in projects aimed at better trilateral understanding and cooperation. As Atlantik-Brücke's chairman from 1984 to 2000, and since 2004 as honorary chairman, I am proud that I have been able to play a leading role in these efforts, where I can call on the many friends and acquaintances

I have made over the years and rely on personal relations long established. I can hardly think of a more important task.

Of course, the personal friends and acquaintances I have in China are all to be found among the economic and political elites, from Ma Yi and Zhu Rongji to plant managers and government officials. But there is one very important exception: Lotus Flower. I first met Xuelian when she was four years old. I was in Beijing, on my way from the German embassy to a fancy dinner meeting around the corner, and had decided to walk the short distance. In an underpass I heard a child crying. As I rushed past, I saw the child, lying face-down on some newspapers, back bare of clothing, a woman squatting nearby begging for money. I went on to my dinner, but the image of the miserable child in the underpass stayed with me. Afterward, I took the same way home, determined to take a closer look. The child was still there, obviously in bad shape, whimpering and crying, the woman still begging. Something needed to be done. I went back to the embassy and told the Ambassador Dr. Konrad Seitz—an old friend—about the child and my determination to help. The ambassador gently pointed out that there were hundreds, if not thousands, of such children to be found all over Beijing; surely I couldn't help them all. I insisted that we take care of that one child. The ambassador agreed to let me use the embassy car (with driver and interpreter) to see if we could get medical treatment for the child. Mrs. Seitz kindly went along.

The woman certainly did not hesitate to accept our offer of help. After all, that was what she was begging for. Her child was suffering from a dreadful disease affecting her back—spina bifida, as it turned out, "split spine" or "open back," a birth defect leading to permanent disability. The poor woman was from a small village in Sichuan province in southwest China. Her husband was among the hundreds of millions of migrant workers, constantly on the road searching for temporary work. With medical care unavailable in her village, and left all alone to care for a seriously suffering child, the woman had taken the desperate step of illegally traveling to Beijing with her child, where she hoped to be able to beg for enough money to afford medical treatment. All of her personal belongings were in a plastic bag that she carried with her.

I received a lesson on the darker sides of life in China. We took Xuelian (Lotus Flower)—which we soon learned was her name—and her mother to a nearby hospital, which flatly refused to even look at the child unless payment was made up front, in cash. I explained that I would act as a kind of godfather to the child and was willing to pay for the treatment. After I had paid up, the child was finally admitted. Her mother, of course, wanted to stay with her. Nothing doing, the hospital told us, unless we also paid for the mother's stay in the child's hospital room. At that point I was happy to pre-pay the second expense as well. Late that night, Xuelian was finally receiving medical treatment. I can only imagine how her mother must have felt.

The following morning two ladies came to visit me in my hotel room, claiming to represent the Chinese Red Cross. They informed me that my intervention regarding the child was not viewed favorably; in other words, it was none of my business. Furthermore, my support for a woman who had violated Chinese laws by illegally traveling to Beijing and begging for money was not appreciated. It took my last reserves of self-control at that point to get up, thank the ladies for their visit, show them to the door, and wish them a good day.

Fortunately, that was the last I heard from Chinese officialdom about my efforts to help a Chinese child in desperate need of medical attention.

My self-appointed duties as godfather to Xuelian did not end after I returned to Germany. I had called on my old friend Wenpo Lee to ask whether he might look after Lotus Flower. He and his lovely wife immediately promised that they would do so, generously assisted by Mrs. Seitz. They made sure that Lotus Flower received proper medical care, for which I continued to pay. Once the immediate treatment had come to a successful conclusion, the question arose: what now? Mrs. Seitz suggested that Xuelian could best be taken care of if the family were enabled to go back home, as long as a decent home and adequate living conditions could be provided. We gave her family sufficient funds to build a home, acquire some land for agricultural use, afford medical care in the nearest hospital, and eventually allow Lotus Flower to attend school. The Lees took it upon themselves to supervise these arrangements.

I came to visit regularly, at least once a year, which required a somewhat arduous trip (the final part by four-wheel-drive vehicle) into one of the most remote provinces. Progress was not always what I had hoped for or expected. For instance, while the house that was built represented a great improvement over the hovel that Xuelian had lived in before, it was still sparse and not well-suited for her disease and disability. It did, however, have a television set: a major acquisition. I was very surprised one year to see the family watching a Formula 1 race: was that what they really needed? But gradually conditions improved. Xuelian's father was able to stay home, tending to his vegetable and tea plots and masting a pig, whose sale would provide additional cash. Her medical problems well under control, Xuelian was in good enough shape to attend middle school in the next larger village; her mother stayed with her there during the week. And to round out the family's good luck, they were allowed to have a second child (since the first child was disabled, the one-child-only policy did not apply). Xuelian now has a brother. The Lotus Flower story has not yet come to a happy end, but I am very grateful indeed with how it has progressed so far. I can only hope that Xuelian will continue to blossom.

Automobiles are half the story of my life. It began at Ford in Cologne, where, as a twenty-two-year-old intern working in the marketing department, I was lucky enough to acquire a truck with practically valueless post-war money and then be able to sell it a few days later for the new hard currency, the deutsche mark. That stroke of good fortune led me into buying and selling cars, from where I branched out into the car insurance business. Before too long, and after a highly successful stint with an American insurance company, I found myself in the insurance brokerage business, where I stayed for the rest of my professional life. A good number of my clients were from the automobile industry. The most important one was Volkswagen, which was then rapidly expanding into the US market. One of my jobs was to provide insurance coverage for that effort. Much later, I came to serve on the Volkswagen supervisory board. Almost from the beginning, then, Volkswagen and the United States were among the main anchors of my life. When the two came into conflict, I felt a strong obligation to step in and try to prevent larger damages, not only to Volkswagen, but to German-American relations in general. That protracted episode took place in the mid-1990s. I consider it a high point in the story of my life.

The automobile industry is a highly competitive business, long dominated by American carmakers. In Germany, the Ford Motor Company had already established its own production facilities by 1925. The Cologne factory, eventually Ford's main production plant and its European headquarters, began operation in 1930. General Motors entered the German automobile business in 1929, when it bought a majority stake in the then largest German automobile manufacturer, Opel. Two years later, the Opel family—which had built up its car and truck business from its humble origins as a sewing machine and bicycle manufacturer—sold its remaining shares to General Motors, but was able to insist that the Opel name be maintained and that Opel design and produce its own cars. Opel as well as Ford continued to produce automobiles in Germany even as the Nazi regime took over; substantial profits were returned to the United States until 1941 (a significant source of controversy). During the war, both carmakers—now no longer under US ownership or control—produced cars and trucks for the German war effort. Their production plants suffered extensive damage from Allied bombing raids. After the war, General Motors and Ford resumed ownership of their properties and began producing automobiles again for the burgeoning post-war market. In a very real sense, their products were the peoples' cars—affordable, reliable, and unpretentious. Other German carmakers—above all Mercedes-Benz and Porsche—occupied the high-end niche in German and international automobile markets.

Of course, Volkswagen emerged as the predominant carmaker in Germany after World War II. Its only and winning entry in the market was the Beetle, based on the original 1930s design by racing car designer Ferdinand Porsche. Volkswagen owed its success not only to the shortsightedness of American, British, and French carmakers—all of which thought the car too ugly and inefficient and therefore refused to take over the Volkswagen production facilities in Wolfsburg—but also to its first post-war director. Heinrich Nordhoff was an engineer by training and passion, who had learned the car business at Opel, where he had risen to a top-level management position during the course of the war. Too tainted (in American eyes) to return to Opel after the war, Nordhoff was put in charge of the Volkswagen resuscitation effort by less sensitive (or more realistic) British occupation authorities. He improved the Beetle's design so that it became efficient, likeable, and thereby marketable; its unique looks and solid reliability—loved by Americans—soon made it iconic for post-war Germany's *Wirtschaftswunder*.

Nordhoff also established a tradition of forceful and colorful chief executives at Volkswagen. For far too long, he insisted that Volkswagen stick with the Beetle and refused to allow frequent design changes or development of a new model altogether. Nevertheless, his strategy and charismatic leadership propelled Volkswagen from a zero position in 1945 to a leadership position. Eventually, it was the Beetle that also financed the transition to an entirely new design, which required a totally different capital stock by Volkswagen and its supplier companies.

Heinrich Nordhoff announced in 1967 that he would retire as VW's chief executive officer the following year. As his handpicked successor, he introduced an outsider. In April

1968, Nordhoff died of a heart attack. His successors were faced with the difficult task not only of having to function in the shadow of a giant, but also of having to steer Volkswagen in a new direction, away from the now outdated Beetle toward a more modern direction. They succeeded spectacularly with the introduction of the Golf as the Beetle's follow-up model, as well as with larger and more luxurious car models. VW was greatly helped by the engineering and styling prowess of Audi, which VW had acquired in 1965, and NSU, maker of a revolutionary Wankel engine limousine, which was brought into the growing VW industrial empire in 1969. Under the leadership of Carl Horst Hahn, who had left VW in 1973 to become CEO of tire-maker Continental but who returned to VW as its CEO in 1982, VW branched out internationally, not only in China, but also to Spain (with the acquisition of SEAT in 1986), the Czech Republic (with the takeover of *Škoda* in 1990), Slovakia, and Hungary. Hahn made the Volkswagen Group a multi brand, global player—the number one choice of Europe East and West and China. His singular strategy for global leadership in the twenty-first century seems to have made Volkswagen expansion unstoppable. After the Board had prolonged his contract beyond the retirement age of sixty-five, he agitated and convinced the Board to vote for Piëch as his successor.

Ferdinand Piëch, grandson of Ferdinand Porsche, was driven to follow in his grandfather's footsteps, indeed to outperform him. After obtaining an engineering degree (with a PhD thesis on Formula 1 racing car engines), he started work at the family's Porsche racing car business, where he quickly made an impact on the company's products. By the early 1970s, he had risen to the position of technical director. The Porsche and Piëch families, never on the best of terms with each other, then decided, in the interest of maintaining family peace and Porsche profitability, that no member of the family should be in a Porsche company leadership position. That forced Ferdinand Piëch out of Porsche and into Audi. In 1988, having almost single-handedly succeeded in establishing Audi as a brand with the most modern and best-engineered cars, Piëch became CEO of Audi after Hahn had proposed him a second time. He had now achieved the overriding goal of his life: to be head of a company larger than the one his grandfather had directed. His reputation as a skillful engineer and manager was unsurpassed; his interpersonal skills, however, were rumored to be less than sterling. Some wagging tongues claimed that he communicated better with cars than with people. Still, Hahn saw him as the obvious choice to succeed him. He took on his duties as chairman of the board of management of VW on January 1, 1993.

Piëch's most urgent task was to steer VW through the recession, which could only be achieved with drastic cost-cutting measures, and he knew just the right person to help him achieve that goal. Sometime in December 1992, even before he had formally taken over the reins at VW, he got in touch with José Ignacio López de Arriortúa, executive vice president at General Motors in Detroit, where López was in charge of worldwide purchasing. López and Piëch had much in common, from their status as foreigners from small European countries working in huge international companies, to rigid lifestyles (no alcohol, for instance) and questionable interpersonal skills. Most of all, however, they shared a passionate commitment both to engineering and to ruthless management. Together, they were going to cure Volkswagen. In the process, they set off a battle of giants.

López was a Spaniard with deep emotional roots to his native Basque homeland. A specialist for the rationalization of work processes, he first gained fame when he helped to build a new General Motors production plant in Spain that showed immense productivity gains. Soon he was working for Opel in Germany and in charge of production and purchasing. From there he went to the General Motors European headquarters in Zurich and then on to Detroit. He was known for the brilliance, paired with extreme ruthlessness, with which he forced suppliers to lower their prices—again and again and again. When he met resistance, he would swoop into the suppliers' plants to show them where and how they could produce more efficiently and, thus, more cheaply. His fame, or notoriety, grew with his rise in the GM hierarchy. His success was undeniable (though eventually studies would show a "López effect" of customer dissatisfaction due to unreliable and difficult-to-replace parts). His methods raised more than a few eyebrows: from the brutal pressure put on suppliers (earning him nicknames such as "Strangler of Rüsselsheim" at Opel or "López the Terrible" in Detroit) to the "warrior spirit" with which he and his small group of coworkers pursued their campaigns (relying on special diets, for instance) or celebrated their triumphs. But as long as he was successful, these eccentricities did not matter. When López arrived at GM headquarters in early 1992, having been hired by newly installed CEO John F. Smith, he was unassailable.

The two passions of López's life produced one overwhelming desire: to establish an automobile production plant in his Basque hometown—a plant that would be built and operated strictly according to his design and production principles and thus demonstrate the superiority of his approach (and possibly of his fellow Basques). López felt that GM had promised him as much when he took on the job at its headquarters, but GM appeared to be dragging its feet in fulfilling that promise. Louis Hughes, head of GM Europe, was particularly opposed, arguing that GM did not need and could not afford a new production facility in the Basque hinterlands. López grew increasingly frustrated, dissatisfied with GM, and ever more determined to achieve his dream. This is where Piëch came in.

After initial contacts had revealed that López might be interested in leaving GM (and the United States) and coming to VW (back in Europe), Piëch arranged for a highly secret visit by López to Wolfsburg in January 1993. López was to see with his own eyes how much VW needed his special expertise, how great the challenge was, how much he could achieve in purchasing, and how well he might be remunerated. López was duly impressed, as well as delighted that VW offered to make him a member of the board of directors, to quadruple his salary, and to give the idea of a new factory in Spain serious consideration. Secret negotiations continued through February, with López maintaining publicly that rumors about his leaving GM were totally unfounded. On March 9, 1993, López signed his contract with VW. The following day he presented John F. Smith with a handwritten letter of resignation, in which he told the head of GM: "You know how much I admire you and love you." He went on: "I must materialize this dream of building this plant . . . because it is critical for my country. They need me." López—and VW—also needed some of his coworkers at GM to join him in Wolfsburg. In the end, six of his "warriors"—all Europeans—became part of the hiring package, their VW counterparts were to be fired.

Needless to say, John F. Smith and his subordinates at GM were stunned. There followed days of intense efforts to persuade López to stay, in the course of which López was promised more money than VW had offered, a promotion to head of North American operations—and yet another promise to build the Basque plant. By March 15, López had changed his mind and agreed to remain at GM; however, something happened to make him change his mind again (allegedly he was asked to sign a five-year employment contract, which he thought discriminatory, as it was required of no other top GM executive). Later that Monday morning, he told GM about his decision, went home to collect his family, and stepped onto an afternoon flight to Germany. He left behind a thoroughly humiliated GM leadership, which had called a press conference to announce López's retention and promotion, but was now forced to admit defeat. It was, of course, even more devastating that López had joined Volkswagen, GM Opel's fiercest competitor in Europe. López was in a position to strengthen VW not only through his cost-cutting acumen, but also through his knowledge of GM plans and procedures. Whereas Jack Smith felt personally insulted, Louis Hughes, head of GM Europe in Zurich, thought that larger GM interests were at stake. Both were livid and determined to get even. The battle lines had been drawn.

I first learned of Piëch's coup in hiring López away from General Motors in the course of a VW supervisory board meeting on March 16, where a dead-tired López was introduced as VW's likely savior, ready to begin his new duties the following day. He had come as a European, he told us, fully prepared to help Europe's preeminent carmaker to prevail against Japanese and American competition. He promised speedy results. We were all impressed. Soon we were more than impressed. Not only was López able to lower VW's purchasing costs drastically, but he also succeeded in winning over VW's workforce to his ideas of more efficient production. By involving them directly in developing the necessary changes—and by involving himself personally in production line visits and meetings—López gained almost fanatic support among VW workers. They, of course, realized that López was their savior as well: had it not been for the massive productivity gains, many jobs at VW would have been lost. Piëch's coup brought immediate dividends, which in turn earned López the unshakable loyalty of VW's boss and its workers.

In Detroit and Zurich, GM's top managers never stopped fuming over the disloyalty shown by López. Jack Smith termed it a tragedy; Louis Hughes, a crime. They initiated extensive investigations to determine whether López and his "warriors" had taken sensitive GM documents with them, going so far as to employ private detectives in Germany to snoop on them. GM, through Opel, sued López and VW in Germany for its allegedly criminal activities in stealing GM property, which set in motion exhaustive police investigations. In searches of VW offices and homes of the "warriors," investigators discovered that they were indeed in possession of a large number of GM documents, a fact that forced López to claim that they were his personal property and of no value to VW (besides, they were in the process of being shredded). Now the simmering conflict between General Motors, America's largest automaker, and VW, its largest European counterpart, rapidly escalated, with GM claiming that López had strung GM along in order to be able to amass and ship off as many documents as possible, while Piëch told a press conference that GM operatives most likely had planted the incriminating documents in VW offices and on VW computers. In Zurich,

Hughes attributed this claim to a "psychosis-like bunker mentality." In Wolfsburg, arguments could be heard that General Motors was out to destroy Volkswagen and thus hurt Germany economically. "We are in an economic war," Piëch declared. "We will avail ourselves of all means to emerge from this battle as the victor." Things were getting ugly.

Efforts were made on a number of fronts to dampen the escalating conflict and to settle it harmoniously before more damage was suffered by the two car companies. Increasingly, there were concerns that German-American relations might be seriously jeopardized in this battle of the auto giants. Piëch thought he might be able to settle the conflict directly with his counterpart at GM, but when he reached Jack Smith, who was vacationing on his luxury yacht, he was brusquely told to deal with Opel—that is, with Louis Hughes. A German judge considering GM's suit urged both sides to seek an out-of-court settlement. The two companies' legal teams soon agreed on the terms of such a settlement, only to be thwarted in their efforts when Hughes, at the last moment, intervened. He refused to accept any settlement that did not provide for the removal of López and an apology by VW. Piëch, fully backed by his supervisory board as well as his workers, adamantly rejected both demands. The main players had dug in their heels.

I got involved in this battle of the giants early on. As the conflict escalated over the summer of 1993, the chairman of the supervisory board, Klaus Liesen—at the time CEO of *Ruhrgas*, a major energy company—asked me to go to the United States to determine how damaging the possible fallout might be and how it could conceivably be avoided. I agreed to do so out of my own concerns regarding the fate of VW and the state of German-American relations. In mid-August I went to Washington, DC, where I had a series of intense meetings with old friends and acquaintances, most of whom thought that VW—having been caught with its "hands in the cookie jar"—was in deep trouble. A number of proposals emerged from these discussions. One was for VW to have an outside review of its dealings with López. Such a review, conducted by the management consulting firm KPMG, eventually cleared VW of any wrongdoing. Another proposal was to hire a top US law firm for legal advice and public relations help. For that purpose, I met with prominent lawyer and Clinton administration adviser Vernon Jordan, whose partner Robert Strauss (a well-known lawyer and Washington insider) eventually acted as VW's chief counsel in the United States. Finally, there was a proposal to seek contact with GM's board in an effort to establish a back-channel and thus bypass the seemingly irreconcilable differences between the chief executive officers. Eventually, that turned out to be the solution to the GM-VW conflict.

In the meantime, I tried a more direct approach. I considered Lou Hughes an old friend, with whom I had worked closely on a number of occasions, particularly in activities involving Atlantik-Brücke. So I sought him out to see if there was room for reason and some compromise. Hughes, however, would not budge. Most memorable was a breakfast meeting in December 1993 in Wiesbaden—the third such meeting. As I noted in my diary afterward: "He is completely fanatic, totally fixated, unreasonable, animated with an almost missionary zeal. He stands for law, order, and purity. The VW supervisory board should make use of what little time remains: Piëch and López must go, then we could talk about everything else. A hopeless talk. He is beyond the point of no return and seems to fight for his existence." The direct approach did not work.

It took another year for the indirect approach to show some promise. During that time, police investigations in Germany went forward, while grand jury investigations in Detroit were initiated. The two sides' chief lawyers, Bob Strauss and Ira Millstein, were working on a compromise, but without success, as GM continued to insist that López be fired and that VW issue an abject apology along with an admission of guilt. To ratchet up its legal campaign, GM prepared a lawsuit charging López and VW with collaborating in an "ongoing criminal enterprise." This was the heaviest gun of all: a suit brought under the "Racketeer Influenced and Corrupt Organizations Act"—RICO, for short. RICO was originally meant to bring the Mafia under control, but had since been used more broadly to pursue just about any kind of organized criminal activity. It allowed not only for criminal punishment, but also for triple damages in a civil suit. If applied to VW, it would brandish its directors as racketeers and make VW potentially liable for billions of dollars in punitive damages. It would not be an easy case to make and would drag on for years with no assurance of success. Apparently, GM's leadership thought long and hard about actually filing a RICO suit in federal court in Detroit. In the meantime, however, it was thought that the mere threat of such a suit might serve to bring VW to heel.

It was at this point, in January 1995, that I had an "electrifying" (so my diary term) telephone conversation with another old friend of mine. Tom Wyman, a former president of CBS television, had been a member of the GM board since 1985. I had gotten to know him while we were both serving on the board of ICI. He was my back-channel to the GM board. I had called him to express my growing concerns about recent developments and to hear his thoughts about possible ways out. Now he told me that it was his impression that the GM board was eager to settle the conflict. Hughes' extreme position was generally not shared. Nobody was thinking about seeking a billion dollars' worth of damages. What might help to bring the matter to a close was a letter of regret and apology by VW. Perhaps, he suggested, two representatives from each side, none of whom directly involved, could secretly meet to draft such a letter.

I shared Wyman's impressions and proposal immediately with Liesen and Piëch, who agreed that it was an approach well worth pursuing. Even Chancellor Kohl, who was increasingly worried about the political ramifications of the GM-VW spat, offered his heartfelt support when I informed him about this development. Wyman and I agreed to meet in London—in the ICI guesthouse—in early February to hash things out. We talked for more than four hours, but failed to reach an agreement. Wyman had come with a formal negotiating mandate from GM and, contrary to his earlier pronouncements, now insisted that a mere apology would not suffice: López still had to be dealt with. This should be the topic of another round of high-level talks. I told him that VW considered this to be an unacceptable demand and that any such talks should be forward-looking and not dwell on the past. He promised to raise the issue again when he reported back to GM. We also agreed to bring in our high-powered lawyers to let them try to work out a solution. But a few days later, it became clear that our efforts had been for naught. Neither side was willing to budge.

Wyman and I continued our discussions. He reported that GM was no longer interested in pursuing a settlement—GM management was willing to await the outcome of the German police investigations, which it was assumed would soon lead to a formal indictment of López and VW. Until then there was little room for maneuver. That was also true for VW. The company let it be known that it was willing to have López publicly apologize, while Piëch would retract his claim that GM documents had been deliberately planted. VW even signaled that it was willing to discuss López's potential departure from the company, but only after his indictment. These minor concessions were not enough to move things forward, but in the meantime VW continued to profit from the cost-cutting efforts of López and his "warriors." López even got to build his automobile production plant, not in Spain, where VW subsidiary SEAT was having such difficulties that another plant seemed outright folly, but in Brazil, where VW's business was booming.

For General Motors, the fact that López was finally building his plant, the plans for which had been drawn up while he was at GM, offered ultimate proof of VW's alleged treachery. It now decided to fire its big gun. On March 7, 1996, GM filed its RICO lawsuit, naming López and Piëch as main defendants. The ninety-nine-page document was unusually detailed, clearly intended not only as justification for the suit, but also as a major weapon in the ongoing public relations war. VW reacted accordingly, seeking on the one hand to have the suit declared invalid by the Detroit court, while on the other hand filing a countersuit in a German court for defamation of character. Possibly the only people happy about this development were the lawyers on both sides, who, it seemed to me at times, were unduly protracting the process in an effort to enhance their substantial fees.

The "car war" had now reached a new high—or low. It certainly had its absurd moments. The RICO defendants needed to be served their court papers. As it happened, Piëch and López were in Vancouver in late May 1996 for an international management meeting. They succeeded in avoiding the GM agents who tried to serve them the court papers. The agents then proceeded to throw the hefty files at them from a distance. It must have been quite a spectacle, unworthy of the two renowned car companies. If RICO was not enough, this episode brought home the importance of seeking a quick solution to an increasingly ugly conflict. In June, Klaus Liesen asked me again to try another effort at behind-the-scenes mediation. Tom Wyman, equally troubled by the unseemly escalation, immediately agreed to meet with me. Something needed to be done, quickly, before things got completely out of hand. VW feared the possibility of losing the RICO case in Detroit, GM's hometown after all—who knew how a local jury might decide such a case? But GM needed to consider the likelihood of collateral damages as well, from costly court proceedings that would keep its leadership preoccupied for years, to a nationalistic backlash in Germany that might redound to Opel's disadvantage. It was far better to get the conflict settled. In that sense, GM's drastic action—filing the RICO lawsuit—had the desired effect.

But bringing clashing titans to a negotiating table was by no means easy. Wyman and I worked endlessly during the summer of 1996 to convince the main protagonists to agree on procedures for exploratory peace talks. It took some doing and a great deal of persuasion to impose what we thought were some necessary conditions for the meeting to be successful. First, the chief combatants should not participate; neither Piëch nor Jack Smith or Lou Hughes could be present, as their undiminished animosity could easily prevent fruitful talks. Second, the chief lawyers needed to be excluded, though they pushed hard to be present—their apparent delaying tactics might derail any movement toward an agreement.

Third, the meeting must take place on neutral ground under maximum secrecy—any publicity would likely spoil the effort. It was finally agreed, then, that the meeting should take place once again in London, in the ICI guesthouse, with GM represented by its chairman, John Smale, and Tom Wyman, and VW by its chairman, Klaus Liesen, and me. In addition, Gerhard Schröder, Lower Saxony's minister-president, was to be a member of the German delegation, as Wyman had strongly suggested his presence: "After all," he argued, "he practically owns the place."

We met on Monday morning, September 16, and got off to a rocky start, with worn-out accusations flying heavily in both directions, but eventually we got down to business, aided by some breaks that allowed more private discussions. Schröder joined us later, arriving in the early afternoon after having been delayed in Hanover due to some unexpectedly poor election results for his party the day before. The framework for an agreement began to take shape. Our side accepted that López's tenure at VW had become untenable. Liesen made clear that VW was prepared not to renew his contract once it expired in 1998. GM still wanted an apology; VW maintained that it had grievances, too. The two sides then agreed that an exchange of carefully drafted letters could settle that issue. GM also insisted on some compensation for the damages it allegedly suffered. Without going into specifics—especially regarding numbers—we explored some less obvious and onerous ways for VW to provide such compensation through cooperation schemes. Finally, we agreed that all legal actions initiated by both sides would stop and all lawsuits would be withdrawn, except for the criminal case pursued by German authorities against López. At the end of the day, we were sufficiently pleased with what we had achieved that we thought we could leave it to the lawyers to work out the details, once the deal had been approved on the executive level. Wyman and I had originally hoped for the process to move swiftly, perhaps even within a day or two, so that the chairmen could sign off on the details of a comprehensive package while still in London. That, unfortunately, turned out to be impossible. As a result, the agreement reached in London almost fell apart again.

Not surprisingly, perhaps, it was López and Hughes who presented major obstacles to the conclusion of the London compromise. The lawyers went to work almost immediately, apparently making good progress. But then the GM lawyers received a call from Hughes, who instructed the lawyers to insist on "reparation" payments by VW, to seek the formal dismissal of López and his "warriors," and to obtain an admission of guilt by Lopez. The negotiations ground to a halt, as another round of frantic telephone calls ensued among the London participants, who tried to clear up the situation.

Then López struck again. Immediately after the London meeting, Liesen had informed López that he would have to leave VW as part of the pending agreement with GM. López accepted that decision graciously enough. But then, a few days later, he happened to meet a former GM colleague at an auto show in Paris, to whom he mentioned almost off-handedly that he was leaving VW to set up his own consulting firm, which would continue to do business with VW—including the supervision of GM-VW cooperation projects. GM's leadership was stunned and angry, believing that López and VW were getting off far too easy, in violation of the spirit of the agreement reached in London. They also feared that López's soft departure from VW might cause the German prosecutors investigating his case of industrial espionage to refrain from bringing him to trial. As a consequence, the GM bargaining position hardened considerably. At a minimum, GM wanted to wait until López was formally indicted, or his case dismissed, before signing off on the details of any agreement with VW. There was little we could do to move the process along, especially since in the meantime VW found itself under additional pressure after the Detroit court had rejected VW's motion to dismiss the RICO suit. GM seemed to be sitting pretty.

López was formally indicted on December 13, 1996. Anticipating that step by the prosecutors, he had severed his relationship with VW two weeks earlier, allowing him and VW to claim that his departure from VW was motivated by the necessity to focus on his legal troubles. It was a claim that pleased GM none too much. Once the indictment was handed down, however, VW could claim at least a moral victory. The prosecutors explicitly stated that they had found no evidence that VW had been involved in any industrial espionage activities. They also pointed out that GM had apparently not suffered any measurable damages. Wyman and I agreed that these determinations tended to strengthen VW's bargaining position to a point where both sides should now, once again, see the advantages of a quick out-of-court settlement. We suggested that the chairmen confer and instruct their lawyers to resume negotiations over the details of an agreement. This they did, indeed with success.

GM's opening position was that VW needed to pay GM $400 million as compensation for damages suffered. Informally, GM lawyer Millstein let VW lawyer Strauss know that the non-negotiable bottom line for GM was exactly $100 million—not so much as compensation, but rather as a symbol of VW's fault in its dealings with López. VW grudgingly agreed to pay GM that amount, insisting, however, that it represented no admission of guilt, but rather a realistic assessment of the potential costs of dragged-out legal proceedings. In addition, VW committed itself to discontinuing dealings with López and his "warriors" for at least three years. Letters were to be exchanged that expressed "regret" over what had happened, but avoided the term "apology." Finally, VW agreed to buy about $1 billion worth of spare parts from GM subsidiaries over a period of seven years: an amount actually less than what VW would have purchased under ordinary circumstances. That part of the agreement also covered cooperation in other markets, especially in China, where GM had encroached on VW territory by setting up a joint venture with VW's partner Shanghai Automotive Industry Corporation—a move initially much resented and resisted by VW. On January 9, 1997, the agreement was signed and delivered. The "car war" had come to an end, ingloriously, not with a bang, but with a whimper. It was not a proud moment for the two car companies and their stubborn leaders. I, however, was proud that I had been able to contribute to preventing a worse outcome—an outcome that could have hurt the overall state of German-American relations much more than the economic health of Volkswagen or General Motors. I was in Switzerland when I learned of the successful conclusion to my efforts. I was finally able to enjoy some of my precious vacation time. It felt good.

Making peace was one thing. Restoring fractured personal relationships was another. When I learned that Gerhard Schröder, who was already looking ahead to the chancellorship, was going to visit the United States in May 1997, I immediately thought it would be a good idea for him to travel to Detroit and meet with the GM leadership. The chairman of Opel, David Herman, agreed to make the arrangements. John F. Smith generously set aside a Sunday evening to meet with the delegation. I flew directly to Detroit to accompany Schröder. Once at the hotel, we were asked to present ourselves in a meeting room at eight o'clock that evening. The minister-president and I appeared punctually, but we were all alone in the room as our hosts had not yet shown up. We admired the artwork on the walls until the door opened and John F. Smith entered, accompanied not by David Herman, who I knew was in town, but by Lou Hughes. It was quite a shock to face my former friend and VW's nemesis. After some awkward moments of introduction, a waiter appeared to ask what we wanted to drink. Schröder and I each opted for a glass of California Chardonnay while Smith and Hughes took water. In the course of the ensuing small talk, we managed to empty our glasses. The waiter promptly reappeared, asking whether we wanted another drink. I looked questioningly at John F. Smith, who paused for a moment, then laughed and ordered some Chardonnay. Hughes, sensing that he did not have much of a choice, followed suit. The ice was broken and the rest of the evening was a success.

We soon joined a large number of GM executives and Schröder's delegation—including a sizeable number of German CEOs—for a festive dinner. It was here that I met some of the other actors in the GM-VW drama for the first time, particularly the GM lawyers who had done most of the footwork. All in all, it was a satisfying conclusion to an ugly episode. Schröder even succeeded in convincing our American hosts that Germans can be witty, too, when he opened his remarks by pointing out that "my German friends tell me that my English is a little bit better than the English of Helmut Kohl, but not good enough for a speech, so I speak in German," and then continued with a thoughtful, but entertaining after-dinner speech, perfectly translated into English. He helped lay to rest any lingering animosities.

After twenty-one years of fascinating service, I retired from the supervisory board of Volkswagen shortly thereafter, in June 1997. But, of course, I remained interested in everything having to do with automobiles in general, and with developments in which I had played a role in particular. I was touched by the fate of Ignacio López, who had gone back to his beloved Basque country, where he continued to pursue his dream of a model automobile production plant while setting up a consulting firm. Tragically, in 1998 he was involved in an automobile accident that left him badly injured and incapable of sustained work, bringing his brilliant, if controversial, career to an early end, which nevertheless has left positive traces in the European industry. Throughout this ordeal, his court case in Germany dragged on, until the prosecutors finally agreed to drop all charges upon payment of a hefty fine. GM, however, would not let the matter rest there. In 1999, it persuaded a Detroit grand jury to indict López for alleged misappropriation of trade secrets. US prosecutors then sought his extradition from Spain so that he could stand trial in the United States. In 2001, the Spanish High Court refused to extradite López, citing his bad health and the fact that the matter had long been settled by VW and GM.

Ferdinand Piëch fared much better. He remained CEO at Volkswagen until 2002, when—following German business traditions—he became chairman of the VW supervisory board. Martin Winterkorn replaced him as CEO of Volkswagen. During his tenure, VW secured its position as Europe's preeminent carmaker. The introduction of the (Mexican-produced) new Beetle in 1998 proved to be one of his biggest successes, not least because it helped to reestablish VW as a major player in the American automobile market, to the point where VW has once again opened a production facility in the United States. Under his chairmanship, the Porsche company—owned by the Porsche and Piëch families—acquired nearly half of the outstanding VW shares, making Porsche a majority stockholder and thereby giving Piëch a nearly unassailable position of power. At a time when the international automobile market is in turmoil, Volkswagen appears to be in excellent shape to survive the looming shakeout. The same cannot be said of General Motors. Volkswagen may yet emerge as the ultimate victor of the "car war."

# Chapter 7

## My Bridge across the Atlantic

Good relations between countries, contrary perhaps to established wisdom, do not just depend on common interests, shared values, eager businessmen, or skilled diplomats, though all of these are important. Good relations require a strong underpinning in each society—pillars, as it were, for the bridges that connect these countries with each other. As former President George H. W. Bush once pointed out, these "don't just appear—they need to be artfully designed, carefully built, and constantly maintained. Otherwise, they won't serve a need, or they are in danger of creeping corrosion or sudden collapse." The former president's remarks were addressed specifically to Atlantik-Brücke—"that bridge across the Atlantic conceived and constructed fifty years ago [which] has stood the test of hard times and rough weather." He further explained that "the bridge across the Atlantic as built and maintained by Atlantik-Brücke is not a highly visible one. Rather, it functions in a myriad of quiet ways, just like the many individual strands that make up the cables holding up such magnificent structures as the Brooklyn Bridge or the Golden Gate Bridge." For more than twenty-five years, I have worked with and at Atlantik-Brücke to help maintain the transatlantic bridge. These years were among the most satisfying of my life.

Atlantik-Brücke was founded in 1952 by Eric M. Warburg, a member of a prominent German banking dynasty. Forced to flee Germany in 1938, Warburg went to the United States, where he set up a successful banking business. He returned to Germany as an officer in the US Army Air Force and served as a translator and investigator in the main Nuremberg trials, in particular for questioning Nazi Reichsmarschall Hermann Göring. He decided to stay in Germany, partly in order to take care of Warburg family interests, but mostly because he felt that it was extraordinarily important that Germany be rebuilt as a democracy with a fully functioning economy. Together with some allies, not least his friend "Jack" McCloy, Warburg played an important role in preventing the "Morgenthau Plan" for the deindustrialization of Germany from being put into practice. In the process, he realized that Americans needed to be made aware of the positive developments taking place in Germany, while Germans should learn more about the United States. Thus was born the idea of Atlantik-Brücke as a private organization with a limited membership of influential opinion-makers that would promote mutual understanding through the establishment of personal contacts and public educational activities. On the American side, Warburg was instrumental in the founding of the American Council on Germany as a counterpart to Atlantik-Brücke.

Besides facilitating a broad range of private contacts, Atlantik-Brücke focused its initial efforts on providing information about Germany to American troops stationed in Germany. Its publications *Meet Germany* and *These Strange German Ways* soon became required reading for GIs. A weekly English-language insert for newspapers distributed to American soldiers, appropriately titled *The Bridge*, offered up-to-date information and commentary about events and developments in Germany. Atlantik-Brücke also began to organize regular seminars on Germany and transatlantic relations to officers serving in Germany. Eventually, these seminars attracted an ever higher level of participants, to the point where top-level commanders became regular participants (and good friends of Atlantik-Brücke). In addition, Atlantik-Brücke sponsored regular seminars for teachers in the extensive school system run by the Department of Defense for the children of soldiers and dependents. Finally, Atlantik-Brücke organized regular study tours of Germany for American journalists. While the immediate impact of these efforts was hard to measure, there can be no doubt that Atlantik-Brücke performed invaluable services and contributed greatly to bettering German-American understanding among groups in which it mattered most.

In 1959 Atlantik-Brücke, in cooperation with the American Council on Germany, held its first conference involving high-ranking German and American officials, policy experts, and decision makers; thereafter, these conferences took place every other year, with venues alternating between Germany and the United States. Conference topics reflected the important issues of the day, of which there was a never-ending supply. The informal character and friendly atmosphere of these conferences soon made them invaluable, as they allowed conference participants not only to freely speak their minds, but also to seek out their counterparts for follow-up discussions and intensive consultations. They thus fulfilled Atlantik-Brücke's original intent, namely to foster transatlantic understanding on personal—and very high institutional—levels. All discussions were off the record, but summary reports from the different discussion groups were presented in a plenary meeting at the end of each conference. These reports, together with formal presentations and official speeches, were published soon after each conference's conclusion. They now represent documents of great historical value, full of fascinating insights and observations, all reflecting the peculiar circumstances prevailing at the time. Unfortunately, the last Biennial Conference took place in Berlin in May 2003. Appropriately enough, the conference topic was "Fissures and Frictions of War: Repairing, Rebuilding, Rethinking," and it focused on the issues and tensions arising from the war in Iraq. It might have been due to those tensions that participation on the American side was unusually sparse. Over the years, Atlantik-Brücke's partner, the American Council on Germany, had found it increasingly more difficult to attract high-level American participants to their joint conferences. Both organizations therefore decided, with some misgivings, to suspend the Biennial Conferences, hoping that they might be revived in the future.

One joint activity that continued unimpeded was the annual Young Leaders Conference, where carefully chosen future leaders from Germany and the United States meet to get to know each other—and each other's countries—and to discuss critical issues of the day. First organized in the early 1970s out of concern that not enough young people were interested in transatlantic relations, active in respective organizations, and available for future leadership positions, the Young Leaders program has since become successful far beyond original expectations. Participants in these conferences have made many lasting friendships and established important professional contacts. The alumni from the past thirty-seven years of Young Leaders Conferences maintain an active international network. Atlantik-Brücke regularly holds alumni gatherings, known as Atlantic Talks, in all major cities in Germany, as well as in London, New York, and Washington. Not only are the Atlantic Talks an opportunity for alumni to reconnect with one another and maintain friendships and professional networks, they also benefit from hearing featured speakers at the events, including prominent figures from business, politics, journalism, and academia. In June 2010, Atlantik-Brücke officially launched the Young Leaders Alumni Association, Atlantik Forum, to further strengthen this important and lively network, widely considered one of the most accomplished on the international stage.

I became chairman of Atlantik-Brücke in 1984. I had long been a member and was familiar with its activities, but when the offer was extended, it came as a big surprise and evoked some initial hesitation. Atlantik-Brücke had become somewhat stale over the years, and its membership perhaps a bit too old. Its chairman, much to his credit, realized that an infusion of new blood was needed. In 1981, as a first step, he hired a new program director, the person effectively in charge of running Atlantik-Brücke. He could not have made a better choice. Beate Lindemann, then a research associate at the Research Institute of the German Council on Foreign Relations in Bonn, threw herself into her new job with uncommon enthusiasm, incredible verve, unlimited energy, and astounding competence. A second step taken by Chairman Karl Klasen was to announce his resignation and to entrust Beate Lindemann with finding a suitable successor. She checked around for possible candidates, contacting, among others, Horst Teltschik, a friend from her studies at the Otto-Suhr-Institute of the Free University in Berlin, who was then Chancellor Kohl's foreign policy adviser. Teltschik, after consulting with his boss, recommended me. He also suggested that it might be appropriate for Kohl to talk with me directly about this, which the chancellor did in early 1984.

I familiarized myself with the tasks I was asked to take on and accepted the chairmanship; however, I set my misgivings and concerns aside once I got to know the new program director better. Beate quickly convinced me that together we could breathe new life into Atlantik-Brücke and make it the exciting institution it had once been—the preeminent player on the German side of German-American relations. It was a challenge that appealed to me. So in July 1984, I was elected by the members of the organization to be Atlantik-Brücke's new chairman. It was a decision I never regretted, not for a single moment.

Once I took my position, we moved quickly to revitalize Atlantik-Brücke, aided by an extremely lean—and therefore all the more effective—support staff and a reenergized and enlarged membership. I made a point of establishing contact with the American Ambassador to Germany at that time, Arthur F. Burns. The close relationship and intense cooperation that I established with Burns during his last year in Germany fortunately continued with his successors, particularly with Richard R. Burt, Vernon A. Walters, Robert M. Kimmitt, Richard Holbrooke, John C. Kornblum, Daniel R. Coats, William R. Timken, and Philip D. Murphy, whom I met many years ago when he was the head of Goldman Sachs in Germany. Naturally, I established close contacts with our German ambassadors to America, who were extremely helpful in supporting our activities in the United States: Günther van

Well, Jürgen Ruhfus, Immo Stabreit, Jürgen Chrobog, Wolfgang Ischinger, Klaus Scharioth, and Peter Ammon.

Returning to the beginning of my chairmanship of Atlantik-Brücke: already in September 1984, we convened an *Arbeitskreis USA* under the leadership of deputy chairman of Atlantik-Brücke, Arend Oetker—a workshop comprising high-level German policymakers, representatives of business, and experts from academia and the media for regular discussions about issues facing German-American relations. The purpose of this workshop, which has continued to meet three times a year ever since, is to allow those in Germany dealing with the United States to compare notes, to gather information, to exchange ideas, and to formulate new approaches—all on a strictly nonpartisan level. It proved to be one of our most successful innovations.

Another huge step forward took place in November 1986 with Atlantik-Brücke's first German-Canadian Conference in Toronto. We had long felt that Atlantik-Brücke was not quite living up to its name by neglecting that other big country across the Atlantic: Canada. At that time, I was a member of the International Advisory Board of the Bank of Montreal, where I developed not only a deep interest in Canada, but also close relations with the bank's leadership, namely William D. Mulholland and Allan J. MacEachen. With their help, we were finally able to establish a regular meeting of German and Canadian decision-makers and opinion-leaders, much like the biennial meetings with our American counterparts. The German-Canadian conferences—convened annually in alternating venues—quickly became a high point of our activities. Discovering Canada in places such as Montebello, Lake Louise, Niagara-on-the-Lake, Banff, and Whistler Mountain proved fascinating in many ways, partly because we came to appreciate North America's "true North," and partly because it offered us new perspectives on the United States. Our Canadian friends, in turn, took as much delight in widening our horizon and getting to know Germany. As we deepened our relations and made many new friends, Atlantik-Brücke added an important new span to its bridge across the Atlantic.

At the same time, we doubled our efforts to strengthen ties with the United States by looking for new cooperation partners. Over the years, we instituted regular conferences and workshops with research institutions and think tanks such as the RAND Corporation in Santa Monica, California (with James A. Thomson), the Woodrow Wilson International Center for Scholars in Washington, DC (with Congressman Lee Hamilton), the Southern Center for International Studies in Atlanta, Georgia (with Peter White), and the Pacific Council on International Policy in Los Angeles, California (with Lawrence J. Ramer). We deliberately wanted to broaden our perspectives, not only intellectually, but also geographically, by moving away from the East Coast, where we had traditionally focused our efforts. Just as North America is more than the United States, the United States are more than New York and Washington, DC. Atlantik-Brücke had already applied that principle to the choice of its Biennial and Young Leaders conference sites; now we were eager to establish more permanent working relationships with institutions in the middle of the country and on the West Coast.

One of the most difficult aspects of German-American relations is the question of how to deal with the Holocaust, its survivors in the United States, and American Jewish communities in general. I was only too aware of these difficulties—the *faux pas* by Franz Josef

Strauss when he addressed the American Jewish Committee and spoke of the American Jews' "prime minister" (in Israel) is burned deeply in my memory. When representatives of the American Jewish Committee (AJC) approached Atlantik-Brücke in the mid-1980s with a proposal to establish a closer working relationship, we immediately accepted. I did not fully share the concerns expressed on the American side that anti-Semitism was on the rise in Germany and needed to be confronted. Nor did I agree with suggestions heard occasionally in Germany that American Jews exerted a powerful influence in American life and on American politics and should, for that reason, be engaged. I did feel strongly, however, that both sides needed to address their difficulties in relating to each other openly, in a spirit of friendship, and with the goal of improving their understanding of each other. Atlantik-Brücke was ideally suited for that purpose.

In November 1987, the AJC and Atlantik-Brücke held their first meeting in Bonn. One year later, another conference took place in New York. These meetings—highly informative and deeply moving—were inspired by the unforgettable leadership of AJC President Theodore Ellenoff (who unfortunately passed away much too early at age seventy in 1995) and the diligent organizational work of William Trosten. Out of these meetings (which were followed by less-formal get-togethers and workshops) emerged some important initiatives. In 1989, Ellenoff and Trosten founded the Armonk Institute for the promotion of better understanding between American Jews and Germans. Under the leadership of Trosten, the Armonk Institute developed a program in cooperation with Atlantik-Brücke to bring American social studies teachers to Germany. They teach American high school students the history of the Holocaust from 1933 to 1945, and therefore these trips should familiarize them with Germany and how it has established itself since the Third Reich. Starting with a pilot effort in Ohio, this program quickly expanded to other states and grew into an intensive series of preparatory seminars and workshops. Along the same lines, efforts began to supplement high school curricula with courses about post-war Germany. All too often, American teaching about Germany ended with World War II and the Holocaust. We fully shared the concerns expressed by Ellenoff and Trosten that such a narrowing of perspectives regarding Germany was not only historically inaccurate, but also detrimental to German-American understanding in general, and also to the understanding of Jews in America in particular. Bill Trosten, unfortunately, also died much too early in 2001, which led to the closing of the Armonk Institute. But the work that he and Ellenoff began lives on, now supported by Atlantik-Brücke alone—a tribute to their foresight and their ceaseless efforts on behalf of better German-American relations.

The year 1989, of course, was one of radical change in Germany and Europe. Atlantik-Brücke was already running at full speed. Now it kicked into overdrive. The opening of East Germany and then, one year later, the unification of Germany confronted Atlantik-Brücke not only with the challenge of expanding its activities into what used to be the German Democratic Republic, but also with the need to comprehend and then share its understanding of what was happening. Atlantik-Brücke proceeded on a number of avenues. It identified members of the now emerging East German elite and brought them into Atlantik-Brücke activities—a difficult undertaking not least due to many East Germans' lack of familiarity with the English language. It intensified its program of informal meetings and workshops in order to allow for more interchanges and discussions. Based on my long-standing contacts in Japan, Atlantik-Brücke broadened its reach, even to the point of opening a new series of international conferences with Japanese counterparts Keidanren (the Japanese Federation of Industry), the Keizai Koho Center, and the Fuji Research Institute (known after their first meeting site as the Gotemba conferences).

Two new initiatives proved to be particularly successful and satisfying. One involved a close partnership with the Technical University and Mining Academy of Freiberg in Saxony. Founded to promote the science of mining in a silver-mining city (where mining activities ended only recently and the remaining mines are now a major tourist attraction), Freiberg University had sunk into relative obscurity during the GDR regime. After reunification, its rector—eager to reestablish the university's good name and secure its survival—had turned to Atlantik-Brücke for help (pointing out that the reputation of the university once was such that it had more American than German students enrolled). We were intrigued and soon got involved as best we could. We began to organize regular events in Freiberg, including some of our international conferences (such as a Gotemba meeting and a German-Canadian conference). In many ways, we were able to put Freiberg back on the map. After all of my efforts at the height of the Cold War to help East Germans achieve better living conditions, it was gratifying to me that now, after the end of the Cold War, I was able in such a small but direct way to help Freiberg emerge from the disasters of Communist rule. Additionally, I was deeply moved when, in the course of an elaborate ceremony that brought together many of my friends, the Technical University of Freiberg awarded me an honorary degree in recognition of my contributions to its reemergence.

The other unification-related initiative was the establishment of a high school student exchange program geared specifically toward the former East Germany, where young people had an immense need—as well as an extraordinary desire—to catch up with the Western world and to learn all they could about their alleged former archenemy, the United States. It was Beate who had the brilliant idea of setting up such a program on the fly. She was already on the board of trustees of Youth for Understanding, a Washington-based high school exchange program. Now, in January 1990, even before the formal unification of Germany, we set up the Youth for Understanding Foundation to fund East German students who wanted to spend a year in the United States. We expanded the program in 1995 to allow American minority students to visit Germany for a year, and in 2010 we began inviting young Germans with minority background (mainly Turkish) to spend a year in the United States. Later that summer, we were able to send a group of thirty-five high school students to America—the first of several thousand since then. The joy, but also critical eye, with which they experienced their host country was exciting to behold and in itself a great reward. We felt like we had hit the jackpot.

In a more real sense, we also hit the jackpot when it came to long-term financing of our Youth for Understanding Foundation. Taking our cue from the best American practices, we concentrated our fundraising efforts on a gala dinner in New York—an event that by now has become a solidly established annual pre-Christmas tradition known as the "Enchanted Holiday Evening." We did not quite know what to expect when we organized our first gala event in late fall of 1991, but we certainly tried to pull out every stop. Chancellor Kohl and President George H. W. Bush agreed to serve as patrons of the evening. Kurt Masur, former conductor of the world-famous *Gewandhausorchester* in Leipzig (where he had played an important role in the peaceful protests that led to the fall of the Wall) and later appointed conductor of the New York Philharmonic, lent his renown and prestige to our effort by speaking to our guests and having members of the *Gewandhausorchester* and the New York Philharmonic perform together (for the first time). Two of our first group of exchange students reported their impressions and experiences. Everyone was indeed enchanted.

Most enchanted of all, perhaps, was John W. Kluge. Born in Saxony in 1914, Kluge was a little boy when his mother immigrated to the United States. It was there that Kluge became eminently successful in the media business, eventually achieving billionaire status. Having heard about his background but not knowing him personally, Beate thought that he should be invited to our event. With relentless insistence, she tracked down his private address in Charlottesville, Virginia. As we learned later, we were lucky that his future wife, Maria Tussi, also of German origin, saw our letter of invitation. She immediately warmed to our idea of promoting high school exchanges from the former East Germany and persuaded John to come to New York. At the end of our evening, in December 1992, Kluge informed us that he would contribute $1 million, for the specific purpose of sending students from Saxony to America. Hundreds of "John W. Kluge Fellows" from Saxony have since been sent to the United States. For his ninetieth birthday, we put together a book titled *John W. Kluge: The Man Who Touched Lives*, in which some of the "Kluge Fellows" described their feelings and experiences when they first confronted America. It is an extraordinary document of lives positively impacted in so many ways. These students, as well as the families who so graciously hosted them, will help to maintain our bridge across the Atlantic.

Atlantik-Brücke felt compelled on other occasions to touch lives in direct and indirect ways. In August 1990, Saddam Hussein occupied Kuwait. President George H. W. Bush, determined that such aggression should not stand, organized an international coalition to force Iraq out of Kuwait. Germany, inhibited by its constitution from contributing troops (which would, in any case, not have been prepared for desert warfare), eventually chose to show its support through financial contributions. But there was widespread and very vocal resistance in Germany to any support for military efforts, especially on the left side of the political spectrum, where pacifist convictions were tinged with increasingly anti-American sentiments. In this situation Atlantik-Brücke decided to offer a loud voice in support of the United States. On January 29, 1991, we placed advertisements in a number of leading German newspapers in which we pledged our support and appealed for demonstrations of solidarity with the United States and its troops deployed in the Gulf. Specifically, we asked that Germans provide aid and comfort to the families of deployed soldiers remaining behind in Germany. The response was overwhelming. Our phones rang off the hook with offers of help and requests for more information. Within a short time we also collected a significant amount of money. We then coordinated with the Army Emergency Relief Agency for optimal distribution of our funds. Eventually, we set up an endowment in support of the education of children who had lost a parent in the Gulf War. This endowment is still active today, helping now college-age children to pursue their academic dreams.

Atlantik-Brücke's success with its spontaneous and non-bureaucratic efforts to help children in need inspired us to similar efforts after the tragedy of September 11, 2001. For several years we supported four children whose fathers died in the collapse of the Twin Towers of the World Trade Center. In addition, every year Atlantik-Brücke sponsors sixteen children selected by the program "Children of 9/11" for a vacation visit to picturesque Hohenzollern Castle in southern Germany, home of what was once Germany's ruling dynasty. There, they are hosted by the Princess Kira of Prussia Foundation and its chairman, a "real prince," Georg Friedrich of Prussia—an impressive experience for the young folks from New York.

German-American relations took a serious turn for the worse soon after 9/11. The determination of President George W. Bush to go to war against Iraq in order to deprive Saddam Hussein of weapons of mass destruction and to eliminate his regime aroused strong resistance in Germany, where the government was unwilling to go along (even though it had once pledged "unconditional solidarity") and the public was unconvinced of the legitimacy of such a war. Many in Atlantik-Brücke shared these sentiments. At the same time, however, we worried about the future of transatlantic relations, as mutual recriminations set in and the tone of accusations grew harsher. We did not want decades of hard work to have been for nothing. German-American friendship should be able to survive such rough times. But how could we get that point across? We thought back to our activities during the first Gulf War and decided to try a similar approach again. It was primarily our Young Leaders, who had gathered for a reunion in Berlin in late January 2003, who enthusiastically endorsed this idea. Their suggestion: place an advertisement in the *New York Times* highlighting the strong bonds of continuing friendship between the United States and Germany.

Our "Message from Germany" appeared in the *New York Times* on Sunday, February 16, 2003. But before this whole-page advertisement could be placed, an incredible amount of work needed to be done, from drafting the text to negotiating a favorable advertising rate and then securing the signatures (and financial contributions) for our "Message." Once again, the response overwhelmed us. More than 600 persons, including a former president and chancellor, agreed to support us. As word spread and the media got wind of our effort, requests for interviews started pouring in, keeping Beate and me busy. Then the major German newspapers told us that they wanted to carry our advertisement as well—for free. *Bild-Zeitung*, Germany's most widely read tabloid, offered to produce the layout. As preparations for the invasion of Iraq intensified, readers of the Sunday *New York Times* soon read our "Message from Germany":

> The partnership between Germany and the United States forms the backbone of modern Germany. A democratic, united Germany within a unifying Europe at peace with itself and its neighbors embodies that partnership . . . Three generations of Americans and Germans have joined hands to ensure that our countries may live in peace, freedom, prosperity and security. For the overwhelming majority of Germans, the relationship with the United States remains of vital importance. Current differences of opinion between governments over the question of Iraq must not be allowed to sever that bond. We . . . will do our utmost to preserve that bond for future generations.

The many responses we received from Americans and from Germans—which kept us busy for a while longer—confirmed our conviction that we had chosen the right time, as well as the right way, to reemphasize the enduring importance of solid and friendly German-American relations.

In the summer of 2005, Hurricane Katrina flooded New Orleans. We were, at that time, meeting in North Dakota with our Young Leaders Conference, watching a catastrophe of immense proportions unfold. On the spot, we offered our help. In cooperation with the governor of North Dakota and the German embassy in Washington, we took on sponsorship of a number of families from New Orleans, whom we helped to relocate to North Dakota and to establish a new life there. When we visited New Orleans later and saw firsthand the incredible damage that the hurricane had wreaked, we realized that more help was needed. Back home, we launched a fund drive, which brought over $1 million to help rebuild the gymnasium of the Lusher Charter School in New Orleans. Again, the response was overwhelming and extremely gratifying. Since 2007, "our" Atlantik-Brücke Community Resource Center is up and running—another element in what we like to call the "Bridge of Hope."

There were other bridges that we in Atlantik-Brücke tried to build. Of particular importance was a program we named "Investment Bridge." Over the years, German industry had established a strong foothold in North America, not just such well-known giants as the German car manufacturers and their suppliers, but also many smaller firms. Their role in the overall course and conduct of transatlantic relations can hardly be overestimated, yet it is a role with which many are unfamiliar, not least the politicians on both sides of the Atlantic, who are wont to get caught up in the minutiae of political issues without being aware of the importance of routine business relations that take place under the radar of political relations.

In order to help overcome such shortsightedness, Atlantik-Brücke instituted a program that brings German policymakers (especially younger members of the *Bundestag*) to the United States and Canada for visits at German firms operating there. German investment exceeds $210 billion in the United States, whereas US firms have invested $110 billion in Germany, making Germany the ninth largest recipient of US direct investment abroad. German companies employ more than 650,000 Americans, second only to British investments in the United States. In 2008, Germany became the fifth largest export market of the United States, for the first time replacing Great Britain with a total of almost $55 billion. In the course of these visits, they also meet with local counterparts, who are often unaware of the important roles German investments play in their states or districts. Thus policymakers not only get to know each other, but they also develop a deeper understanding of German industries, and of the political difficulties they occasionally face. Since its inception in 1997, our "Investment Bridge" trips have taken us deep into the North American continent, from the two coasts to the Mexican border and all the way up to Fort McMurray in Alberta Province (where synthetic fuel is extracted from the world's largest oil-sands deposits). It is a unique way to get to know other countries better.

The positive experiences with "Investment Bridge" efforts in North America led Atlantik-Brücke to an experiment in expanding its activities beyond North America. As described earlier, I had played some role in getting Volkswagen established in China. My Chinese counterparts, having learned from me about "Investment Bridge," encouraged me to launch a similar effort in China. Given the importance of China for foreign investments, I was certainly willing to give it a try, and the German business community and policymakers were happy to join us for excursions to China. Along the way we made it a point, however, not to lose sight of our primary mission, the maintenance of good transatlantic relations. Wherever and whenever we could, we made it clear to our Chinese counterparts that German-Chinese relations should not proceed at the cost of reducing German-American relations. More important yet, we also sought to establish a program of trilateral German-American-Chinese discussions with the Chinese People's Institute of Foreign Affairs, now under the chairmanship of Ambassador Yang Wenchang, with the goal of ensuring that Germany and the United States coordinate their dealings with China. We are moving cautiously along the way of expanding the reach of Atlantik-Brücke programs. We have also set our sights on Russia (where we have established a cooperative effort with the university in St. Petersburg belonging to the Russian trade union, represented by its President Mikhail Shmakov) and on India (where the inaugural meeting of our International Advisory Council [IAC] took place at the invitation of our IAC member Ratan N. Tata). But we will never neglect our primary mission: to build and maintain bridges across the Atlantic.

In June 2000, after sixteen years of immensely rewarding work as chairman of Atlantik-Brücke, I resigned from my position. I was then seventy-four years old and felt it was time to pass on the baton to someone younger. My resignation was not entirely voluntary, and I lack the energy required for performing the duties of a chairman, but it was clearly the right thing to do in view of my near-arrest and indictment for alleged tax evasion. I could not, in good conscience, represent Atlantik-Brücke while defending myself against these serious charges. Resigning from this chairmanship (as well as from other functions such as president of the European Business School, which I had helped found) was one of the many painful consequences of this unfortunate episode in my life. Once the indictment had been dropped and I had been exonerated—as I knew I would be—the members of Atlantik-Brücke were gracious enough to make me their honorary chairman in June 2004. In the meantime I had, of course, remained active in Atlantik-Brücke affairs. My activities intensified again after my name had been cleared. I considered it a duty to help out where I could, but it was far more than that: a distinct pleasure in the service of a cause to which I remain fully committed.

America has always played a decisive role in my life. It is even part of my name: Leisler refers to one of my paternal forefathers who was an early American revolutionary, when he took on the British Crown in 1689 and sought to gain direct representation and intercolonial cooperation. I grew up in a family with close personal and business connections to America—from Averell Harriman (the first American I remember meeting as a small child) to Otto Kiep, my godfather, who, as the German consul general in New York, welcomed Albert Einstein to America and eventually paid the ultimate price for his disrespect of the Nazi regime. After the war and all of the disasters it had brought to Germany, one of my first thoughts was to immigrate to the United States. For bureaucratic and personal reasons, this never took place. Instead, I ended up working for an American insurance company that wanted me to pursue a career in the United States, but at that point I was too settled in Germany to accept such an offer. Nevertheless, once I had achieved financial security for myself and my family, I was committed to entering politics in order to contribute to Germany's recovery. When I did so, it was with American politics as my model and inspiration, beginning with my first election campaign in 1965, during which I was quickly branded as "the German Kennedy." Throughout my political career, as well as in the years beyond, I preached and practiced my firm conviction that good relations with the United States must form a second, unwritten constitution of the Federal Republic of Germany. The previous chapters described some of my efforts to make sure that this constitutional demand would be maintained.

I have long lost track of how often I have visited the United States and how much time I have spent there. Political, business, and private missions have taken me to every corner of that vast country. Yet as much as I was fascinated by the United States and admired it, I often had difficulty understanding and approaching the country. Huge social and racial gaps baffled me; income disparities disappointed me; and the American way of doing business occasionally frightened me with its "quarterly thinking" and seeming lack of social responsibility. The political process produced great leaders and farsighted policies, yet it also generated politicians of stunning ineptitude and policies that appeared maddeningly shortsighted. One thing was certain, though: America was never boring, and dealing with it was always a challenge—one that I gladly took on.

Over time, I learned that the United States will always have one strong redeeming quality: the ability to correct its costly mistakes. Others have made similar observations (Alexis de Tocqueville, for instance, in his masterful analysis *Democracy in America*, published in 1835). I came to this conclusion not long after I had begun traveling to the United States. My first visit in 1952 was a carefree, joyous, and exciting trip, highlighted by my precocious appearance at the Philadelphia headquarters of the insurance company whose car insurance policies I was selling to American soldiers in Germany. But I did become aware of the mania that was then sweeping through American society and politics: McCarthyism. How, I wondered, could a country that had just brought liberty to Germany and was in the process of installing the basics of democracy there, treat some of its own citizens so indiscriminately and ruthlessly, putting them on blacklists and sending them to jail for alleged Communist leanings or connections? I began to follow this disconcerting aspect of American politics more closely. As the activities of the senator from Wisconsin gradually became discredited and McCarthyism finally disappeared by the late 1950s, I realized that America did indeed have the inner strength to resist and eventually overcome such serious digressions from its proper path, even if it took some time for this kind of self-control (as Tocqueville had called it) to exert itself. That realization strengthened my belief in America and confirmed my conviction that good relations with such a country were of primary importance.

My faith in America—as well as my own determination to enter the world of politics—received a considerable boost in 1960. I happened to be in San Francisco in early November on company business (organizing insurance for VW imports). I noticed a poster announcing a speech by Senator John F. Kennedy in the Cow Palace on November 2, a week before the elections. As told in an earlier chapter, I had met the senator from Massachusetts two years before in New York through the initiative of a mutual friend, who had insisted that I should get to know an up-and-coming political star. I remembered fondly our meeting in a New York restaurant, for I had indeed found Kennedy fascinating and charismatic. Now he was running for president of the United States, the first Irish-American and Catholic with any chance of winning. I had to go and see him in the Cow Palace.

It was an unforgettable event. The future president had the crowd fully on his side, delighting them with his youthful appearance and wit, challenging them to pick up the country and to "start to move forward again, [to] demonstrate what a free society, freely moving and working can do." I was astonished to hear him say: "The generation which I speak for has seen enough of warmongers. Let our great role in history be that of peacemakers." (He promised to focus his attention on arms control and disarmament issues, and to set up an arms control agency for that purpose—a promise he fulfilled once in office.) And without using the later fashionable term "soft power" or resorting to the slogan "ask not what your country can do for you, ask what you can do for your country" (which he must have saved for his Inauguration Address), Kennedy made very much the same points when he argued, "We are going to have to have the best Americans we can get to speak for our country abroad" and suggested the establishment of a volunteer Peace Corps, whose members would serve as "ambassadors of peace." I came away deeply moved and inspired. I felt that with Kennedy as president, America would be on the right path again. And so it was, though only for a brief time.

President Kennedy came to Germany in June 1963 for a triumphant visit. The high point, of course, was his speech in Berlin in front of nearly half a million people, with that most memorable sound bite: "*Ich bin ein Berliner.*" He also paid a visit to Frankfurt, where he spoke in the venerable *Paulskirche*. In this speech, he emphasized the importance of establishing a true Atlantic community. I had the pleasure of being in the audience. In my diary, I later noted that his speech was perhaps too abstract, geared more to German professors than to a broader audience. Still, it was a thoughtful speech, and the excitement over the president's visit was palpable. It reinforced my decision to enter politics, with JFK as my inspiration. I admired his style, which I sought to emulate (with some success, at least in running my election campaigns), and I took his political messages to heart, from the importance of public service to the requirements of "soft power," the necessities of negotiating and compromising with adversaries, and the need for an Atlantic community. His assassination in November 1963 only deepened my admiration and determination.

I was elected to the *Bundestag* in October of 1965. Soon thereafter, I took on the duties of chairman of the *Bundestag*'s committee for economic development. One of the pleasures of that job was that it allowed me to visit many parts of the world that I might otherwise never have seen. But it did restrict my regular travels to the United States. It was not until the early summer of 1966 that I was able to go to America—this time, however, as a member of the *Bundestag* and therefore with a good deal of political clout. It turned out to be quite a memorable trip.

The highlight of this trip was a visit with Averell Harriman. He and my father had remained friends over the years, so it only seemed right that I should look him up. Of course, I was also curious about that rich American whom I had met so briefly as a child. Harriman, in the meantime, had served as US ambassador to the Soviet Union and the United Kingdom, as secretary of commerce in the Truman administration, and as chief administrator of the Marshall Plan in Europe. In 1952 and again in 1956, he was also a presidential hopeful for the Democrats, though his hopes were dashed both times when he lost the primary campaigns to Adlai Stevenson. From 1955 until 1958, he served as governor of New York, where he was succeeded by Nelson Rockefeller, another scion of one of America's richest families. After Kennedy took over the White House in 1961, Harriman joined the State Department, first as ambassador-at-large and then as assistant secretary for Far Eastern Affairs. In April 1963, he became undersecretary of state for political affairs, a position he held until March 1965, when he reverted to being ambassador-at-large until the end of the Johnson administration in 1969. The fact that he was willing to serve in these less-than-top positions in the State Department is testament to his patriotism and to his commitment to selfless public service. However, Harriman was not just another bureaucrat in the State Department, as I was pleased to discover in the course of my trip to Washington in June 1966.

Now that I was in politics myself, I hoped to gain from Harriman's incredible experience and accumulated political wisdom. So I contacted him, explained who I was, and asked to see him during my forthcoming visit. My father's old friend—apparently delighted that the child he had once met had now matured into a budding politician and eager public servant—went into action. He arranged for me to stay in Blair House, the president's guest quarters across Pennsylvania Avenue from the White House—an unusual privilege for a parliamentary newcomer, but a gracious gesture apparently not out of reach for Averell Harriman.

Being hosted by Harriman in this fashion confirmed for me what I no longer doubted: that our butler in Hamburg was wrong in questioning Harriman's wealth. He clearly liked to live the good life, even if that included a preference for German beer. I told him that story when I met him again in 1966, and he was greatly amused. He still preferred German beer to other drinks, he claimed. It may have been a typically American overstatement to a foreign visitor, or perhaps an equally typical understatement of old wealth. Nevertheless, I took him at his word and from then on sent him a crate of *Holstenbier* every Christmas. It helped to facilitate a relationship that grew into friendship over the years. We saw each other frequently until his death in 1986 at age ninety-four. I owe Averell Harriman far more than could ever be compensated with some choice bottles of beer.

Harriman arranged for a series of foreign policy briefings for me. The most pressing issue at the time was, of course, the war in Vietnam, so he brought in the State Department's experts on Vietnam to give me their views on the war's progress. Harriman joined us. At the beginning of the briefing, he demonstratively turned down the volume of his electronic hearing aid (the nearly invisible hearing aids of today were not yet available then). After the briefing—which did indeed emphasize the progress America was making—Harriman took me into his office and bluntly declared that everything I had just heard was "bullshit." The war was not going well and political progress appeared out of reach. More important yet, Americans at home were losing patience with the war effort. He predicted that the United States would eventually tire of the military engagement in Vietnam and withdraw, even if that meant ultimate defeat. He did not think that this would be the great catastrophe others were confidently predicting. Neither would it give rise to a massive right-wing reaction at home, nor would it lead to the collapse of "dominoes" around the world—countries under threat of Communism and relying on American support to prop them up. Harriman was not a misty-eyed idealist. He took great pains to tell me how he had tried to convince President Roosevelt toward the end of World War II that Stalin was no "Uncle Joe" and that the Soviet Union under his leadership could not be trusted to live up to American expectations regarding Soviet conduct and post-war settlements. No, he was a realist, and as such he could clearly see that Vietnam was a lost cause. Two years later, President Johnson sent him to Paris for exploratory peace talks with North Vietnam that, unfortunately, did not come to fruition at that time. Harriman had given his best to bring the war to an end, both within the administration and then in his negotiations with the North Vietnamese. I greatly admired him for his efforts and rued his lack of success.

Harriman, graciously enough, wanted to make sure that I heard all sides of the Vietnam War story, so he arranged a visit for me at the Pentagon. I met with Secretary of Defense Robert McNamara, who at that time was still very confident. Ever the former Ford executive and technocrat in the Department of Defense—the "whiz kid"—McNamara spelled out in precise details why the United States was engaged in Vietnam and how it was going to win that war. McNamara was very nice and open with me, so I asked him whether he saw any problem with the United States following in the footsteps of France as an imperial power. No, no, he replied, America had no imperial aims or designs, but if Vietnam fell to the Communists, a wave of Communism would roll all over Asia, and the United States simply had to ensure that this would not happen; in the end, even Berlin might be at stake. I thought the whole "domino theory" was ridiculous, but I did not press the point. He had his staff present a briefing that showed where the war was going well (those body counts!), where the war efforts had its weaknesses, and how those weaknesses would be addressed. It was all so rational, so technically precise, and so wrong. I met repeatedly with McNamara and others in the Pentagon during the remainder of the Johnson administration and never heard a different line. Some years later our paths crossed again, when McNamara was president of the World Bank and I was engaged in a rescue effort for the Turkish economy. McNamara appeared a completely different person, full of regret and remorse over his conduct during the war in Vietnam, willing to shoulder a good deal of the blame for this American foreign policy disaster. I admired him for it and only wished that he had seen much earlier how wrong his technocratic approach to the American engagement in Vietnam had been. America might have been spared many problems and a lot of grief.

I experienced the political convulsions caused by the Vietnam War in 1968. My party, the CDU, had asked me to serve as its official observer for the 1968 US presidential elections. I gladly agreed to do so, as it allowed me yet another, far more intimate look at a country I felt so close to, yet which at times seemed so frustratingly foreign. My observations began in early August with the Republican National Convention in Miami Beach. Nelson Rockefeller, then the governor of New York, was a family friend (as in the case of Harriman, the Rockefellers had shipping interests that had brought them into business contacts with my father). I had gotten in touch with Rockefeller in the early 1960s, and over the years our relationship had grown into a friendship. He was an open and generous person, always accessible to me. In 1968, he was running for the nomination as presidential candidate of the Republican Party. Once I knew that I was going to be an observer at the convention, I let him know that I would be there. He immediately invited me to stay in his hotel and to observe the process up close from his perspective. It was an invitation I was not inclined to refuse.

The event began with a huge party, with perhaps as many as 5,000 people. I watched with great fascination as the waiters poured champagne, racing along rows of glasses without stopping at each person. Somehow, this seemed like a typical American approach to something as dignified as serving a glass of champagne. I used the occasion to chat with the delegates. What were Rockefeller's chances, I wanted to know. It quickly became apparent that they were not very good. Everybody liked Rockefeller; he was, after all, a genial and generous person with a lot of experience behind him. But he was also a Rockefeller—a founding father of the "Eastern Establishment." Nixon, I was told, was a man of the people: always approachable and ready to offer help in some form or other. Rockefeller, on the other hand, was a member of the elite, nice enough in his own right, but not as easily approachable or as helpful as Nixon. So the delegates thought that Nixon, the former vice president and unsuccessful candidate for the governorship of California—the man who, after his defeat there, had famously declared: "You won't have Dick Nixon to kick around anymore"—would end up winning the nomination, which he did, rather convincingly. Nixon was helped by the fact that he was able to present himself as the candidate of the political center. Rockefeller stood for the traditionally more liberal eastern wing of the party, while the more radical right wing was represented by the rising star in the west, the governor of California and former Hollywood actor, Ronald Reagan.

The convention of the Democratic Party took place in late August in Chicago. The Democrats were bitterly split over the two most trying issues of the time: the war in Vietnam and the promotion of civil rights. President Johnson had announced in March 1968 (after he had won the New Hampshire primary election so narrowly that his victory was widely interpreted as a defeat) that he would no longer seek reelection. Only five days after Johnson's announcement, Martin Luther King, Jr., the icon of the civil rights movement, was assassinated on April 4, 1968. His murder led to widespread rioting and thus reopened the public debates over the rights and wrongs of race relations in the United States. Two months later, Robert Kennedy, President Kennedy's brother, who by then appeared to be the frontrunner among the Democratic candidates, was killed just after he declared victory in the California primary. Kennedy's murder took away the Democratic Party's most charismatic and credible candidate, someone who had both a strong civil rights record and had come out against a continuation of the war in Vietnam. The Democrats were now left with a sitting vice president, Hubert Humphrey, who had remained loyal to Johnson, but was therefore burdened with the unpopular president's legacies, and Senator Eugene McCarthy, whose pacifist campaign had garnered the support of the nation's young people. On the far right, the Democratic governor of Alabama, George Wallace—an unrepentant segregationist and typical Southern populist—had formed a third party and was threatening to take vital votes away from the Democrats. It was not a good situation for the Democratic Party as it gathered for its convention in Chicago.

I was in Chicago with my good friend and colleague from Great Britain, Peter Walker, who was there as the official election observer for the Conservative Party. We stood together on a balcony of the Chicago Club overlooking Michigan Avenue, watching a great American tragedy unfold below us. Chicago's mayor, Richard Daley (infamous for his corrupt iron grip on the city), wanted to show his country and the world how to run a "clean" party convention. All kinds of dissident groups and protest movements had announced their intent to disrupt the proceedings in order to make their protests heard and their anger felt. Mayor Daley had made it equally clear that he would not allow that to happen. This led to an inevitable clash, with a massive number of protestors (as many as 10,000) confronting an even larger number (some 23,000) of police and National Guard members. Taunted by the demonstrators, the police struck back, indiscriminately clubbing anybody in their way and spraying a massive amount of tear gas in order to disperse the crowds. Much of that action took place on Michigan Avenue, right below us. "My God," Peter exclaimed to me, "America is falling to pieces." He said it just as we were being forced back into our rooms because the tear gas had reached us. I was inclined to agree with him; it did appear that America was coming apart at its seams. Never before had I seen anything like this. How would America ever recover from this ugly display of disunity, much less deal effectively with its underlying causes? I left Chicago deeply discouraged.

Even though most of the primary voters had expressed their antiwar sentiments, the Chicago Convention selected Humphrey—who had not run in a single primary—as the presidential candidate of the Democratic Party. I was very fond of the vice president, whom I had gotten to know in my function as chairman of the *Bundestag*'s committee for economic development. I experienced him as a thoughtful, kind, and energetic person, always willing to help where he could. Back in 1967, he had even accepted an invitation from me to participate in a conference in Bonn on international development and foreign aid. The appearance of the American vice president at an event organized by me was quite a coup, for it helped not only to raise the conference's profile, but also to increase my standing among my colleagues. (Humphrey's visit to Germany made the headlines in other ways as well. A group of leftist radicals plotted to protest against the vice president by throwing a "custard bomb" at him. The plot was foiled by police before it could be carried out, which led to rioting by left-wing student radicals. An incensed Ulrike Meinhof, then a journalist, complained: "Napalm yes, custard no." The incident may well have been a contributory factor in the growth of the "68" protest movement and the eventual rise of terrorism in Germany.)

As an official election observer, I was invited to join each party's candidate for a week of campaigning. This allowed unusual access to the candidates, which in Humphrey's case was even closer because of our prior acquaintanceship. I was, of course, not unfamiliar with the rigors and demands of an election campaign. But the trials and tribulations of an *American* election campaign were an experience of a different dimension. We could barely catch our breath, much less gather our thoughts, crisscrossing the country and hopping from event to event. Organization seemed the key to a successful campaign, and Humphrey's campaign appeared not well-organized at all. But he was by far the better speaker, able to connect with his audiences on an emotional level—Humphrey was the only politician I ever knew who could come to tears over his own rhetoric—as well as on an intellectual one. His speeches were invariably thoughtful and interesting. I witnessed one exception, though, and it highlighted his integrity as a person while revealing his shortcomings as a campaigner.

We were in Pittsburgh in mid-September. Humphrey was scheduled to speak to a group of union members, generally the most supportive of Democratic candidates; however, before Humphrey's speech, the group had been addressed by George Wallace, now running as the candidate of the "American Independent Party." Wallace had roused this audience to great excitement with his usual vitriolic attacks on the follies of leftist liberals and the foibles of hippie protestors (who, he liked to assert, were ignorant of only two four-letter words: work and soap). It was a tough act to follow. Humphrey tried as best he could, but was not able to elicit any response but a frosty silence. After a few minutes he had had enough. He broke off his speech with this parting shot: "I will leave you with one message. Jobs here will not be safe until the last black man in America has a job." Hisses and boos accompanied him as he left the stage. At the bottom of the stage, Humphrey turned to me and said: "Walther, I really gave it to them, didn't I?" I could only agree in admiration for his courage in telling his audience an uncomfortable truth, but I did wonder whether this was any way to win an election. As it turned out, it was not. Humphrey lost to Nixon, unable to overcome the burden of the war in Vietnam on the one side, and his (well-deserved) reputation as a liberal in favor of social reforms on the other. America had missed a chance to make a thoroughly decent man its president.

Richard Nixon was cut of a different cloth. I had a chance to observe him up close during a few days of campaigning with him. His campaign was organized perfectly: events took place on time, local arrangements were impeccable, and when we got back on the plane to head for the next campaign stop, the martinis were fresh (shaken or stirred), cold, and delicious. Nixon's speeches were carefully drafted and delivered without much passion. Compared to Humphrey's speeches, they also appeared strangely devoid of much substance. When it came to foreign policy—Nixon's main interest and undoubtedly his forte—he spoke with great diplomatic skill, but offered few details. Regarding the war in Vietnam, he claimed to "have a plan" for ending it, but did not spell it out. He barely addressed any of the pressing domestic issues, such as widespread poverty and shameful race relations; instead, he preferred to speak about the need for law and order.

Surprised and bothered by this approach to campaigning in what surely were extraordinarily troubled times, I asked Ron Ziegler, who took care of us observers (and later served as President Nixon's press spokesperson), why this was so. Ziegler gave a straightforward and, in the end, entirely plausible (though disturbing) explanation. Campaign events were scheduled only in places where an appearance by the candidate might actually make a difference. For a Republican candidate, that precluded areas of poverty and places with large racial minorities. Potential Nixon voters were neither black nor poor, therefore there was no need to address such issues as poverty reduction or racial equality. Later, Nixon came to call this foundation of his public appeal the "silent majority." To get their votes, the candidate pursued a strategy of silence on uncomfortable issues. It worked for Nixon in 1968.

Nixon was a deeply troubled person, as was already evident in the few private exchanges I had with him during the 1968 campaign. He could be very charming and forthcoming, especially when he could talk about his favorite topic: foreign policy. He explained with some passion and much insight how he was going to end the war in Vietnam by pursuing an opening with China, thereby putting strategic pressure on the Soviet Union to improve its relations with the United States—both developments designed to limit outside support for North Vietnam and thus bring the war to a successful end. It was not least on the basis of these conversations with Nixon and his advisers that I came to the conclusion that, should Nixon be elected, the United States was going to pursue a policy of détente vis-à-vis the Soviet Union, to which the Federal Republic needed to adjust accordingly. My own approach to *Ostpolitik* rested on that realization. In that sense, I had absolutely no problem with Nixon. It was the personality he projected in domestic affairs that I found deeply troubling. He spoke in very vindictive, almost hateful terms about his political opponents, all those Rockefellers and Kennedys, who represented a snotty Eastern elite that allegedly despised him. It was my impression that he displayed a deep sense of insecurity about his own standing, which he compensated with internalized rage and venom. He left no doubt as to who was on his list of enemies.

Nixon's conflicted personality led him to the abyss of the Watergate scandal—the result of which made him the first president to be forced to resign from office. I had no contact with him after he became president, but I was a frequent visitor to the White House, where I met with Henry Kissinger and his staff at the National Security Council. This allowed me to observe the gradual and eventually tragic demise of Nixon as president. Alcohol became one of his biggest problems, though it was not well-known outside the White House. Inside, it eroded his authority and his ability to function. Once I was sitting in Kissinger's office; his deputy, Alexander Haig, was also there. The phone rang. Kissinger looked at Haig and said: "You take it. The drunk is calling." I was shocked, as much about the president's alcohol problem as about his advisers' cynical comments, in the presence of a visitor no less. Later, Haig told me that steps had been taken to make sure that Nixon could not abuse his powers as commander-in-chief while intoxicated. These were truly dark times for the United States.

Years later, in 1982, I met Richard Nixon again. He had come to Germany to promote the German version of one of his books. I was invited to a publication party in Hamburg. Afterward, the former president joined a small group of guests for dinner, and I was seated next to him. We engaged in pleasant small talk. Searching for topics to breach, I asked whether he was going to get involved in the Congressional election campaigns that were about to start. Nixon turned to me, raised his voice, and snarled: "Me? Campaign for these bastards? Never!" He went on to complain how badly he had been mistreated, even by members of his own party, despite the fact that he had given everything for his country. His rage toward the disloyal and ungrateful elites spilled out of him again. Other conversations stopped around the dinner table as fellow guests watched this outburst with amazement and embarrassment. More than anything, I felt sorry for a man who had, in fact, achieved so much for his country (not least by opening up to China and pursuing a policy of détente vis-à-vis the Soviet Union, though neither policy contributed to an honorable end of the Vietnam War), but who, because he lacked control over his inner demons, had fallen so far from grace.

Henry Kissinger was Nixon's closest adviser. He played a role that, to this day, is not quite clear. Was he the brilliant mind behind Nixon's foreign policy or merely the president's National Security Advisor who translated Nixon's ideas into policies and then helped to implement them? How deliberate, or realistic, was that approach, which came to be known as the "madman strategy," whereby Kissinger acted as the rational statesman with whom others should cooperate lest they wanted to deal with that unpredictable "madman" Nixon? Was he the loyal executioner of the president's policies, or did he act on his own? For that matter, did Kissinger prevent worse things from happening, or could he have done more to prevent some of Nixon's excesses that led to Watergate? How is it that Nixon, who enjoyed a reputation as the ultimate American politician, had to resign his office in disgrace, while Kissinger not only emerged unscathed, but with a reputation that reached stratospheric dimensions? If nothing else, Henry Kissinger is a fascinatingly multifaceted person who played the best game in town. I never tired of watching him in action.

I first got to know Henry Kissinger as Nelson Rockefeller's foreign policy adviser. Rockefeller had done a lot to promote the young Harvard professor with the heavy German accent (Kissinger had fled to the United States as a teenager in the 1930s). By the time Rockefeller ran for president in 1968, Kissinger—who had published a number of brilliant books on national security (as well as a historical study of Metternich and Castlereagh)—was widely recognized as one of the foremost strategic thinkers in America. Not known at that time was the fact that he had also gained some practical experience in highly secret negotiations with the North Vietnamese over a possible settlement of the war in Vietnam. I met him in Miami Beach during the 1968 Republican National Convention as the person who, in some form or other, would be in charge of the foreign policy of Rockefeller, should he become president. As I saw it, Kissinger jumped ship as soon as it became clear that Rockefeller would not be nominated, and made himself available to Nixon. I thought it an outrageous act of disloyalty, but Rockefeller assured me that he saw it differently and harbored no ill feelings. Not many days later, I ran into Kissinger again as he accompanied Nixon on some of his campaign swings. He now played the much-appreciated role of interpreting Nixon's foreign policy ideas to me. I was highly impressed by the nimbleness of his career move and even more so by the broad reach of his foreign policy expertise.

Henry Kissinger remained a good friend over the years, though I did not always share his assessments. For instance, I found his insistence on the validity of the "domino theory" regarding Vietnam (which he expounded every time we talked) less than credible. I was disappointed that he advised President George W. Bush to stay on course in Iraq and not let the United States suffer another defeat (and in the process have some other "dominoes" toppled); to me, that seemed historically incorrect and in nobody's interest, least of all that of the United States. But such disagreements never had any impact on our relationship. Kissinger was always available when I sought information or advice, which proved particularly important over the course of *Ostpolitik* while trying to steer my own party away from its overly confrontational course and any resulting clashes with American intentions. In later years, after I had become chairman of Atlantik-Brücke, Kissinger readily participated in many of the organization's events, generously offering his insights and willingly lending his name to our efforts, increasing their importance and appeal. Kissinger could easily and understandably have turned his back on the country that had forced him to flee to the United States. Instead, he maintained a special interest in German affairs and in the maintenance of good German-American relations. One could argue that this was merely another demonstration of his keen strategic sense, given the importance of Germany today. I knew that it was much more, and I will never cease to admire him for it.

Alexander Haig, whom I had first met in Nixon's White House, also remained a reliable friend. He was ever the military man, highly decorated for courageous service in Korea and Vietnam, with a straightforward personality. Having been a reserve officer in the German Navy, I am no stranger to dirty language and questionable jokes; however, I experienced Haig as the ultimate master of both—he seemed to have a limitless store of the vilest and dirtiest jokes I have ever heard, which he relished telling in what he deemed appropriate company. Maybe he figured that as a sailor I would enjoy this kind of humor. I didn't mind, because I appreciated the accompanying camaraderie. Haig, by now a four-star general, was Supreme Allied Commander Europe during the Carter administration. When I took on the mission to collect international support funds for Turkey, I informed Haig. He immediately invited me to his headquarters for a thorough briefing on Turkey from SACEUR and NATO perspectives, and he offered me his personal and institutional help. It was yet another example of the importance of personal relationships in the conduct of difficult political tasks.

Nelson Rockefeller never made it to the presidency, but he came close. Throughout his unsuccessful efforts in 1960, 1964, and 1968, he continued to serve as governor of New York, where he successfully introduced far-reaching reforms ranging from education to the environment. He also promoted massive infrastructure projects, including the Twin Towers of the World Trade Center in New York City, which led some of his detractors to accuse him of suffering from an "edifice complex." He finally resigned from the governorship in December 1973 in order to devote himself to other pursuits, including another run at the presidency in 1974. But Richard Nixon resigned as president in August that year, making Gerald Ford—his vice president (the former Minority Leader in the House of Representatives who himself had come into the office after Vice President Spiro Agnew resigned in disgrace in October 1973)—president of the United States for the remainder of Nixon's second term. The country was now without a vice president. Ford's choice for vice president was Nelson Rockefeller, who, after extensive confirmation hearings in Congress, took office in December 1974. Rockefeller was now just "a heartbeat away from the presidency," but as Ford's vice president, he had to write off his own presidential ambitions for the 1976 elections.

When Ford took office, he announced that the "long national nightmare" was over. That might have been true as far as Watergate was concerned, but the Vietnam issue was still unresolved, even though the United States and North Vietnam had agreed on a peace settlement in January 1973 (for which Kissinger and his Vietnamese counterpart, Le Duc Tho, were awarded the Nobel Peace Prize that year). South Vietnam was unable to defend itself against continued Vietcong and North Vietnamese military pressure; the United States, tired of the long conflict, was unwilling to come to its aid. When Saigon was about to fall in April 1975, President Ford declared an end to American involvement in Vietnam (pointedly not informing his Secretary of State Henry Kissinger about this momentous announcement). America had finally come to its senses and corrected one of its worst foreign policy errors. No "dominoes" fell, there was no right-wing reaction at home, and America's standing around the world improved—rather than suffered—and restored—rather than destroyed—its credibility. The lessons learned in and after Vietnam lasted for quite a while. Unfortunately, they did not last long enough to prevent the United States from committing yet another serious mistake when it went to war against Iraq in order to eliminate its dictator, Saddam Hussein. One can rely on eventual error corrections, but one must also face the fact that errors will be made again. Dealing with the United States is a challenge.

Nelson Rockefeller played an inconspicuous role in the two remaining years of the Ford administration. "It's not much of a job," he once told me with a wistful smile. When Ford ran for reelection in 1976, Rockefeller begged off the ticket; the life of an underemployed vice president was not for him. I continued to see him regularly, usually in his magnificent office on Capitol Hill (the vice president is the presiding officer in the Senate). He and his wife, Happy, also came for a private visit to our home in Kronberg. We always had intensely serious discussions, but also shared many laughs, as he had an infectious sense of humor. He may not have been "much of a student of history," as he claimed at one point, but he had a keen sense of what was happening around him. He saw through the follies of his contemporaries and was willing to share his insights with me. I learned a lot from him. When he died of a heart attack in January 1979 at age seventy, it was reported that a young woman was with him in his Manhattan townhouse. Sad as I was upon learning of his death, I had to smile: if the (never fully confirmed) reports were true, this was the Nelson Rockefeller I had also come to know—full of love of life and not above some mischievous adventures. The Rockefellers are an incredibly enterprising and philanthropic family, who have set themselves many monuments. The one I like best is a little church in the village south of their estate above the Hudson River. David Rockefeller once proudly showed it to me. Its ten stained-glass windows are stunningly beautiful. Two were designed by Henri Matisse and installed by the Rockefeller brothers in honor of their mother, who was a great patron of modern art (she founded the Museum of Modern Art in New York). After their father died, the brothers thought it would be a fitting memorial to have additional stained-glass windows put into the church, so they commissioned Marc Chagall to make windows that would complement Matisse's work. Union Church in Pocantico Hills now stands as a jewel-like testament to the Rockefellers' generosity, their spirituality, their sense of beauty, and their love of life.

In 1976—two-hundred years after the founding of the United States with the Declaration of Independence—the American voters decided that they did not want four more years of Gerald Ford. He was a thoroughly decent, rock-solid man, who could not quite overcome his image of a less-than-sure-footed politician (who, during a crucial election debate, did not seem to know that Poland was not a free country). His well-motivated, unconditional pardon of his predecessor also continued to hurt him with public opinion. America turned instead to a former Navy engineer, a peanut farmer, a lay preacher, and a governor of Georgia, who promised to be a "president as good as the American people": Jimmy Carter. He seemed the perfect choice for the post-Watergate and post-Vietnam era, of humble background and without lofty ambitions for his country, other than to always do the right thing. As it turned out, he was not quite up to the job. The economy turned sour during his presidency, while abroad the United States was pushed around, first by the Soviet Union (which invaded Afghanistan) and then by Iran (whose newly installed revolutionary Islamist regime allowed radicals to storm the American embassy and to hold its personnel as hostages). Unfortunately, humility and moral righteousness did not prove to be the right approach in securing American interests around the world. Carter's European colleagues found it hard to work with him. German Chancellor Schmidt treated him with barely disguised contempt. Transatlantic relations suffered accordingly.

My own experiences with the Carter administration were quite positive. I got to know President Carter in the course of my Turkey rescue mission and found him to be knowledgeable, personally kind, and politically helpful. I also established a good working relationship with Zbigniew Brzezinski, his Assistant for National Security Affairs (who followed in the very big footsteps of Henry Kissinger). Brzezinski was the son of a Polish diplomat. As a child he spent four years in Nazi Germany while his father was stationed there. In 1938, his father was posted in Canada, where the family had remained after Poland was occupied by Germany and then, after the end of the war, taken over by the Communists. At Harvard, where he was a colleague (and competitor) of Kissinger, Brzezinski developed the theory of totalitarianism. Because of this background, Brzezinski had a reputation of being fiercely anti-Soviet and anti-German. It was a reputation not entirely undeserved (and therefore not helpful in his dealings with a prickly German chancellor), but in my dealings with him, I found him invariably open-minded and helpful. I also came to appreciate him as a brilliant strategic thinker and masterful manager of power in the White House. Admittedly, though, it was at times hard to understand how Brzezinski's *Realpolitik* approach to foreign policy meshed with the president's more idealistic inclinations (evident, not least, in Carter's push for human rights around the world). The resulting confusion did a good deal of damage to the Carter administration's standing and thus to its foreign policy.

Years later, I had my own moment of confusion with Brzezinski. I was president of a newly established private business school in Germany. One day I learned that one of its professors, named Brzezinski, was about to celebrate his fiftieth birthday. As I was rushing out of my office, I asked the secretary to draft a congratulatory letter to Professor Brzezinski and signed a blank sheet of paper for that purpose. That is never a good idea, as I should have known. A few weeks later I received a very kind and humorous letter from Zbigniew Brzezinski, who thanked me for thinking of him on his fiftieth birthday, but pointed out that, unfortunately, I had made him much younger than he really was. Not that he minded, but . . . I could see the twinkle in Brzezinski's eyes as he wrote this letter. It very much reminded me of the Brzezinski I had gotten to know as a member of the Trilateral Commission and remained in contact with ever since. Every time I see him, I am amazed at the brilliance of his analyses, in particular on China.

Speaking of unforgettable people and moments, a good friend had introduced me to the American "financial genius" Paul Volcker, whom I got to know extremely well and whom I visited many times at his office during his long reign as chairman of the board of governors of the Federal Reserve System from 1979–1987. I am a great admirer of his intense engagement and success in very difficult times. What I like most is that he never ever seems to lose his deep-seated genuine sense of humor.

By 1980 the American public had grown weary of Carter, whose stature seemed ever more diminutive and whose policies less than successful. "Are you better off than you were four years ago?" asked his Republican challenger, who also promised to lay the "Vietnam syndrome" of remorse and reticence to rest and make America strong again. Ronald Reagan was elected overwhelmingly, carrying forty-four states. Twelve years before, I had sat in the Miami Beach convention hall—right next to Mrs. Reagan—observing the California governor's futile attempt to win his party's nomination. Now, at age seventy, he had finally achieved his goal, becoming the oldest president on taking office.

Reagan brought new glamour and style to the presidency. He was the "Great Communicator," having honed his speaking and performing skills as an actor in Hollywood, as governor of America's most populous state, and as a sought-after speaker on the political lecture circuit. I experienced him in action only once while he was president. The occasion, in April 1985, was a Rose Garden ceremony honoring John J. McCloy on his ninetieth birthday. "Jack" McCloy was known not only as the "Chairman of the Eastern Establishment," but also as a bedrock of German-American relations. He was deeply influenced by Eric M. Warburg, who had to leave Germany in 1938 and soon met McCloy after his arrival in the United States. They remained friends ever since. As a student at Harvard, McCloy had taught the Rockefeller boys how to sail; later he worked for the Rockefeller family in various positions. As a young lawyer, he was at one time legal counselor to IG Farben. In World War I, he had served as an officer with the American forces in France. In World War II, he was assistant secretary of war, playing a major and eventually highly controversial role in policymaking (such as ordering the internment of American citizens of Japanese descent or rejecting bombing raids on Auschwitz). After the war, in 1949, he became the US High Commissioner for Germany during the three crucial years that saw the establishment of the Federal Republic of Germany. McCloy's conciliatory and forward-looking approach to German rehabilitation and reconstruction may well have been crucial in putting Germany on the right track. He is, in any case, fondly remembered for it, and richly deserved the honors bestowed upon him that day by the American president, who was joined by the German president, Richard von Weizsäcker (whose father, convicted at Nuremberg, had been pardoned by McCloy).

Reagan's opening remarks were appropriately brief and gracious. "It would take too long to recite for you the rest of John McCloy's many important contributions to our country and to the cause of peace and freedom. From wartime intrigue and espionage to European reconstruction after World War II, to disarmament negotiations spanning more than thirty years, John McCloy's high intellect and selfish heart..." at which point the small audience stood in shock: the president was calling his guest of honor selfish? A simple mistake? A Freudian slip? An indicator of Reagan's rumored onset of Alzheimer's disease? But Reagan, ever the "Great Communicator," recovered quickly and with the best display of his "aw shucks" charming grace: "*selfless* heart; I shouldn't have mispronounced that word above all!" He then went on to explain that McCloy's "selfless heart has made a difference, an enduring difference, in the lives of millions." McCloy took it all in good humor, telling the president in his reply that "compared to me, what a spring chicken you are."

The Rose Garden ceremony in honor of McCloy took place a few weeks before the commemoration of the fiftieth anniversary of Nazi Germany's unconditional surrender on May 8, 1945. The controversy surrounding Reagan's visit to a military cemetery in Bitburg, where some SS soldiers were also buried, revealed some of the unhealed wounds in German-American relations. The Kohl government was grateful to the American president for insisting on this gesture of reconciliation. Otherwise, German-American relations were not always the best. Germany was uncomfortable with Reagan's seemingly rigid anti-Soviet stance that denied the importance of détente, stressed the priority of rebuilding military strength, and sought to force Europe to limit its exposure to the Soviet Union (by imposing sanctions on a gas pipeline deal, for instance). When Reagan campaigned for letting "Poland be Poland," and then when he stood at the Brandenburg Gate and exhorted "Mr. Gorbachev, tear down this wall!" Germans reacted squeamishly. Such a confrontational approach was not to their liking and thought to be counterproductive; an easing of tensions, rather than a heightening of them, was the preferred German way of dealing with the Soviet Union. Yet two and a half years after Reagan's Brandenburg Gate speech, the Wall did come down. Reagan—the president with firm convictions and a long-term perspective—may have been right after all. When I had a chance to talk with Mikhail Gorbachev not long after the fall of the Wall, he grudgingly conceded that it was Reagan's policy of strength, and especially his pursuit of a Star Wars shield against nuclear missiles, which had brought the Soviet Union to its knees. To me, that was a valuable lesson in humility regarding the pitfalls of assessing political leaders and their policies.

I had the pleasure of making the acquaintance of Ronald Reagan's vice president, George H. W. Bush. Before too long, we established a long and friendly relationship that lasted well beyond the presidency of "Bush 41." I first met Vice President Bush when I was on yet another delicate mission for Chancellor Kohl. In 1972, Chancellor Brandt was looking for an appropriate and adequate way to commemorate the twenty-fifth anniversary of the Harvard commencement speech by Secretary of State George C. Marshall, the speech that served as the origin of the Marshall Plan; he was also looking to express Germany's gratitude for that unprecedented and highly successful demonstration of American generosity. He decided to give the American people a gift in return—the German Marshall Fund (GMF) of the United States. The idea was to establish a foundation, entirely under American control, that would honor the memory of George Marshall and the largesse of the American people by engaging in activities that focused on problems common to industrialized societies. The expectation was, of course, that this foundation would thereby contribute to transatlantic relations in general, and to German-American relations in particular. At a ceremony at Harvard University in June 1972, Willy Brandt formally handed over the first installment of a DM 150 million commitment, which was to be paid out over a period of fifteen years. (A portion of that initial contribution was allocated to Harvard's Center for West European Studies, whose director, Guido Goldman, had played an instrumental role in conceptualizing and finalizing these arrangements.)

Fifteen years later, the question arose as to whether the Federal Republic should renew its financial commitment to the GMF, which by that time had become solidly established in Washington, DC, and a major player among American foundations. On the German side, however, there was a good deal of dissatisfaction with the GMF. Many members of the *Bundestag*, especially among the CDU/CSU faction, felt that the GMF had not focused enough on German-American relations, had awarded too few grants to German applicants, and was altogether too insistent on demonstrating independence from its German sources. The terms of the gift had specified that independence, but there was a general feeling that the GMF should not bite the hand that fed it—a hand that was now asked to feed it some more. Kohl needed the *Bundestag*'s approval to commit another contribution to the GMF. Faced with resistance, he asked me to work out a deal with the GMF and members of the *Bundestag* that would result in the necessary support.

These negotiations turned out to be surprisingly difficult, as German lawmakers insisted on some kind of German influence on the disbursement of the money they were asked to provide, while the GMF resolutely rejected any such change in its charter. There was, however, strong pressure for continued support of the GMF; not to do so could have been interpreted as a deliberate slight of the United States (at a time when relations were already strained), or, worse yet, as an expression of German ingratitude toward the United States. In the end, I was able to work out a compromise, whereby Germany agreed to commit another DM 100 million for a period of ten years, while the GMF conceded to setting aside an unspecified amount of money strictly for German projects, to be administered by a German advisory committee. Eventually, this proved to be an unworkable procedure because of tensions between the advisory committee in Germany and the GMF headquarters in Washington. Its funding secured, the GMF emerged from these tensions as a much stronger institution, somewhat to my surprise, but certainly much to my satisfaction. The credit for this success goes to the presidents Frank E. Loy and Craig R. Kennedy. The GMF now has an impressively broad reach, not least in Eastern Europe, where it became heavily engaged after the end of the Cold War. Having set aside a significant portion of its annual contributions, it succeeded in building up an endowment that allows it to operate the way the original gift had envisaged: as an independent American foundation honoring the memory of George Marshall and his plan. Willy Brandt, I should think, would be very pleased with his creation.

The renewal of the German financial commitment to the GMF in 1986 called for a high-level formal event, especially due to all the bad blood that had been spilled before. Helmut Kohl asked me to deliver the first installment as his personal representative; it was to be formally accepted on behalf of the American people by the vice president of the United States. So I met with George H. W. Bush in the vice president's ornate office in the Senate building to hand over a check for DM 10 million. Bush graciously and gratefully accepted the check, ever the perfect vice president in handling such ceremonial duties. After the obligatory pictures had been taken, he took me aside for a friendly chat. Soon we were engaged in intense political discussions that ran far beyond the allotted time. We hit it off. When I finally said good-bye, Bush gave me a friendly pat on the shoulder and said, "Do come again." I gladly took him up on this invitation whenever I could.

Bush achieved a rare feat in American political history when he ran for president in 1988 and won; the last sitting vice president to be elected president had been Martin Van Buren in 1836. Bush was, of course, supremely qualified, especially in the area of foreign policy, having been a member of the House of Representatives, ambassador to the United Nations, the first Chief of the US Liaison Office to the People's Republic of China (which later became an embassy), and director of the Central Intelligence Agency. As president, he exceeded every expectation concerning his foreign policy expertise. His administration's management of the collapse of the Soviet empire was brilliant, with its emphasis on deliberate speed toward the achievement of maximum goals while refraining from any triumphant gloating. Nowhere were these qualities more evident than in his handling of the issue of German reunification.

President Bush visited Germany in May 1989, at a time when Gorbachev was advocating *perestroika* and *glasnost*, Hungarians had cut through the barbed wire separating them from Austria, and Poles were organizing their first free elections. Change was coming to Europe, but what would it bring? Bush provided an answer when he gave a speech in Mainz: a Europe whole and free. He proclaimed:

> As president, I will continue to do all I can to help open the closed societies of the East. We seek self-determination for all of Germany and all of Eastern Europe. And we will not relax, and we must not waver. Again, the world has waited long enough . . . Just as the barriers are coming down in Hungary, so must they fall throughout all of Eastern Europe. Let Berlin be next—let Berlin be next! Nowhere is the division between East and West seen more clearly than in Berlin. And there this brutal Wall cuts neighbor from neighbor, brother from brother. And that Wall stands as a monument to the failure of Communism. It must come down.

He invited the Federal Republic to become a "partner in leadership" in order to bring about these changes, but Germans were still skeptical about the American president's large goals, and they were hesitant to join him as a partner in bringing them about. Caution in the interest of stability seemed the more appropriate way to proceed. His speech in Mainz was applauded politely. Afterward, he and Chancellor Kohl boarded a ship for a leisurely trip down one of the most spectacular portions of the Rhine River. I was among the select few who had been invited to join the two leaders. It offered me the chance for a brief chat with Bush as an old acquaintance. I ascertained that he was very serious indeed about working toward a Europe whole and free, which at its core would require a united Germany. At that point, I still did not see reunification coming, but I refrained from sharing my skepticism with the president. In principle, we all wanted a Europe whole and free; in practice, we were sure that it would take decades to achieve.

The Wall came down less than six months later. Kohl was reluctant to press for speedy reunification, but the American president pushed him to make use of this opportunity while he could. In the process, he worked hard not only to overcome opposition by leaders in London and Paris (who showed little excitement over the prospect of a reunified Germany), but also to lay the groundwork in negotiations with the Soviet Union. Bush's optimism, paired with strategic foresight and diplomatic skill, prevailed. When reunification was finally achieved only a year later, Germany knew who to thank. Never had the importance of Germany's "second unwritten constitution" been more evident, and rarely have German-American relations been better.

While the United States appeared preoccupied with Europe, Saddam Hussein thought he could exploit that situation by occupying Kuwait; a somewhat uncertain American diplomacy may, in fact, have given him reason to believe that the Bush administration would tolerate such an act of outright aggression. Now it was British Prime Minister Margaret Thatcher who warned the American president not to go "wobbly." After careful diplomatic and military preparations, American forces, supported by a broad coalition of other forces, liberated Kuwait in February 1991. Germany had contributed no troops, but offered a substantial financial contribution to help offset American costs. (Some time later, I had occasion to ask General Schwarzkopf, the commanding general and mastermind behind the operation to free Kuwait, what he would have done had German troops been offered. "Oh," he replied with disarming honesty, "I would have found a safe enough place for them." German troops were, in fact, ill prepared and poorly trained for such a mission, which is why they were not offered in the first place. This highlighted a problem of increasing importance for NATO, namely the growing gap between American military capabilities and those of its allies.) The ground war was over after one hundred hours, with Iraqi forces in panicked retreat from Kuwait. Bush ordered a halt of operations, claiming that he had no authority to move to Baghdad and dislodge the regime of Saddam Hussein, nor the military power to sustain an occupation of Iraq. The wisdom of this decision continues to be hotly debated. I, for one, thought—and still think, now even more strongly—that Bush did exactly the right thing, both strategically and diplomatically.

On June 12, 2001—his seventy-seventh birthday—I visited the former president in his vacation home in Kennebunkport, Maine. I was accompanied by Beate Lindemann, executive vice chairman of Atlantik-Brücke. We wanted to inform him in person that Atlantik-Brücke had decided to award him its Eric M. Warburg Prize in recognition of his invaluable contributions to the reunification of Germany. Bush expressed his delight at this honor and immediately agreed not only to accept the prize, but to come to Berlin for the award ceremony. We were thrilled over this turn of events, for which we had only dared to hope. The more formal part of our visit over, we then sat down for some friendly talk. Soon he became restless, looking outside to the beautiful day by the sea, and he asked whether we would like to join him for a stroll on the beach. We were not properly dressed for such an excursion, so he dug up some wind-proof jackets we could wear. Properly—and quite colorfully—outfitted, we set off for a lengthy boat trip along Maine's spectacular coast.

Bush was still very much interested in—and very well-informed about—everything having to do with German reunification. He criticized the way the processes of reunification had played out in practice. The "Two-Plus-Four" agreement, he explained, had sought to make certain (on his insistence) that the two German states would have a free hand in determining the details of unification. His intent and expectation were that a unified Germany would abide by all the principles governing a free and democratic state. Yet in one important respect, he complained, Germany had failed to do so: "You should at least have taken care that all private property expropriated by the German Democratic Republic be returned to its rightful owners." His point was well taken; property rights issues plagued the reunification process for many years (pitting former owners against longtime users).

Of course, we also talked about China, a topic of great interest to both of us. Bush emphasized the extraordinary importance of China for the United States and hinted that under the then current administration—which happened to be that of his son, George W. Bush ("Bush 43," in contrast to "Bush 41," a playful distinction that was even expressed on the jackets the two distinguished members of the Bush family wore in private)—relations with China did not receive sufficient attention and were, perhaps, not very well managed. He hastened to add, however, that he was in general extremely reluctant to offer any kind of foreign policy advice to his son. In the course of our discussion, I mentioned that I was going to travel straight on to China after our visit to Maine. In Beijing I was scheduled to meet with my old acquaintance Zhu Rongji, the premier of the State Council, whom Bush also knew. He was duly impressed and decided on the spot to write Zhu Rongji a personal letter that I could deliver. Back in the house after our invigorating walk, the former president immediately sat down at his desk to write what became a three-page letter. He asked me to read it. It was basically a reiteration of his argument that good relations with China were of primary importance to the United States and that he would do his best to make sure that they would be maintained. He then sealed the envelope and handed it to me, wishing me good luck. Little did I know that I would sorely need it.

Once I arrived in Beijing, I learned that I would not be able to hand over the personal letter by the former president to Zhu Rongji directly. Our meeting had been canceled because the premier had to go on an urgent foreign trip. Following standard diplomatic protocol, I thought of turning the letter over to the American ambassador in Beijing, who would then formally present it to the head of the Chinese government. But as bad luck would have it, the US embassy was just then without an ambassador, as the Clinton administration's ambassador had already departed, and the newly appointed ambassador had not yet arrived. I determined that it would have been improper to give the former president's personal letter to an embassy underling, so I looked for another delivery method. I asked the German ambassador whether he would be willing to serve as a diplomatic letter carrier. He was shocked over my ignorance of the niceties of diplomatic protocol. It would cause a major diplomatic incident, with unforeseeable implications for all involved, if a German ambassador were to present a letter by a non-German dignitary to the Chinese head of government. There was simply no way that he could complete the task.

During my visit in Beijing, I was invited to dinner with my old friend Ma Yi, who, as deputy chairman of the Economic Planning Committee, had long ago opened my way to China. The dinner took place in the usually festive environment of the Forbidden City, with exquisite food served by equally exquisite young ladies (and accompanied by frequent toasts with Maotai, an exclusive liquor distilled from fermented sorghum that takes some getting used to—Ma Yi had gotten me used to it over the years). Apparently, word had spread that I was carrying a letter by the former American president and that I had been unable to deliver it. In the course of our dinner, Ma Yi suggested that perhaps he might be the mailman of choice—he would consider it a pleasure and privilege to accept the letter from me and pass it on to Zhu Rongji. As fond as I was of Ma Yi, and as much as I wanted to see the letter delivered into the hands of Zhu Rongji, this hardly seemed proper either, so I politely declined his offer.

But now I was really worried: what should I do with the letter? I was afraid that Chinese intelligence operatives, who surely were on my trail in any case, might be tempted to get hold of it, now that its existence was common knowledge. From then on, I carried the letter with me at all times and put it under my pillow at night, just to be sure. In the end, I never was able to deliver the letter to its intended recipient. I took it back home with me and sent it back to Bush, with profuse apologies that I had failed in my duties as letter carrier. I don't know whether Zhu Rongji ever received the letter written so spontaneously by "Bush 41." Chinese-American relations, in any case, did not appear to suffer.

The Warburg Prize ceremony took place in Berlin on April 17, 2002. It was a particularly festive occasion because Atlantik-Brücke was also celebrating the fiftieth anniversary of its founding. Preparations were accordingly complicated and hectic, but I wanted to make sure that our honoree, the former president, was treated with the light touch that I knew he would find enjoyable. From our many conversations, I knew that he, like me, was crazy about cars. I arranged for him to be picked up at the airport in Berlin with a brand-new Audi A8, one of the first coming off the production line. My little ploy worked as anticipated. After Bush disembarked from the plane, his security detail rushed him to the limousine and urged him to get inside. But the once mightiest man in the world had other ideas. "That's a fantastic car," he exclaimed, as he slowly walked around it, inspecting every detail, "mind if I have a look at the engine?" The perplexed driver, not used to such requests, looked at me, and after I had nodded imperceptibly, opened the hood. Bush took his time taking a good look, absorbing every detail. "A smart engine," he finally noted approvingly, as his security detail watched with expressions of concern, humor, and admiration. They were visibly relieved when Bush finally disappeared in the car. I was quietly happy that his visit had gotten off to an excellent start.

Some 450 guests convened that evening in Charlottenburg Palace, Berlin's oldest and largest palace dating back to Hohenzollern times. For ceremonies such as ours, it is by far one of Berlin's finest venues. Among the guests was Chancellor Schröder, accompanied by his wife Doris, a journalist by profession who had once worked for a while in the United

States. Former Chancellor Kohl was, of course, also there. Foreign Minister Joschka Fischer gave a speech honoring the recipient of the Warburg Prize. It was quite a spectacle hearing the once radical leader of the 1968 protest movement and then founding member of the anti-establishment Green Party praising an American president. "Without you, Mr. President," Fischer rightly pointed out, "the changes that overtook Europe would have been quite different and, who knows, perhaps even much less peaceful. . . . The policies pursued by the United States contributed directly and decisively to the reunification of Germany in peace and liberty." He praised the "outstanding statesmanship" that had made it possible to have the Soviet Union "be involved as a recognized power and given a realistic perspective for the future," while respecting "at the same time the legitimate desire of Germany to have the same status as other nations and regain its full sovereignty, including a free choice of alliances." I could hardly believe my ears: Fischer had, at the time, been one of the more outspoken skeptics about the need for, and likely success of, reunification. Maybe the Bible had it right, I thought: there is more joy in heaven over one repentant sinner than over ninety-nine righteous hypocrites.

There certainly was a lot of joy that evening. The foreign minister received rousing applause, as did Helmut Kohl, who shared his deeply felt emotions and sincere appreciation for the help and support that had been extended by President Bush. The honoree expressed his gratitude for the prize and all the accolades that came with it, pointing out that he was no longer used to such treatment: usually he was either introduced as the husband of Barbara Bush, who had just published her third book, or as the father of the current president (who, in fact, sent a gracious message of congratulations to his father). It was all done in good humor, but with solemn purposes behind it. It was the social event of the year, everyone agreed afterward. Atlantik-Brücke had done itself proud.

"Bush 41" had good reason to be proud that day, but it would also have been understandable if his pride were mixed with nostalgia and sorrow. His foreign policy achievements were undeniable, but when he was running for reelection in 1992, America's voters focused more on the failures of his stewardship of the economy than on the triumphs of the commander-in-chief in Europe and the Middle East. "It's the economy, stupid!" was the unofficial, yet definitive, slogan of his Democrat rival, William Jefferson Clinton, the governor of Arkansas—the man from Hope. The country was experiencing an economic downturn and rising unemployment, both of such sufficient severity that Bush's public approval deteriorated rapidly. Clinton was able to exploit that weakness (aided by the third-party candidacy of the eccentric Texas billionaire, Ross Perot, who gained 19 percent of the votes). Clinton was elected with a majority of 43 percent, versus 37 percent for Bush. It was an ignominious defeat for Bush, who only a year earlier had seemed unbeatable.

I had experienced the young candidate at the Democratic National Convention in New York and must admit that I would have voted for him as well, even though I admired Bush and considered him a friend. Incredibly charming, Clinton had the rare gift of "peaceful conviction," as I liked to call it—the ability to win over people through the sheer force of his personality. I had the chance to talk with him while the convention was in full swing. If he was nervous and tense at that moment, his anxiety did not show. He appeared relaxed, fully focused on his counterpart, eager to learn all he could about him. He succeeded in making me feel as if I were, right then and there, the most important person in the world to him. We talked about Germany, about which he was very knowledgeable, praising its post-war and post-reunification achievements and arguing that the German system of a "social market economy" could be a model for the United States as well—less emphasis on limiting the role of the state, more emphasis on making sure that the state promoted social equality and justice. (He would later call this the "Third Way" and seek the cooperation of European leaders committed to social-democratic policies.) I was flattered and impressed. Over the course of his presidency, I continued to be impressed by his openness for new solutions under changing conditions, regardless of prior convictions or prevailing ideologies. I liked that in a politician.

Having bombed politically four years before with an overly bombastic speech, Clinton now delivered a brilliant acceptance speech that drove the delegates to wild enthusiasm. I was similarly moved. At the end of his speech, which concluded with the promise of a "New Covenant" with the American people, where such problems as racial inequality and inadequate health care would finally be solved, I was convinced that Clinton would be the better choice for the United States. I am not easily taken in by political rhetoric, but on that day Clinton won me over. Over the course of his two terms in office, he did not entirely disappoint me. To be sure, he failed in his efforts to reform the system of health care in the United States, and social inequalities of all kinds hardly disappeared during his presidency; however, he presided over the longest peacetime expansion of the economy, creating millions of new jobs in the process, and producing the first budget surplus in a long time. In foreign policy, he steered a reasonably steady course, with efforts at expanding NATO, pacifying the Balkans, and expanding international trade (the North American Free Trade Agreement, negotiated by Bush, was finally ratified during his administration). He worked tirelessly to bring about a Middle Eastern peace settlement, though an ultimately successful agreement proved unreachable. The only dark spot on his record—for which he took the unusual step of apologizing long after he had left office—was his failure to get the United States and the rest of the world involved in stopping a dreadful genocide in Rwanda. Clinton, who established excellent relations with both Chancellor Kohl and, later, Chancellor Schröder, was highly popular in Germany. The (in my view) insignificant personal transgressions that came to light in the course of the scandal involving the young White House intern Monica Lewinsky did little to harm his popularity in Germany, though it did much to make Germans wonder about the state of American politics: a president should be impeached and removed from office because of a sexual affair? What a strange country America was after all.

These strange American ways got worse. Most Germans would have liked to see Vice President Al Gore win the 2000 elections, in the hope that he would keep the United States on the course charted by President Clinton. Europe and America appeared to be in sync; there was a strong interest in maintaining that state of affairs. Gore seemed to have won—he certainly gained a majority of the popular vote—but the final election outcome got hung up in Florida, literally. How to count "hanging chads" on machine-readable paper ballots would determine who had prevailed in Florida, and thereby determine who was president by a two-vote majority in the Electoral College. What followed was an unseemly spectacle, which the rest of the world watched in amazement: was that any way for the world's oldest democracy to elect its leader? It finally took a narrow decision—itself highly controversial—by the Supreme Court to stop the wrangling in Florida. The result was the election of George W. Bush as the forty-third president of the United States.

There is no need to dwell on the disastrous impact that "Bush 43" had on German-American relations, or for that matter, on America's standing in the world in general. His conservatism did not go over well in more socially inclined and liberal-minded Europe. His unilateralism—evident early on in the United States' withdrawal from the Kyoto Protocol for dealing with the dangers of climate change, from participation in the International Criminal Court set up to prosecute war crimes and genocide, and from the Anti-Ballistic Missile agreement with Russia that precluded a potentially destabilizing missile defense—was considered an affront to the spirit of international cooperation that Europe was trying to foster. Such steps, justified strictly in terms of narrow American interests, were also seen as threats to security and world peace. Initial hopes that "Bush 43" might follow in his father's footsteps, or at least rely on his counsel, were dashed when it became apparent that he seemed more interested in besting his father than in acting like him. (At one point, when asked whether he ever sought his father's advice, George W. Bush replied that he relied on the help of a "higher father.") As the president swore to fight an international "axis of evil," the image of "Bush 43" as the Texan cowboy acting like "Rambo" guided by simplistic ideas about good and evil took hold.

Then al-Qaeda terrorists struck on September 11, 2001. For a short time, America could rely on the world's sympathy. In Berlin, 250,000 people gathered to demonstrate their support. In Paris, *Le Monde* declared that "We Are All Americans." But that wave of sympathy and support soon ebbed as the Bush administration went its own way in fighting international terrorism. When the "war on terror" turned into a dubiously justified war against Iraq, Europe parted ways with the United States (with the exception of Great Britain, where Prime Minister Tony Blair thought he might be able to restrain the American ally). The establishment of a prison for "enemy combatants" and "detainees" at Guantanamo in Cuba—where the Bush administration could claim that, because of its extraterritorial status, American legal safeguards and international laws did not apply—did great damage to trust in America's sense of justice. When pictures of the abusive treatment of prisoners in Abu Ghraib prison in Iraq emerged, the impression deepened that America had not only started an illegitimate war that it failed to win, but that it was in danger of losing its soul.

The errors of the president's way were not lost on an increasing number of Americans. "Bush 43" won reelection in 2004, when the costs and failures of the Iraq War were not yet overwhelmingly evident, but disapproval of the president's policies grew—in the 2006 Congressional elections, the Republican Party lost its majorities in both houses of Congress. The process of "self-control"—of correcting mistakes before they become absolute disasters—took hold. It certainly tested my patience as I observed that drawn-out process, but I never lost confidence that America would, before too long, master this crisis as well.

America did not disappoint. The election of Barack Obama as president of the United States constitutes not only a decisive renunciation of the path on which "Bush 43" had taken his country, but it is also a spectacular reaffirmation of American values. To be sure, his electoral success was aided in the end by a spiraling recession that threatened to become a depression (itself the result of the kind of corrupt excesses and regulatory failures that the Bush administration had allowed, if not encouraged). But it seems to me that the American voters would have turned to him even in the absence of this catalyst, precisely because he promised to take America on a new path (something his Republican opponent, seventy-year-old John McCain, could not credibly do). I fully shared the almost giddy enthusiasm with which the majority of Americans and most everyone else around the world anticipate the Obama presidency. What an incredible turn of events: the first African American president, son of a Kenyan father and a (Caucasian) Midwestern mother, who grew up in Indonesia and Hawaii, graduated from Harvard Law School, worked his way into the American consciousness—and conscience!—with brilliantly conceived and delivered speeches, and finally promised his country: "Yes, we can!"

The necessary efforts to rescue the economy will not only bind resources for a long time to come, but also will keep the president and Congress preoccupied. Political realities will inevitably intrude and prevent the realization of some of the more lofty goals. But where basic policy changes are concerned, President Obama should be able to proceed. There should be a new tone in Washington, much less confrontational, more consensus-oriented. There should be a new openness to the world, much less unilateralist, more cooperative in spirit and execution. There will be less emphasis on military power and more attention paid to what is now fashionably called "smart power." And priority will be given to making sure that America acts in accordance with its own best values and traditions. As former President Clinton put it at the Democratic National Convention that nominated Barack Obama: "People the world over have always been more impressed by the power of our example than by the example of our power." President Obama echoed this message five months later in his historic Inaugural Address when he said, "Our power alone cannot protect us, nor does it entitle us to do as we please. [It] grows through its prudent use; our security emanates from the justness of our cause, the force of our example, the tempering qualities of humility and restraint."

During my visits to the United States in 2010 and 2011, I witnessed a deterioration of public support for President Obama in spite of legislative advances, particularly in the passing of the health insurance bill. I was struck by the reaction of Republican members of the House and Senate, who alleged the health insurance bill amounted to the "introduction of socialism" in America. When I argued that health insurance in Germany was introduced in 1875 by the most conservative first chancellor, Prince Bismarck, in order "to prevent socialism from succeeding," I received no sensible reply.

Barack Obama, the "first Pacific President" of the United States as some Americans call him, has had little exposure to life in Europe. However, we do vividly remember and admire his famous speech in Berlin on July 24, 2008, which earned him the enduring support of millions of Germans. The numerous exchanges between Barack Obama and Angela Merkel, who had moved from West Germany to East Germany as a child when her father, a Protestant pastor, was transferred to a parish there, were intensive and personal in the light of their very different origins.

Chancellor Angela Merkel deserves great credit for having rescued German-American relations after President George W. Bush launched his war against Iraq in March 2003, supported by the United Kingdom under Prime Minister Tony Blair. After becoming German Chancellor in November 2005, she paid several visits to Washington and developed an effective working relationship with Bush and Secretary of State Condoleezza Rice, which brought to an end the most serious deterioration in bilateral relations since World War II.

In 2009, the board of Atlantik-Brücke decided to honor Chancellor Merkel with the organization's highest award, the Eric M. Warburg Prize. The ceremony was held in a packed auditorium at the Library of Congress in Washington on June 25, 2009, and it was followed by a gala reception and a VIP dinner. On the next day, Chancellor Merkel paid her first official visit to President Barack Obama at the White House. At the ceremony, Chancellor Merkel delivered a substantive foreign policy address in German with simultaneous translation, which was received with great applause. Senator Chuck Hagel, an old friend, was Merkel's choice to deliver the speech honoring her. I had the privilege of speaking at the dinner, thanking her for her great success in managing German-American relations, and wishing her a productive first official session with President Obama. I also had the pleasure to greet Sarah Warburg-Johnson, who represented the Warburg family at the award ceremony that commemorates her grandfather, the founder of Atlantik-Brücke, Eric M. Warburg. As we mentioned in our invitation to the prize ceremony, it was thanks to the generous financial and logistical support of Volkswagen AG in Wolfsburg that this memorable event became reality. As always, it was a great pleasure to have the chairman of Atlantik-Brücke Tom Enders (CEO of Airbus) at my side.

# Epilogue

## America In Me

For Germans of my generation, who experienced Nazi tyranny and the horror of World War II, it was the United States of America that liberated Europe from the terror regime of Adolf Hitler in 1945. The end of World War II was the darkest hour in our lives, but soon after 1945, the United States paved the way for Germany to get an unexpected second chance to become a democracy. Economic recovery set in. America, the conqueror, became the ally and eventually the friend that preserved the freedom of Berlin when it was threatened by strangulation during the blockade of 1948–1949.

Democracy, economic recovery, and US leadership helped bring a peaceful end to the Cold War and the liberation of Eastern Germany and the other nations of Eastern Europe. The leadership of President George H. W. Bush was directly responsible for the unification of Germany firmly anchored in the free world and the community of Western democracy. When I addressed the thirty-second annual German-American Young Leaders Conference of Atlantik-Brücke in Hamburg in August 2010, I cited the long path from the darkness of 1945 to the globalized world of 2010. Many Young Leaders, German and American, conveyed their gratitude to me for having reminded them of what America had done for us. In spite of my conviction that the European Union must continue to unify to become a potent and active partner of the United States, we at Atlantik-Brücke and Atlantik Forum—members and Young Leaders Alumni alike—recognize that German-American friendship is and will continue to be of paramount importance. We are committed to cherishing and strengthening our partnership forever.

As I mentioned in my preface, Maine played a crucial role in convincing me to write this book. In the summer of 2011, at eighty-five years old, I was again spending the summer on Vinalhaven. When I looked back on my "Over Sixty Years in Post-war Reconstruction, International Diplomacy, and German-American Relations"—part of the title of this autobiography—one particular highlight stands out, because it shows the international recognition my work has found. I want to finish my memoirs with the description of this highly emotional event.

In June 1994, I had been chairman of Atlantik-Brücke for ten years. I thought little of that anniversary and paid no attention to it. Two days before the annual membership meeting of Atlantik-Brücke I had arranged for some meetings in Bonn, but Beate Lindemann had other ideas. Totally unknown to me, she had arranged a series of celebratory events. That she was able to keep these secret from me is one of her major achievements and speaks of her organizational skills. I thought that I was going to a routine meeting in the Foreign Office that afternoon, when I was led instead to its main conference room, the *Weltsaal*. I was floored, for here I saw gathered around the huge conference table many of my best friends and colleagues from the United States and Germany, who greeted me with thunderous applause. The surprise was perfect and complete. A meeting was called to order for the purpose of conducting a symposium on the future of transatlantic relations. It was a good thing that I was there mostly to listen, for I was nearly speechless (which, I must admit, is rarely the case). Henry Kissinger, Richard Holbrooke (then the American Ambassador to Germany), and others proceeded, under the chairmanship of my friend and deputy chairman of Atlantik-Brücke, Arend Oetker, to discuss the current state and future direction of German-American relations, which were then somewhat strained because of unfolding events in the Balkans.

Later that evening, I was on my way to a black-tie dinner at the residence of the Canadian Ambassador William T. Delworth. But no, I was not. Instead, I was taken to the *Redoute* in Bad Godesberg, Bonn's most delightful formal setting for a ceremonial event. Here, a large crowd of close friends and colleagues awaited me. It turned into an unforgettable summer evening. I recovered more quickly from my absolute surprise, happily circulating among the guests. Even more surprises were waiting. First, Rita Süssmuth, president of the *Bundestag*, presented me with the Federal Republic's second-highest order, the *Großes Verdienstkreuz mit Stern und Schulterband* (Grand Cross with Star and Sash). Then the British ambassador announced that Her Majesty the Queen had made me a "Commander of the British Empire." Now I was nearly speechless again.

Much as I appreciated these honors, the best was yet to come. Toward the end of the evening, after some very thoughtful remarks by Henry Kissinger, Beate Lindemann came to the real point of this event: my ten years as chairman of Atlantik-Brücke. Her remarks were moving enough, but then she presented me with the manuscript of a collection of essays entitled "America Within Us." She had asked many of those who had accompanied me over the years on my own personal bridge across the Atlantic to reflect about what America and its relations with Germany meant to them. Some fifty contributors had accepted this invitation, including Kenneth W. Dam, Theodore Ellenoff, Carl Horst Hahn, Josef Joffe, Robert M. Kimmitt, Henry A. Kissinger, John C. Kornblum, Paul H. Nitze, Volker Rühe, Wolfgang Schäuble, Theo Sommer, Paul A. Volcker, and James D. Wolfensohn.

The result—soon published as a book in both German and English—is an often highly personal account of how much America is indeed in all of us, how much that means to us, and how important it is that we never lose that connection. It was a deeply felt, highly moving, and greatly appreciated acknowledgment of my own life's work: America in us, and America in me.

# Name Index

# Subject Index